The Cambridge Companion to Native American Literature

Invisible, marginal, expected – these words trace the path of recognition for American Indian literature written in English since the late eighteenth century. This Companion chronicles and celebrates that trajectory by defining relevant institutional, historical, cultural, and gender contexts, by outlining the variety of genres written since the 1770s, and also by focusing on significant authors who established a place for Native literature in literary canons in the 1970s (Momaday, Silko, Welch, Ortiz, Vizenor), achieved international recognition in the 1980s (Erdrich), and performance-celebrity status in the 1990s (Harjo and Alexie). In addition to the seventeen chapters written by respected experts – Native and non-Native; American, British, and European scholars, the Companion includes bio-bibliographies of forty authors, maps, suggestions for further reading, and a timeline which details major works of Native American literature and mainstream American literature, as well as significant social, cultural, and historical events. An essential overview of this powerful literature.

JOY PORTER is a lecturer in the Department of American Studies at the University of Wales, Swansea, UK where she teaches American and Native American history and literature. Previously she was Senior Lecturer in American History at Anglia Polytechnic University, Cambridge. She is the author of *To Be Indian: the Life of Seneca-Iroquois Arthur Caswell Parker, 1881–1955* (2002). Her work can be found in a variety of books such as *The State of US History* (Berg 2002) and journals such as *New York History* and *Presidential Studies Quarterly*. Her next book is *Native American Freemasonry*, the research for which is supported by a Leverhulme Research Fellowship.

KENNETH M. ROEMER, an Academy of Distinguished Teachers Professor at the University of Texas at Arlington, has received four NEH grants to Direct Summer Seminars and has been a Visiting Professor in Japan, a guest lecturer at Harvard, and lectured in Vienna, Lisbon, Brazil, and Turkey. His articles have appeared in journals such as *American Literature*, *American Literary History*, and *Modern Fiction Studies*. His *Approaches to Teaching Momaday's* The Way to Rainy Mountain (ed.) was published by the MLA; his *Native American Writers of the United States* (ed.) won a Writer of Year Award from Wordcraft Circle. He has written four books on utopian literature, including *The Obsolete Necessity* and *Utopian Audience*. His collection of personal narratives, verse, and photography about Japan is entitled *Michibata de Deatta Nippon* (A Sidewalker's Japan).

THE CAMBRIDGE COMPANION TO

NATIVE AMERICAN LITERATURE

EDITED BY

JOY PORTER

and

KENNETH M. ROEMER

CAMBRIDGE
UNIVERSITY PRESS

CAMBRIDGE UNIVERSITY PRESS
Cambridge, New York, Melbourne, Madrid, Cape Town, Singapore, São Paulo

CAMBRIDGE UNIVERSITY PRESS
The Edinburgh Building, Cambridge, CB2 2RU, UK
Published in the United States of America by Cambridge University Press, New York

www.cambridge.org
Information on this title: www.cambridge.org/9780521529792

© Cambridge University Press 2005

First published 2005
Reprinted 2006

Printed in the United Kingdom at the University Press, Cambridge

A catalogue record for this book is available from the British Library

ISBN-13 978-0-521-82283-1 hardback
ISBN-10 0-521-82283-1 hardback
ISBN-13 978-0-521-52979-2 paperback
ISBN-10 0-521-52979-4 paperback

To
Mildred Allison Roemer, 1906–2003
Brooklyn and East Rockaway, New York
Arthur Kenneth Roemer, 1912–2005
East Rockaway, New York
and
Kathleen and John Porter,
Derry/Londonderry, N. Ireland.

CONTENTS

ILLUSTRATIONS

Figures

Maps

The maps are taken from *American Indians: Answers to Today's Questions* by Jack Utter. (Reproduced by permission of the University of Oklahoma Press.)

CHADWICK ALLEN is Associate Professor of English at Ohio State University and Associate Editor of Studies in American Indian Literatures. He is the author of *Blood Narrative: Indigenous Identity in American Indian and Maori Literary and Activist Texts*, which was a finalist for the MLA First Book Prize, and articles and book chapters on the discourses of indigenous activism, postcolonial and indigenous theories, and popular representations of US frontiers. He is a past President of the Association for the Study of American Indian Literatures and a recipient of two Fulbright research awards to Aotearoa/New Zealand.

KIMBERLY M. BLAESER (Anishinaabe), a Professor of English at the University of Wisconsin-Milwaukee, teaches Native American Literature, Creative Writing, and American Nature Writing. Blaeser is an enrolled member of the Minnesota Chippewa Tribe and grew up on the White Earth Reservation. Her publications include two collections of poetry, *Trailing You*, which won the 1993 First Book Award from the Native Writers' Circle of the Americas, and *Absentee Indians and Other Poems* (2002). She is the author of *Gerald Vizenor: Writing in the Oral Tradition* and the editor of two anthologies: *Stories Migrating Home: a Collection of Anishinaabe Prose* (1999) and *Traces in Blood, Bone, and Stone: Contemporary Ojibwe Poetry* (2004). Her poetry, short fiction, essays, and scholarly articles have appeared in widely read Canadian and American collections, including *Reinventing the Enemy's Language* and *Nothing but the Truth*.

LAURA COLTELLI is full professor of American literature at the University of Pisa. Her works include essays on American poetry and analyses of colonial journals and travel literature. She has published numerous studies on Native American literature, including *Winged Words. American Indian Writers Speak* (1990) and Joy Harjo's *Spiral of Memory* (ed., 1999). Her recent

books include *Voci dal Sudovest. Terra e identità negli scrittori indianoa-
mericani* (2002) and a volume on radical women writers, *Le radici della
memoria. Meridel Le Sueur e il radicalismo americano degli anni '30* (2002).
She has edited Italian translations of works by Silko, Momaday, Harjo, and
Ortiz, as well as an anthology of contemporary American Indian writers.
She is the general editor of the series "Crossroads" devoted to American
writers, recently inaugurated with a collection of poems by Sherman Alexie.

ANN HAUGO, an Assistant Professor in the School of Theatre at Illinois State
University, teaches theatre history, literature, and criticism, including
courses on American Indian theatre. Her publications on American
Indian theatre have appeared in books such as *American Indian Theatre:
a Reader, The Color of Theatre: Race, Culture, and Contemporary
Performance*, and *The Blackwell Companion to American Drama*, and
in various academic journals and periodicals. She has served as Project
Associate with Project HOOP (Honoring Our Origins and People through
Native Theatre, Education, and Community Development) and as
Consultant to the Native American Women Playwrights' Archive.

DAVID L. MOORE is Associate Professor of English at the University of
Montana. He teaches and publishes on Native American and American
literatures, and has taught previously at the University of South Dakota,
Salish Kootenai College, and Cornell University. He was the recipient of a
Post-Doctoral Fellowship at the Society for the Humanities at Cornell
University and of the Faculty Research Fellowship in Western Studies at the
O'Connor Center for the Rocky Mountain West. His publications include
an edited volume of *American Indian Quarterly* as well as numerous articles
and essays in key journals and collections from Cambridge, Prentice Hall,
Gale, Nebraska, New Mexico, Smithsonian, and other publishers. Currently
he is working on a book on Native American redefinitions of America.

DAVID MURRAY is Professor of American Literature and Culture in the
School of American and Canadian Studies, University of Nottingham,
England. He is the author of *Forked Tongues: Speech, Writing and
Representation* in North American Indian Texts (1992) and *Indian
Giving: Economies of Power in Early Indian–White Exchanges* (2000),
and has edited *Literary Theory and Poetry* (1989) and *American Cultural
Critics* (1995), as well as essays and articles on Native American topics.

ROBERT M. NELSON is a Professor of English at the University of Richmond,
where he teaches a variety of courses in Native American literature. He is a

former co-editor of *Studies in American Indian Literatures* and is current editor of the online *Guide to Native American Studies Programs* in the US and Canada. In addition to his book, *Place and Vision: the Function of Landscape in Native American Fiction*, he has authored many critical essays on contemporary American Indian writers. His previous work on Silko includes several published articles, and he has a book in progress on the embedded texts in Silko's novel *Ceremony*.

BERND PEYER is a lecturer at the Center for North American Studies, Johann Wolfgang Goethe-Universität, Frankfurt, Germany. He has taught at D-Q University, Dartmouth, and the Technische Universität Dresden. He has received ACLS and Ford Foundation Fellowships, the latter to the McNickle Center for the History of American Indians; a Gordon Russell Visiting Professor Grant to Dartmouth; and a Mellon Postdoctoral Research Fellowship to the Newberry Library. His publications in the US include *The Singing Spirit: Early Short Stories by North American Indians* and *The Tutor'd Mind: Indian Missionary-Writers in Antebellum America*. His anthology of American Indian nonfiction prose from the 1760s to the 1920s is forthcoming from the University of Oklahoma Press.

JOY PORTER is a lecturer in the Department of American Studies at the University of Wales, Swansea, UK, where she teaches American and Native American history and literature. She is the author of *To Be Indian: the Life of Seneca-Iroquois Arthur Caswell Parker, 1881–1955* (2002). Her work can be found in a variety of books such as *The State of US History* (2002) and journals such as *New York History* and *Presidential Studies Quarterly*. Her next book is *Native American Freemasonry*, the research for which is supported by a Leverhulme Research Fellowship.

CATHERINE RAINWATER is Professor of English at St. Edward's University in Austin, Texas. Her essays have appeared in journals such as *American Literature*, *Philological Quarterly*, and *Modern Fiction Studies*. Her most recent books are *Dreams of Fiery Stars: the Transformations of Native American Fiction* (1999), and *Figuring Animals: Essays on Animal Images in Art, Literature, Philosophy, and Popular Culture* (co-edited with Mary S. Pollock, 2004). She won the MLA Norman Foerster Prize (1990) for her work on Louise Erdrich and the Penelope Niven Creative Nonfiction Literary Award (2004) for a personal essay called "My Father's Clothes." She is president of and newsletter editor for the Ellen Glasgow Society and has also served on the editorial boards of *Canadian Literature* and, currently, *Modern Fiction Studies*.

KENNETH M. ROEMER, an Academy of Distinguished Teachers Professor at the University of Texas at Arlington, has received four NEH grants to Direct Summer Seminars and has been a Visiting Professor in Japan, a guest lecturer at Harvard, and lectured in Vienna, Lisbon, Brazil, and Turkey. His articles have appeared in journals such as *American Literature*, *American Literary History*, and *Modern Fiction Studies*. His *Approaches to Teaching Momaday's* The Way to Rainy Mountain (ed.) was published by the MLA; his *Native American Writers of the United States* (ed.) won a Writer of Year Award from Wordcraft Circle. He has written four books on utopian literature, including *The Obsolete Necessity* and *Utopian Audiences*. His collection of personal narratives, verse, and photography about Japan is entitled *Michibata de Deatta Nippon* (A Sidewalker's Japan).

A. LAVONNE BROWN RUOFF is Professor Emerita of English, University of Illinois at Chicago, and former interim director of the D'Arcy McNickle Center for American Indian History, Newberry Library. She received the MLA's Lifetime Scholarly Achievement Award (2002) and a Lifetime-Achievement Award from the American Book Awards of the Before Columbus Foundation (1998). She directed four NEH Summer Seminars for College Teachers and has received an NEH research grant and fellowship. General editor of the American Indian Lives Series for the University of Nebraska Press, Ruoff is the author of *American Indian Literatures* (1990), and the co-editor, with Jerry W. Ward, Jr., of *Redefining American Literary History* (1990). She has published annotated editions of books by S. Alice Callahan (Muscogee-Creek), George Copway (Ojibwe), Charles Eastman (Dakota), and E. Pauline Johnson (Mohawk).

JAMES RUPPERT is the President's Professor of Alaska Native Studies and Cultures working in the English, Alaska Native Studies, and Northern Studies departments at the University of Alaska Fairbanks. He is a past-president of the Association for the Study of American Indian Literatures and has won three Fulbrights. His published work includes *Mediation in Contemporary Native American Fiction*, *Nothing but the Truth: An Anthology of Native American Literature* (with John Purdy), and *Our Voices: Native Stories from Alaska and the Yukon*.

KATHRYN W. SHANLEY is chair of the Native American Studies Department at the University of Montana and an enrolled Assiniboine (Nakota) from the Ft. Peck Reservation in Montana. She has also taught at the University of Washington and Cornell University. Shanley focuses on the intersections between educational institutions, Native communities and groups, and

Native political movements. She has published widely in the field of Native American literary criticism on issues of representation of Indians in popular culture, as well as about authors such as James Welch, Maria Campbell, Leslie Marmon Silko, Linda Hogan, Thomas King, and N. Scott Momaday. She recently edited *Native American Literature: Boundaries and Sovereignties* (2001) and has a forthcoming book on the writings of James Welch.

PATRICIA CLARK SMITH (Micmac) is Professor Emerita at the University of New Mexico. She has written essays on Native American literature, is one of five editors of *The Bedford Anthology of World Literature*, and has published two books of poems. She has been awarded a Woodrow Wilson Fellowship, a Rockefeller Research Grant, and a Fulbright Faculty Development Grant. She and Michael Running Wolf retell stories of their people in *On the Trail of Elder Brother: Glous' gap Stories of the Micmac Indians*. She has written two books for young people on Native subjects, *As Long as the Rivers Flow: the Stories of Nine Native Americans* (with Paula Gunn Allen of Laguna Pueblo) and *Weetamoo, Heart of the Pocassets*.

ANNETTE VAN DYKE is an Associate Professor of Interdisciplinary and Women's Studies at the University of Illinois at Springfield where she teaches Native American Women's Literature and other women's literatures. She is the author of *The Search for a Woman-Centered Spirituality* (1992) and numerous essays in *SAIL, MELUS* and elsewhere on Native authors. She served as President of the National Women's Studies Association from 2000–2001 and received the 2004 Naomi B. Lynn Award for her outstanding contribution to women at the University of Illinois at Springfield.

NORMA C. WILSON, Professor of English at the University of South Dakota, where she has taught since 1978. She moved to South Dakota soon after completing a Ph.D. in English at the University of Oklahoma with a dissertation on "The Spirit of Place in Contemporary American Indian Poetry." Her book of poems, *Wild Iris*, was published in 1978 by Point Riders Press, Norman, Oklahoma. She has published numerous essays on Native literature in journals such as *Studies in American Indian Literatures*. In 2001 The University of New Mexico Press published her book, *The Nature of Native American Poetry*. She was a writer in residence at Fundacion Valparaiso, Mojacar, Spain in 2002.

HERTHA D. SWEET WONG is Associate Professor in the English Department at the University of California, Berkeley. She is author of *Sending My*

Heart Back Across the Years: Tradition and Innovation in Native American Autobiography, published by Oxford University Press (1992), as well as numerous articles on Native American literature, autobiography, and environmental non-fiction. She is editor of Louise Erdrich's *"Love Medicine": A Casebook*, also from Oxford (2000) and, with John Elder, co-editor of *Family of Earth and Sky: Indigenous Tales of Nature from around the World* (1994). Currently, she is co-editing an anthology of contemporary short fiction by Native North American women and working on a book on visual autobiography.

ACKNOWLEDGMENTS

The editors of this volume thank Ray Ryan, of Cambridge University Press, David Murray, and A. LaVonne Brown Ruoff for their help and professional direction with this project. Special thanks are also due to the volume's Cambridge University Press editor Sarah Stanton and to Lesley Atkin. Joy Porter also thanks David S. Berman and Muffy Roxy Porter, who made the editorial task enjoyable. Ken Roemer thanks his wife Micki for her patience.

A NOTE ON INDIVIDUAL AND TRIBAL NAMES
IN THIS VOLUME

The variety in number and type of name Indian individuals and groups possess can sometimes seem confusing, however, rather than dismiss this complexity, it pays to embrace it. Names, and their uses and development over time provide vital keys to understanding. They bring people, places, groups, and their interactions into immediate and sharp focus in ways other sorts of information do not.

A fundamental reason for complexity in Indian names and naming is that many tribes and individuals have, and have had in the past, more than one name. Some Indian names may be intended only for group or family use and yet others reserved for use outside the family or group. People of a single area sometimes have more than one name. The same name was sometimes given to people who lived far away from each other and a single group could be known by a series of names as they traveled from one area to another. Furthermore, often tribes were known by names given to them either by other tribes or by non-Indians. The Cherokee, for example, are known by perhaps fifteen designations and the name Cherokee is itself a name bestowed by others. Further examples are the Ojibwe who are also known as the Ojibwa, Chippewā, Anishinabe, Mississauga, Anishinabeg, and Saginaw; the Diné, who are also known also as Navajo, Dineh, Tenuai, and Navaho; and the Mohican from the Hudson Valley in New York who are also known as Mahican and Mahikan (and often confused with Mohegan of the Thames River in Eastern Connecticut as a result of James Fenimore Cooper's muddling of tribal names in his 1826 novel, *The Last of the Mohicans*). Understandably, as time has progressed, various tribes have ceased to recognize names by which they have been generally known because those names were never their actual names to begin with. Likewise writers over time have changed how they identify themselves, as when Louise Erdrich moved from identifying herself as Turtle Mountain Chippewa to Turtle Mountain Ojibwe. Yet further complexity comes from the fact that as well as there being variation in tribal designation, there have also been changes in how those designations have been spelt.

Our policy has been to use the designation writers use to refer to themselves, but, where known, to further specify tribal affiliation when nineteenth-century writers have simply been identified using general terms that encompass large groups, such as the designation Sioux. Generally, where tribal affiliation is known it appears as the full tribal name in parenthesis; where an individual is identified as possessing heritage from more than one tribe both tribes are listed in parenthesis separated by a slash. Some writers prefer that a dash separate their tribal designations and every effort has been made to respect that preference. Where an individual is known by a name in an Indian language, this is given in the text first, where possible with an English language translation and alongside any commonly used non-Indian name(s).

For further information on tribal names, consult the following web sites: http://anpa.ualr.edu/; http://americanindian.net/names.html and http://www.nativeculture.com/lisamitten/nations.html. The latter site can be reached through the Bureau of Indian Affairs website http://www.doi.gov/bureau-indian-affairs.html.

KENNETH M. ROEMER

Introduction

I

In 1969 Vine Deloria, Jr.'s (Yankton-Standing Rock Sioux) *Custer Died for Your Sins* appeared. In 2001 W. S. Penn (Nez Perce / Osage) published *Feathering Custer*. Both are witty books by talented Native American writers. Juxtaposing them suggests the rapid development of the study of American Indian literatures. One of Penn's targets is the academic literary critic, while Deloria aims at anthropologists. Why the difference? One obvious explanation is that an invisible target is hard to hit. In 1969 academics specializing in Native literatures were practically non-existent. Anthropologists (along with folklorists and historians) controlled academic Indian country. Today anthropologists, folklorists, and historians still occupy much of the territory. But the dramatic increase in the visibility of Native American literatures has inspired the growth of a substantial body of criticism worthy of recognition, praise, and, as Penn demonstrates, at times, ridicule. Since 1969 in libraries, in classrooms, and on the Internet the study of American Indian literatures has progressed from invisible to marginal to expected status.

The recognition of literature written in English by American Indians (the focus of this volume) was long overdue. The Mohegan minister Samson Occom published a best-selling sermon in 1772, which he followed in 1774 with a collection of hymns, thus initiating the significant tradition of collecting and writing hymns in English and tribal languages. Novels, poetry, essays, and autobiographies written by Native Americans have appeared since the early nineteenth century; John Joseph Mathews's (Osage) *Wah'Kon-Tah* (1932) was a Book of the Month Club selection; Will Roger's (Cherokee) syndicated *New York Times* columns and "correspondence" for *The Saturday Evening Post* reached millions of readers – despite these and many other "facts" of Native American literary production and recognition, writing by American Indians was rarely included in university literature courses before the 1970s.

This disciplinary barrier to teaching Native American texts as literature collapsed during the 1970s and 1980s. Broad social and academic movements – Civil Rights and Ethnic Studies, in particular, but also feminism and Women's Studies – combined with specific literary events help to explain the change. 1969 witnessed two of the events: the previously mentioned publication of Deloria's *Custer Died for Your Sins*; and the awarding of the Pulitzer Prize for fiction to an unknown Kiowa author, N. Scott Momaday, for his first novel, *House Made of Dawn* (1968). The 1970s witnessed the appearance of a popular paperback reprint of the collaborative life narrative *Black Elk Speaks* (1972); the establishment of Harper & Row's Native American Publishing Program (1971), which published Simon Ortiz's (Acoma) *Going for the Rain* (1976); Reynolds Price's front-page *New York Times Book Review* rave review of James Welch's (Blackfeet / Gros Ventre) *Winter in the Blood* (1974); the publication of Gerald Vizenor's (Anishinaabe) *Bearheart* (1978, 1990); and the acclaim accorded to Leslie Marmon Silko (Laguna) for *Ceremony* (1977). The numbers of American Indian authors grew dramatically during the 1980s and 1990s. Louise Erdrich (Turtle Mountain Ojibwe) has an international reputation and has won major awards, including a National Book Critics Circle Award for *Love Medicine* (1984, 1993). Other Native American novelists, poets, playwrights, and essayists including Paula Gunn Allen (Laguna / Sioux), Michael Dorris (Modoc), Joy Harjo (Muscogee / Cherokee), Linda Hogan (Chickasaw), Greg Sarris (Coast Miwok / Pomo), Diane Glancy (Cherokee), and Sherman Alexie (Spokane / Coeur d'Alene) achieved national reputations and, in Alexie's case, even celebrity status.

The increased visibility of writing by Native American authors inspired the types of scholarly, institutional, and publishing support necessary to foster and sustain the growth of a new field. As the "Further Reading" section of this volume indicates, bibliographies and reference works began to appear in the 1970s. By the 1990s reference books on American Indian literatures were plentiful. The benchmark work was A. LaVonne Brown Ruoff's *American Indian Literatures* (1990), followed by Andrew Wiget's *Handbook of Native American Literature* (1994, 1996) (which was preceded in 1985 by Wiget's survey *Native American Literature*), Janet Witalec's *Native North American Literature* (1994), my *Native American Writers of the United States* (1997), Kathy J. Whitson's encyclopedia *Native American Literatures* (1999), and Suzanne Eversten Lundquist's *Native American Literatures* (2004). Important recent specialized reference works include Dorothea M. Susag's *Roots and Branches* (1998) for high school teachers; Bruce A. Goebel's *Reading Native American Literature: a Teacher's* Guide (2004) and Eric Cheyfitz's *The Columbia History of Native American Literature since 1945*

(2005). The bibliographies, handbooks, and encyclopedias are grandly complemented by the online and hard-copy Native American Press Archives directed by Daniel Littlefield (Cherokee) at the University of Arkansas at Little Rock.

Reference works and archives made visible the existence of the literature and scholarship; anthologies facilitated the texts' entry into the classroom. Collections of English translations of songs, ceremonial chants, prayers, and narratives date back into the nineteenth century. Since the awarding of the Pulitzer to Momaday, there has been a marked increase of anthologies devoted to writing composed in English, beginning with modest collections published by regional presses, for example, John Milton's *The American Indian Speaks* (1969) and culminating in the late twentieth century and opening the twenty-first with sophisticated, multi-genre anthologies, for example, Joy Harjo and Gloria Bird's (Spokane) *Reinventing the Enemy's Language* (1997) and John L. Purdy and James Ruppert's *Nothing But the Truth* (2001).

Critics and scholars need testing grounds and outlets for their ideas; they need sessions, conferences, journals, and publishing programs. Since the early 1970s the Modern Language Association and an affiliated organization, the Association for the Study of American Indian Literatures, have fostered national discussions at MLA conventions. The early meetings culminated in a 1977 National Endowment for the Humanities Summer Seminar in Flagstaff, Arizona; the MLA's most recent recognition of the field came in a Lifetime Achievement Award (2002), a tribute to one of the field's founders A. LaVonne Ruoff. Now there are other organizations supporting the field, including the Wordcraft Circle of Native Writers and Storytellers, and other gatherings, including the Native American Literature Symposiums. Critical debates are encouraged by specialized journals – especially *Studies in American Indian Literatures* and the new journal *Indigenous Journeys*, but also by *American Indian Quarterly*, *American Indian Culture and Research Journal*, and *Wicazo-sa*. Even the widely distributed newspaper *Indian Country Today*, routinely includes discussion of contemporary Native authors in their "Lifeways" section. Today the best-known authors frequently publish with prestigious commercial companies like HarperCollins, Norton, and St. Martin's. Other novelists, poets, and scholars find support from several university presses, notably the University of Nebraska, the University of Oklahoma, the University of Arizona, and UCLA.

From ignored to required, from dry bed to mainstream – the rise of American Indian literature deserves much attention and praise while also inviting some perplexing and even troubling questions. What exactly is Native American or American Indian or Indigenous literature? My multi-labeled statement of that question obviously raises another: what should we call this literature? Also, are there characteristics that distinguish the literature? In this introduction I will only be skimming the surfaces of the many possible responses to these questions. I hope my comments will, nevertheless, encourage teachers and students to place their study of particular texts within the contexts of these questions.

II

When addressing the question, "What is Native American literature?," two words come to mind: immensity and diversity. It is appropriate that the most important reference work (Ruoff's *American Indian Literatures*) and the one journal exclusively devoted to Native literary studies (*Studies in American Indian Literatures*) both add an "s" to literature, as I will in this introduction when referring to the body of written and oral literatures. The oral literatures certainly deserve the plural form. Before the arrival of Columbus, there were thousands of narratives, ceremonies, songs, and speeches performed by experts trained in performance and interpretation. Each of these traditionally used categories can, of course, be subdivided into numerous related forms. For example, creation, trickster, hero, and animal stories for narratives. In *Native American Literature,* Wiget offers a useful way to differentiate between various ceremonial performances by discussing the relative emphases on the individual, the tribe, and healing and renewing of the world. Songs can encompass almost every aspect of human life. The Navajo celebrate their culture heroes Monster Slayer and Child of Water in song; they also sing of weeding. As useful as these genre categories can be, they mask another type of diversity. Anyone who has studied a particular narrative, speech, song, or ceremony knows that the genre boundaries are quite porous. For instance, the Navajo Nightway, an elaborate nine-day ceremony, does indeed focus on the healing of one (or a small number of) individual(s). But the words of the prayers extend *hózhó* (beauty, order, happiness, harmony) far beyond individuals to encompass Navajo old men and old women, young men and young women, boys and girls, and children and chiefs, as well as many colors of corn. Furthermore, certain songs sung during the Nightway can also be sung "separately" outside of the ceremonial context.

Cultural and regional variety multiplies the genre diversity. Conservative estimates place cultural counts at more than three hundred cultural groups and more than two hundred languages in North America when Columbus arrived.[1] And this was (and still is) a dynamic cultural diversity. Even if we limit our view to cultures within the boundaries of the United States, evidence of extensive trade routes, which often extended far beyond those boundaries, suggest that more was traded than "goods." The prevalence of hero twins in the Southwest, the flood episodes and recurring emergence of earth diver motifs in creation narratives, and numerous other parallels demonstrate the vibrant borrowing and reinventions that went on for hundreds, even thousands, of years. Of course, this dynamism continued after the arrival of Europeans. In one famous late nineteenth-century account of inventive borrowing, Frank Hamilton Cushing collected an imaginative blending of a traditional Zuni story about a girl tending her flock of turkeys and the Cinderella story.[2]

The diversity of Native oral literatures encompasses more than a cataloguing of the diversity of cultures, languages, and region; the diversity of genres (which can include tribal genres quite different from Euro-American typologies), and the dynamics of cross fertilizations. The diversity also includes how the literatures are experienced. For most students, encountering Native oral literatures means reading paragraphs in standard English or reading what look like poems. These are limited and misleading encounters. Not only do they often hide the central role of mediation by translators, editors, and publishers, they hide the tremendous diversity of written and performance forms used over the past five centuries to represent oral literatures. Spanish priests and French Jesuits offered some of the first versions, preceded, of course, by Mayan non-alphabetical forms of inscription. As tribal languages took modern written form (Cherokee was an early example), there were written versions in tribal languages. In the nineteenth-century Henry Rowe Schoolcraft and other "collectors" of oral literatures often offered three versions of a text: a representation in the tribal language, a literal translation, and a more literary translation. In the twentieth century collections such as Dennis Tedlock's *Finding the Center* (1972) and Larry Evers and Felipe S. Molina's (Yaqui) *Yaqui Deer Songs* (1987) offered sophisticated combinations of bilingual representations framed by linguistic and cultural contexts.

Even if we limit our view to English translations there is a tremendous variety. For example, for narrative texts, translations range from Franz Boas's huge blocks of prose punctuated by pause lines and parenthetical numbers indicating five-line units, to Anthony Mattina's attempts to use "Red English" representations to capture the grammar and diction of his English-speaking storytellers, to Dell Hymes and Tedlock's use of narrative verse forms and typography to represent dynamics. If we move beyond the "reading" experience to audio tapes, videotape series (such as Larry Evers's *Words and Place: Native Literature from the American Southwest*), and live performances – all of which can vary with the skills and personality of the performer and the composition of the audience – the diversity of experiencing American Indian oral literatures is truly immense. Thus the decision to limit our focus to literature written in English.

Nevertheless, at the outset of the volume it is important to acknowledge the grand importance of the performed literatures as a major (possibly The Major) part of Native American literatures. This acknowledgment will be continued throughout the volume, often explicitly as in discussions of oral narratives by Joy Porter, translation mediations by David Murray, and collaborative life narratives by Hertha Sweet Wong, as well as implicitly in the examinations of the influence of storytelling traditions in works by many of the authors and in the mention of the numerous echoes and reinventions of family and community voices that appear in the essays, fictions, plays, and poems.

III

There is no need to survey the different written genres in English here, since the contributors to Part 2 provide overviews of genres and genre mixing. I do, however, want to highlight a problem that tends to obscure the extent of the immensity and diversity of Native American literature written in English. Anyone who has read Ruoff's *American Indian Literatures* or Helen Jaskoski's *Early Native American Writing* (1996), or visited Littlefield's Native American Press Archives knows that for more than two hundred years Indian authors have written many forms of non-fiction prose, as well as fiction, poetry, and, more recently, drama. One literary event and a powerful academic prejudice tend to obscure that diversity. The event was the awarding of the Pulitzer for *House Made of Dawn;* the prejudice was and still is a privileging of fiction and poetry over drama and non-fiction prose. The predilection for fiction and poetry (and to some degree autobiography) combined with the focus on contemporary novels inspired by Momaday's Pulitzer tends to obscure the importance of the non-fiction, drama, and pre-1968 literature.

This is unfortunate because, as indicated in several essays in this volume, the less privileged genres and the earlier literature can offer so much to students of American literature and culture. In essays, bibliographies, and books, several scholars – in particular Jack Forbes (Renape / Lenape), Robert Warrior (Osage), Daniel Littlefield, Vine Deloria, Chadwick Allen, Joanna Brooks, and Maureen Konkle – have emphasized the significance of the non-fiction prose, including the sermons, treaty / council documents, political essays and speeches, humor, intellectual / academic writing, histories, and journalism outlined in Bernd Peyer's essay. For instance, Allen argues convincingly in *Blood Narrative* (2003) that non-fiction, especially treaties, have helped to shape rhetorical and narrative strategies in the fiction and poetry. Furthermore, in terms of word count and number of readers (especially

Indian readers) non-fiction genres are the most significant forms of Native American writing. Therefore, students hoping to gain insights on key issues such as tribal sovereignty and how this concept translates on national, tribal, and local levels would be wise to consult Littlefield's Native American Press Archives, as well as newspapers such as *Indian Country Today,* the *Navajo Times,* and local newsletters. A paper like *Indian Country Today* also introduces students to some talented and provocative writers, especially in the "Perspectives" section; for example, Suzan Shown Harjo (Muscogee / Cherokee) has contributed lively articles on the harmful effects of words such as "plight," "roamed," and "squaw" (for example see the 28 February and 4 July 2000 issues).

Audiences for drama and pre-1968 poetry and fiction certainly cannot rival the size of readership of the popular non-fiction. An acquaintance with both is, nevertheless, essential to a knowledge of Native American literature. Early twentieth-century plays like Lynn Riggs's (Cherokee) *Green Grow the Lilacs* (1931) and *Cherokee Night* (1936) deserve attention in their own right. The former is especially interesting because of its transformation into the popular musical *Oklahoma!* in 1943 and all the implied issues about musical adaptations and the appeal of the West, the range, and small towns. Drama is significant, moreover, because, as Ann Haugo's essay demonstrates, it is one of the fastest growing "new" genres for Indian writers and because of its connections to an even "newer" genre – film, most notably seen in the national distribution and video and DVD availability of *Smoke Signals, The Fast Runner,* and *Skins,* but also in less widely distributed films like *Naturally Native* and the video versions of Spiderwoman Theater productions.

D'Arcy McNickle's (Métis Cree / Salish) *The Surrounded* (1936) is an obvious example of a pre-1968 novel worthy of study "on its own" as a sophisticated psychological study of a mixed-blood protagonist, Archilde Leon, surrounded by conflicting Salish, Old World Catholic, and "new" American cultures. Together the early novels also remind us that long before *House Made of Dawn, Ceremony,* and *Love Medicine,* Native American authors were exploring complex mixed-blood identity issues in *Surrounded,* Mourning Dove's (Colville / Nicola / Okanogan) *Cogewea* (1927), John Joseph Mathews's *Sundown* (1934), and John Milton Mathews's (Cherokee) *Brothers Three* (1935); and examining the controversial issue of the role of women in S. Alice Callahan's (Muscogee) *Wynema* (1891) and *Cogewea.*

Furthermore, the pre-1968 writing forces us to consider basic questions about content and perspective. Consider two mid-nineteenth-century authors, Betsey Guppy Chamberlain (Algonkin) and John Rollin Ridge (Cherokee). Does Chamberlain bring a particular "Indian" viewpoint to her essays on working conditions in New England Mills? Should Ridge's *The Life and Adventures of Joaquín Murieta* (1854) be part of Native American literature despite its focus on a legendary Mexican bandit? Louis Owens' (Cherokee / Choctaw) responds positively to the latter question. He sees the novel as "a disguised act of appropriation" that is as much about the oppression of Indians as it is about a romantic Mexican figure?[3] Similar "Indian content" questions might be applied to many later works and settings by American Indian authors – the distinctly white Oklahoma landscape of Riggs' *Green Grow the Lilacs,*[4] Momaday's poems about Russia, and the Moscow and Tokyo worlds of Martin Cruz Smith's (Senecu del Sur / Yaqui) *Gorky Park* (1981) and *December 6* (2002). Is it forcing the issue to define such works as Indian literature, or is excluding them from this rubric as narrow-minded as "wishing Joseph Conrad had written [only] 'Polish' novels."[5] This type of question, implied 150 years ago by Ridge's novel, should remind us that it is best to avoid overly rigid notions of appropriate "content" for Indian literature. "About Indians" should be defined flexibly enough to include the huge diversity of the topic and the possibility of appropriation of seemingly non-Indian subjects by Native viewpoints. Most important, it is crucial to examine each author within the contexts of his or her cultural and physical environment and his or her development as a reader and writer.

Several of the early novels also demonstrate that long before the mixed-genre creations of Momaday's *The Way to Rainy Mountain* (1969), Ortiz's *Fight Back* (1980), Silko's *Storyteller* (1981), Joy Harjo's *Secrets from the Center of the World* (1989), Diane Glancy's *Claiming Breath* (1992), and, more recently, Anita Endrezze's (Yaqui) *Throwing Fire at the Sun, Water at the Moon* (2000) and Carter Revard's (Osage) *Winning the Dust Bowl* (2001), American Indian novelists were pushing genre boundaries. One of the most interesting examples is Ella Deloria's (Yankton Nakota) *Waterlily,* which was completed in the 1940s but not published until 1988. Deloria considered herself a translator, linguist, and ethnographer, but she felt that her academic form of writing limited her audience and forced her to suppress her personal viewpoints. With the encouragement of the famous anthropologists Franz Boas and especially Ruth Benedict, she attempted to harness the form of historical fiction in the service of spreading ethnographic information about kinship and social relations of the Tetons (Lakotas). At times the result can be a contrived narrative that creates "ethnographic opportunities" – the death of a beloved grandmother is a ready-made opportunity to educate the reader about Ghost Keeping rituals and customs. But the overall effect is a convincing undercutting of stereotypes about "primitive hunting and gathering" societies. The networks of interpersonal relations represented are just as, if not more, complex than the workings of family and community groups in European and mainstream American societies.

IV

It is certainly accurate to speak of the immensity and diversity of the many forms of spoken, sung, and performed literatures and of the many forms of written texts, including more than two hundred years of writing in English. But when it is necessary to converse with colleagues and students and to give titles to courses, articles, and books, relying on "Immense and Diverse Literature" will be viewed with much suspicion. Unfortunately, there is no entirely satisfactory answer to the naming question. The typical labels – American Indian literature, Native American literature, native literature, Indigenous literature, Amerindian literature – all pose ethical and descriptive problems because they impose European concepts and language that are inaccurate and transform diversity into a vague generic essentialist category that can be used to marginalize or misrepresent a diversified people and a complex intercultural history. "American" evokes the name of the Italian explorer Amerigo Vespucci, and it can be applied to North and South continents, whereas the term is typically misused to mean only the United States. As Gerald Vizenor often reminds readers, "Indian" reflects Columbus's confused sense of geography (unless one believes that *Indios* derives from Columbus's positive response to the Taino people – *una genta in Dios,* a people in God).[6] "Native" could apply to anyone born in the United States, though capitalizing the "N" may suggest the primacy of the first "natives." "Native," indigenous, and Amerindian risk negative connotations of stereotypical notions of the "primitive," and the latter two terms risk the dehumanizing connotations of social science jargon.

There have been many praiseworthy attempts to find alternative labels. In 1972 in the national periodical *Akwesasne Notes,* Jack Forbes recommended replacing the colonizers' names with several possible Native names, including the Algonquian words *Anishinabe-weli* (the equivalent of Indian country), though he admitted the problem of using one language group name when there were so many tribes.[7] Another possibility would be to use the term "First Nations," since it would emphasize the historical primacy of the peoples and the concept of sovereignty, which is so important today. Through usage, First Nations has, however, become almost exclusively associated with Canadian tribes. In *The Voice in the Margin* (1989), Arnold Krupat offers five interrelated definitions reflecting the diversity of the literature: "Indian" literature (a "local literature"), the "ongoing oral performances of Native people"; "indigenous" literature, involving interactions between Indian and Euro-American literary forms; "ethnic" literature, created by minority populations not historically indigenous to the United States; "national" literature, the sum of Indian, indigenous, ethnic, and Euro-American literatures; and "cosmopolitan" literature, the intersections of the national literatures.[8]

Three decades of dialogue about the naming issue have not produced consensus among literary scholars and academic publishers. Even this volume bears witness to the disagreement: the editors inclined toward American Indian literature, the publisher toward Native American literature. There is rising consensus in favor of American Indian among reservation Indians, newspaper editors, and many contemporary authors, who have taken a misnomer and re-inscribed it to represent a source of pan-tribal unity and pride. Negative responses to Native American, the most frequently used alternative to American Indian, can range from gentle humor about grant seekers cultivating politically correct language to hostility from Alaskans, Hawaiians, sovereignty activist groups, and those with strong tribal roots. On the other hand there are substantial numbers of urban and suburban Indians and academics, critics, and publishers who prefer Native American and, like one of the first Native autobiographers, William Apess (Pequot), find great offence in the term Indian. In *Manifest Manners* (1994) and other writings, Vizenor presents "Indian" as an irreparably tainted term that must be challenged by "postindian warriors" who in new stories create terms of survival and vitality.[9] Of course, the complexity of the naming issue is highlighted by Vizenor's use of "indian" as the root of his re-invented term.

Because of this complexity and because there is no consensus, the editors of this volume have not imposed naming guidelines on the contributors, hence the variety of terminology in the essays. In this introduction, I have used American Indian and Native American interchangeably, though, as noted earlier, when referring to the totality of oral and written texts, I have used the plural literatures; when referring only to texts written in English, I have used the singular literature.

As unsettling as it is, a workable approach to the naming question (there is no "best" approach) is to use American Indian or Native American literature(s) when referring to the immense and diverse bodies of oral and written texts, but to be more precise about the historical, cultural, and generic contexts when referring to specific texts. Defining Momaday's *House Made of Dawn* as a novel informed by Kiowa storytelling, Navajo ceremonialism, Jemez Pueblo landscapes and social/spiritual values, Modernist (especially Faulknerian) concepts of the novel, Emily Dickinson's and Yvor Winter's concept of the lyric, and rural and urban post WW II socio-economics, may seem rather long-winded compared to calling the novel Native American literature. But the multi-layered naming helps us to understand how an author like Momaday creates a vibrant literature from many sources. Stressing the multiplicity by using multiple naming – whether it be for a twentieth-century novel or a trickster narrative that displays borrowing from several tribal oral and written non-Indian sources – helps to emphasize the dynamic nature of the literatures and to counter labelling that seeks a non-existent static and "pure" indigenous literature. The latter approach leads to what Vizenor calls "Terminal Creeds." The former may be unsettling and unending, but it points toward a living continuum of literary voices.

V

Are there characteristics that distinguish literature written in English by American Indians from other forms of written literature? Considering the diversity of writing in English by Native Americans, it is not surprising that responsible critics have avoided defining specific issues that distinguish the literature. Still, critics are aware that the process of literary canonization typically demands that newcomers (an ironic misnomer in this case) define their distinctiveness (or at least shared concerns) as a prerequisite for adding examples of a "new" literature to the canon. Even if, as Craig Womack (Muskogee / Cherokee) argues in Red on Red (1999), Native literary canons are best studied as separate tribally based literatures, there is a need to articulate characteristics that define those canons.

Especially since the publication of House Made of Dawn several attitudes, issues, and concerns have surfaced in interviews with authors and in the criticism: for example, attitudes about a shared history – attitudes reflecting complex mixtures of post-apocalyptic worldviews, an awareness of the miracle of survival, and a hope that goes beyond survival and endurance to senses of tribal and pan-tribal sovereignty and identity. Other points of interconnection include complex concepts of communal identity and of language and place/time.

The historical perspectives often challenge popular notions of spe-cific events and figures; for instance, in The Heart is a Drum (1999) Robin Riley Fast examines how Erdrich, Paula Gunn Allen, and Maurice Kenny (Seneca / Mohawk) revise images of Mary Rowlandson's captivity, Pocahontas, Sacagawea, and the Jesuit priest Isaac Jaques in their poetry. But the historical revisioning goes beyond reconstructions of specific events and figures to encompass an alternative worldview. In Captured in the Middle (2000) Sidner Larsen (Gros Ventre) writes of a secular post-apocalyptic historical sense of a people who have already experienced a near extinction, survived, and carry on. Although this historical perspective shares some characteristics with the end-time oral narratives and syncretic messianic movements catalogued in Jace Weaver's (Cherokee) Other Worlds (2001), it is strikingly different in its secular orientation and in its belief that the destructive phase of the apocalypse has already occurred. In her essay "Where I Ought to Be" Erdrich offers dramatic hypothetical comparisons for the destructive, near extinction phenomenon: "Many Native American cultures were annihilated more thoroughly than even a nuclear disaster might destroy ours ... " It was "as if the population of the United States were to decrease from its present level to the population of Cleveland."[10] The numbers support Erdrich's comparisons. As Joy Porter notes in her historical contexts essay, estimates of the North American population in 1492 range from approximately one million to more than eighteen million. By 1900 diseases and military encounters had reduced the population to approximately 250,000.[11] The loss of land – through military defeats, treaties, legal and suspect leases, purchases, and misguided policies (such as the 1887 Dawes Act discussed in Joy Porter's essay in this volume) – contributes to the post-apocalyptic sense. In the poetry, fiction, and non-fiction the sense of loss persists. Beginning in 2002, the front page of every issue of *Indian Country Today* featured two small maps of the United States: one labelled "Indian Country – 1442" is entirely red; the other labelled "Indian Country Today" is dotted with small-to-tiny red spots representing remaining Indian land. In the wake of these catastrophic losses of life, land, and culture (and the continuing effects of losses manifested in poverty, disease, substance abuse, crime, and suicide), it is not surprising that so much of the fiction, poetry, drama, and non-fiction express the sorrow, pessimism, and bitterness about a people defined in Joy Harjo's poem "Anchorage" as "those who were never meant / to survive."[12]

But as that same poem proclaims, they did survive and more. In "A Good Story" Alexie offers an intentionally understated and ironically humorous observation on the post-apocalyptic worldview when the mother of one of his narrators, Junior, comments: "'You know,' ... 'Those stories you tell, they're kind of sad, enit?'" Reflecting the responses of many non-Indian and Indian readers to Native American literature, she justifies her request for a "good story" by adding that "'people should know that good things always happen to Indians, too.'"[13] One of the hallmarks of the best American Indian writing is an unflinching awareness of the impact of tragic losses and a persistent articulation, even celebration, of the good stories of survival, including a strong will to defend tribal and cultural sovereignty and identity.

The expressions of survival come in many different forms. In Momaday's multi-genre life narrative *The Way to Rainy Mountain,* he acknowledges, in the opening pages and throughout the historical voice of the twenty-four sections, the brutal realities of the destruction of human, buffalo, and horse lives and of deicide (the outlawing of the Sun Dance). And yet the powers of

Kiowa storytelling and of memory and the imagination can create beauty and a vitality – "As old as I am, I still have the feeling of play" sings the old woman of the Epilogue.[14] Building on Momaday's testament to endurance and vitality, in *Blood Narrative* Chadwick Allen identifies a nexus of blood/land/memory that has grounded powerful concepts of identity in many forms of Indian writing. But even authors far removed from traditional sources of blood/land/memory have discovered means of countering hard times and misrepresentations. For example, in the midst of Brooklyn's row houses, of family tensions (a father's alcoholism), and of economic hard times, the three sisters of Spiderwoman Theater can, in *Sun, Moon and Feather*, gain hilarious forms of empowerment by reinventing as childhood games the Canadian love songs and lines of Hollywood Mounties and princess stereotypes.

Like the post-apocalyptic senses of history articulated in Native American literature written in English, the senses of community are complex and multidimensional. Three dimensions that are particularly important are communal senses of identity, authorial senses of responsibility to the community, and communal senses of authorship and literature reflected in the uses of oral traditions. Of these concepts, communal senses of identity may be most obvious to non-Indian readers because they contrast so markedly with the mainstream senses of individualism. One of the most elaborate fictional presentations of the interconnective nature of communal identity appears in Ella Deloria's *Waterlily*. The protagonists Blue Bird and her daughter Waterlily define themselves within complex networks of monogamous and polygamous families, within *tiyospaye* (which Deloria's narrator calls "tipi groups"), within camps, and within broader culture groups , as well as within complex networks of "social parents," friendship vows, and gender and age roles. The narrator proclaims, "Almost from the beginning [of life] everyone could declare, 'I am not afraid; I have relatives.'"[15] In other novels, poems, plays, and life narratives the articulation of communal identity is less elaborate and less specific. But it is common for characters, poetic personae, and the "speakers" and writers of life narratives to identify themselves (or be defined by narrators) as embodiments of families, clans, bands, single tribes, and multiple tribes.

But even in the (almost) pre-Euro-American contact world of Waterlily there are fractures in the communal networks. Over time the break lines become gaping wounds. One of the central motifs of the post-apocalyptic worldview of communal identity is the fracturing, decentering, and confusing multiracial expanding of communal identities. One distressing result of these disruptions is the "restless-young-men-with-nothing-to-do" syndrome examined in several important twentieth-century novels by Robert Dale

Parker in *The Invention of Native American Literature* (2002). These male characters are "so lonely, so nonsocial"; they avoid or lack traditional community guidance that could offer restorative alternatives to the Euro-American concepts of "work" and "doing" that foster self-hatred.[16]

The enormous realities of disease, war, and governmental control often transformed supportive community networks into destructive forces. In Erdrich's North Dakota saga of twentieth-century Chippewa (Anishinaabe), interfamily hatreds between the Puyat-Morresseys-Lazarres and Pillagers-Nanapushes-Kashpaws are expressed in acts of cheating and violence (including the scalping/shaving of Margaret Kashpaw's hair). To survive, family, friends, and lovers turn on each other. Voluntary and forced abandonment and separation abound, leaving children motherless in Silko's *Ceremony* and Linda Hogan's *Solar Storms* (1995); sons fatherless in Alexie's *Lone Ranger and Tonto Fistfight in Heaven* (1993); fathers deprived of sons in Elizabeth Cook-Lynns's (Dakota-Crow Creek Sioux) *The Power of Horses* (1990); sons and daughters foster-parentless in Vickie L. Sears's (Cherokee) "Grace" (1989); and friends friendless in Hanay Geiogamah's (Kiowa / Delaware) play *Body Indian* (1972). Mixed-blood family identity adds confusing types of communal identity that extend far beyond the kinship networks Waterlily learned causing painful fragmentations dramatized in the previously mentioned early fiction as well as in powerful contemporary poetry, especially poems by Linda Hogan and Wendy Rose (Hopi / Miwok) about their divided identities.

If *Waterlily*'s narrator were reincarnated in twentieth-century fiction, poetry, or drama written by American Indians, (s)he might change his/her proclamation from "I am not afraid: I have relatives" to either "I am afraid: I have relatives" or "I am afraid: I've lost relatives." But if the crisis of the communal identity is at the core of the post-apocalyptic worldview, so is the message of the survival and adaptation of communal identity. Though often small scale, the adaptations are humane, sometimes humorous, and genuinely miraculous: Alexie's recovering alcoholic who cares for a child no one wants; Sarris's Alice, a young girl whose practical budgeting, dependability, and, when necessary, ability to point a gun, hold a multiracial urban family together; Erdrich's fierce rivals Lulu Nanapush and Marie Kashpaw become political allies in their senior years fighting for tribal sovereignty and traditional culture. The new communal identities are not as secure or as predictable as Waterlily's or Black Elk's communal identities. But they reflect a resilience at the center of the survival message of Native American literature.

The writers' interrelated senses of responsibility to community and communal concepts of authorship and literature – which grow out of the senses of communal identity – also reflect powerful acts of resistance, adaptation, and survival. In *That the People Might Live: Native American Literatures and Native American Community* (1997), Jace Weaver stresses the former: "the single thing that most defines Indian literatures relates to [a] sense of community and commitment to it." He terms this phenomenon "communitism," which blends the words community and activism. Although he doesn't mention Jane Tompkins, his concept of communitism articulates her emphasis on distinguishing a text by the "cultural work" it does, in this case especially for Indian readers. Weaver points in general to the "participation in the healing of grief and sense of exile felt by Native communities," and in particular to how the authors "help Indians imagine themselves as Indians."[17] My previous discussions of the examples of survival and vitality suggest how these acts of helping can be accomplished even when Indian communities suffer grief and exile.

Irony, even paradox, characterizes the communal concepts of authorship. With the exceptions of a few forms of oral presentation – for instance, particular speech traditions such as the Plains coup narratives – most forms of Native American oral literatures are communal. The individual performing the song, ceremony, or narrative is usually not considered the "creator" of the "text." Hence there is the irony of authors drawing authority and authenticity from traditions to which individualized concepts of authorship are foreign, a phenomenon that Catherine Rainwater and I among others have examined.[18]

In much of the essay writing and journalism by Native American authors this tension is not as obvious because authors, for instance, Will Rogers, often do not explicitly draw upon communal oral traditions, though writers such as Rogers, the Lakota humorous writer Jake Herman, and certainly Alexander Posey (Muskogee) mimicked Native speech patterns as Posey does in his "Fus Fixico Letters" (1902–08).

In historical writing, autobiography, poetry, and fiction, Indian writers have found creative ways to incorporate the paradoxes of communal-oral and individual-written authorship into their texts. In one of the earliest histories by an Indian, George Copway (Ojibwe) used communal oral narratives as the foundation of his tribal history *Traditional History and Characteristic Sketches of the Ojibway Nation* (1850). From William Apess's *A Son of the Forest* (1929) to the popular *Indian Boyhood* (1902) by Charles Eastman (Santee Sioux) to the more literary and experimental autobiographies by Mathews (Osage) (*Talking to the Moon*, 1945), Momaday (*The Way to Rainy Mountain*, 1969), Silko, (*Storyteller*, 1981), and Diane Glancy (*Claiming Breath*, 1992), Indian writers have incorporated oral traditions into their life stories. In poetry, communal oral traditions are often reflected in chant-like cadences of repetition with variation as in Joy Harjo's frequently anthologized poems "I Give You Back" and "She Had Some Horses" or in other writers' successful attempts to capture the cadences of "Red English." Examples in novels of the importance of communally shared oral narratives are obvious: for instance, in King's *Green Grass, Running Water*, Vizenor's *Bearheart*, and Silko's *Ceremony*, major characters, narrative structures, and implied reading experiences reflect communal oral traditions of trickster stories and ceremonial healing.

In their discussions of Native American writing authors and critics repeatedly refer to important concepts of language and of place/time that have grown out of communal oral traditions. Traditional Native American word concepts move far beyond describing, communicating, and explaining to encompass generative powers of creating and interconnecting. In their essays and fiction, Momaday, Silko, and Erdrich have offered especially provocative articulations of these concepts. Momaday stresses the generative force of words. In *House Made of Dawn* Tosamah's " *In principio erat Verbum* " sermon links Abel's disease and potential for curing to the absence and the development of a voice. In "The Man Made of Words" (1970) Momaday recalls how writing about the old, one-eyed woman Ko-sahn enabled her to step out of the language and appear before him and how, in a Kiowa story, an arrow maker was willing to allow his and his wife's lives to depend upon the effects of a few spoken words. Silko and Erdrich often stress generative powers of interconnection. In "Language and Literature from a Pueblo Perspective" (1979), Silko proclaims that each word can generate stories and every story can begin other stories in an infinite web of living words. In Erdrich's *Tracks*, Nanapush, in an attempt to explain his talkativeness, offers a moving statement of the connecting and healing powers of storytelling in a post-apocalyptic world: "During the year of the sickness, when I was the last one left, I saved myself by starting a story ... I got well by talking. Death could not get a word in edgewise, grew discouraged, and traveled on."[19]

Word power and sense of place are intimately connected in Native American literature. In a letter to James Wright reproduced in *The Delicacy and Strength of Lace* (1986), Silko observed that "it was as if the land was telling the stories" in *Ceremony*.[20] Native American writers of non-fiction frequently draw attention to the importance of place in both spiritual and secular realms. In *God Is Red* (1973; 1992) Vine Deloria argues that one of the fundamental differences between Native American and Western Christian worldviews is that the former is grounded primarily in spatial relationships; the latter is historically ("linear time") grounded. In his life narrative *Talking to the Moon*, Mathews offers an ecological variation on the interconnections between people, place, and spirit. He grounds Osage religion firmly in thoughts and feelings inspired by northeastern Oklahoma's prairie grass and blackjack oak country.

Besides the variations of networks of specific places and timeless spirituality, the diverse senses of "Indian place" can be suggested by indicating three other perspectives: the traditional grounding of oral literatures and worldviews in place, the "homing" motif in nineteenth- and twentieth-century writing, and landscape defined by a strong awareness of the absence of Indian possession of former Indian places.

Momaday dramatizes the grounding of stories in place in the Introduction to *The Way to Rainy Mountain*. He imagines that the Kiowa responded to their first view of Devil's Tower (or Bear Lodge) in Wyoming by creating a story "because they could not do otherwise."[21] The nature of the landscape thus often determined the nature of the stories that oriented Indian cultures. Sometimes this profound sense of place is addressed in descriptions of monumental settings such as McNickle's vast Montana landscapes in *Surrounded*. Simon Ortiz and other Native poets have shown how it can be evoked with images of small ordinary places and objects – as small as a juniper root in a New Mexico dry wash.

The "homing" motif,[22] is crucial to many genres of Native writing, for instance, in life narratives as different as Zitkala-Ša's (Yankton-Dakota) "A Trip Westward" and "My Mother's Curse Upon White Settler's" and Mary TallMountain's (Athabascan) "You *Can* Go Home Again"; in poetry, the many departures (Oklahoma, Kansas, Hawaii) and returns (Navajo Country) of Lucy Tapahonso's (Navajo) *Sáanii Dahataal* (1993); and in numerous works of fiction from Wynema Harjo's nineteenth-century return from the White South to the Creek Nation in Callahan's *Wynema* (1891) to Adair and Tema's return to Oklahoma in LeAnne Howe's (Choctaw) *Shell Shaker* (2001). The homing motif presents a distinctive alternative to the "lighting out for the territory" and "frontier" narratives of non-Indian American literature, and the complexity of this motif is increasing as the concept of "home" expands to include non-American locales as in Welch's *The Heartsong of Charging Elk* (2000) whose protagonist makes France his home.

But what about the many Native Americans whose sense of place is not as firmly grounded as Ortiz's juniper or Mathews's blackjacks or Tapahonso's Navajo country, or Charging Elk's France? (According to the US 2000 Census more than half of the 4.1 million Americans who identified themselves as having Indian heritage live in urban areas.) Do the senses of place articulated by Native writers have something to say to and for them? Many of the contemporary writers demonstrate sympathy for the difficulty of establishing a sense of place by stressing a paradoxical presence of absence: an awareness of the continuing presence of the absence of former tribal lands and of the limits of Indian sovereignty in Indian Country. This awareness can take the form of a painful daily consciousness of places lost. In *Ceremony*, Betonie reminds Tayo that "Indians wake up every morning of their lives to see the land which was stolen, still there, within reach, its theft being flaunted."[23] The awareness can address the effects of past and present removals and relocations from place, as is the case in many of Wendy Rose's powerful "half-breed chronicles" poems that dramatize San Francisco-Hopi connections and disconnections. And in some of the bleakest depictions, the absence of traditional place/community implies the desperate need for combinations of old and new senses of place. For example, in Geiogamah's play *Body Indian*, which is set in a noticeably unsacred and grubby apartment, the abuse suffered by Bobby at the hands of his Indian friends (including their theft of his artificial leg), obviously implies that "if Indian people are to survive with a measure of decency and dignity, they must stick together."[24] Place must still mean community.

The crucial link between landscape and community identity, the post-apocalyptic sense of land lost, the spatial emphasis in many Native religions, the organic ties between storytelling and place, and the central belief that the "environment" is not a place way out there but instead a place in the middle, a community home – all these senses of place challenge modern Indian and non-Indian readers to (re)consider their concepts of the American landscape.

VI

Indeed, all the characteristics typical of many works of American Indian literature written in English challenge modern readers. The secular post-apocalyptic senses of loss, survival, and sovereignty remind non-Indian readers that there is a group of Americans for whom near extinction is an historical reality, not a hypothetical worry for the future or an event that happened elsewhere. The survivors' and sovereignty tales may be extremely relevant to all twenty-first-century Americans as they confront threatened or actual disasters and attempt to define their sovereignty and identity in a global culture. The senses of communal identity certainly challenge the way many non-Indian readers define authors and the characters they create. They also help Indian and non-Indian readers to understand why governmental policies intended to foster individualism often fail. The emphasis on discovering ways to preserve traditional and to discover new forms of family and community interconnectedness in a world of fragmented families and communities can be a challenging guide for any American readers experiencing "dysfunctional" families and impersonal workplaces and neighborhoods. The powerful concepts of language and place heighten awareness of what Native Americans have lost. They can also invite readers to consider generative powers of language and land that address problems of disorientation identified by Momaday three decades ago when he wrote "The Man Made of Words": "We may be perfectly sure of where we are in relation to the supermarket and the next coffee break, but I doubt if any of us knows where he is in relation to the stars and the solstices. Our sense of natural order has become dull and unreliable."[25]

The distinctive characteristics are challenging in another way. Like the "facts" of increased visibility of Native American literature and the growth of Native American literary scholarship, the characteristics outlined in this introduction raise further questions. Weaver's community-activism emphasis raises the question of the role of the American Indian author. Should s(he) be a committed and independent artist, a representative, a mediator, an advocate? The ethical pull toward representation and advocacy is strong. But how can one voice represent more than 560 federally recognized (and several hundred hoping-to-be-recognized) tribes?

And there is the related question of the authority to represent. This authority is primarily grounded in the experience of "being Indian." Ever since (and probably before) the 1854 Publisher's Preface to John Rolling Ridge's *Joaquín Murieta* announced that the author was a "'Cherokee Indian,' born in the woods,"[26] readers have privileged writing about Indians that originated from "insiders." (Ironically this novel is not explicitly "about" Indians.) But defining who is an "insider" today can be difficult. Considering the diversity of tribal cultures and the fact that more than half of the Native American population lives in diversified cities and suburbs, it is not surprising that different groups of Indians and non-Indians emphasize different Indian identity criteria, especially blood quantum, tribal membership, community opinion, commitment, and self concept. These different emphases combined with valid anger about "pretend Indians" and their publishers and with sometimes less-than-valid hostility fueled by personal motives can generate great tensions within the community of Indian writers. It is not surprising that there have been challenges to the Indianness of some authors; *Indian Country Today* even ran a series on the topic in the early 1990s.[27]

Although not as public as the author-Indianness controversy, the appropriate criticism debate attracts significant attention. Several scholars question the application of specific critical approaches. For example, in *Blood Narrative* Chadwick Allen convincingly questions the appropriateness of using early manifestations of postcolonial and multicultural theories to interpret

American Indian literature, since the former was initially developed to understand Southeast Asian, Caribbean, and African experiences and the latter to interpret experiences of groups who voluntarily or involuntarily emigrated from their homelands. In *American Indian Literature, Environmental Justice, and Ecocriticism* (2001) Joni Adamson examines the senses of place in selected contemporary poetry and fiction and concludes that ecocriticism based on wilderness preservation models are inadequate tools for understanding Native American literature. Other critics address broad interpretive issues. In *Voice in the Margin* (1989), Arnold Krupat challenges interpreters of Native literature to abandon their aversion to literary theory. He argues that the complexity of Native American literature calls for the types of new historical and poststructuralist theories (notably Mikhail Bakhtin's concept of polyvocality) that are being applied to mainstream literatures around the world. More recently, Craig S. Womack in *Red On Red* advocates using critical models that grow out of the author's tribal land, language, and stories. Though it preceded Womack's, Krupat's, Adamson's, and Chadwick Allen's books, Paula Gunn Allen's "Kochinnenako in Academe" from *The Sacred Hoop* (1986) suggests a cross-cultural alternative that avoids the oppositional tribal / non-tribal, Indian / Euro-American binaries. She indicates insights and distortions that result from traditional tribal and modern feminist readings of the Keres Yellow Woman stories. Her alternative offers a combination of tribal and feminist orientations that minimize distortions and takes advantage of contemporary critical insights. Considering the diversity of Native American literature, there will never be one critical approach capable of adequately interpreting all the literature. But Paula Gunn Allen's approach signals a critically sound and ethically praiseworthy model.

VII

The editors of this *Cambridge Companion* hope that the combinations of descriptive and critical perspectives offered by Native American, non-Indian American, and European scholars in this volume will help beginning and advanced students of American Indian literature to appreciate the qualities and diversity of the literature. Because most courses, anthologies, and scholarship focus on well-known contemporary authors, and, more significantly, because several Indian authors are among the most respected living American authors, we provide one section of individual author studies, beginning with N. Scott Momaday. Determining which authors to feature was difficult; many of the authors listed in the index merit separate essays. Momaday, James Welch, and Leslie Marmon Silko were obvious selections; their initial novels, and to a lesser degree their poetry, attracted national attention and helped to make the study of literature by American Indians legitimate in English Departments. Simon Ortiz deserves inclusion with these three; he is the poet who attracted national attention to contemporary Native American poetry written in English. Furthermore, his strong influence on Silko's and Joy Harjo's writing and his innovative experimentation in multi-genre writing offer insights into Native American writing communities and contemporary Native American authors' attempts to combine oral and written, artistic and political literature. Gerald Vizenor may well be the most prolific contemporary Native American author whose writing in many genres – including award-winning haiku poetry and a screenplay – invites readers to consider the dark, ironic, zany, and wonderful sides of mixed heritages. Few contemporary novelists, or novelists of any period, have created a series of novels as consistently brilliant as Louise Erdrich's North Dakota Saga, which has repeatedly and deservedly been compared to Faulkner's Yoknapatawpha County Saga. Selecting authors who achieved national reputations in the last decade was especially difficult because there are so many. The inclusion of Harjo and Alexie points toward the past and the future of Native American literature. Harjo has close contacts with two of the "founders," Ortiz and Silko, and like them has achieved powerful combinations of tribal oral literature, personal conversational expression, and written poetic forms. Alexie's fast-paced combinations of brutal realism and satiric humor bring to mind nineteenth- and twentieth-century Native protest literature and humorous writing. Harjo and Alexie have also established national reputations as multi-media performers. They reach wide audiences through live performances, narration of major television series (Harjo narrated Ted Turner's *Native Americans* series) and a nationally distributed film (Alexie's screenplay for *Smoke Signals*).

The number and talent of the contemporary authors might have justified filling most of this volume with post-1968 individual author studies. We decided not to do this but instead to allot most of the collection to historical, cultural, gender, and genre contexts that would counter the disproportionate attention paid to individual author studies of contemporary writers and that would offer students and instructors contexts useful to the study of many well-known and emerging writers.

Part 1, together with this introduction, provides important historical, cultural, and gender contexts. Chapter 1 demonstrates how pre-Columbian values and oral narratives of historical origins, as well as European inventions of the concept of "Indian," colonial and national governmental policies, international wars, and a phenomenon as recent as the tribally owned casino can shape writing by American Indians. The second chapter addresses significant issues raised by mediations between Native and non-native cultures: for instance, the implications of translations, the cultural work of fiction read by Indians and non-Indians, the degree to which Indians have been portrayed as active agents or as victims, and the complexities of modern Indian identity. Throughout the volume there are discussions of women writers and women collaborators, and three of the eight individual author chapters are devoted to women. Nevertheless, we believe that it is important to have a separate chapter on Native American women writers. Even though their contributions to the literature written in English began in the early nineteenth century, their works were often underrepresented in the scholarship and unnoticed by the general reading public until the late twentieth century. Chapter 3 is one more attempt to counter that under-representation.

The focus of Part 2, specific genres, raises a legitimate question: if one of the significant contributions of Native American writers is the creation of mixed-genre works of literature, why devote so much of the volume to examinations of individual genres? One obvious response to this question is to remind readers that all the writers examined were inspired (and constrained) by genre conventions they learned from their own reading experiences – a learning process that was reinforced by their publishers' and readers' genre expectations. Having a section devoted to genre also highlights the diversity of forms of Native writing. Since fiction and poetry are the two genres most often taught in literature classes that include Native American texts, it is important to include examinations of each. There are two chapters on fiction in part because there are so many novels and short stories; the extra space devoted to fiction, especially since 1968, also reflects the essential role recent fiction played in gaining respect for all forms of oral and written American Indian literatures. The two chapters on non-fiction respond to historical and pedagogical situations. As indicated earlier, Samson Occom's best-selling execution sermon, the syndicated journalism of Will Rogers, and Deloria's popular *Custer Died for Your Sins* demonstrate that some of the most widely read and influential works by American Indians have been non-fiction. Furthermore, some of the most frequently taught texts are life narratives (for example, *Black Elk Speaks*). A separate chapter on life narratives (which discusses both collaborative and single-author works) introduces students to the continuing importance of oral performance and the crucial mediative roles of non-Native editors, as well as introducing them to important concepts of communal selves and cross-cultural authorship that differ from the individualistic identities represented in many mainstream autobiographies.

For reasons noted earlier, drama is taught less frequently, but drama anthologies such as Hanay Geiogamah and Jaye T. Darby's *Stories of Our Way* (1999) and Mimi Gisolfi D'Aponte's *Seventh Generation* (1999), collections of commentary such as Geiogahah and Darby's *American Indian Theater in Performance* (2000), and the inclusion of plays in general anthologies such as Purdy and Ruppert's *Nothing But the Truth* and Gerald Vizenor's *Native American Literature* (1995) are making plays readily available for classroom use. The rapid growth of Native American theater groups and the obvious connections between the worlds of Native American drama and film also suggest that the study of drama and theater will be a crucial element of future Native American literary studies.

The editors and contributors hope that the discussions of historical, cultural, and gender contexts, the overviews of genres and genre mixing, the essays on individual authors and the brief bio-bibliographies section will help those new to American Indian literature to appreciate why its study has moved from invisible to expected status. We also hope that this *Cambridge Companion* will engage those familiar with the subject and encourage them in their classrooms and in their writing to expand the recognition of America's oldest and newest literature.[28]

Notes

1. A. LaVonne Brown Ruoff, *American Indian Literatures: an Introduction, Bibliographic Review and Selected Bibliography*, New York: Modern Language Association, 1990, p. 1. For less conservative estimates, see Joy Porter's essay.
2. Kenneth M. Roemer, "Native American Oral Narratives: Context and Continuity," in Brian Swann, ed., *Smoothing the Ground: Essays on Native American Oral Literature*. Berkeley: University of California Press, 1983, pp. 48, 54, note 30.
3. Louis Owens, *Other Destinies: Understanding the American Indian Novel*. Norman: University of Oklahoma Press, 1994, p. 33.
4. See Craig Womack, *Red on Red: Native American Literary Separatism*. Minneapolis: University of Minnesota Press, 1999, pp. 271–88.
5. Geary Hobson, ed., *The Remembered Earth: an Anthology of Contemporary Native American Literature*. Albuquerque: Red Earth Press, 1979, p. 9.
6. Peter Matthiessen, *Indian Country*. New York: Viking Press, 1984, p. 3.
7. Jack Forbes, "It's Time to Throw Off the White Man's Names," *Akwesasne Notes* 4.2 (March 1972), p. 31.
8. Arnold Krupat, *The Voice in the Margin: Native American Literature and the Canon*. Berkeley: University of California Press, pp. 209–16.
9. Gerald Vizenor, *Manifest Manners: Postindian Warriors of Survivance*. Hanover: Wesleyan University Press, 1994, pp. 10–12.
10. Louise Erdrich, "Where I Ought to Be: a Writer's Sense of Place," *The New York Times Book Review* 28 July 1985, p. 23.
11. Jack Utter, *American Indians: Answers to Today's Questions*, 2nd edn. Norman: University of Oklahoma Press, 2001, pp. 39, 43.
12. Joy Harjo, *She Had Some Horses*. New York: Thunder's Mouth Press, 1997, p. 14.
13. Sherman Alexie, *The Lone Ranger and Tonto Fistfight in Heaven*. New York: Atlantic Monthly Press, 1993, pp. 139–40.

14. N. Scott Momaday, *The Way to Rainy Mountain*. Albuquerque: University of New Mexico Press, 1969, p. 88.
15. Ella Deloria, *Waterlily*. Lincoln: University of Nebraska Press, 1988, p. 20.
16. Robert Dale Parker, *The Invention of Native American Literature*. Ithaca: Cornell University Press, 2003, p. 29.
17. Jace Weaver, *That the People Might Live: Native American Literature and Native American Community*. New York: Oxford University Press, 1997, pp. 42–45.
18. Catherine Rainwater, *Dreams of Fiery Stars: the Transformations of Native American Fiction*. Philadelphia: University of Pennsylvania Press, 1999, pp. 6–9; Kenneth M. Roemer, "The Heuristic Powers of Indian Literatures: What Native Authorship Does to Mainstream Texts," *Studies in American Indian Literatures*, Ser. 2, 3.2 (Summer 1991), pp. 8–21.
19. Louise Erdrich, *Tracks*. New York: Henry Holt, 1988, p. 46.
20. Anne Wright, ed., *The Delicacy and Strength of Lace: Letters Between Leslie Marmon Silko and James Wright*. Saint Paul: Graywolf Press, 1986, pp. 27–28.
21. Momaday, *Way to Rainy Mountain*, p. 8.
22. See William Bevis, "Native American Novels: Homing In," in Brian Swann and Arnold Krupat, eds., *Recovering the Word: Essays on Native American Literature*, Berkeley: University of California Press, 1987, pp. 580–620.
23. Leslie Marmon Silko, *Ceremony*. New York: Viking Press, 1977, p. 127.
24. Jeffrey Huntsman, "Introduction" to Hanay Geiogamah, *New Native American Drama*. Norman: University of Oklahoma Press, 1980, p. xvii.
25. N. Scott Momaday, "The Man Made of Words," in John L. Purdy and James Ruppert, eds., *Nothing But the Truth: an Anthology of Native American Literature*. Upper Saddle River: Prentice Hall, 2001, p. 86.
26. John Rollin Ridge [Yellow Bird], *The Life and Adventures of Joaquin Murieta, the Celebrated California Bandit*. San Francisco: W. B. Cooke, 1854, p. 2.
27. See especially the three-part series "Indian Writers: Read or Imagined," which began with the 8 September 1993 issue.
28. I would like to thank my co-editor Joy Porter for making excellent suggestions for revising this introduction, especially in the discussion of naming the field. Several paragraphs in this introduction are revised versions of my introduction to *Native American Writers of the United States*. Detroit: Gale Research, 1997.

KENNETH M. ROEMER

Timeline: literary, historical, and cultural conjunctions

In several ways the following timeline is similar to previously published timelines for American Indian literature: it lists significant books in English by Native American authors (thus the 1772 beginning date) and relevant government policies, legislation, and historical, social, and cultural events. Wars are listed, not only because Indian participation in the Revolutionary and 1812 Wars was significant, but also because of the high enlistment rate among Native Americans in the twentieth century and the impact war experiences had on Indian communities. Like Gretchen Bataille's time line in the anthology *Nothing But the Truth* (2001), my list includes books by non-Indians, in part because these books helped to shape popular (mis)conceptions of Indians and because Native American authors often explicitly or implicitly responded to the stereotypes popularized by works such as *The Last of the Mohicans* (1826), *Nick of the Woods* (1837), or *Hanta Yo* (1979).

In one significant way this timeline differs from earlier chronologies: it includes books by non-Indians that do not explicitly address "Indian" issues. I hope these inclusions will inspire (or provoke) meaningful comparative questions. For example what are the implications of the similarities and differences in war and postwar experiences as represented in novels by Momaday, Silko, and Owens and in works such as *Catch 22* (1955), *No-No Boy* (1957) and *Bless Me, Ultima* (1972)? When it is placed within the contexts of imagist and modernist poetry published between 1916 and 1922, to what degree does the collection of translations *Path on the Rainbow* (1918) represent a celebration or an exploitation of Indian oral traditions? In 1902 both Alexander Posey and Finley Peter Dunne captured spoken dialect (Muskogee-English / Irish-English) in print. In 1903 and 1911, W. E. B. DuBois and Charles Eastman (Santee Sioux) both used the word "soul(s)" in their titles. What do these early twentieth-century coincidences suggest about capturing the voices and spirit of marginalized groups? In 1920 to 1921 we discover three strikingly different "main street" identities offered by an Anglo American, a Jewish American, and a Yankton Dakota. What do these voices suggest about the possibility or desirability of ever articulating a unified "American" identity? The juxtapositions also raise questions about literary canon formation; for example, how might discussion of John Rollin Ridge's (Cherokee) popular *Joaquín Murieta* (1854) alter perceptions of the "American Literary Renaissance" of the 1850s?

In other words, I hope that the time line will be a source of information and context, as well as a heuristic device inviting examination of the implications of juxtaposing Native and non-native literatures and histories.

Major sources: Chadwick Allen, "Integrated Time Line," *Blood Narrative* (2002), pp. 220–39; Gretchen M. Bataille's "Selected List," in John L. Purdy and James Ruppert, eds., *Nothing But the Truth* (2001), pp. 620–32; Lee Francis, *Native Time* (1998); Frederick E. Hoxie, *Encyclopedia of North American Indians* (1996); Judith Nies, *Native American History* (1996); A. LaVonne Brown Ruoff, "Important Dates," *American Indian Literatures* (1990), pp. 191–93; and Jack Utter, *American Indians: Answers to Questions*, 2nd edn., (2001). The decade-by-decade descriptive timeline series by Barbara Bad Wound that began with the 1–8 November 1999 issue of *Indian Country Today* was very useful. I would like to thank Joy Porter and Kenneth Philp for making suggestions about the timeline, though I take responsibility for any errors.

Key: A = autobiography; CA = collaborative autobiography; CT = collection of translations of oral literature; D = drama; F = fiction; NF = non-fiction; P = poetry; S = speech or sermon. An asterisk indicates an American Indian author.

1772	Samson Occom,* *Execution of Moses Paul* (S)
1774	John Woolman, *Journal* (A)
1775	American Revolution begins (ends 1783)
1776	Thomas Paine, *Common Sense* (NF) Declaration of Independence
1782	Crevecoeur, *Letters* (NF, A)
1786	Secretary of War placed in charge of Indian affairs
1790	Susanna Rowson, *Charlotte Temple* (F)
	First US Census, US population: 4 million, Indian population: est. 600,000. Pre-Columbian population estimates for North America range from 1 to 18 million.
1791	Benjamin Franklin, *Autobiography* Pt. 1 (A) in French
1798	Charles Brockden Brown, *Wieland* (F)
1799	Handsome Lake (Seneca) religious movement
1803	Louisiana Purchase
	Lewis and Clark expedition

1812	War with England (ends 1814)
1819	Washington Irving, *Sketch Book* (NF, F)
1824	Bureau of Indian Affairs (BIA) est. in the War Department
1826	First issue of *The Literary Voyager or Muzzeniegun*, Jane Johnson Schoolcraft,* co-ed.
	James Fenimore Cooper, *Last of the Mohicans* (F)
1827	David Cusick,* *History of the Six Nations* (NF)
1829	William Apess,* *Son of the Forest* (A)
	Andrew Jackson inaugurated
1830	Indian Removal Act
1832	Office of Commissioner of Indian Affairs est.
1833	Black Hawk,* *Black Hawk, an Autobiography* (CA)
1834	Indian Intercourse Act
	Indian Territory est. in Eastern Oklahoma
1835	William Apess,*
	Indian Nullification of the Unconstitutional Laws of Massachusetts (NF)
	William Gilmore Simms, *The Yamassee* (F)
	Seminole War begins (ends 1842)
1836	Ralph Waldo Emerson, *Nature* (NF)
1837	Nathaniel Hawthorne *Twice-Told Tales* (F)
	Robert Montgomery Bird, *Nick of the Woods* (F)
	Republic of Texas recognized by US
1838	Cherokee Trail of Tears removal to Oklahoma (ends 1839)
1841	Act for preemption of public lands: 160 acres, $1.25 per acre
1845	Frederick Douglass, *The Narrative* (A)
	Edgar Allan Poe, *The Raven and Other Poems* (P)
	Florida and Texas annexed
	Most Seminoles removed to Indian Territory
1846	War with Mexico (ends 1848)
1847	George Copway,* *Life, History, and Travels of Kah-ge-ga-gah-bowh* (A)
1848	Treaty of Guadalupe Hidalgo
	SW and California tribes under US control
1849	California gold rush
	Office of Indian Affairs moved to Dept. of Interior
1850	George Copway,* *Traditional History . . . of the Ojibway* (NF)
	Ralph Waldo Emerson, *Representative Men* (NF)
	Nathaniel Hawthorne, *The Scarlet Letter* (F)
	California admitted as state
	Fugitive Slave Law passed
1851	Herman Melville, *Moby-Dick* (F)

1852   Harriet Beecher Stowe, *Uncle Tom's Cabin* (F)
1854   John Rollin Ridge,* *Joaquín Murieta* (F)
        Henry David Thoreau, *Walden* (A, NF)
        Kansas-Nebraska Act establishes "squatter sovereignty"
1855   Henry Wadsworth Longfellow, *Hiawatha* (P)
        Walt Whitman, *Leaves of Grass* (P)
1861   Civil War begins (ends 1865)
1863   Kit Carson's campaign begins against Navajos and Apaches
        (ends 1864)
        Abraham Lincoln, "Gettysburg Address" (S)
1864   Massacre of Cheyenne at Sand Creek, Colorado
1865   13th Amendment abolishes slavery
1866   First Civil Rights Act
1867   Board of Indian Commissioners established
        Alaska purchased from Russia
1871   Indian Appropriation Act nullifying treaty making
1872   Modoc War
1876   Little Big Horn Battle
1877   Nez Perce revolt, Chief Joseph leader
1879   Carlisle Indian School established
1881   Henry James, *Portrait of a Lady* (F)
1882   Indian Rights Association established
1883   Sarah Winnemucca,* *Life among the Piutes* (A)
        Indian Rights Association established
        Buffalo Bill's Wild West Show begins
1884   Helen Hunt Jackson, *Ramona* (F)
        Mark Twain, *Huckleberry Finn* (F)
1885   William Dean Howells, *The Rise of Silas Lapham* (F)
        Last buffalo herd exterminated
1886   Geronimo surrenders
        Haymarket Riot in Chicago
1887   General Allotment Act or Dawes Act (repealed 1934)
1888   Edward Bellamy, *Looking Backward* (F)
1889   North and South Dakota and Montana statehood
        Oklahoma land rush begins
1890   Emily Dickinson, *Poems* (P)
        Adolph Bandelier, *The Delight Makers* (F)
        Massacre at Wounded Knee
1891   S. Alice Callahan,* *Wynema* (F)
1893   Frederick Jackson Turner, "Significance of the
        Frontier" (NF)

1895	Emily Pauline Johnson,* *White Wampum* (P)
	Stephen Crane, *The Red Badge of Courage* (F)
1898	Spanish-American War
	Curtis Act
	Oklahoma allotment
1899	Simon Pokagon,* *Queen of the Woods* (F) authorship debated
	Kate Chopin, *The Awakening* (F)
1900	Francis La Flesche,* *The Middle Five* (A)
	Theodore Dreiser, *Sister Carrie* (F)
	US population: 76 million; Indian population: 237,000
1902	Charles A. Eastman,* *Indian Boyhood* (A)
	Alexander Posey begins writing "Fus Fixico Letters" (F)
	Finley Peter Dunn, *Observations by Mr. Dooley* (F)
	Edith Wharton, *The House of Mirth* (F)
1903	W. E. B. DuBois, *Souls of Black Folk*
1907	Henry Adams, *Education* (NF) (1918 republished for public)
	Oklahoma statehood
1909	Gertrude Stein, *Three Lives* (F)
	NAACP est.
1910	Alexander Posey,* *Poems of Alexander Posey*
1911	Charles Eastman,* *Soul of the Indian* (NF)
	Society of the American Indian established.
1912	New Mexico and Arizona statehood
	Jim Thorpe (Sauk / Fox) Olympic champion
1913	Emily Pauline Johnson,* *Moccasin Maker* (F)
	Willa Cather, *O Pioneers* (F)
	Robert Frost, *A Boy's Will* (P)
	Indian Head nickel issued
1914	World War I begins in Europe (US entry 1917, War ends 1918)
1916	H. D., *Sea Garden* (P)
1917	William Carlos Williams, *Al Que Quiere!* (P)
1918	*The Path of the Rainbow* (CT), George Cronyn, ed.
	Influenza epidemic
1919	Will Rogers,* *Rogers-isms* (NF)
	Sherwood Anderson, *Winesburg, Ohio* (F)
1920	Sinclair Lewis, *Main Street* (F)
	Anzia Yezierska, *Hungry Hearts* (F)
1921	Zitkala-Ša,* *American Indian Stories* (A, F)
	Eugene O'Neill, *Emperor Jones* (D)
1922	T. S. Eliot, *The Wasteland* (P)
1924	Congress grants citizenship to Indians

1925   F. Scott Fitzgerald, *The Great Gatsby* (F)
1926   Ernest Hemingway, *The Sun Also Rises* (F)
        National Council of American Indians established.
1927   Mourning Dove,* *Cogewea* (F)
1928   Meriam Report criticized policies on Indians
1929   William Faulkner, *The Sound and the Fury* (F)
        Oliver LaFarge, *Laughing Boy* (F)
1931   Lynn Riggs,* *Green Grow the Lilacs* (D)
        BIA begins off-reservation placement foreshadowing
        later Relocation program
1932   John Joseph Mathews, *Wah'Kon-Tah* (F)
        John Neihardt and Nicholas Black Elk,* *Black Elk Speaks* (CA)
        Santa Fe Indian School established
1934   John Joseph Mathews,* *Sundown* (F)
        Indian Reorganization Act
1935   John Milton Oskison,* *Brothers Three* (F)
        Indian Arts and Crafts Board established
1936   D'Arcy McNickle,* *The Surrounded* (F)
        Ruth Underhill and Maria Chona, *Autobiography of a Papago
        Woman* (CA)
1937   Zora Neale Hurston, *Their Eyes Were Watching God (F)*
1939   John Steinbeck, *The Grapes of Wrath* (F)
        Pope declares Kateri Tekakwitha (Mohawk) venerable
1940   Richard Wright, *Native Son* (F)
1941   Frank Waters, *The Man Who Killed the Deer* (F)
        US enters World War II (War ends 1945)
1942   Navajo "Code Talkers" established
1944   Ella Deloria,* *Speaking of Indians* (NF)
        Ruth Muskrat Bronson,* *Indians Are People, Too*
        National Congress of American Indians established
1945   John Joseph Mathews,* *Talking to the Moon* (A)
        Ira Hays Iwo Jima flag photo
1946   *The Winged Serpent,* (CT) Margot Astrov, ed.
        Indian Claims Commission Act (disbanded in 1978)
1947   Tennessee Williams, *A Streetcar Named Desire* (D)
1948   Crazy Horse Mt. Memorial project dedicated
1949   Arthur Miller, *Death of a Salesman* (D)
1950   US troops in Korea (armistice signed 1953)
        Relocation program begins
        US population: 150.7 million; Indian population: 358,000
1951   A. Grove Day, *The Sky Clears* (CT)

1952   Ralph Ellison, *Invisible Man* (F)

1953   Termination policy resolution (HCR 108) passed in Congress (repealed 1988)

1954   Indian Health Services moved from the BIA to Public Health Service

1955   Joseph Heller, *Catch-22* (F)

1956   Indian Vocational Training Act

1957   John Okada, *No-No Boy* (F)

1959   D'Arcy McNickle,* *Indians and Other Americans* (NF)
        Navajo Times established
        Alaska and Hawaii statehood

1960   John Barth, *Sot-Weed Factor* (F)
        Flannery O'Connor, *The Violent Bear It Away* (F)
        US population: 180 million; Indian population: 52,400

1961   American Indian Chicago Conference "Declaration of Indian Purpose"
        National Indian Youth Council established

1962   Institute of American Indian Arts established

1963   Hal Borland, *When the Legends Die* (F)
        Martin Luther King, "I Have a Dream" (S)
        John F. Kennedy assassinated

1964   Thomas Berger, *Little Big Man* (F)
        Saul Bellow, *Herzog* (F)
        Indian Historian (journal) established
        Billy Mills (Lakota) Olympic Champion
        Civil Rights Act
        Gulf of Tonkin Resolution
        Vietnam War (ends 1974)

1968   N. Scott Momaday,* *House Made of Dawn* (F) (awarded a Pulitzer in 1969)
        American Indian Movement established
        Indian Civil Rights Act
        Navajo Community College established (opens in 1969)
        "Fish-ins" in Pacific Northwest
        Martin Luther King and Robert Kennedy assassinated

1969   Vine Deloria, Jr.,* *Custer Died for Your Sins* (NF)
        N. Scott Momaday,* *The Way to Rainy Mountain* (NF, A, P)
        Arthur Kopit, *Indians* (D)
        Akwesasne Notes established
        National Indian Education Association established
        Alcatraz Island occupation

1970   Dee Brown, *Bury My Heart at Wounded Knee* (NF)
Native American Rights Fund established
North American Indian Women's Association established
Nixon's "Self-Determination without Termination" speech
Return of Blue Lake to the Taos
Convocation of American Indian Scholars (Momaday's "Man Made of Words" lecture delivered)
US population: 203 million; Indian population: 793,000

1971   *The Magic World* (CT), William Brandon, ed.
Red Power (NF), Alvin Josephy, Jr., ed.
Alaska Native Claims Settlement Act
American Indian Press Association established
BIA headquarters occupation

1972   John Lame Deer,* *Lame Deer, Seeker of Visions* (CA)
Shaking the Pumpkin, (CT) Jerome Rothenberg, ed.
Rudolfo Anaya, *Bless Me, Ultima* (F)
Indian Education Act

1973   Vine Deloria,* *God Is Red*
Thomas Pynchon, *Gravity's Rainbow* (F)
Wounded Knee, SD occupation
University of Oklahoma drops "Little Red" mascot

1974   James Welch,* *Winter in the Blood* (F)
Man to Send Rain Clouds (F) Kenneth Rosen, ed.
Gary Snyder, *Turtle Island* (P, NF)
Women of All Red Nations established
Studies in American Indian Literatures established as newsletter, later becomes a journal
American Indian Quarterly established
American Indian Culture and Research Journal established

1975   *Carriers of the Dream Wheel* (P) Duane Niatum,* ed.
Voices of the Rainbow (P) Kenneth Rosen, ed.
Maxine Hong Kingston, *The Woman Warrior* (A, F)
Indian Self-Determination Act
Educational Assistance Act
Council of Energy Resource Tribes established

1976   Simon Ortiz,* *Going for the Rain* (P)
N. Scott Momaday,* *The Names* (A) and *The Gourd Dancer* (P)
Peter Blue Cloud* *Turtle, Bear, and Wolf* (P)
Indian Health Care Improvement Act
William Sampson (Creek) nominated for Oscar, *One Flew Over the Cuckoo's Nest* based on Ken Kesey's novel (1962)

1977   Leslie Marmon Silko,* *Ceremony* (F)
        Martin Cruz Smith,* *Nightwing* (F)
        Gary Soto, *The Elements of San Joaquin* (P)
        NEH / MLA Indian Literatures Seminar, Flagstaff, AZ

1978   Gerald Vizenor,* *Darkness in St. Louis Bearheart* (F, rpt. 1990)
        American Indian Religious Freedom Act
        Indian Child Welfare Act
        Tribally Controlled Community College Assistance Act
        American Indian Science and Engineering Society established

1979   James Welch,* *Death of Jim Loney* (F)
        Ruth Beebe Hill, *Hanta Yo* (F)
        Archaeological Resources Protection Act

1980   Ray Young Bear,* *winter of the salamander* (P)
        Hanay Geiogamah,* *New Native American Drama* (D)
        Maine Indian Claims Act
        US population: 227 million; Indian population: 1.36 million

1981   Leslie Marmon Silko,* *Storyteller* (F, P, A)
        Lakota Times, later retitled *Indian Country Today,* established,
        Tim Giago (Lakota), ed.

1982   Alice Walker, *Color Purple* (F)

1983   Joy Harjo,* *She Had Some Horses* (P, reissued, 1997)
        Studies in American Indian Literature (NF), Paula Gunn Allen* ed.

1984   Louise Erdrich,* *Love Medicine* (F, rev. ed. 1993)
        Sandra Cisneros, *The House on Mango Street* (F)

1985   Janet Hale Campbell,* *Jailing of Cecilia Capture* (F)
        Wilma Mankiller, first woman principal chief of the Cherokee

1986   Paula Gunn Allen,* *The Sacred Hoop* (NF)
        James Welch,* *Fools Crow* (F)
        Louise Erdrich,* *Beet Queen* (F)

1987   Michael Doris,* *Yellow Raft in Blue Water* (F)
        Gerald Vizenor,* *Griever* (F)
        Gloria Anzaldúa, *Borderlands /La Frontera* (A, NF, P)
        Toni Morrison, *Beloved* (F)

1988   Louise Erdrich,* *Tracks* (F)
        Ella Deloria,* *Waterlily* (F, written in 1940s)
        Anna Lee Walters,* *Ghost Singer* (F)
        *Harper's Anthology of Twentieth Century Native American
        Poetry,* Duane Niatum,* ed.
        Tony Hillerman, *A Thief in Time* (F)
        Indian Gaming Regulation Act

1989   Michael Dorris,* *The Broken Cord* (A)
        N. Scott Momaday,* *The Ancient Child* (F)
1990   Linda Hogan,* *Mean Spirit* (F)
        Thomas King,* *Medicine River* (F)
        Native American Grave Protection and Repatriation Act
        Native American Languages Act
        US population: 249 million; Indian population: 1.9 million
1991   Leslie Marmon Silko,* *Almanac of the Dead* (F)
        Custer Battlefield name changed to Little Bighorn Battlefield
        Persian Gulf War
1992   Sherman Alexie,* *The Business of Fancy Dancing* (P, F)
        Diane Glancy,* *Claiming Breath* (A)
        N. Scott Momaday,* *In the Presence of the Sun* (P, NF)
        Simon Ortiz,* *Woven Stone* (P, NF)
        Louis Owens,* *The Sharpest Sight* (F)
        First "Returning the Gift" gathering, Norman, OK
        Ben Nighthorse Campbell (Northern Cheyenne), first American
        Indian senator
        Foxwood Casino dedicated by Mashantucket Pequods
1993   Sherman Alexie* *The Lone Ranger and Tonto, Fistfight in
        Heaven* (F)
        Thomas King,* *Green Grass, Running Water* (F)
        Wilma Mankiller,* *Mankiller* (A)
        Lucy Tapahonso,* *Sáanii Dahataal* (P)
        Wordcraft Circle of Native Writers and Storytellers established
1994   Louise Erdrich, *Bingo Palace* (F)
        Susan Power,* *Grass Dancer* (F)
        Wendy Rose,* *Bone Dance* (P)
        Greg Sarris,* *Grand Avenue* (F)
1995   Linda Hogan,* *Solar Storms* (F)
1996   Louise Erdrich,* *Tales of Burning Love* (F)
        Discovery of the Kenniwick Man
1999   Leslie Marmon Silko,* *Gardens in the Dunes* (F)
        Stories Our Way, (D) Hanay Geiogamah,* ed.
        Seventh Generation (D)
        Mimi Gisolfi D'Aponte, ed.
        Sacagawea dollar issued
2000   James Welch,* *The Heartsong of Charging Elk* (F)
        Anita Endreszze,* *Throwing Fire at the Sun* ... (NF, F. P)
        US population: 281.4 million; Indian population: 2.5 million
        "Indian" + 1.6 million mixed heritage = 4.1 million

2001	Sherman Alexie,* *The Toughest Indian* (F)
	Louise Erdrich,* *Last Report on the Miracles* ... (F)
	LeAnne Howe,* *Shell Shaker* (F)
2002	Debra Magpie Earling,* *Perma Red* (F)
2003	Louise Erdrich,* *The Master Butchers Singing Club* (F)
	Sherman Alexie,* *Ten Little Indians* (F)
	Iraqi War
	John Herrington (Chickasaw), first tribally enrolled astronaut in space
	Indian Memorial at Little Bighorn Battlefield dedicated
2004	Louise Erdrich,* *Four Souls: a Novel* (F)
	United States vs. Lara recognizes tribes' legal power over non-member Indians on their territory
	The National Museum of the American Indian opens
	Cecilia Five Thunder, first woman elected leader of the Oglala Lakota

PART I

HISTORICAL AND CULTURAL CONTEXTS

I

JOY PORTER

Historical and cultural contexts to Native American literature

Literature tells truths about the past that history cannot articulate. This is a truism with particular resonance in the Native American context because until the watershed years of the late 1960s and early 1970s Indians were either ignored or grossly misrepresented by conventional histories. Typically, histories that did focus exclusively upon Indian concerns limited their approach, either to the history of Indian policy or frontier conflict, or, in the case of anthropological studies, to tribal histories with narratives that ended before 1900. By comparison, Native American literature across time has voiced a different experience of American history. It has voiced a different relationship to historical "facts" and a different consciousness of the past itself. Therefore this chapter does more than simply orientate the reader through setting out a version of the Indian past in outline and linking it to aspects of Indian literature. Just as importantly, it considers how the past is conceptualized within Native cultures at the tribal and cross-tribal level and how this has informed the literary projects of specific Native writers.

The great transformative power of Indian literature from any era derives in part from its ability to invoke a past with direct implications for the present. Indians, after all, are not just fictional, they are real. The strength and agency of Indian America today testifies to the survival of diverse Indian nations and individuals in spite of a brutal colonial past. However, the larger context for Indian urban and reservation life remains one of endemic disadvantage rooted firmly in the history of colonialism. Such impoverishment stacks the odds against Native peoples throughout the United States, including within the richer states like Alaska, home to 86,000 natives. The National Academy of Public Administration reported in 1999 that 31 percent of all Indians lived below the poverty line, compared to 13 percent within the US population as a whole. Again in October 2002 the US Census Bureau reported that the lowest US median household income of all was at Buffalo County, South Dakota, home of the Crow Creek Indian Reservation. The recent economic and social factor of Indian gaming has not displaced poverty as the specter haunting

Indian America and in particular, single-parent Indian women remain acutely affected by what has been called the "feminization" of American poverty since the 1970s. The historically large disparities in the health statistics between Indian and non-Indian populations persist, with Indians much more likely than non-Indians to die from tuberculosis, liver disease, diabetes, pneumonia, and influenza and from accidents, homicide, and suicide.

Thus the battles for Indian survival are far from over. Contemporary Indian communities face acute ongoing threats to the sovereignty of their remaining land base and to the ecological balance of Indian environments from, amongst other things, nuclear testing, nuclear waste disposal, coal strip mining and oil, logging, and uranium extraction. Indian communities also face threats to the integrity of their tribal, national, and ethnic representation and they suffer the internal conflicts created when a diverse set of peoples survive massive depletion in numbers, progressive engulfment by foreign cultures, repeated displacement, and fundamental attack upon their spiritual life. These facts are noted at the outset because for readers to form an understanding of Indian literatures and their development, the best foundation is undoubtedly engagement with Indian peoples themselves, even if initially that engagement is confined to awareness of these kinds of basic structural realities within contemporary Indian life and a sense of the urgent need for these to alter for the better.

Literature is part of the web of cultural strength that has allowed Indian peoples to demonstrate remarkable resilience over time. Indian literary voices flourish today in spite of the loss of 70 to 90 percent of the indigenous population of the Americas in the first century of contact, the expropriation by non-Indians of over 95 percent of the pre-contact Indian landbase, the subsequent limitations placed on Indian control over the resources of the residual Indian territory and the extreme poverty and disadvantage Indians have experienced since contact. US Indian population numbers reached an all-time low of 237,000 in 1900. Depending on conflicting professional sources, one, eighteen, or perhaps tens of millions of North American Indians perished following "discovery" in 1492. As the poet Joy Harjo once put it, there has been the "destruction of grandchildren" resulting in a "famine of stories," that is, a sustained attack over centuries upon Indian populations with a corresponding impact upon the Indian imagination.[1] Since 1900 however, Indian numbers have increased dramatically. In 1990 the US census enumerated 1.9 million Native Americans while in the 2000 Census 4.1 million people reported as American Indian and Alaskan Native alone or in combination with one or more other races. 538,300 reported as living on reservations or trust lands meaning that by far the majority of

Indians in the United States now live in urban environments. Thus current levels of understanding and appreciation of Native American literatures should be seen in the context of a gradual renaissance of Native American numbers and of a rebirth of the collective and individual purchase Native Americans exert, within nations, bands, and as individuals.

Indian literature and early contact

Today there is wider recognition of the fact that American literature did not begin in 1492 or 1776, but is in fact a continuum of voice that began with the first human expression of language in the landscape we now think of as the United States. However, where the first Americans expressing language came from and how long they have existed within that landscape is not universally agreed upon.

When Europeans first encountered Native American peoples they speculated that they had been there only a few hundred years. Estimates grew to 5,000 years in 1900 and recently leapt again with the discovery of a human record on an island off the California coast, dated to 28,000 BCE. Since the eighteenth century, most scientists have been convinced that the first Americans were migrants from Northeastern Asia. Contemporary scholars like Michael Crawford (*The Origins of Native Americans: Evidence from Anthropological Genetics*, 1998) think the first peoples in the Americas might have come from Siberia. The theory is that the earliest inhabitants crossed a land or perhaps ice "bridge" exposed during the last glacial period between Siberia and Alaska in an area called the Bering Strait. Vine Deloria, Jr. has taken particular exception to this idea however, noting the political implications of an Indian "discovery" of the Americas and suggesting that traditional accounts of indigenous origins would be a much more fruitful focus for study (Deloria, 1973, 1989, 1995). Deloria's general concern about the social and political implications of this "origins" scholarship seemed to be borne out in 1999 when anthropologists suggested that the earliest North Americans were neither Indian nor Asian but were in fact Western Europeans who arrived around 18,000 years ago. That said, some Native American writers have accepted the Asian origins theory, including the first to gain recognition and acceptance at the very centre of American literature, the Kiowa writer and painter N. Scott Momaday.[2]

But however the distant past is imagined within the United States, Indians belong there since Indian peoples had formed a close relationship with the spirit of the land long before first contact with Western Europeans. Indians belong to America, as the Sioux spokesman Luther Standing Bear put it in his 1933 book *Land of the Spotted Eagle*, because of repeated birth and rebirth, because their bodies are "formed of the dust of their forefather's bones."[3] Indian oral literatures, too, have undergone repeated birth and rebirth on American soil and they continue to provide a foundational heritage for Indian literature of all sorts. Categorized into four porous genre groupings: ritual dramas, including chants, ceremonies, and rituals themselves; songs, narratives, and oratory, these sacred and non-sacred storied expressions of language articulate, amongst many other things, Indian understandings of the fundamental truths of creation and the origins of human beings and their relationship to the universe. They continue to develop and undergo extension across time in various contexts. An example is the Laguna writer Leslie Marmon Silko's novel *Ceremony* (1977). The narrator begins by telling the reader that "Thought-Woman, the spider," created the world through thought and is thinking the story about to be told.[4] Silko draws upon a Laguna oral tradition that can encompass both the ancient remembered past and the realities of a novel written in 1977 because it is not confined by a linear understanding of time: it speaks not just to a history of the past but to a consciousness that is ongoing. Another example of oral tradition informing contemporary work is Anishinaabeg writer and academic Gerald Vizenor's use of trickster tales in *Bearheart* (1978, 1990).[5] Often considered the first Indian postmodern novel, *Bearheart* uses trickster discourse to evoke liberating parody, doubt, and wonder so as to escape all kinds of boundaries. As the Laguna, Sioux, and Lebanese scholar Paula Gunn Allen puts it, in Indian literature, Indian oral tradition and Western tradition can interact just like the wings of a bird in flight.[6]

When Europeans first arrived in the Americas, they faced a new conceptual landscape expressed through oral tradition, but they failed to comprehend the different, sophisticated ways of understanding human existence they encountered or the languages and dialects that articulated them. They came upon a continent that was home to over two thousand cultures with their own significantly differing ways of functioning. These cultures inhabited a great variety of landscapes, engaged in a range of sometimes interlinked economies, cherished their own shared memories of the past, and spoke languages often unintelligible not just to Europeans, but to their own Indian neighbors. In all, there were perhaps five hundred languages in what is now the United States and Canada: over five centuries later less than two hundred are still spoken.

Even so, Indian oral traditions are not fragile: in spite of tremendous adversity they survive and continue to grow, reflecting change and diversity within the cultures that produce them and those cultures' relationships over time both with other Indians and non-Indians. It is not possible to do justice even in outline to their magnitude and complexity here, but it is possible to isolate aspects of belief thought of as common to most traditional Indian lifeways. These include a sense of the interconnectedness and relationship between all things, between animals, land, peoples and their language, and a requirement to seek individual, communal, and environmental balance. This quest for balance, whether it is between various tribal, non-Indian, or social imperatives, drives a number of Indian protagonists within contemporary Indian literature, including the narrator of James Welch's *Winter in the Blood* (1974), Abel in Momaday's *House Made of Dawn* and Cyprian, the professional balance-artist in Louise Erdrich's 2003 novel, *The Master Butchers Singing Club*.

Balance is linked to the survival of community within specific landscapes. Thus the self in oral traditions has unlimited context: it benefits from a profound sense of kinship to all animate and inanimate forms of being and there is no split between the sacred and the secular or between humanity and the rest of creation. Place, self, and community are so intimately linked that loss of territory is a deprivation of psychic strength. To some extent, this puts the contemporary Indian author in a complex position. If he or she draws upon oral tradition, he or she is, as noted in the introduction to this volume, almost inevitably invoking a tradition to which individualized notions of authorship are foreign. This is because oral tradition is essentially inclusive; it is, as Simon Ortiz describes it, "the actions, behavior, relationships, practices throughout the whole social, economic, and spiritual life process of people."[7]

Oral traditions involve more than just what is spoken, they are a living dynamic practice that includes an interactive and spiritual relationship to specific places that is expressed and perpetuated through forms of ritual and ceremony with the power both to heal and cause harm. Integral to this is a reverence for the fundamental creative and transformative power of language, symbol, and thought. Correspondingly significant is reverence for the power of silence: silence, in a sense, as the climate for the performative act of expressing language. In the oral as opposed to the written tradition, N. Scott Momaday tells us, "language bears the burden of the sacred, the burden of belief" and silence is "the dimension in which ordinary and extraordinary events take their proper places."[8] Performance is at the core of the oral tradition; therefore the meaning of a linguistic expression is not created just by the linguistic expression on its own. For critics like Susan Berry Brill de Ramirez, this means that contemporary writers whose works are informed by their respective oral traditions produce work that is at heart a conversation. Often there is a close relationship between the work, the writer, and a traditional community and the reader must, as she puts it, "conversively interact" with the world of the story told.[9]

In sum, Indian literature informed by oral tradition operates within a different epistemology or way of knowing. Thus, when N. Scott Momaday opens *House Made of Dawn* with "Dypaloh" and closes with "Qtsedaba," words used to signal the beginning and the end of a story within the Jemez Pueblo oral tradition, he is urging readers of a book primarily written in English to do much more than recognize a different language. He is invoking another way of categorizing meaning. Critics like Alan Velie and Gerald Vizenor have suggested that storytelling in the oral tradition establishes a dialectical relationship between "text and interpretation," something that unites Native American literature with postmodernism.[10] This dialectical relationship is one of the most radical things about Native American litera-ture because it stimulates epistemological reconsideration and powerful imaginative engagement with the processes of textual creation. Even so, many Native writers who draw upon oral tradition transcend postmodern-ism through the spiritual dimension of their work. The different ways of seeing and being in the world invoked, for example, by the stories surround-ing Mabel McKay, the relative and informant of Greg Sarris (Coast Miwok / Pomo), could never be limited by any single interpretative framework (Greg Sarris, *Mabel McKay: Weaving the Dream*, 1994).

An understanding that Indian linguistic and/or artistic expression is often culturally specific, embedded within sacred practice, and fundamentally orientated around specific homelands has been a long time coming.[11] Indeed, Columbus's sense of cultural and religious superiority was such that because the Indians he first encountered did not speak his own language, he deemed them to have no conceptual language at all. He was so convinced of his own worldview that he told the Spanish monarchs who were his employers that he would bring six Arawak natives to them "in order that they might learn to speak." He went on to progressively rename and recon-textualize the islands he encountered so as to mark non-Indian possession of them, and to rename all the indigenous peoples of the Americas with one single collective descriptor, Indian. He applied the term because he mistakenly believed he had landed among islands off Asia and at the time, India was a synonym for all of Asia east of the river Indus. In his novel *Green Grass* (1993), Thomas King satirizes the European renaming and hierarchizing process Columbus began through juxtaposing Christian and Native origin myths. His character Ahdamn, first son of the Christian God, lives with First Woman in a garden created by Thought Woman and preposterously, he starts renaming everything he encounters after preconceived images from American consumerism; telling Elk he is in fact a microwave oven and Old Coyote he is a cheeseburger.[12] William Apess, in one of the earliest native autobiographies, *A Son of the Forest* (1829), was so incensed by this non-Indian desire to rename and recontextualize he wrote, "I know of nothing so trying to a child as to be repeatedly called by an improper name." Since the word "Indian" was not in the Bible, he concluded that it must be "imported for the special purpose of degrading us."[13] Gerald Vizenor extended this point in his 1998 book *Fugitive Poses*, arguing that *"indians"* are, "the romantic absence of natives ... a simulation and loan word of dominance ... the other in a vast mirror."[14]

Just as Columbus ignored indigenous sovereignty of expression, he ignored the sovereignty of indigenous rights to indigenous lands. He applied a doctrine formalized by non-Indians in the eleventh century known as "discovery" largely so as to avoid conflict amongst European nations over claim to Indian land. The United States would officially embrace this same doctrine in an 1823 Supreme Court case as the foundation of its own legal claim to sovereignty over Indian lands. Thus 1492 began the long and hotly resisted history of attempts to translate Indian lands into non-Indian property and Indian cultures and expression into forms that met the needs of non-Indians. However, it also marked the beginning of a history of ongoing reciprocal influence between Indian and Western European cultures and it intensified the history of ongoing change in intertribal relationships amongst Indian communities themselves.

The most powerful colonizing nations in the Western hemisphere were Spain, France, and England and each nation persisted with the fiction that the indigenous peoples they encountered were homogeneously "Indians" even as they penetrated Native homelands and encountered and negotiated with greater numbers of diverse, and sometimes divided, sets of peoples. As the fifteenth and sixteenth centuries progressed, colonizing countries increasingly thought of themselves as "European" and perceived indigenous peoples not on their own terms but as counter-images of aspects of themselves. European culture was considered superior to Indian culture of any sort, but from the beginning non-Indians differentiated Indians into "good" and "bad," with "good" Indians having noble, innocent, and virtuous qualities and "bad" Indians having fiendish, warlike, and occult ones. Non-Indians understood Indians in antithesis to themselves: because they thought themselves civilized, dynamic, and *in* history they judged Indians to be culturally static and somehow *outside of* history. Thus any change within Indian culture away from the basic image of the Indian invented during the period of early contact, especially toward attributes deemed to be "civilized," came to be seen by non-Indian culture as degraded and less authentically "real." Even from before contact, the non-Indian image of the Indian always said much more about how non-Indians understood themselves than about the actual diversity of Indian cultures and Indian cultures' own responses to change over time.[15]

There were differences in how each colonizing nation related to Indians, but these differences were more to do with the different social and governmental organization of the native societies they encountered and the different terrains they inhabited than they were to do with essential divergence in approach. Spain, France, and England all competed to raise national and personal prestige through colonization, to maximize public and private wealth through trade, and to spread their version of the Christian faith through conversion. Each impetus radically affected cultural cohesion within Indian communities through eroding traditional politics and economics, displacing traditional gender roles, and imposing conflicting allegiances within Indian spiritual life. No government in Europe suggested that Indians had no claim whatsoever to their land, but they all found ways to claim title to it by emphasizing some aspect of Indian deficiency relative to European standards. Land deemed "empty," either because it was not inhabited by a Christian prince or because it was occupied seasonally as part of a Native economy, was therefore open for occupation by Europeans for their "higher" use. A doctrine of conquest evolved that legitimated, in European eyes, seizure of Indian lands peacefully or militarily for "just" cause according to Christian "civilized" criteria. "Civilization" proved to be a perniciously flexible concept. Over time it would be used to justify diverse abuses against Indian land and peoples, acts conducted against Indians ostensibly "for their own good" since they were deemed likely to bring Indians closer to a "civilized" ideal.

Initially, Spain was awarded dominion over the entire Western hemisphere by Pope Alexander VI, and irrespective of clerical intervention, it proceeded in practice to augment its wealth through a system of "legal" Indian enslavement and two other means of exploiting Indian labor and resources known as the *encomienda* and the *repartimiento*. From 1512, the *encomienda* system allowed Spanish colonists to extract labor from native workers if they paid a head tax and taught the natives assigned to them Christianity and Spanish ways. In practice this was almost as exploitative as slavery and by 1600, it was being replaced by the *repartimiento* system, which required Indian leaders to supply male Indian labor to work on Spanish projects for set periods. Spain's grip over land, resources, and Indians was regularly challenged in what Europeans called the "New World," but Spain remained the dominant imperial power for most of the colonial period. Until 1750, France was its most serious rival. From foundational settlements in the St. Lawrence River Valley from 1608, it dominated large chunks of present-day United States in its quest for lucrative fur-trading territories. The French attempted a less brutal version of the Spanish impetus to totally transform Indian lifeways called "Francization" but the more successful assimilation took place in the other direction. Many of their own traders, known as *coureurs de bois*, exiled themselves to the freedom of Indian ways. French–Indian relations have often been thought of more positively than those of other imperial nations because the French officially recognized Indian diversity, learnt Indian languages, and saw the efficacy of understanding the nuances of Indian diplomatic practices nation to nation. However, the French empire was fundamentally like any other colonizing the Americas; it used coercion and cruelty, obliterated Indian populations and enslaved them, in the French case most effectively through debt.

The French fur trade can be seen as emblematic of the unequal Indian/non-Indian trade relationships and the fundamental gap in comprehension between the two sets of cultures that characterized the period. Most tribes saw animals not as a commercial resource but as a species of persons with their own powers and understood trade as part of reciprocal exchange with its own symbolism and matrix of obligation. Admittedly, some tribes did well for a limited time out of the fur trade, but the overall effect on Indian peoples was for them to become dependent on the manufactured items needed for the commercial exploitation of valuable animals, on trade goods in general, and on adulterated alcohol in particular. It is noteworthy that when the first Indian autobiography appeared in 1829, it gave a moving account of the abuse the Pequot writer William Apess had endured at the hands of his alcoholic grandparents. Apess made it clear in *A Son of the Forest* (1829) that he held whites responsible for the blight alcoholism brought upon Indian life. Overall, the fur business for Indians generated a cycle of trade, violence, dependence, and poverty. Non-Indian trappers brought epidemic disease to which native peoples had no resistance; over-hunting caused severe ecological disruption and species elimination, and trade severely eroded Indian social cohesion and dominated tribal relationships.

Having faced serious resistance to their rule from the great Iroquois Confederacy, from the Fox, the Natchez, and the Chickasaw, the French surrendered their empire to the British in 1763. The British had begun with a tiny settlement at Jamestown, Virginia in 1607, but by 1763 controlled, in the European worldview, Florida, Canada, and the trans-Appalachian lands up to the Mississippi River. Like previous empires, the British came to America to exploit all things Indian, but unlike previous empires, their hold on the land, because it was based around family-based settlement and agriculture, was much less transitory. Although British–Indian relations varied with place and time, British Indian policy provided the United States with the foundations of its Indian policy after the birth of the new nation in 1776. For example, in 1638 Puritans set up the first reservations, called "plantations," as segregated areas where it was intended Indians would live, detribalize, and convert to Christianity. In 1652, Puritans passed the first allotment act, where plantation Indians deemed sufficiently "civilized" were allotted land for farming and stock raising. In the 1760s, British Indian policy officially articulated the kind of bias against mestizo or mixed-blood peoples that eventually characterized American culture. By 1763, the separation of Indian and British societies was codified in royal proclamation; a vast west was reserved for Indians and British–Indian relationships were defined by treaties.

The colonial exploits of Spain, France, England, together with those of Holland and Russia, caused massive demographic and ecological change and exchange within Indian homelands. The depletion in Indian numbers mirrored the depletion and supplanting of American animal and plant species. Indeed, European penetration of the American interior was often heralded by Indian sightings of "English flies" (the honey bee) and of other domesticated European creatures as well as of highly aggressive European weeds and pests. Environmental historians such as Alfred W. Crosby have pointed out that in the Americas and elsewhere, European domination was due, not so much to military superiority or to superiority of any kind, but to environmental factors that spelt success for European agriculture and death to aboriginal peoples as well as to the species that sustained them.[16] Contact initiated biological catastrophe in Indian country because Europeans spread diseases unknown in America. Recurrent epidemics of smallpox, measles, pneumonia, scarlet fever, typhus, and, after 1840, cholera, alongside loss of livelihood and land coupled with the effects of alcohol were what principally reduced tribal populations, rather than military engagement.

This is not to suggest that Indian peoples were strategically or militarily insignificant during the colonial period; on the contrary, Indians controlled most of America west of the Appalachians until 1783. Many tribes helped Europeans to fight four bloody imperial wars from 1689 to 1763 and Indians fought a litany of battles resisting colonial encroachment. For example, King Philip, also known as Metacomet, waged war from 1675 to 76 against British expansion and exploitation; 1680 saw the successful Pueblo Revolt against the Spanish; for two years from 1711 the Tuscaroras lashed out against Carolina slave raids, trade fraud, and land seizure; Aleuts revolted against sickeningly brutal Russian colonizers for four years from 1762; and in 1763 Pontiac waged a war for Indian independence in the Northwest, killing more than 2,000 British troops and settlers. Tribal and intertribal resistance to non-Indian encroachment was, and continues to be, variously military, political, and/or religious. Pontiac used the "Delaware Prophet's" message to unite Indian military resistance; the Mohawk Joseph Brant (Thayendanega) tried to create a political–military confederacy in the Old Northwest at the end of the eighteenth century; at the beginning of the nineteenth Tecumseh, the Shawnee orator and statesman, along with his brother the prophet Elskwatawa, led an intertribal movement resisting assimilation and demanding restoration of Indian land which finally erupted into military action. Although heavily mediated by context and non-Indian translation, many examples of Indians questioning settlers' motives in oratory persist. One of the earliest was made in 1609 by Wahunsonacock, or King Powhatan, who asked colonists, "What should you take by force that from us which you can have by love?" and, "What is the cause of your jealousy?" Tecumseh, in 1811, saw there was little point in negotiation with the invaders and asked his fellow southern tribesmen, "Will we let ourselves be destroyed in our turn, without making an effort worthy of our race?," concluding "I know you will say with me, Never! Never!"[17]

Perhaps the most successful Indian strategy for resisting Anglo-American conquest was the move to further settle the relatively isolated Great Plains region of the North American heartland. Around 1700 a hybrid culture developed as over thirty tribes entered the Plains, joining tribes like the Plains Apaches, Wichitas, and Pawnees. The horse, gained from the Spanish along the Rio Grande, along with the buffalo became the mainstay of Plains economic culture. A common sign language developed to allow intertribal communication. Settling the Plains allowed tribes to avoid consistent direct contact with non-Indians for about a century and to selectively adapt aspects of non-Indian culture to their own needs over time. Prosperous Plains peoples were to prove powerful obstacles to non-Indian Westward expansion.

Indian literature and the United States

Tribes on the North American periphery faced European colonialism first. After 1775 to 83 the new nation, the United States, set about applying essentially the same colonial principles to the tribes of the interior. British attempts to manage Indian affairs centrally and to limit colonists' progressive encroachment into Indian Territory had, after all, been one of the causes of the American War for Independence. With American victory, the desire for coexistence waned and the drive to possess Indian lands east of the Mississippi increased. For Indian peoples in eastern North America, the whole century was an age of revolution; they were engulfed by waves of Europeans and Africans, their spiritual lives were challenged and forcibly split, their political structures disrupted, and at every level violence increased in intensity. Even so, the American Revolution was an especially dark time for Indians. Most tribes involved fought for the British as their best chance for protecting their freedom but the British eventually betrayed their Indian allies when forced to make peace with the thirteen colonies. Victorious Americans saw Indians as guilty and defeated and set about grabbing their land citing American right of conquest. The history of Indian peace and interdependence with Europeans was forgotten as Americans created a national mythology that consigned Indians to a "savage" past. Indian absence, either through death or the cultural death of complete assimilation, was deemed necessary to the future of the new republic. It was a wholly contradictory vision of "freedom," since, as the Pequot writer William Apess put it, "the Revolution which enshrined republican principles in the American commonwealth, also excluded African Americans and Native Americans from their reach."[18] By 1795, even the Indian battle for Ohio was lost as settlers pushed west. Meanwhile in Alaska, from 1784, natives were murdered or enslaved as part of the Russian drive to gain fur, until from 1799, the establishment of the Russian American Company brought several decades of peace but also further expansion of the fur trade.

"Ethnic cleansing" is how Anthony F. C. Wallace describes the calculated strategy to purchase Indian lands linked to President Jefferson that applied throughout the period 1801 to 1829, even though Jefferson justified the process of removing Indians from their homelands as a means of ultimately "civilizing" them.[19] British defeat in the War of 1812 meant that Indian peoples lost their military leverage as potential allies to competing imperial powers leaving the United States free to set about forcing Indian peoples to relocate from their homelands using treaties. As the great authority on Indian treaties Francis Paul Prucha has pointed out, treaties are a political anomaly that began in 1778 with the last one completed in 1868, making a grand total of at least 367. As formal, international agreements between recognized states, what is important about them is that they rest upon a concept of Indian sovereignty, they recognize special legal status for Indians and, even though Indian rights have frequently been disregarded, they give Indians a protected existence.[20] US/Indian treaties have an ugly history, not least because the concept of buying and selling land is alien to traditional Indian thinking and because the treaties struck were repeatedly broken or renegotiated to meet the pressure for new land for non-Indian settlement. Treaty-making with war as an alternative created bitter divisions within Indian societies often geared toward consensus government; yet further internal tensions arose as a result of the massive movement of missionary stations west of the Mississippi after 1819 funded by Congress.

1830 saw the passage by Congress of the Indian Removal Bill, which legitimized the federal appropriation of Indian lands east of the Mississippi and the exile of Indians living there to the trans-Mississippi West, mostly to Indian Territory, now Oklahoma. President Jackson and his supporters gave this plan a philanthropic gloss, but their deeply patronizing and intensely paternalistic rhetoric did little to hide their desire for Indians to disappear so the country could fulfil what was thought of as its Manifest Destiny to expand to the Pacific. Recurring tribal relocations simply could not keep up with the American settlers' lust for land. The Five Civilized Tribes (the Cherokees, Chickasaws, Creeks, Choctaws, and Seminoles) were forced to relocate even though they were highly structurally assimilated to nineteenth-century American ways, including owning slaves, having constitutional government, and producing the founding organ of Indian journalism, the *Cherokee Phoenix*. The Cherokee's corpse-strewn forced winter migration, the "Trail of Tears," goaded by both the Georgia militia and federal troops, reduced the tribal population by 25 percent. This happened despite the Supreme Court 1831 ruling in their defense, whereupon Indian tribes were deemed "domestic dependent nations" with a unique government-to-government relationship to the United States, resembling that of a ward to a guardian. Predictably, the best seller of this era was anti-Indian, Robert Montgomery Bird's *Nick of the Woods* (1837). However, by 1847 George Copway (Ojibwe) had published one of the earliest Indian autobiographies; and by 1850, *The Traditional History and Characteristic Sketches of the Ojibway Nation*, showing the central importance of place and oral tradition to the Ojibwe.

The US completed its continental spread through treaties with Britain in 1846, Mexico in 1848, and with the Gadsden Purchase of 1853. This brought many new Indian nations under its control. The discovery of gold in 1848 stimulated an invasion of miners into California, causing appropriation of tribal lands and a terrible decline in Californian Indian numbers. A flavor of the oppression and cruelty experienced by Indians in this era was deeply encoded in the Cherokee writer John Rollin Ridge's 1854 western adventure, *The Life and Adventures of Joaquín Murieta, the Celebrated California Bandit*. As settlers streamed west, more and more tribes were engulfed and the pattern of compression of tribal territories and the relocation of survivors to reservations that was federally applied in Texas, Oregon, and California was in time applied to all Western tribes. The Civil War slowed Western migration, but its conclusion left the West thoroughly militarized and spurred even greater settler thirst for Indian land. The Great Santee Sioux Uprising of 1862 in Minnesota, the Five Civilized Tribes' treaties with the Confederacy and the support provided to the

Confederacy by the Comanches and Kiowas were all the justification federal powers needed for further removal and reduction of Indian territories. Notoriously, at Sand Creek, Colorado, in 1864 two hundred Cheyennes, mostly the elderly and women and children, were massacred by US troops. In the Southwest, Navajos and Mescalero Apaches were forced onto reservations, as were tribes throughout the West as the buffalo and Indian winter food supplies were systematically destroyed. The surrender of Goyahkla, also known as Geronimo, on behalf of his western Chiricahua Apache band in 1886 marked the end of Indian military power in the nineteenth century. The following year saw the purchase by the United States of Alaska, and the ensuing decades saw a marked decline in Alaskan Native numbers as Alaskan resources were exploited as never before by unprecedented numbers of non-Native incomers.

Indian reservations varied in size from the tiny to the twenty-five thousand square mile Navajo reservation covering parts of Arizona, New Mexico, and Utah. For many Indians, the reservations they had been forced onto were alien, poor lands where they were expected to transform culturally from being hunters to farmers using inadequate equipment whilst surrounded by various threatening expansionist interests. Systematic non-Indian destruction of wildlife made subsistence economics unviable. Such impossible conditions led to demoralized dependence on government agents for rations and further subversion of the main supports of tribal life. The Bureau of Indian Affairs, which had been part of the War Department until it transferred to the Department of the Interior in 1849, gained considerable power over Indian life, administering federal programs and acting as a "trustee" for Indian resources.

With Indians no longer a military threat, the United States set about attacking Indian tribalism and Indian values at their core. The rhetoric of the time stressed Indian assimilation to the American way of life. This justified a brutal educational program implemented within Indian boarding and day schools that aimed to totally annihilate Indian culture. The "boarding school experience" from 1875 to 1928 was, as David Adams has called it, an "education for extinction." Essentially, it was a new form of war, both ideological and psychological, waged against children.[21] It was part of a pattern of erosion of Indian family life, augmented by child placement and adoption within non-Indian families that was not formally or comprehensively halted until the passage in 1978 of the Child Welfare Act. Reservation education for about two decades was dominated by the thinking of one army captain, Richard H. Pratt, whose motto was "Kill the Indian and save the man!" However, even though the schools forbade Indian languages, religion, and customs, Indian children still managed to resist these regimes and to generate positive intertribal community at places like Chilocco Indian School, Oklahoma. Pratt's model school at Carlisle Barracks, Pennsylvania opened in 1879 and educated many of the key Indian intellectuals active during the 1920s. Their generation were encouraged to think that wholesale abandonment of Indian ways would guarantee Indians' full incorporation into the mainstream of American society and the fulfillment of America's "final promise" of compensation for the loss of Indian land. However, by the early decades of the twentieth century it would become clear that Indians, along with other non-white minorities, were to be granted only partial assimilation and would be relegated to the periphery of the nation's hierarchy.[22]

The primary piece of legislation of the assimilation era, the General Allotment or Dawes Act of 1887, was promoted as a means of rapidly assimilating Indians in a generation through imposing individualism and breaking up tribal ownership of land in common. Under the Act each head of household was allotted one hundred and sixty acres of land with eighty acres being given to single persons over eighteen and to orphans. The land was to be held in trust by the Secretary of the Interior for twenty-five years until it became fully the Indian's property and the Indian subject to all state and federal laws. The Act authorized the federal government to buy up the remainder of the land after allotments had been made and to use the money, or keep it in trust, for the benefit of the tribe. In practice, most reservations were unsuitable for farming and the allotments too small to be economically viable. Many Indian farmers quickly found themselves in debt and when the land was finally theirs, were forced to lease or sell it to non-Indians. In 1891, further legislation permitted the leasing of allotted lands in trust for agriculture, grazing, and mining. This placed even more Indian land and economic resources in non-Indian control. The primary overall effect of the Dawes Act was not to create Indian homesteads and foster the assimilation of Indians as fully integrated individuals into American society. Instead, the Act made a great many Indians landless and assimilated around two-thirds of the Indian landbase into to non-Indian ownership. Indian land holdings went from 138 million acres in 1887 to 48 million acres, much of it desert, in 1934 when the policy was changed. Indian figures such as Charles Eastman (Santee Sioux) and Sarah Winnemucca (Paiute) had thought the 1887 Act would foster Indian independence and give Indians citizenship, but its effect was to take Indian land out of tribal ownership and to plunge Indian peoples further into economic dependence on the federal government. In fact citizenship, even when it was universally applied to Indian Americans in 1924 in response to the valor and patriotism of the Indian contribution to World War I, never had the kind of transformative effect reformers had hoped.

Fortunately, a few reservations escaped the partitioning process and as a consequence, fared better as the twentieth century progressed. Fortunate y, Alaska's remoteness allowed its Native peoples to escape the intensity of t1e Americanization process although missionary schooling still continued to have its impact.

Forced onto reservations, subject to a repressive bureaucracy, and unable to practice traditional modes of economic, social, and religious life, Indian peoples looked for ways to regenerate their communities. Once again, various religious leaders provided an answer to the distress, the most significant being the Paiute Wovoka (Jack Wilson) son of the prophet Tavibo, who promised Indian deliverance and the return of the buffalo by 1891. The songs of the intertribal Ghost Dance movement recorded by James Mooney in *The Ghost Dance Religion and the Sioux Outbreak of 1890* (1896) reveal the depth of Indian desires to reunite in peace with lost loved ones and to see the return of the buffalo. Wovoka's Ghost Dance religion spread across the West, and for the Sioux, it took on an active and insurgent rather than peaceful hue. This culminated in the 1890 massacre at Wounded Knee Creek, northeast of Pine Ridge Agency, when US cavalry gunned down 150 Indians including women and children: another 100 or more died escaping into the snow. The Wounded Knee atrocity retains great significance within Indian life and literature. The as-told-to biography *Black Elk Speaks* (John Neihardt, 1932) deals explicitly with the event while the more recent *The Master Butchers Singing Club* (2003) by Louise Erdrich has a central backstory about Wounded Knee that haunts the main characters.

Three years after Wounded Knee, as American history was finding its disciplinary feet, the non-Indian historian Frederick Jackson Turner famously recorded the American frontier "closed." An idea of Indians having "vanished" solidified within United States history as it did within American life. Fascination with frontier conflict and with a dime novel and movie version of the West that never existed, rather than with actual Indian cultural adaptation and development, would characterize American life until at least the middle of the next century. As non-Indian Indian reformer Helen Hunt Jackson pointed out in 1881, the way in which Indians had been treated made the nineteenth century America's *Century of Dishonor*.[23]

A new dawn: the twentieth century

In many ways, the 1890s marked the darkest point before the beginning of an Indian dawn within the United States. By 1900, conquest, seizure, disease, war, abuse, trickery, treaties, and statutes had reduced the Indian estate from its pre-contact magnitude of nearly three billion acres and reduced Indian peoples themselves to less than 250,000 in number. But from 1900 on, each year more and more Indian children attended school and by 1920 6 percent of Indians would live in urban environments. The Native American Church, which had succeeded the Ghost Dance in the reservation era, fought off Christian opposition to its sacramental use of the peyote cactus, gave many Indians hope, and fostered cultural cohesion. 1911 saw the birth of the Society of American Indians, a secular reform group of Indian intellectuals or "Red Progressives." The group eventually declined due to internal faction-alism, but it nevertheless provided Indian leadership at a crucial point in twentieth-century Indian regeneration. The Alaskan Native Brotherhood and Alaskan Native Sisterhood founded in 1912 also focused upon accul-turation and rights, but proved longer lasting. Americans were surprised during World War I by Indian support for the war effort. 10,000 joined the US army for conflict overseas, 2,000 more joined the Navy, millions of Indian dollars were spent on war bonds and reports reached home of the bravery of Joseph Oklahombi (Choctaw) in the trenches. By the mid-1920s the ideal of America as a "melting pot" had lost currency. Social science gained sway and, with it, ideas of cultural pluralism. Modern American life seemed increasingly hollow and atomized and, nostalgically, intellectuals began to perceive ethnic cultures as having greater integrity. Reformers such as John Collier idealized Indian culture, especially the agricultural commu-nities in New Mexico and Arizona, for the very qualities non-Indians had once decided marked Indians out as inferior. Community, the centrality of religion, and a perceived lack of an historical dynamic were now admired as positive, rather than denigrated as "primitive" attributes.

By the early 1930s print was emerging as a strong new vehicle for Indian oral traditions. In 1934 John Joseph Mathews published *Sundown* and D'Arcy McNickle completed his novel, *The Surrounded* (1936). Both novels have male protagonists who struggle to reconcile ideas about economic "progress" and Indian life, *The Surrounded* dealing more explicitly with the economic collapse that the allotment process forced upon Indian country. Another of McNickle's novels, *Wind From An Enemy Sky*, not published until 1978, would deal in greater political focus with the crises caused on reservations by the imposition of the market economy and the failures of the next change in policy, the Indian New Deal. As Commissioner of Indian Affairs, Collier secured the passage of the New Deal's founding piece of legislation, the Indian Re-organization (or Wheeler–Howard) Act in 1934. The Act was accepted by 192 of the 263 tribes who voted on it; by 1936 aspects of the Act were applied to Alaskan Natives and a separate Oklahoma Indian Welfare Act had been passed. The Indian New Deal was perhaps the first genuine attempt to improve Indian life that was not also a pretext for taking Indian land. It ended the policy of individual allotment of land, re-established tribal government with "certain rights of home rule," and established a revolving credit fund to improve reservation economics. Collier was criticized for trying to ossify Indian culture and push Indians "back to the blanket" and for fostering tribal self-governments that promoted "progressive" white-orientated Indians rather than "traditional" leadership. The increased role of the Bureau of Indian Affairs also focused complaints that, overall, the Indian New Deal was cripplingly paternalistic even if its intentions were benevolent. Significantly however, policy from 1934 to 1947 helped to increase the Indian land base by nearly four million acres and to save many Indians from starvation during the Depression.

The Indian New Deal gradually lost funds after 1941 as the war effort intensified. Once again, during this time of national crisis, Indian men and women showed patriotism greatly disproportionate to their numbers within the general population and Indians in service showed exemplary ability in battle. Perhaps 25 million Indian dollars were spent on war bonds and over 800 Indian women served as nurses or in the military's auxiliary branches. 25,000 Indians served in integrated units on all fronts in Europe and Asia with at least 215 receiving medals for bravery. Their service, which often benefited from the ceremonial and ritual support of their communities, perpetuated the illustrious warrior traditions of various tribes. Ironically, although Indians had been punished for using their languages in schools, in time of war, tribal speakers proved invaluable to their country. Indian "code talkers," especially Diné (Navajo) marines, converted military radio traffic into a special classified version of their own language, an encryption that proved impenetrable to the enemy. In Arizona, reservation homelands were commandeered for use as Japanese–American internment camps; in the Aleutian Islands, the Japanese invaded and the US sent 200,000 military personnel there in response. Indian willingness to shoulder the burden of agricultural and industrial war support brought many out of the reservations and into factory work in cities like Los Angeles, Tulsa, Denver, and Albuquerque. After the War, the GI Bill allowed significant numbers of Indian veterans access to college. Indian patriotism in time of war continues into the twenty-first century. 41,500 Indians served during the Vietnam War, around 3,000 served in the Persian Gulf during the War with Iraq, and 24,000 Indian men and women were in service prior to Operation Desert Storm. The first female US soldier to be killed during the US–British assault on Iraq during 2003 was Lori Ann Piestewa (Hopi).

Following World War II, with America the pre-eminent power in the world, the pendulum of non-Indian thinking about Indians swung back. The Cold War gave the presentation of an homogeneous America a new significance and the drive to quickly make Indians independent citizens reasserted itself. Indian leadership responded through the formation of what was essentially a strongly tribal Washington pressure group, the National Congress of American Indians, formed in 1944. In 1946, a government Indian Claims Commission was set up to decide and settle financially claims against the federal government for broken treaties and agreements. It was a sign of the times that many non-Indians saw its role as facilitating the end of federal responsibility for Indians once and for all. By the early 1950s, such thinking was formally enshrined in Termination policy. Between 1952 and 1962, sixty-one tribes, groups, bands, and communities were stripped of federal services and protection. They lost health and education services and became liable for tax on their lands. The Menominees and Klamaths, who owned valuable timber, became destitute as a result.

Overall, Termination was negative for Indian tribes: it poisoned Indian/non-Indian relations and it placed all Indian groups in a double bind. If they were successful and escaped the paternalism of the Bureau of Indian Affairs, they also risked arbitrary and sudden termination and the loss of recognition as Indians at the federal, state, or local governmental level. Arguably, a more positive aspect of Termination was relocation. Indians had been urbanizing for half a century, but the specific relocation programs of the 1950s allowed them to settle in big cities like Los Angeles and Chicago. Many retained a satellite relationship to homeland reservations. By 1960, 35,000 Indians had relocated, a settlement shift that fostered greater cross-tribal cohesion and provided a basis for the activism that was to come. However, the relocation programs were badly organized and often, Indian urban life simply meant poverty and alienation without the support of extended family. The problems of relocation, and of the articulation of a Native self in an urban landscape were a powerful central theme within N. Scott Momaday's story of a returned veteran, *House Made of Dawn*. Increasingly, the reservations that had been viewed by Indians as prisons in the nineteenth century were seen in the twentieth as Indian cultural strongholds.

The 1960s, like the 1920s, were a decade of investigation into Indian conditions and, as in the 1920s, reform pressure stimulated policy change that led to ongoing improvement in Indian conditions, economics, and population levels. Various studies brought the grim and unwholesome conditions Indians experienced into sharp relief. They called for Self-Determination to replace the drive for Termination, a plea echoed in the 1961 "Declaration of Indian Purpose" produced by the American Indian Chicago Conference. New activist groups echoed the theme, including the National Indian Youth Council, founded in 1961 by young, radical, college-educated Indians, the controversial American Indian Movement (AIM) formed in 1968 and the Alaskan Federation of Natives (AFN) formed in 1966. The AFN helped spearhead the 1971 Alaska Native Claims Settlement Act, which, along with significant monetary compensation, granted Alaskan Natives more land than was held in trust for all non-Alaskan US tribes combined. However, the Act was structured around corporate, rather than Native, forms of governance and its long-term implications in this regard remain of deep concern to many. Overall, the call for Indian self-determination, for tribal control over social, legal, and educational issues provided a new focus for more networked and cooperative forms of tribal nationalism. Furthermore, the domestic programs of the 1960s and Indian administrative control over federal funding brought many more Indians into a bureaucratic relationship to federal agencies. Eventually Self-Determination would wholly supplant Termination, which ceased formally in the late 1970s.

About one in four of all eligible Indians served in south-east Asia between 1965 and 1973 and there is evidence that those experiences were a spur to the indigenous activism of the period.[24] The poet Wendy Rose registered some of the parallels between Indian and Asian experience in "The Long Root" (1972), when she wrote "there is no way to shake / Cambodia from my Wounded Knee."[25] 1969 to 1973 saw Indian insurgency ranging from non-violent political demonstrations to occasional armed resistance. Indian activism, dubbed "Red Power," often used the same tactics as the Black civil rights movement but added humor and wit. A good example is the 1969 occupation of Alcatraz. Indian activists claimed Alcatraz by right of discovery and promised faithfully to create a reservation on uninhabitable land for the Natives, to be administered by a Bureau of Caucasian Affairs. The tone of the event mirrored that of Vine Deloria's witty and biting book *Custer Died for Your Sins*, published the same year.[26] AIM organized the "Trail of Broken Treaties" to Washington in 1972; it culminated in the Bureau of Indian Affairs headquarters coming under Indian occupation and AIM demands receiving national press coverage. AIM members also symbolically occupied Wounded Knee on Pine Ridge Reservation in 1973 and defied a long violent siege there against federal and state forces.

Since Wounded Knee II, the focus of Indian activism has been increasingly local and global. Civil disobedience over local issues involving land and subsistence fishing rights, even in the face of acute hostility, has yielded dividends, as have numerous Indian court battles at the state and federal level. Key legislation includes the 1972 Indian Education Act, which provided a basis for comprehensive funding of Indian education; the 1978 Religious Freedom Act, which went some way toward protecting Native religions and the 1991 Native American Graves Protection and Repatriation Act, a broad national reburial and repatriation policy for Indian human remains and sacred objects that has proved highly controversial in implementation.

Indian sovereign, treatied, and humanitarian rights have also been promoted within international frameworks such as the Organization of American States, the World Council of Indigenous Peoples, and the United Nations' Working Group on Indigenous Populations. However, the United States has generally tried to dismiss indigenous rights issues with the claim that Indian self-determination is already guaranteed because of the 1975 American Indian Self-Determination and Educational Assistance Act. Yet the cultural consciousness indigenous coalition expresses continues to grow in global significance. At its core is the claim to specific homelands, to sovereign nationhood, and to the sovereignty of indigenous representation – an inseparable triad that Chadwick Allen calls the blood/land/memory complex.[27]

Native American literature has also broadened its context in recent decades and there has been much critical debate over its position relative to other national and transnational discourses. It is sometimes grouped with postcolonial literatures, but recently critics have found this to be too simple a conflation. Given some of the chronic conditions many Indian peoples live under and the structural limitations placed upon Indian development by non-Indians, they suggest that Indians in fact live under paracolonialism and that it is more appropriate to think of Indian literature as part of resistance literature, with attributes in common with the literatures of places like Palestine.[28] As previously mentioned, Alan Velie and Gerald Vizenor have suggested that the oral tradition strongly links to postmodernism. Postmodernism, however, along with other intellectual developments, can place sophisticated and severe limitations upon the intellectual bases to Indian claims to literary and extra-literary voice and agency. As Louis Owens has pointed out, inevitably, Indian voices must perform complex and shifting negotiations that are "never simple or free of cost" in order to make a strategic and subversive impact upon literate Euro-America.[29] Greg Sarris has attempted to transcend some of these debates by collapsing the distinction between criticism and its object of study, while Craig Womack has made the case for "tribally specific" literary criticism.[30] A linked question that has vexed writers and critics alike is whether the English language is a suitable vehicle for Indian literature. Some writers, like John E. Smelcer, are acutely aware of the fact that almost all Native American literature has been written in English. "It's time," he suggests, "for a canon in our grandmothers' tongues." However, Leslie Marmon Silko has pointed out that Pueblo people at least "are more concerned with story and communication and less concerned with a particular language," while the contributors to a recent volume of Native Women's writing are comfortable that English serves their purposes, since they argue they are *Reinventing the Enemy's Language*.[31]

The fact that Indians and non-Indians have been living in intimate juxtaposition for almost five centuries is evident both in contemporary Indian literature and in Indian life. One indicator of this is the way in which, when novelists draw upon oral tradition, they often look not just to living forms but also to earlier incarnations mediated through non-Indian anthropological sources. Thus Momaday's *House Made of Dawn* makes use of Washington Matthews's *The Night Chant* (1902) and his *The Way to Rainy Mountain* (1969) of James Mooney's *Calendar History of the Kiowa* (1898).[32] Today most Indians, including most Indian writers, are of mixed heritage: they are crossbloods, to use Gerald Vizenor's term, the products of a long history of intertribal marriage and of Indian intermarriage with non-Indians. Unsurprisingly, versions of a crossblood identity are central to numerous works within Native American literature, including Mourning Dove's *Cogewea* (1927), James Welch's *The Death of Jim Loney* (1979), Maria Campbell's *Halfbreed* (1973) and Gerald Vizenor's *Griever* (1987). Some writers tend toward separatism. Sherman Alexie's *Reservation Blues* (1995) concludes with a character's candid remarks, "Those quarter-bloods and eighth-bloods get all the Indian jobs, all the Indian chances, because they look white." Alexie's character Chess finally decides that the answer is to have lots of brown babies that "look up and see two brown faces."[33] Other Indian literary characters advocate other perspectives. "Nothing is that simple," the mixed-blood medicine man in Leslie Marmon Silko's *Ceremony* reminds us, "you don't write off all the white people, just like you don't trust all the Indians."

Today over 60 percent of Indians live in urban or suburban, rather than reservation, contexts. Perhaps in part because such large concentrations of Native peoples now live in places like New York City, Los Angeles, Tulsa, Oklahoma City, Seattle, Phoenix, and Honolulu, there has been an explosion of the, often pan-tribal, expression of Indian heritage, known as the powwow. Powwow (Algonkian for "making medicine"), is a way in which Indian people come together to celebrate their tribal identities. The blend of humor, community, and dance so often integral to powwow is powerfully affirmed in Hanay Geiogamah's play 49, published in her *New Native Drama* (Oklahoma, 1980). Humor has a central, healing role within many aspects of Indian cultural life, not just powpow. It is notoriously culturally specific, but as Kenneth Lincoln's book *Indi'n Humor* (Oxford University Press, 1993) explains, Native American literature and life are replete with humor's dancing, psychic strength and it has always provided a valuable bridge between Native and non-Native ways of seeing the world.

The strength of Indian humor can surprise since, from the outside, it can sometimes seem as though there is little to laugh about in modern Indian America. The Reagan administration's severe cuts in social services put tribal politics under acute financial and factional strain and pushed tribes toward relationships with multinational corporations seeking to extract resources from reservation lands and to dump toxic waste. But at the same time, the administration's efforts to dismantle the Great Society served to strengthen Indian sovereignty and to stimulate a new phenomenon, the growth in Indian gaming. Successive tribes have taken advantage of the federal trust status of reservation land to bypass state gaming laws and open high-stake bingo and gambling businesses. Under the Indian Gaming Act of 1988 the right of tribes to establish gambling and gaming on their reservations was recognized as long as the states in which they are located have some form of legalized gambling. Gaming, especially for small tribes close to major urban or tourist areas, has been a business success story because it has allowed reservations to gain a small slice of the nation's commercial gaming revenue. Indian gaming seems set to play a fundamental role in tribal economics in the future, even though conflicts persist over issues surrounding tribal and state sovereignty and over its moral, social, and spiritual implications within communities. Gaming has produced a new popular stereotype of the casino-rich Indian but the larger picture of endemic disadvantage within Indian America remains in place. Problems surrounding corruption and the fact that AIDS, alcoholism, and diabetes stalk urban and reservation Indian communities far outweigh the spectacular success gaming has brought to a limited number of tribes.

This chapter has presented a seemingly straightforward outline of Indian history, but in truth the relationship between mainstream history and many Indian approaches to the past is far from uncomplex. Indian epistemological perspectives on history are often inclusive of story, myth, and symbolism and therefore inevitably clash with conventional history rooted in the search for verifiable facts and committed to rational plausibility. One way of accessing these issues further is to study the non-fictional and fictional histories by Indians that present alternatives to conventional narratives about the past. These can be found in mixtures of autobiography and history like George Copway's *The Life, History and Travels of Kah-gepga-gah* (1850) and N. Scott Momaday's *The Way To Rainy Mountain* (1969); in the journal *Indian Historian* launched in 1964 by the American Indian Historical Society and in histories such as D'Arcy McNickle and Harold Fey's *Indians and Other Americans* (1959, 1970). In her book *The Heart is the Drum: Continuance and Resistance in American Indian Poetry* (1999), Robin Riley Fast discusses revisionist history across a number of selected works including poems by Louise Erdrich, Paula Gunn Allen, and Maurice Kenny. Fast also considers novels like

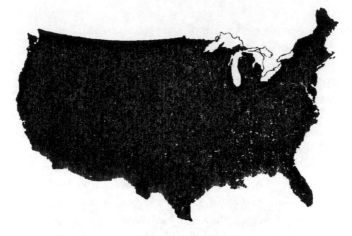

Map 1. Indian country in the year 1492

Map 2. Indian country in 1776

Ella Deloria's *Waterlily* (1988, completed 1940s) describing the pre-contact Lakota, James Welch's *Fool's Crow* (1986) focusing on the Blackfeet in the late 1860s and beyond and Linda Hogan's *Solar Storms* (1995) which invokes the early 1970s Canadian James Bay hydroelectric project controversy. Many other Indian books make history and its processes central in other ways. For example, Robert J. Conley (Keetowah Cherokee) used song, legend, and documentation to create his love story *Mountain Windsong: a Novel of the Trail of Tears* (1992, 1995) set at the time of Cherokee removal from North Carolina to Indian Territory, while LeAnne Howe's *Shell Shaker* (2001) juxtaposes two significant

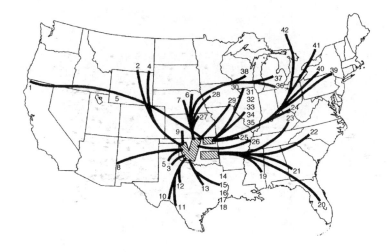

LEGEND
Numbers correspond to tribal groups forced to relocate in Oklahoma.

1 Modoc	12 Tonkawa	23 Shawnee	34 Piankashaw
2 Arapaho	13 Waco	24 Chickasaw	35 Wea
3 Kiowa	14 Tawakoni	25 Quapaw	36 Sac
4 Cheyenne	15 Caddo	26 Osage	37 Potawatomi
5 Comanche	16 Hainai	27 Kaw	38 Fox
6 Ponca	17 Kichai	28 Iowa	39 Delaware
7 Pawnee	18 Anadarko	29 Oto-Missouri	40 Seneca-Cayuga
8 Apache	19 Choctaw	30 Kickapoo	41 Wyandot
9 Wichita	20 Seminole	31 Kaskaskia	42 Ottawa
10 Lipan	21 Creek	32 Miami	
11 Kickapoo	22 Cherokee	33 Peoria	

Map 3. Indian "removals" to Oklahoma

periods in Choctaw history, French and British colonial hostilities during the 1730s and 1740s and casino corruption and tribal politics during the early 1990s. Even so, as Thomas King has pointed out, in general Native writers have "assiduously avoided" writing historical fiction. Rather than supplant, for example, non-Native imaginings about the nineteenth century, Indian writers have tended to focus upon the present, with an eye upon possibilities for influencing the future.[34]

In many ways, the future for Native American literature looks bright and the potential for growth in understanding about the Native American past across cultural boundaries equally so. As the new century unfolds, Indian literature and Indian cultures themselves retain their strength, as Simon Ortiz put it, "like stone woven together."[35]

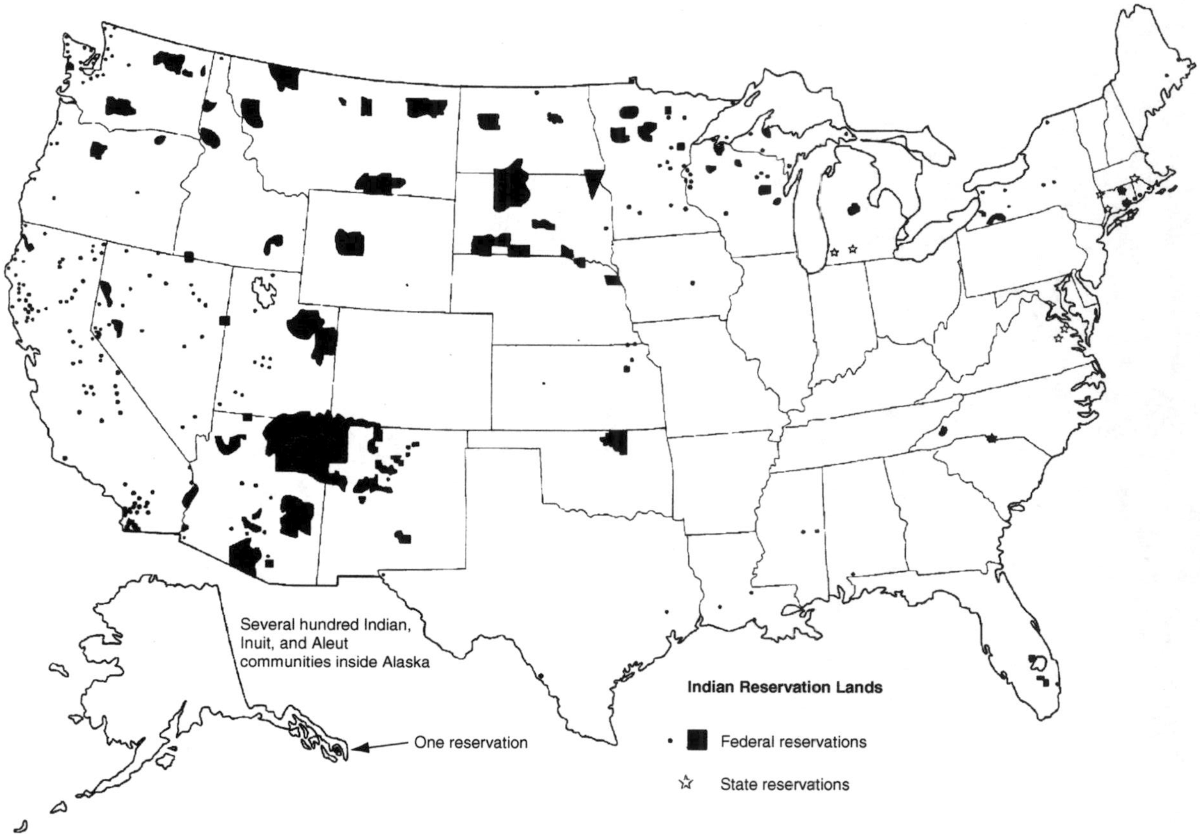

Indian Reservation Lands

■ Federal reservations

☆ State reservations

Several hundred Indian,
Inuit, and Aleut
communities inside Alaska

One reservation

Map 4. Federal and state Indian reservation lands

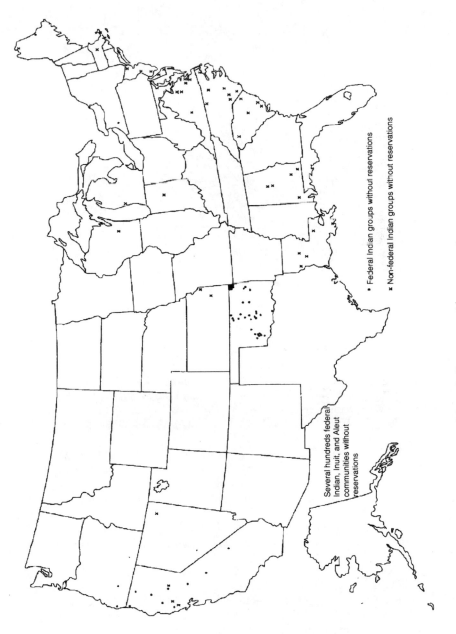

Map 5. Indian groups without reservations

Several hundreds federal Indian, Inuit, and Aleut communities without reservations

• Federal Indian groups without reservations

× Non-federal Indian groups without reservations

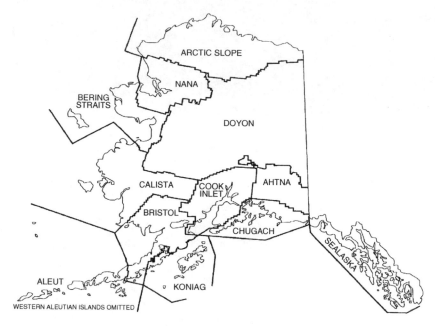

Map 6. Alaska Native regional corporations

Notes

1. Joy Harjo, *In Mad Love and War*, Middleton, CT.: Wesleyan University Press, 1990, p. 14.
2. Michael H. Crawford, *The Origins of Native Americans: Evidence from Anthropological Genetics*, Cambridge: Cambridge University Press, 1998, p. 3–4; Vine Deloria, Jr., *God is Red*, New York: Grosset and Dunlap, 1973; "A Simple Question of Humanity – The Moral Dimensions of the Reburial Issue," *Native American Rights Fund Legal Review* 1989, 14(4), p. 1–12; *Red Earth White Lies: Native Americans and the Myth of Scientific Fact*, New York: Scribner, 1995; N. Scott Momaday, *The Man Made of Words: Essays, Stories, Passages*, New York: St Martin's Griffin, 1997, p. 40.
3. Luther Standing Bear, *Land of the Spotted Eagle*, Boston: Houghton Mifflin, 1933, p. 248.
4. Leslie Marmon Silko, *Ceremony*, New York: Viking, 1977, p. 1.
5. Gerald Vizenor, *Bearheart: the Heirship Chronicles*, Minneapolis: University of Minnesota Press, 1990.
6. Paula Gunn Allen, *Voice of the Turtle: American Indian Literature, 1900–1970*, New York: Ballantine, 1994, p. 7.
7. Simon J. Ortiz, *Woven Stone*, Tucson: University of Arizona Press, 1992, p. 7.
8. N. Scott Momaday, *The Man Made of Words: Essays, Stories, Passages*, New York: St. Martin's Griffin, 1997, p. 104, 16.
9. Susan Berry Brill de Ramirez, *Contemporary American Indian Literatures and the Oral Tradition*, Tucson: University of Arizona Press, 1999, p. 31.

10. Alan Velie and Gerald Vizenor in *Native American Perspectives on Literature and History*, Norman: University of Oklahoma Press, 1994:10; Tedlock, Denis, *The Spoken Word and the Work of Interpretation*. Philadelphia: University of Pennsylvania Press, 1983, p. 236.
11. Craig S. Womack, *Red on Red: Native American Literary Separatism*, Minneapolis: University of Minnesota Press, 1999, p. 16.
12. Christopher Columbus, *The Four Voyages*, trans. and ed. Walter Cohen, New York: Penguin Books, 1969, p. 56; Thomas King, *Green Grass, Running Water*, 1993, p. 41.
13. William Apess, *A Son of the Forest*, 1829, p. 7.
14. Gerald Vizenor, *Fugitive Poses: Native American Indian Scenes of Absence and Presence*. Lincoln: University of Nebraska Press, 1998, pp. 14, 15, 37.
15. Robert F. Berkhofer, Jr., *The White Man's Indian: Images of the American Indian From Columbus to the Present*, New York: Random House, 1979.
16. Alfred W. Crosby, *Ecological Imperialism: the Biological Expansion of Europe*, New York: Cambridge University Press, 1986.
17. Wahunsonacock in Peter Nabokov, ed., *Native American Testimony: an Anthology of Indian and White Relations: First Encounter to Dispossession*, New York: Harper, 1975, p. 88; Tecumseh in Virginia Armstrong, ed., *I Have Spoken: American History through the Voices of the Indians*. Athens: Swallow Press/Ohio University Press, 1971, p. 45.
18. Barry O'Connell, ed., *On Our Own Ground: the Complete Writings of William Apess, a Pequot*, Amherst: University of Massachusetts Press, 1992, I xix, I xxiii; Colin G. Calloway, *The American Revolution in Indian Country*, Cambridge: Cambridge University Press, 1995.
19. Anthony F. C. Wallace, *Jefferson and the Indians*, Cambridge, MA: Belknap Press, 1999, pp. 18–21.
20. Francis Paul Prucha, *American Indian Treaties: the History of a Political Anomaly*, Berkeley: University of California Press, 1994, pp. 1–3.
21. David W. Adams, *Education for Extinction: American Indians and the Boarding School Experience, 1875–1928*, Lawrence: University Press of Kansas, 1995, p. 27.
22. K. Tsianina Lomawaima, *They Called It Prairie Light: The Story of Chilocco Indian School*, Lincoln: University of Nebraska Press, 1994; Frederick E. Hoxie, *A Final Promise: The Campaign to Assimilate the Indians, 1880–1920*, Cambridge: Cambridge University Press, 1984.
23. Frederick Jackson Turner, "The Significance of the Frontier in American History", *Proceedings of the State Historical Society of Wisconsin*, 1893; Helen Hunt Jackson, *A Century of Dishonor*, New York, 1881.
24. See Tom Holm, *Strong Hearts, Wounded Souls: Native American Veterans of the Vietnam War*, Austin: University of Texas Press, 1996.
25. Wendy Rose, "The Long Root", in *Bone Dance: New and Selected Poems, 1965–1993*. Tucson: University of Arizona Press, 1994, p. 4.
26. Vine Deloria, Jr., *Custer Died for Your Sins: An Indian Manifesto*, New York: Avon, 1970.
27. Chadwick Allen, *Blood Narrative: Indigenous Identity in American Indian and Maori Literary and Activist Texts*, Durham: Duke University Press 2002, p. 220.
28. Jace Weaver, *Other Words: American Indian Literature, Law and Culture*, Norman: University of Oklahoma Press, 2001.

29. Louis Owens, "As If An Indian Were Really An Indian," *Para Doxa: Studies in World Literary Genres* 15, p 182.

30. Greg Sarris, *Keeping Slug Woman Alive: a Holistic Approach to American Indian Texts*, Berkeley: University of California Press, 1993; Craig Womack, *Red on Red: Native American Literary Separatism*, Minneapolis: University of Minnesota Press, 1999.

31. John E. Smelcer in *Here First: Autobiographical Essays by Native American Writers*, eds., Arnold Krupat and Brian Swann, New York: Modern Library, 2000, pp. 321–336; Leslie Marmon Silko, "Language and Literature from a Pueblo Indian Perspective" in Leslie Marmon Silko, *Yellow Woman and a Beauty of the Spirit: Essays on a Native American Life Today*, 1996; Joy Harjo and Gloria Bird, eds., *Reinventing the Enemy's Language*, New York: Norton, 1997.

32. Washington Matthews, *The Night Chant: a Navajo Ceremony*, American Museum of Natural History Memoirs, Anthropology Series no. 5 (New York, 1902); James Mooney, *Calendar History of the Kiowa*, in The Seventeenth Annual Report of the Bureau of American Ethnology for the Years 1895–96, Washington, D.C.: Smithsonian Institution, 1898, pp. 141–44.

33. Sherman Alexie, *Reservation Blues*, New York: Warner Books, 1995, pp. 283–84.

34. Thomas King, ed., *All My Relations*, Toronto: McClelland and Stewart, 1993, pp. xi–xii.

35. Simon Ortiz, "A Story of How a Wall Stands" in Gerald Vizenor, ed., *Native American Literature*, New York: Longman, 1995, p. 259.

Major secondary sources

Alfred, Taiaiake, *Peace, Power, Righteousness: an Indigenous Manifesto*. Oxford: Oxford University Press, 1999.

Axtell, James, *The Invasion Within: the Contest of Cultures in Colonial North America*. Oxford: Oxford University Press, 1985.

Deloria, Philip J. and Neal Salisbury, eds., *A Companion to American Indian History*. Oxford: Blackwell Publishers, 2002.

Krupat, Arnold, *Red Matters: Native American Studies*. Philadelphia: University of Pennsylvania Press, 2002.

Mihesuah, Devon Abbott, *Indigenous American Women: Decolonization, Empowerment, Activism*. Lincoln: University of Nebraska Press, 2003.

Silver, Shirley and Wick R. Miller, *American Indian Languages: Cultural and Social Contexts*. Tucson: University of Arizona Press, 1997.

Trigger, Bruce and Wilcomb Washburn, eds., *The Cambridge History of the Native Peoples of the Americas*, 2 vols. Cambridge: Cambridge University Press, 1996.

Warrior, R. A., *Tribal Secrets: Recovering American Indian Intellectual Traditions*. Minneapolis: University of Minnesota Press, 1995.

White, Richard, *The Middle Ground: Indians, Empires, and Republics in the Great Lakes Region, 1650–1815*. Cambridge: Cambridge University Press, 1991.

2

DAVID MURRAY

Translation and mediation

Whereas other chapters of this book deal with various aspects of the field of Native American literature and offer ways to approach it, this chapter is designed to encourage questioning, not only of the boundaries and particular nature, but even of the separate existence of such a thing as Native American literature. This may seem rather perverse, but in fact it is important to see that such a category is by no means self-evident or obvious. It is also important to examine what is at stake for outsiders and insiders in establishing lines of difference between Indian and other literatures, as this is related not only to larger questions of cultural difference but also to the independent and sovereign political status of Indians. Thus, while the key terms of this chapter, translation and mediation, might suggest a bridging and connecting of two different entities, the intention is also to explore and challenge that assumption of clear-cut differences.

Let us take one rather simple idea of difference, perhaps the most obvious to an outsider. This would contrast the written expressions of individuals in modern Western literature to the communal oral traditions and forms of expressions of pre-contact traditional cultures and their continuation in present-day Indian communities. But if we think of this oral tradition, however dynamic and continuing, as the original Indian culture, then it follows that anything we encounter as Indian literature is already some steps removed from this, in that it is in textualized form and is either translated or written by someone in English who is some distance from that tribal and oral situation. In other words we could say that in reading Indian literature we are always dealing with a process of mediation and translation. One major mistake, though, would be to assume that therefore this literature is less authentically Indian, because this would be to assume that there was only one way of being Indian, and that was to be traditional, oral, and communal. So we need to keep clearly in view both that the literature we encounter is always, and inevitably, at some distance from a communal and oral traditional culture *and* that this does not give it a lesser claim to be called Indian literature. Of course there is a great difference between writers like Simon Ortiz, a full-blood who speaks his native Keresan as a first language, or Luci Tapahonso, who writes in Navajo as well as English, and others, like Louis Owens or Sherman Alexie who are writing from a mixed-blood position with less knowledge of an Indian language. It would be wrong to ignore these differences, but it is worth beginning with Arnold Krupat's insistence that "in varying degrees, all verbal performances studied as 'Native American litera-ture,' whether oral, textualized, or written, are mixed, hybrid; none are 'pure' or, strictly speaking, autonomous. Native American written literature in particular is an intercultural practice."[1]

This chapter will give a sense of the many forms of that "intercultural practice" and the ways in which issues of translation, both linguistic and cultural, are at the heart of longstanding concerns over authenticity. I begin with the oral expressions of traditional Indian communities, and the ways that they have been made accessible and consumable as literature, which raises the question of translation in its most clear form, and then I will move selectively through the novels and poetry written by Indians in English, which constitute most of what we think of as Indian literature, to the present complex debates over the representativeness and legitimacy of some of these writings.

Oral traditions

While early travelers, missionaries and settlers sometimes recorded Indian myths and stories in translation as curiosities, or evidence of superstition, there was little interest in their form, or sense of their value as literature. With the development in the nineteenth century of anthropological interest in other cultures came a growing sense in America that whole cultures were disappearing. Even those who accepted the inevitable disappearance of "lesser" or "primitive" cultures felt the need to preserve some record of what was disappearing, and a part of this exercise in what has been called 'salvage ethnography' was the collection of many volumes of myths, tales, ritual chants, or songs, an activity that has continued to the present. These volumes present an interesting problem in that in many ways they give us a scrupulous attempt at a faithful recording of Indian cultural practice, but they also fail to make it accessible to the general reader as literature, and it's worth looking at what has to happen to it to make it accessible, as it reveals what literature is expected to be. In its most off-putting and un-literary form, as in the many volumes produced under the auspices of the Bureau of American Ethnology by major figures such as Franz Boas and Frances Densmore, the ethnographic approach gives us, for instance, a text transcribed from a native language, with an interlinear translation, which translates each word exactly, then a looser translation into more correct and fluent English, plus accompanying notes explaining context and even sometimes a musical transcription, using Western notation. (Increasingly in later collections, audio recordings also provide another record of the storytelling or musical event.)

The aim here is authenticity – to give as complete a record of the relevant information as possible, rather than shaping it to white literary expectations, but later scholars have pointed out that one ignored area was the performance aspect of many of these stories within their community. The tales would be shaped and adapted in the telling by the expectations, knowledge, and responses of the audience, and recent work has tried to incorporate such an awareness in modern transcriptions or reconstruct it to supplement these older versions.[2] The original concern was ethnographic, documentary, and scientific, and so was in sharp contrast with the more popular presentations of Indian literature at the time and later, which drew on ideas of the doomed nobility of a simple people. The same Romantic enthusiasm which was shown for the natural products of folk culture in Europe extended to the supposedly simple and natural effusions of primitive peoples, with the result that through the later nineteenth century and onwards versions of Indian songs and poems were popular, but what passed as Indian was often just recirculated clichés of Indian nobility and harmony with nature, sometimes given an extra pathos by the idea that Indians were doomed to extinction.

It may be easy to dismiss some of this, but the issue becomes more complex when we have serious attempts by poets to use the ethnographic sources and make them accessible by bringing out their aesthetic dimensions. In claiming that they were literature these white writers were making a claim that specific expressions of Indian culture could communicate with other cultures at an aesthetic level – that is, that something transcended their particular form and language, and could be communicated in the new versions. What is clear to us as later readers, though, is the extent to which, in bringing out what they thought of as the universal aesthetic qualities, these writers were in fact reduplicating their own very culture-bound idea of what the poetic and the universal was. In the case, for instance, of attempts made by poets influenced by modernist ideas, ethnographic texts which involved narrative elements and repetitions were stripped down to resemble a Japanese haiku form, and then this similarity to other forms was claimed as evidence of its universality! There was also the idea that it was legitimate to strip down and select from something created by a specific person and in a specific time and place and present it simply as a Navajo poem, or even more generally an Indian lament, because the products of such cultures were assumed to be anonymous and communal, and therefore the part could always stand for the whole. In this case what is actually a fragment of a whole becomes reconstituted as part of a different whole, that of tribal unity, and universal poetry, and this is because the primitive art-object was supposed to be able, because of its provenance in a culture which was undivided, to synthesize everything in that culture. We can still see this same assumption at work in New Age and other appropriations of Indian ideas or artworks under a larger umbrella of the spiritual or beautiful.

There is an investment here in the idea of the aesthetic as an area of experience which transcends the local and specific, and this needs discussing, as it remains a potent idea. At its most basic it stems from an idea that all people share common experiences and common responses to the most fundamental and spiritual aspects of our lives, and that our cultural and artistic expressions share common denominators. There is certainly something heartening in the idea that what we share as human beings can be communicated across our cultural and linguistic differences. Indeed it can be an important element in dispelling the idea of unknowable and primitive Otherness, which can feed fear and justify exploitation. But simply to invoke art as the category that can do this is problematic. For a start, the category of art and the aesthetic itself is a Western concept rather than a universal given, and on the evidence of past attempts we have every reason to suspect any claims for universality or the capacity to communicate easily across cultures. American writers and ethnographers have long grappled with this issue, and one of the most interesting debates has been around what has come to be called ethnopoetics. Put simply, how much is it possible to translate and communicate of an original storytelling or ceremonial event? How many elements can be translated? Jerome Rothenberg developed the idea of "total translation" in which he used all the resources he had, including oral performance, and visual and typographic effects on the page to translate as many aspects of the original as he could be aware of from working with anthropological materials, into a form which would communicate as art within the broader literary world. He has been attacked, along with others like Gary Snyder, for "white shamanism," that is the appropriation of what does not belong to him, and this important idea of cultural property is one I will return to later. While in the end the work of the ethnopoets may be judged as reflecting just as clearly as their Romantic and modernist predecessors the aesthetic values of their *own* culture rather than those of the Indian originals, one important way in which they may constitute an advance is in foregrounding the processes and problematics of translation, rather than obscuring and eliding them under the cloak of art and universality. As Rothenberg puts it, translation can function as "a discourse on its own problematics" and "a commentary on the other and itself and on the differences between them. It is more a kind of question than a summing up."[3]

Although I have outlined some strong reasons for suspecting any claims for translation as carrying over an authentic sense of Indian literature or culture, I do not want to suggest that translation in itself is either impossible or undesirable – or even avoidable. Craig Womack, who has himself produced some of the most interesting attempts at bringing together the oral traditions of his Creek background and his present literary and critical context, points out the pitfalls of denying the importance of translation. "While we assume that every other body of literature in the world is translatable, we seem to hold out a different set of expectations for indigenous literatures." For all other literatures, he argues, we assume that there is something of sufficient merit that will survive and come through the process of translation, and he wants to insist that this same quality in Indian literature has been obscured by treating it as ethnography "with a unique set of rules that apply to static cultures set in the past rather than viable nations facing contemporary political realities." While he acknowledges the dangers of loose universalizing translations of the sort I have outlined above, he is concerned to head us off from the opposite danger. "The problem with the 'translation problem,' with its skepticism and emphasis on literary diminishment, is that it places us within a 'pure versus tainted' framework."[4] This framework would see all development from pre-contact forms as a corruption, so that writing would be less pure than orality, and all other forms of change and mixing would be a diminishment of Indianness.

What Womack is describing here has also been called essentialism, which is a much-used term in discussions such as these. The negative charge behind it is that it assumes a fixed and ahistorical essence or identity which all Indians, or women, or any other group, have in common. As part of a larger critique of fixed categories and binary thinking this has largely been aimed at the repressive racial and sexual stereotyping used by dominant cultures to justify their actions, but the force of the criticism has also been felt, and sometimes resented, by these falsely categorized groups themselves. They have felt that their claims for specific identity and unity based on common experience and culture are threatened by the sweeping use of the term. Gloria Bird has described it as "a convenient term that is used to undermine native people's [sic] unique legal and political position to determine for themselves who are their members."[5] This question of identity and sovereignty will be returned to later, but the problem here is that this binary opposition has much more to do with White preconceptions and idealizations than with Indian experience, and Womack makes the important point that Indian unease over translations is more about who has the power to dictate what is really Indian. As has often been noted, one of the characteristics of many traditional Indian communities was an openness to change and a willingness to adopt and include Whites and aspects of their culture, rather than any sort of cultural or racial exclusivity, so ideas of purity can be seen as largely a product of their colonial and postcolonial situation. Given the many forced changes which Indians have undergone over the centuries it is important to balance what has been done *to* them in forcing change with what has been done *by* them in the form of constructive and chosen adaptations, often under conditions of extraordinary hardship and difficulty.

Indian writing and representation

It is particularly important to bear this in mind as we move to a different sort of Indian literature, that written by Indians themselves, because the whole question of Indian authorship is a complex one. It might seem straight-forward to assume that once we move from the anonymous myths and poems of a tribal past presented through intermediaries, to texts written in English with a named author we have moved to an area not only of Indian authorship but of Indian authority and control, but we need always to ask about the *conditions of production and circulation* of any text. Just how complex questions of authorship can become will be demonstrated in a separate chapter on Indian autobiography, but in any situation where we have a text written by an Indian certain sets of conditions have to have been met. The author either spoke and wrote English or was helped by a translator or editor. Furthermore, in order for the book to have been published it needs to have been in the interests, whether commercial, political, academic, or whatever, of those who controlled the publishing outlets. So the idea that we are getting the unmediated "voice" of Indians needs to be treated with caution.

While many Indians learned some English through trade contacts, those who learned to read and write it mostly did so with the help of the Christian church, and the only things deemed worthy of publishing were those which expressed views consonant with Christian teachings. Thus it is not surprising that the first publications are from Christian Indians, but what might be surprising is how often they express, even within these confines, a distinctive position. Samson Occom's *Sermon at the Execution of Moses Paul*, published in 1772, can be seen as illustrative of the complex issues involved. The speech was instigated, as was its publication, by "many [White] Gentlemen in Town" who no doubt saw a sermon by a Christian Indian to a backsliding Indian about the evils of alcohol to be something worth encouraging. It could therefore be said to represent a white agenda, but Occom uses the occasion to preach not only to the condemned Indian, who has killed a man while drunk, but to the audience who are made up of fellow Indians and white onlookers. What is noticeable is his awareness of these multiple audiences, and the way that he targets different parts of his speech at them (getting in a criticism of those who provide alcohol as well as those who are overcome by it, for instance).

I would suggest that this awareness of being overheard by a white audience, or even of having them as primary audience is an important and continuing feature of Indian literature, perhaps comparable to the "double consciousness" of African Americans described by W. E. B. DuBois. Certainly for almost any Indian writer, with the exception of some Indian journalism, until recently the expectation must have been of a mainly white readership, and though it might seem a large jump we can see this brought out very forcefully in probably the best known work of Indian polemic and protest, which triggered for many the awareness of Indian activism, Vine Deloria, Jr.'s *Custer Died For Your Sins: An Indian Manifesto* (1969). The title of the book plays on the idea of a sermon, and is clearly aimed at a white audience and their misconceptions about modern Indians (parts of the book were first published in *Playboy*), but at the same time it is a consciousness-raising call to fellow Indians. The early writer who most fully exemplifies this tactic is William Apess. A Christian Indian like Occom, his first book, the autobiographical *A Son of the Forest* (1829) follows the pattern of the redemption narrative, though with some startling revisions of conventional Indian identity, but his later works reflect a growing political consciousness as well as a control over his medium. In *An Indian's Looking-Glass for the White Man* (1833) he presents the disastrous effects of white incursions on Indian communities. They have become "a complete place of prodigality and prostitution" and the people "mean and abject" but this has a historical cause, and so he turns attention back onto the white man. Such a shift in focus is indicated in the title, which allows us to read it in several ways. Is the Indian looking at himself for the benefit of the white observer-reader, or is he holding up the looking glass to the white man so that he can see himself? More radically, since the "mean and abject" Indian is just as much the white man's creation as is the civilized and Christianized Indian, who has been created in the white man's image, Apess is holding up several images of the white man as well as the Indian.[6] Postcolonial critics have developed the complex implications of what has been called mimicry – the interplay of identities and the turning back upon the dominant group of its own ideas of identity through imitation, and shown how the play and exploration around similarities by whites depends on an implicit and underlying idea of difference. In the case of Indians there is a fascinating interplay in which, for instance, the borrowing of Indian identity, as in "playing Indian" went hand in hand with efforts to turn Indians into whites.[7]

An awareness of the molding effects of education, and the expectations of a white readership on earlier Indian writers has led later readers to read these earlier texts with an ear for possible subversive elements, trying to locate what has been called a "hidden transcript," and there is certainly a danger of falling into the trap of trying to discern the "true" voice of the author, which is assumed to be more Indian and more critical than is immediately recognized. While often interesting, it may sometimes be inappropriate to try to rescue the text or the author by showing that they were really more subversive than they appear. Rather we need to see the texts as sometimes undecidable, multifaceted, and perhaps multivoiced. This is particularly true of the writings of the late nineteenth and early twentieth centuries, when Indian voices start to be heard, which in varying degrees conform to white Romantic expectations and/or express a distinctive and often sharply critical Indian position. The poems of Pauline Johnson, for instance, often seem to reflect the conventions governing Indian representation both in the verse itself and her performance of it. The performing of a certain sort of Indianness, found in books which emphasize the traditional, often aimed at young people, was, then, not just the province of imposters like Grey Owl, the Englishman who vividly described living in ecological harmony with nature in the wilds of Canada, in widely successful books and lecture tours but felt the need to present himself as an Indian in the process.

Apart from autobiographies, which are dealt with elsewhere, many of the early works were accounts of traditional Indian life, with an emphasis on what was distinctive, traditional and positive, as in the collections of tales by Charles Eastman or Ohiyesa. There was also the concern for what was changing, what did not fit the pattern of clear difference. We can see for instance the stresses and fractures caused by what was supposed to be the positive process of Indian boarding school education in the work of Gertrude Bonnin or Zitkala-Ša, where she describes the experience of feeling, at the moment of greatest success in winning a school prize, that she has also thereby failed her mother. Written by authors who themselves were living the contradictory pressures of progress and tradition, these writings often constitute a shifting and unstable interrogation of the dominant society's assumption that progress and assimilation can and should be achieved.

Broadly speaking, though more Indians were expressing themselves in print more often by the early twentieth century, the expression was predominantly in autobiographies, tribal histories or journalism rather than in strictly literary forms. It is not until the appearance in 1968 of Momaday's *House Made of Dawn* and its critical success heralding a spate of fiction and poetry in what has been called a Native American Renaissance that we have a critical mass of writings of all sorts. This is not to say that there were not important precursors, in, for instance, Mourning Dove's novel *Cogewea: the HalfBlood* (1927), John Joseph Mathews's *Sundown* (1934) or D'Arcy McNickle's *The Surrounded* (1936). These books dealt with the inability on the part of their protagonists to reconcile the conflicting demands of the tribal and the modern, and the focus on the figure of the mixed-blood as a metaphor for larger communal conflicts of identity is one which continues to the present, and will be returned to later. The stance of the authors above, though, is significantly different and more ambivalent than in most later writers. In the case of John Joseph Mathews, for instance, his non-fiction writings reflect his position as a wealthy outsider, educated in Europe and widely traveled. The sophisticated, self-sufficient figure he presents in the autobiographical *Talking to the Moon* in 1945 does not seem to reflect the tragic impasse explored in his fiction, and his tendency to talk of the Osage as "they," rather than "we" is characteristic of the stance – or one of the stances – taken by many of the older Indian writers.

One way of looking at these earlier writers is to see them as struggling with sets of assumptions contained in the language and literary conventions which they are using, and it could be argued that only with Momaday's work and what follows do we have a real expression of Indian worldviews. Kenneth Lincoln sees the literature of what he calls this Native American Renaissance as "a written renewal of oral tradition"[8] but that description perhaps makes it sound more straightforward than it is, and some later writers have problematized the relation between English and this oral trad-itional world. In the title of their collection *Reinventing the Enemy's Language* (1977) Joy Harjo and Gloria Bird suggest both a clear division and a way of exploiting it. The fact of having to use English does not entail a passive adoption of white values. Rather, in the spirit of all those earlier creative and syncretic adaptations of European culture noted by anthropolo-gists and historians and echoing Apess's looking glass referred to above, they see this as an act of cultural and political assertion. "Reinventing" in the colonizer's tongue and turning those images around to mirror an image of the colonized to the colonizers as a process of decolonization indicates that something is coming into focus that will politicize as well as transform literary expression.[9]

The sense here of writers taking control of a situation not of their own making is reflected in their description of themselves as "aware of ourselves as native women (in all our various constructs) in a language that we have chosen to name our own" (23). The extent to which the language itself, as opposed to the subject matter, is made distinctively Indian in this collection or in other writings is an arguable one, in that the incorporation of actual rhythms and expressions of what has sometimes been called Red English presents all the problems and dangers of any vernacular usage, including unwittingly reinforcing and catering to negative stereotypes. What they seem to mean here is the use of more standard forms of English to express Indian worldviews or "a particular way of perceiving the world" (24). The assumption here, then, is of fundamental differences which have been threatened by the loss of Indian speakers but can be creatively sustained and expressed in English.

That the status of this Indian difference has been made problematic by changes in the Indian population itself is suggested by the editors' account of their difficulties in deciding who was eligible to contribute. In requiring contributors to be "tribally identified" they wanted to hear only from "those who have directly experienced being Indian in their everyday lives" (26), but tribal identification, like any other method of defining Indianness leads to the quagmire of criteria based on blood quantum, residence, or particular descent patterns, all of which vary between tribes. This is, of course, in large part the legacy of the racist attitudes of successive governments, but for our purposes Harjo and Bird's difficulties point to a larger issue, which has become a theme in a great deal of recent writing and criticism, which is how to approach the whole question of changing definitions of identity.

One response suggested by the fusion of some postmodern and post-colonial ideas has been to question the necessity or usefulness of fixed boundaries which define identities whether at a personal, racial, or national level. James Clifford has argued that identity need not be predicated on the sort of boundaries of race which have defined Indians. "What if identity is conceived not as a boundary to be maintained but as a nexus of relations and transactions actively engaging a subject? The story or stories of interaction must then be more complex, less linear and teleological."[10] Applied to Indian literature this might mean that, rather than the pattern of finding or losing identity, with the plot movement working around those actions which give a grounding to identity (making connections with tradition, kin, and community, healing ceremonies and so on), we have a less clear direction, with new, less grounded but still satisfactory identities being forged, as in the work of Gerald Vizenor, Sherman Alexie, or Thomas King, and crucial here is the issue of mixed-blood identity.

The figure of the mixed-blood Indian has often been used as a metaphor for the historical processes which were changing and in many ways destroying Indian communities, and is central to a great deal of Indian literature, but the question has been how to see this figure. A negative view has been to see the mixed-blood figure as representing a tragic loss of Indianness, indicative of the demoralized and directionless condition of Indians deprived of the ability to continue in traditional ways. But a more positive way of looking at these figures is to see them as representing ways of mediating and negotiating, rather than being defeated by, contradictions. The mode of presentation then becomes comic rather than tragic and the use of the traditional figure of the shape-shifting trickster who can change identities has been quite widely adopted and circulated as corresponding to postmodern ideas of constantly reinvented identity, and a lack of fixed values or identity. Whether such an easy celebration actually chimes with the lived reality or is more a literary and utopian gesture has been a matter of some debate, as has the reason for its popularity with non-Indian readers. Does it allow for connections to be made across cultures or is it just more easily consumable by white readers because it has lost its specificity and communal identity in a cosmopolitan and postmodern melange?

One of the foremost critics of this has been Elizabeth Cook-Lynn, who has played an influential role in defining and articulating what has been called a nationalist perspective. In a world dominated by white control of the means of representation she wants the tribal position to have, for once, "the last word." Linking this cultural situation with the larger need for political sovereignty, she voices misgivings about the failure of most Indian writers to match the political efforts being made by Indian nations "to defend sovereign definition in the new world."[11] For Indian writers the body of nationalist material made up of myth, history, and earlier cultural expressions "must form the body of the critical discourse that functions in the name of the people; the presence of the Indian nation as cultural force." Instead we have what Elizabeth Cook-Lynn sees as the demoralizing cosmopolitanism of so many contemporary writers, whose popularity with mainstream America seems related to their presentation of Indians as "gatherings of exiles, emigrants, and refugees, strangers to themselves and their lands, pawns in the control of white manipulators, mixedbloods searching for identity."[12]

Cook-Lynn's point of reference is the tribal community or nation, and her criterion is how far any writing promotes its history and continuing values. She aims at "analysis in a tribal voice"[13] and this gives her writing a sharpness of focus, and sometimes an acerbity which is different from the more general claims about Indian literature. Kenneth Lincoln, for instance, reflects a generalized sense when he asserts that "[g]rounded Indian literature is tribal; its fulcrum is its sense of relatedness." He extends the idea of tribe to mean not just extended family but community, "ceremonial exchanges with nature and an animate regard for all creation" and "spiritual balance." As he goes on, then, his definition of tribal becomes more general – in fact, sufficiently so that it can be seen to make easy connections with other traditions, but the nationalist view would take tribal to mean something much more culturally and politically specific.

The challenge to present a nationalist or community-rooted literature is taken up perhaps most inventively by Craig Womack. His book *Red on Red*

(1999) not only demonstrates the wealth of material actually available to draw on in tribal traditions, through accounts of Creek and Cherokee writers past and present, but also makes an argument for the importance of a tribal specificity, as the basis for an assertion of literary as well as political sovereignty. While not trying to claim any absolute historical or psychic purity, Womack also deplores the easy dismissal of native-oriented positions as essentialist. His book "assumes that there *is* such a thing as a Native perspective and that seeking it out is a worthwhile endeavor." Furthermore, rather than arguing for the acceptability of it within an American canon, he sees it as separate and prior to it – not "the branch waiting to be grafted onto the main trunk" but the original tree itself. This means shifting the literary criteria from generalized ones that might apply to all literatures, to a more politicized aesthetic, in which "autonomy, self-determination and sovereignty serve as useful literary concepts."[14] This is a counter to what Womack sees as the depoliticizing and dehistoricizing which has taken place in the critical and popular success of some recent Native American literature.

Another Indian critic, Jace Weaver, has criticized what he calls the "gymnastics of authenticity" by which white critics have denigrated the idea and importance of Native identity and cultural specificity in favor of a universalism.[15] The charge often laid against universalism is not just that it plays down the local, indigenous, and specific but that what it claims as universal in fact actually reflects the values of the most powerful group who can define what is universal. Thus eighteenth-century Enlightenment universalism actually embodied many white European values which were assumed to be of absolute validity, and so was actually Eurocentric rather than universal. Similarly, a white critic who claimed to judge an Indian literary work by standards of universal aesthetic or moral literary value could be open to the charge that he or she was actually smuggling in Eurocentric criteria. Not only that, but in the effort to play down or dismiss what could not be translated or made into a literary or moral lingua franca, the critic could be seen as aiming to keep control of the criteria by which Indian literature is judged. Arnold Krupat has sketched out a map of the different positions, which he sees as going from nationalism through indigenism to cosmopolitanism and these critical positions also correspond to literary approaches, though less precisely as the literary texts themselves are often more multivalent and individual authors like Leslie Silko may change positions.[16]

What we see, then, is a very complicated situation in which every term seems contested. Put simply and crudely, to suggest an unbridgeable difference between worldviews can be seen as a reifying and limiting way of viewing Indians (bad thing), and a response to this would be to stress what is common and communicable across cultures as a way of historicizing and including

Indian cultures and literatures within an enlarged idea of American literature (good thing). On the other hand this itself can be seen as imposing universalist values, as downplaying Indian specificity and cultural uniqueness, and insisting on white centrality and authority (bad thing). In a parallel set of terms, mediation and translation can be seen either as positive actions in aiding communication, and, if carried out by Indian writers themselves as James Ruppert suggests, they can demonstrate an ability to move positively across cultures rather than being stranded in the divide between them. Or more negatively, they can be seen as catering for the white outsider in commodifying Indian culture to make it accessible.

A third set of terms clustered around mixed-blood identity involves the same confusing ambiguities. Either this figure offers a point of common ground on which Indians and others can meet and Indians can celebrate an identity not limited by racist conceptions, and even become a model of how to combine past and present as with Vizenor's trickster heroes, or it is a specious identification which ignores the reality of tribal life and caters for a postmodern consumption of images rather than reality.

Furthermore, hanging over all of these debates is a keen awareness of another issue, that of who has the power or right to speak on these issues? Indian suspicion of the power of white authorities to pronounce on their lives is reflected today not only in political issues of sovereignty and control over their natural resources, but also in disputes over the custody of ancestral skeletal remains, ceremonial objects, and spiritual resources. The suspicion of appropriation extends not only to New Age practitioners and plastic shamans but to academics. It underlies the arguments over universalism and can result in a series of impasses, but perhaps we need to see it also as bringing to the fore the crucial questions of authority and power underlying Indian authorship.

Louis Owens, whose own explorations of mixed-blood identity range across fiction, autobiography, and literary criticism, gives perhaps the best expression of the complexities of the situation. Rather than accepting the tribal or cosmopolitan oppositions, he sees the positive ways in which Indian literature can cater for its different readerships and yet allow a privileged position to the Indian reader as insider. He sees the possibility of "a richly hybridized dialogue aimed at those few with privileged knowledge – the traditionally educated Indian reader – as well as those with claims to a privileged discourse – the Eurocentric reader. One effect of this hybridization is subversive: the American Indian writer places the Eurocentric reader on the outside, as 'other,' while the Indian reader (a comparatively small audience) is granted, for the first time, a privileged position ... [T]he writer is appropriating an essentially 'other' language and thus entering into dialogue with the language itself."[17] Nevertheless such victories need to be put in a larger context in which even books like Momaday"s classic and trailblazing *House Made of Dawn* which are "superbly subversive" and "shifting, hybridized, interstitial, and unstable" are also capable of being received within the metropolitan center as presenting "a carefully managed exoticism." The lesson, and the necessary risk, he suggests, is that "in giving voice to the silent we unavoidably give voice to the forces that conspire to effect that silence."[18]

Notes

1. Arnold Krupat, *The Turn to the Native: Studies in Criticism and Culture*, Lincoln and London: Nebraska University Press, 1996, p. 21.
2. See the pioneering work of Dell Hymes and Dennis Tedlock. For a selection and overview see the several collections edited by Brian Swann, for instance *On the Translation of Native American Literatures*, Washington and London: Smithsonian Institution Press, 1992.
3. Jerome Rothenberg, "'We Explain Nothing, We Believe Nothing': American Indian Poetry and the Problematics of Translation," in Brian Swann, ed., *On the Translation of Native American Literatures*, p. 65.
4. Craig S. Womack, *Red on Red: Native American Literary Separatism*, Minneapolis and London: Minnesota University Press, 1999, pp. 64, 65.
5. Joy Harjo and Gloria Bird (eds.), *Reinventing the Enemy's Language: Contemporary Native Women's Writing of North America*, New York and London: Norton, 1997, p. 27.
6. William Apess, *On Our Own Ground: the Complete Writings of William Apess, a Pequot*, ed. Barry O'Connell, Amherst: Massachusetts University Press, 1992), p. 155.
7. See Philip Deloria, *Playing Indian*, New Haven and London: Yale University Press, 1998.
8. Kenneth Lincoln, *Native American Renaissance*, Berkeley, Los Angeles and London: California University Press, 1983, p. 8.
9. *Reinventing the Enemy's Language*, p. 22.
10. James Clifford, quoted in Ruppert, *Mediation in Contemporary American Literature*, Norman and London: Oklahoma University Press, 1995, p. 22.
11. Elizabeth Cook-Lynn, *Why I Can't Read Wallace Stegner and Other Essays: a Tribal Voice*, Madison: Wisconsin University Press, 1996, p. 82.
12. 'The American Indian Fiction Writers: Cosmopolitanism, Nationalism, the Third World, and First Nation Sovereignty' in Cook-Lynn, *Why I Can't Read Wallace Stegner*, p. 85, 86.
13. Cook-Lynn, *Why I Can't Read Wallace Stegner*, p. 6.
14. Craig S. Womack, *Red on Red*, pp. 11.
15. Jace Weaver, *That the People Might Live: Native American Literatures and Native American Community*, New York and Oxford, Oxford University Press, 1997, p. 14.
16. Arnold Krupat, *Red Matters: Native American Studies*, Philadelphia: Pennsylvania University Press, 2002, pp. 1–24.

17. Louis Owens, *Other Destinies: Understanding the American Indian Novel*, Norman and London: Oklahoma University Press, 1992, pp. 14–15.
18. Louis Owens, 'As If an Indian Were Really an Indian: Native American Voices and Postcolonial Theory' in Gretchen M. Bataille, ed., *Native American Representations: First Encounters, Distorted Images and Literary Appropriations*, Lincoln and London: Nebraska University Press, 2001, pp. 23, 24.

Major secondary sources

Cook-Lynn, Elizabeth, 'The American Indian Fiction Writers: Cosmopolitanism, Nationalism, the Third World, and First Nation Sovereignty' in *Why I Can't Read Wallace Stegner and Other Writers: a Tribal Voice*. Madison: Wisconsin University Press, 1996.

Krupat, Arnold, *The Turn To the Native: Studies in Criticism and Culture*. Lincoln and London: Nebraska University Press, 1996.

  Red Matters: Native American Studies. Philadelphia: Pennsylvania University Press, 2002.

Murray, David, *Forked Tongues: Speech, Writing and Representation in North American Indian Texts*. Bloomington: Indiana University Press, 1990.

Ruppert, James, *Mediation in Contemporary American Literature*, Norman and London: Oklahoma University Press, 1995.

Swann, Brian, ed., *On the Translation of Native American Literatures*. Washington and London: Smithsonian Institution Press, 1992.

3

ANNETTE VAN DYKE

Women writers and gender issues

Although popular culture representations of the Native American woman have tended to focus upon the image of the Indian princess or the "squaw" – "a violent, degraded, and filthy creature,"[1] Native American women writers have attempted to change these stereotypes by recording their stories in English since the nineteenth century. Native women attended reservation schools and boarding schools after the rise of reservations in 1851, but even before that some women like Jane Johnson Schoolcraft were relatively well educated. By the turn of the century, a number of Native women were highly educated and some had college degrees. As writers, they took elements of the oral storytelling tradition that had always been an integral part of their culture and incorporated them into the genres of novels, short stories, essays, and poetry. Some like Winnemucca and E. Pauline Johnson called upon Indian oration techniques to perform for the public, cultivating the Indian princess image to give them authority and to attract white audiences. Native writers extended such elements as the belief in the sacredness of language and earth, attention to place and landscape, propagation of cultural values, and concern for the community welfare as opposed to the concern for the individual into their writings. A novel by a Native American writer is not so much fiction as it is "witnessing" significant events through time.

In addition to the stereotypes of princess and squaw, Native American women writers have had to address the misconceptions about the importance of women in Native culture. As Laguna / Métis scholar Paula Gunn Allen notes:

> However he is viewed – sympathetically or with suspicion and terror – the Indian is always *he* … In the annals of American Indian literary lore there has been no female Red Cloud, Sealth, Logan, Black Elk, Lame Deer, or Rolling Thunder to bear literary witness to the shamanistic traditions of American Indians; there has been no female Sitting Bull, no Crazy Horse, no Handsome Lake, no Wovoka, no Sweet Medicine. And because there have been no great and noble women in that essentially literary cultural memory called tradition, there is no sense of the part that women have played in tribal life either in the past or today.[2]

Allen, who comes from what she calls a gynocratic tribal society, meaning a society in which feminine power is central, believes that if the centrality of women to most American Indian societies was recognized, profound changes would take place in the understanding of Native cultures: "The idea of Indian in the contemporary public mind will shift from warrior/brave/hunter/chief to grandmother/mother/Peacemaker/farmer."[3] The most important change she notes is that if women are seen in the proper perspective as the center of Native American culture, the image of the dying Indian and the extinction of Native American culture would be replaced with an image of a thriving and continuing culture.

The work of early Native American women writers

Early Native American women writers had relatively high status either because of their educational background or their standing in their communities. Most were privileged and acculturated. They sometimes employ "double-voiced discourse" which addresses two audiences from the often-jarring standpoint of being both within and outside Native culture. In addition, they often combine genres and use non-linear structures in their writings to achieve their goals. As a literary critic notes, "Many readers of early Native American women writers may need to suspend ordinary reading practices that value 'consistency' and 'unity.'"[4]

One of the first Native women to publish was the Ojibwe writer, Jane Johnston Schoolcraft or Bame-wa-wa-ge-zhik-a-quay, Woman of the Stars Rushing Through the Sky (1800–41). Born in Sault Ste. Marie, a settlement next to an Ojibwe village in what is now Michigan, to a Scotch-Irish fur trader, John Johnston, and Susan or Osha-guscoday-way-guay or Woman of the Green Prairie, Johnson's early education was at home. Her father taught her and seven siblings literature, history, and the classics while her mother educated them in Ojibwe culture and tribal history. A favorite daughter, Johnson visited Detroit, Montreal, Quebec, and Ireland with her father.

In 1823 she married Henry Rowe Schoolcraft, Upper Great Lakes Indian agent. The couple lived with Jane's family. Several years later Henry started a literary magazine, *The Literary Voyager or Muzzeniegun*, that had circulation in Detroit and New York as well as in Sault Ste. Marie. Jane contributed poetry and versions of Ojibwe stories, using the pseudonyms of "Rose" and "Leelinau." Her writing reflects her educational background – the influence of English poets of the pre-Romantic and Romantic period from her studies with her father, also a poet, coupled with her knowledge of Ojibwe culture from her mother's side of the family. Her work was admired by writers of her time such as Anna Jameson and Harriet Martineau who came to visit her.

Jane was also one of the primary sources for Henry's many works on Native American culture. She is important as an early founder of the Native American literary tradition, combining both European and Native elements.

Paiute writer and orator, Sarah Winnemucca or Thocmetory or Shell Flower, was the first Native woman to publish an autobiography. She wrote her *Life Among the Piutes: their Wrongs and Claims* (1883) to advocate for her people who had been relocated a number of times in conflicts with Euro-Americans over their land. Born about 1844 near Humboldt Lake in what is now Nevada, Winnemucca had less education than Schoolcraft. She attended a Catholic girls' convent school for a few months in 1860 until she was expelled because other parents did not want their daughters associating with Indians. Even so, she knew three Indian languages, English, and Spanish. She was raised in a line of important tribal leaders, her father Old Winnemucca and her grandfather Tuckee, who had a policy of peaceful coexistence with whites. To this end, Winnemucca served as an interpreter and liaison between Paiutes, other tribes, and settlers as well as US government and military leaders. She went on a lecture tour in San Francisco in 1879 to make public the wrongs against the Paiutes and also made over 300 appearances in the East. A consummate performer, she often wore an Indian "princess" costume of her own design.

Winnemucca wrote her autobiography at the insistence of two women educators and reformers in Boston. Mary Mann edited the work and Elizabeth Palmer Peabody raised the money to publish it in time for the next session of Congress. The autobiography begins with Winnemucca's birth year and draws upon her experience as an orator, using a narrator who shifts her perspective as she grows older throughout the work. Although earlier Native writers, William Apess and George Copway had written autobiographies, they focused upon their spiritual journeys to salvation and their Christian missionary work. Like them, however, Winnemucca writes from within the history of the nation and the land, using mixed genres of tribal stories, personal experiences, and contemporary events.[5]

Throughout her work, Winnemucca reminds her readers that the status of women in Paiute society was much higher than in Euro-American society – that Paiute women had complementary roles with men and were included in decision-making. She writes about the Festival of Flowers or coming-of-age ceremony for girls as well as the high accord in which children were held. An important theme is the abusive treatment of Indian women by white men. She was also a victim of differing standards for men and women, criticized for her three marriages and her volatile temper. In her autobiography, she carefully documents her versions of events as much to support her authority as spokeswoman for the Paiutes as to counter the idea that because she was a woman who spoke in public, she had low moral standards. Winnemucca wrote scathingly of so-called "Christian" Indian agents who robbed and cheated her people, but in support of the military who were more likely to treat the Paiutes fairly.

Finally, disillusioned with the unkept promises, Winnemucca decided to open a school for Paiute children with the backing of her editor and publisher, Mann and Peabody. She taught there for four years. Unlike other schools of the time, her school featured bilingual education and attention to Paiute cultural values. With the passage of the Dawes Act of 1887, her students were sent to white-run Indian schools and her school closed. Winnemucca died in 1891, leaving behind a legacy of a warrior woman, educator, and orator, advocating for her people.

S. Alice Callahan, a highly educated Creek (or Muskogee), is not only the first Native woman to write a novel, but also the first to write a novel in Oklahoma, then Indian Territory.[6] Born in Sulphur Springs, Texas, on 1 January 1868, Sophia Alice Callahan was only twenty-three when her novel was published. She was the daughter of Samuel Benton Callahan, who was of Scotch and Irish descent through his father and Creek descent through his mother. Callahan's mother, Sarah Elizabeth Thornberg Callahan, was the daughter of a Methodist minister in Sulphur Springs. Alice Callahan was one of eight children and part of what the newspapers of the time called the "Creek aristocracy" – Native Americans who had amassed a fair amount of wealth and who held prominent positions in both Native American and Euro-American societies.

Long before Callahan's birth, her family had been driven from Alabama on the infamous 1833 Trail of Tears, settling in Sulphur Springs. Her father established a large and prosperous cattle ranch and farm near Okmulgee, Oklahoma, before the Civil War. While he was serving as a representative of the Creek and Seminole Nations to the Confederate Congress, Union sympathizers drove the family out. Her mother and two of her siblings went back to Sulphur Springs where Callahan was born and educated. After the war, her father reestablished himself near Okmulgee, serving the Creek Nation in various governmental positions until the government was disbanded after allotment of the land to individuals in 1887.

Callahan attended Wesleyan Female Institute in Staunton, Virginia, in 1887 and 1888. She taught at Wealaka Mission School in 1892 and 1893 and Harrell Institute in Muskogee in 1893. She had planned to finish her education at Wesleyan so she could open her own school, but she died of acute pleurisy 7 January 1894 when she was only twenty-six.

Wynema was published in 1891, the year before Callahan took over her duties at Wealaka Mission School. Although little is known about the circumstances surrounding its publication, the intent of her novel is described in the dedication: "TO THE INDIAN TRIBES OF NORTH AMERICA Who have felt the wrongs and oppression of their pale-faced brothers, it may serve to open the eyes and heart of the world to our afflictions, and thus speedily issue into existence an era of good feeling and just dealing toward us and our more oppressed brothers."

While Callahan's novel has a Native American theme, it draws upon mainstream literary traditions of the time, couching her reform goals into the genre of women's sentimental fiction. Written to garner the understanding of a white audience, and, in particular, the woman reader, the novel employs the tactic of using a white, Christian woman reformer, Genevieve Weir, as a central character to guide her Indian character Wynema to maturity and "civilization" while Genevieve is being educated about Creek culture and Indian issues at the same time. This tactic employs Callahan's bicultural authorial voice, her mixed-heritage perception of being both within and outside of Creek culture. She also subverts the domestic ethic that women's place is in the home by asserting that the world and the home are one and the world should be ordered by the values of the home. Her ending has Native Americans and Caucasians "nesting in the villages together." Surely this peaceful image is an illustration of Allen's view of how American Indian societies would be thought of if the centrality of women were recognized.

Besides addressing issues important to Native Americans of the time such as the Dawes General Allotment Act of 1887 and the 1890 massacre at Wounded Knee, Callahan comments upon temperance and suffrage for women. Again, these show her concerns, which bridge the boundaries between Native Americans and whites as well as between genders. The novel also crosses the boundaries of history and fiction by discussing such issues in her romantic plot. Unfortunately, Callahan's work did not pass into the public's consciousness as did Winnemucca's and had no discernable impact on government policies. However, as the author of the first novel by a Native woman, Callahan holds an important place in Native American literary history. Her early death cut short her advocacy for her people.

E. Pauline Johnson, or Tekahionwake or Double Wampum (1861–1913), was the first Native woman to publish collections of poetry and short stories. Like Callahan, she came from a privileged background. She was born on the Grand River Reservation of the Six Nations, near Brantford, Ontario, in the family home, Chiefswood. Her father, a Mohawk leader, was a well-known orator and mediator between the Mohawks and the whites. Her mother was British-born, Emily Susanna Howells, a cousin of William Dean Howells, a prominent American novelist of the time. Her mother taught Johnson and her three siblings English literary traditions, especially the English Romantics. From 1874 until 1877, Johnson attended Brantford Collegiate Institute where she had the opportunity to take part in school performances.

In 1884, Johnson's father died after being brutally beaten in his quest to stop the sale of alcohol on the reservation. The family could no longer afford to live at Chiefswood. Like other middle-class women of her time, Johnson turned to writing to support herself and her mother. In 1892, she took up performing her poetry, calling upon her oratory skills from college and the models of her father and grandfather, John "Smoke" Johnson or Sakayengwaraton, also a noted orator. Like Winnemucca, she performed in a fringed buckskin dress of her own making for the first half of the show. She was known as "The Mohawk Princess." However, for the second half, she wore a ball gown, demonstrating her bicultural background and her understanding of the stereotypes held about Native women. Immensely popular, she toured Ontario, the East Coast of the United States, London, and later the Midwest.

In 1895, Johnson published her first poetry collection, *The White Wampum*. Well received, it established her as an Indian writer of some repute. Because she wrote her poetry to be performed, some of today's readers may feel her work is overly dramatic. In 1903, she published her second collection, *Canadian Born*, which reprints some earlier work and has less Indian content than the first collection, possibly causing some critics to like it less. The topics of Johnson's poetry vary widely: nature lyrics, traditional Romantic pieces, drawing upon her early education in the English Romantics, and Indian themes. Her poetry shows the respect for nature and attention to place that we might expect from a Native writer.

In 1911, she branched out into a collection of stories, *Legends of Vancouver*, based upon the Northwest Coast Indians, including a few from the Iroquois, in collaboration with Chief Joe Capilano (Squamish). Like her father, Johnson served as a cultural mediator between Natives and whites, writing numerous articles on Mohawk history and culture. She was particularly outspoken in these on white authors' depictions of Native American women characters as weak and suicidal. A number of her stories depict Native women as strong mothers and protectors of tribal culture. In 1913, as she was dying, her friends published *The Shagganappi* (1913),[7] a collection of stories dedicated to the Boy Scouts, and drawing upon ethnographic information from such groups as the Iroquois, Blackfoot, and Salish.

After her death, Johnson's work about women was collected and published as *The Moccasin Maker* (1913). Like Callahan, she often uses a romantic plot in these to protest the treatment of women and Native Americans. Many of her heroines are mixed-bloods facing problems resulting from their heritage. Besides being responsible for publishing the first poetry collections, Johnson was one of the first writers to explore identity and women's issues.

Zitkala-Ša or Red Bird or Gertrude Simmons Bonnin (Yankton-Dakota, 1876–1938) is the first of the writers considered here to attend a boarding school for Indians. This colored all of her writings. She was born Gertrude Simmons on the Yankton Sioux Agency in South Dakota, the third child of Ellen Simmons or Tate I Yohin Win or Reaches for the Wind, a full-blood, and a white father (Felker) who disappeared before her birth. Zitkala-Ša was raised as a traditional Dakota until 1884 when missionaries came to recruit for White's Indian Manual Institute, a Quaker boarding school for Indians in Wabash, Indiana. The eight-year-old persuaded her mother to let her go. As recorded in her autobiographical stories collected in *American Indian Stories* (1921), this experience changed her life for the worst. She depicts her life on the reservation as idyllic and her entry into the white world as typified by the boarding school as full of cruelty and alienation. Besides discussing the Indian boarding schools which set out "to civilize" the students, Zitkala-Ša recounts a blatant racist episode during a speech contest when a banner was hung denigrating her, the representative of Earlham College, as a "squaw."

She attended six years at White's. When she finally went home, she felt alienated from her tribe and her family. From 1895 to 1897, she attended Earlham College in Richmond, Indiana. In 1897, she taught at Carlisle Indian Industrial School and began to publish her autobiographical stories in the *Atlantic Monthly* under the Lakota name she chose for herself, Zitkala-Ša. Her critical stance on the boarding schools that her writings revealed probably lost her the position. Having discovered her musical talent at Earlham, she went to the New England Conservatory of Music in 1900 and 1901 to study violin. Returning to the reservation to care for her mother, she collected traditional stories for her *Old Indian Legends Retold by Zitkala-Ša* (1901). Many of these stories featured the Dakota trickster, Iktomi, and were aimed at reaching across cultures to teach Indian values to both adults and children. She was one of the first to publish traditional Indian stories without the intervention of white ethnographers.

At the reservation, she worked for the Indian Service and met and married Raymond Talesfase Bonnin, a Yankton Dakota. They moved to the Uintah Ouraye Ute Reservation in Utah where their son, Raymond Ohiya, was born. Zitkala-Ša no longer had time to write, although she collaborated on an Indian opera, *The Sun Dance*. In 1914, she began her political work as an activist for Indian self-determination. A member of the Society of American Indians (SAI), she was elected Secretary-Treasurer in 1916. From 1918 to 1919, she served as editor of the SAI's journal, *American Indian Magazine*, and began writing again – this time overtly political pieces. She continued her political work until her death, founding the National Council of American Indians and serving as president. Criticized by Indian men for her aspirations, she responded by writing on the roles of Indian women as leaders. Zitkala-Ša leaves a potent legacy of political activism and writing as well as preservation of culture in her writings. She is credited with helping to organize the modern pan-Indian reform movement, serving as a model for women's involvement.

Mourning Dove or Humishuma or Christine Quintasket (Okanogan c. 1888–1936) was in the forefront of attempts to preserve Native American culture and language through her novel and collections of traditional stories. Mourning Dove was born on the Colville Reservation in Washington State to Lucy Stuikin (Colville) and Joesph Quintasket (Nicola / Okanogan). She attended school on and off for about four years at the Goodwin Mission School of the Sacred Heart Convent at Ward, Washington. She had another year at the Bureau of Indian Affairs-sponsored Fort Spokane School for Indians before she was called home to care for her three siblings after the death of her mother in 1901. Of the writers we have considered, Mourning Dove is the least literate.

Wanting to continue her education, she went to the Fort Shaw Indian School outside Great Falls, Montana, working as a matron for four years. She married Hector McLeod who was part Flathead Indian in 1908. McLeod was alcoholic and abusive, and Mourning Dove left him, moving to Portland, Oregon. While she was in Montana, she saw the last of the buffalo rounded up by the order of the federal government in 1912. This incident inspired her to write *Cogewea, the Half Blood, A Depiction of the Great Montana Cattle Range*.

She attended business school in Calgary, Alberta, for two years to learn typing and further improve her English skills. She had a typed draft of her novel and had collected twenty-two Okanogan legends when she met Lucullus Virgil McWhorter in 1912. He had been collecting Yakima tales and was particularly interested in her work. This was the beginning of their nineteen-year collaboration. Publication of the novel did not go smoothly. Although the novel was accepted for publication in 1916, it was not actually published until 1927. After publication, Mourning Dove discovered that McWhorter had changed the novel so that it hardly felt like her work. Her focus had been to show the difficulties of being a mixed-blood in the context of a racist society while McWhorter, believing that the Indians were a vanishing race, added many ethnographic notes and railed against white corruption and hypocrisy. He also put unrealistic language into the mouth of the heroine to make her seem better educated than most whites. One critic calls *Cogewea* "a rough-hewn gem in which two people from divergent backgrounds insightfully comment on their times."[8] Nevertheless, the result is often jarring for the reader.

Mourning Dove faced huge difficulties in writing her novel and stories. She mostly supported herself as a migrant fruit picker, typing her manuscripts at night in her tent. She had several serious illnesses, a second alcoholic husband, and cared for numerous relatives. In addition to *Cogewea*, she published *Coyote Stories* in 1933. Another version of her collected stories was published in 1978 as *Tales of the Okanogans. Mourning Dove: a Salishan Autobiography* was published in 1990, fifty-four years after her death. Toward the end of her life, Mourning Dove became an activist. She was the first woman to be elected to the Colville Tribal Council.

Mourning Dove is one of the forerunners of the twentieth-century Native American novelist. She was one of the first to work considerable material from the oral traditions into a work of fiction. The Native American perspective on the sacredness of the earth is also prevalent in her work. Not until the latter half of the twentieth century will these elements appear prominently in a Native American novel.

Ella Cara Deloria, or Anpetu Waste or Beautiful Day (Yankton - Dakota, 1889–1971) is one of the first Native American linguists and, like Mourning Dove, a forerunner in the preservation of oral traditions. Unlike Mourning Dove, she was highly educated. Deloria was born at White Swan on the Yankton Sioux Reservation in South Dakota to Philip Deloria (Dakota) and Mary Sully Bordeaux (part Dakota). Mary was Philip's third wife and Ella was their first child. After being assigned in 1890 to St. Elizabeth's Church on the Standing Rock Reservation to serve the Teton Sioux, Philip was accepted as an Episcopal priest in 1891. Ella started school at St. Elizabeth's. In 1902 she went to All Saints boarding school in Sioux Falls, South Dakota. She won a scholarship to Oberlin College and attended there for two years until she transferred to Columbia University in New York City. There she met Franz Boas, noted anthropologist. She graduated in 1915 with a degree in education.

Deloria spent several years teaching at All Saints. Her mother died in 1916, and she had to become the family mainstay. She also was the inheritor of her family stories and traditions. She did not begin to work with Boas and Ruth Benedict, his student and colleague, until 1928. It was Benedict who suggested that she work particularly on women and family kinship structures. A gifted linguist, Deloria knew all three of the Sioux dialects. In 1929 she published her first scholarly paper, "Sun Dance of the Oglala Sioux," in *The Journal of American Folklore*. She continued to work with Boas and Benedict on an ad-hoc basis, but without any steady monetary support. In 1932, she published *Dakota Texts* and in 1933, she coauthored with Boas, "Notes on Dakota Teton Dialect," in the *International Journal of American Linguistics*. *Dakota Grammar* was published with Boaz in 1941 and *Speaking of Indians* in 1944.

Deloria had also completed a draft of her novel, *Waterlily*, by 1944, but its publishing was delayed until seventeen years after her death. *Waterlily* draws upon Deloria's knowledge of Siouan culture. The novel gives readers an insight into the roles and status of women before European contact. By writing it in the form of fiction, she could add in her personal interpretation of the past. In a time when males without access to female culture were doing most anthropological studies, Deloria's work makes an important contribution to the understanding of Plains Indian women. Taken together with her linguistic work, she leaves a legacy that future generations have built upon in preservation of Native American languages and cultures.

The Native American literary renaissance

Native writers of the mid to late twentieth century were part of a resurgence of writing that some critics called the Native American literary renaissance. Beginning with N. Scott Momaday's *House Made of Dawn* in 1968, Native writers began to publish substantial amounts of fiction, poetry, and critical essays. Of these late twentieth-century writers, women made significant contributions. One of the best known is Leslie Marmon Silko (Laguna, 1948 –) whose novel, *Ceremony* (1977), received wide acclaim.[9] (For more detail, see the Silko essay in Part III of this volume.) Like Momaday's novel, *Ceremony* explores the plight of World War II Pueblo veterans; but unlike Momaday's novel, which has a rather ambiguous depressing ending, *Ceremony* speaks to the continuance of the Pueblo people. Laguna Pueblo critic and writer, Paula Gunn Allen, points to this difference in endings and perspectives on the future of Native peoples as one of the differences between male and female Native writers. Silko weaves the old stories that she heard as a child into the text, paralleling the modern story of her veterans. The novel culminates in a magnificent healing story inspired by and dedicated to Thought Woman, the primary Laguna deity.

In 1981, Silko won a prestigious John and Catherine MacArthur Prize for work in fiction, poetry, and film – $159,000 tax-free over five years. That year, she also published a collection of photographs, short stories, and poetry, entitled *Storyteller*. Most of her previously published short stories and poetry from her chapbook, *Laguna Woman* (1974), appear in this volume. The title story demonstrates the process of storytelling and being a Native American storyteller.

Silko has two other novels to her credit: *Almanac of the Dead* (1991) and *Garden of the Dunes* (1999). *Almanac* is a graphic and disturbing tale of drug dealers, military tyrants, self-serving land developers, and corrupt Native Americans. The controversial novel documents 500 years of European abuse and oppression of Native Americans and the land. In *Garden of the Dunes*, Silko explores threads of European earth-based and Native American women's spirituality among other themes. As in her other works, these novels emphasize traditional story as a model for contemporary behavior and the continuance of Native American peoples.

Paula Gunn Allen (1939 –), Laguna / Métis novelist, poet, theorist, and professor, is a cousin of Silko.[10] As one of the foremost scholars of Native American literature, Allen collects and interprets Native American mythology. She describes herself as a "multicultural event," citing her Pueblo / Sioux / Lebanese / Scottish-American ancestry. Born in Albuquerque, New Mexico, Allen grew up in Cubero, New Mexico, a Spanish-Mexican land grant village abutting the Laguna and Acoma reservations and the Cibola National Forest. For most of her schooling, she attended a Sisters of Charity boarding school in Albuquerque, graduating in 1957. She received a bachelor's degree in English (1966) and a Master of Fine Arts in creative writing (1968) from the University of Oregon. In 1975, she received her doctorate in American studies with an emphasis on Native American literature from the University of New Mexico.

Allen writes from the perspective of a Laguna Pueblo woman from a culture in which the women are held in high respect. The descent is matrilineal – women owned the houses, and the primary deities are female. A major theme of Allen's work is delineation and restoration of this woman-centered culture. She has also been a major champion to restore the place of gay and lesbian Native Americans in the community. Her work abounds with the mythic dimensions of women's relationship to the sacred, as well as the struggles of contemporary Native American women, many of whom have lost the respect formerly accorded to them because of the incursion of Euro-American culture. This tragedy is the subject of her 1983 novel, *The Woman Who Owned the Shadows*. Besides loss of respect, her main character must sort out the various influences that having a mixed ancestry brings in order to reclaim a Native American woman's spiritual tradition. *The Woman Who Owned the Shadows* is one of the first contemporary novels to have a complex Native American female as its central character.

Allen is recognized as a major scholar, literary critic, and teacher of Native American literature. Among her teaching positions are San Francisco State University, the University of New Mexico, and the University of California at Berkeley and at Los Angeles. Allen's 1983 *Studies in American Indian*

Literature: Critical Essays and Course Designs, an important text in the field, has an extensive bibliography in addition to information on teaching Native American literatures. *The Sacred Hoop: Recovering the Feminine in American Indian Traditions*, published in 1986, contains her 1975 germinal essay "The Sacred Hoop: a Contemporary Perspective," which was one of the first to detail the ritual function of Native American literatures as opposed to Euro-American literatures. Allen's belief in the power of the oral tradition embodied in contemporary Native American literature to effect healing, survival, and continuance underlies all of her work.

Allen was awarded a National Endowment for the Arts writing fellowship in 1978, and she received a postdoctoral fellowship grant from the Ford Foundation-National Research Council in 1984. She is active in the anti-nuclear and antiwar movements, the gay and lesbian movements, as well as the feminist movement. She won an American Book Award in 1990 for *Spider Woman's Granddaughters: Traditional Tales and Contemporary Writings by Native American Women*, an attempt to correct the lack of stories by and/or about Native Women in literature collections. She also won the 1990 Native Prize for Literature. In her 1991 *Grandmother of the Light: a Medicine Woman's Sourcebook*, Allen expands her interest in the ritual experience of women as exhibited in the traditional stories. She traces the stages in a woman's spiritual path using Native American stories as models for walking in the sacred way. More recently, she has extended her interest in Native American writing by publishing collections of Native writing: *Voice of the Turtle: American Indian Literature 1900–1970* and *Song of the Turtle: American Literature 1974–1994*. These add to the canon of Native American literature. Through her poetry, novel, essays, collections of stories, and activism, Allen has made a major contribution to Native American literary studies, women's studies, gay and lesbian studies, and American literature.

Joy Harjo (Muskogee / Cherokee 1951 –) is a premiere poet, musician, and screenwriter. Born as Joy Foster in Tulsa, Oklahoma, to Allen W. Foster (Muskogee Creek) and Wynema Baker Foster (French, Irish, and Cherokee), she took the name of her paternal grandmother, Naomi Harjo, in 1970. (For more detail, see the Harjo essay in Part III of this volume.) She has two degrees in creative writing – a bachelor's degree from the University of New Mexico and an M.F.A. from the University of Iowa. She has taught at a number of universities, among them the University of New Mexico and the University of California, Los Angeles.

Harjo is known for the way her poetry creates characters who speak from the earth, removing barriers in time and understanding between the sacred and the profane. She believes that "myth is an alive, interactive event that is present in the everyday."[11] Like Allen she creates strong women's voices in her poetry, countering the dominant culture idea of weak women. In an interview with Joseph Bruchac she says that her women "reach an androgynous kind of spirit where they are very strong people ... They're human beings... It's time to break the stereotypes."[12] Even as a contemporary writer, Harjo has to address these same gender issues which earlier Native women writers had to face.

In this interview, Harjo notes another difference between male and female writing. By dedicating *She Had Some Horses* (1983) in part to Meridel Le Sueur, Harjo notes what she sees as a commonality that American women writers have with each other. She says, "The strongest writing that's going on in the United States today is women's writing. It's like they're tunneling into themselves, into histories and roots ... whereas other writing doesn't often feel it has a center to work from" (101).

In her many books of poetry, Harjo writes of women's relationship to the land, their endurance, their centrality as the mothers of the future among other themes. Her work illustrates her belief in the power of language for change, healing, and continuance, showing the influence of the oral tradition with her often chant-like rhythms. Like Winnemucca and E. Pauline Johnson before her, she is a performer. She plays soprano and alto saxophone, reciting her poetry with the Native American band, Poetic Justice. In an edited collection, *Reinventing the Enemy's Language: Contemporary Native Women's Writing of North America* (1997), Harjo and her co-editor, Gloria Bird, celebrate the "beautiful survival" of Native American women.

Like Allen, Linda Hogan (Chickasaw, 1947–) works to restore the traditional Native American balance between male and female power that was disrupted by the coming of Euro-Americans. Through her writings she seeks to draw upon wisdom from nature and from female powers of regeneration. A prolific poet, novelist, playwright, and essayist, Hogan's work is centered on the preservation of the environment. For instance, the theme of her novel, *Mean Spirit* (1993), a finalist for a Pulitzer Prize, is not only about the mistreatment of the Osage during the 1920s oil boom, but about the destruction of the environment.

Hogan was born in Denver to Charles Henderson (Chickasaw) and Cleona Bower Henderson (white). While the family moved frequently because of her father's army postings, Hogan has always considered her home to be Oklahoma, where her paternal grandparents lived. Her maternal ancestors homesteaded in Nebraska Territory and Hogan draws upon those experiences as well in her writings. She is acutely aware of the difficulties of the working poor of both Indian and non-Indian and this is a constant theme in her writing.

Although Hogan has two degrees – a B.A. obtained as a nontraditional, commuter student and an M.A. in English and creative writing from the University of Colorado, she has felt that much of her education lacked relevance. As a result, she tries to ground her writing in the lives of common people while, at the same time, drawing upon the mythological from her Native heritage. For instance, many of the poems in *Savings* (1988) have to do with the lives of the urban Indian. Set in Minneapolis, the poems speak of the brutality and racism of the city, but woven into the poems is the hope of transcendence offered by the mythic.

She has received many awards such as a D'Arcy McNickle Memorial Fellowship at the Newberry Library (1980), a National Endowment for the Arts grant in fiction (1986), a Guggenheim for fiction (1990), a Five Civilized Tribes Playwriting Award (1990), and an American Book Award from the Before Columbus Foundation (1985) for her poetry book, *Seeing Through the Sun.* She has also taught at many universities, including the University of Minnesota and the University of Colorado at Boulder. She continues to lecture and give readings, especially to Native American groups.

Much of her poetry celebrates the role of caretaking that women do from day to day, extending that caretaking to caring for the earth. She believes that women need "to return to being caretakers ... to offer service to the living and the planet."[13] In her poetry book, *Eclipse* (1983), many of the poems are concerned with issues of war and destruction and their impact upon children. In *Book of Medicines* (1993), it is not the power of God, which holds everything together, but the small tasks which women do. In her novel, *Solar Storms* (1995), her seventeen-year-old protagonist's world is shattered by her biological mother's failure to love, to care, which parallels the destruction of the environment. In order to bring her life back to any kind of balance, she leaves her foster home to seek out her female relatives. She learns that all things are connected and finds that the small things that women do influence the global things. This theme of a mother's failure to love is also explored in her memoir, *The Woman Who Watches Over the World* (2001).

In *Solar Storms*, Hogan has presented the reader with a continuation of what Allen's 1983 novel, *The Woman Who Owned the Shadows*, began. She has created a complex portrayal of the Native American woman as hero, but this time the healing of the protagonist extends to concern for the community – a theme that echoes Silko's work in *Ceremony* with her male protagonist. Hogan's work makes powerful statements about the individual's responsibility to others and to the earth.

Diane Glancy (Cherokee 1941–) is the author of numerous books of poetry, novels, essays, and plays. She was born in Kansas City, Missouri, to Lewis Hall (one-quarter Cherokee) and Edith Wood Hall (English and

German). She has a bachelor's degree from the University of Missouri, an M.A. from the University of Central Oklahoma, and an M.F.A. from the University of Iowa Writer's Workshop. She has been an artist-in-residence in Oklahoma and Arkansas and from 1984 to 1986 was the playwright laureate for the Five Civilized Tribes. She teaches creative writing, script-writing, and Native American literatures at Macalaster College in Saint Paul, Minnesota.

Like the writing of other Native writers of mixed heritage, Glancy's work often deals with identity issues. As she notes, only one of her great-grandparents was Cherokee, but in her writing it is her "Indian heritage that emerges again and again."[14] Her autobiographical non-fiction, *Claiming Breath* (1992) and *The West Pole* (1997), explore this cultural split. Much of her fiction explores the lives of contemporary urban Indians, especially her well-known collection of short fiction, *Firesticks* (1993). These are not romanticized Indians, but well-crafted, complex characters. Glancy's work reflects her statement that Indians' "experience encompasses the span from the pitiful weakness of the derelict on the street to the medicine man who reaches into the universe."[15] Her stories often have Native Americans characters who connect with the majesty of spirit expressed in nature and are changed.

Glancy's work is often a complicated mix of prose, poetry, drawings, photographs, and other media artifacts. For example, in her quest to recover her heritage for herself and her Nation, she reconstructed the journey along the Cherokee Trail of Tears in *Pushing the Bear* (1996). She includes newspaper articles of the day interspersed with the fictional stories of the participants – both soldiers and Cherokees. Her poetic use of language is particularly valuable in capturing the consciousness of the different characters, who are in various stages of assimilation into Euro-American culture. Like the writers before her, she draws upon Native oral traditions and Euro-American written traditions, creating new forms of literature. Despite her many awards, her work has not received the critical attention it deserves.

Any discussion of Native American women writers and gender issues would not be complete without at least a mention of novelist, essayist, and poet, Louise Erdrich. She is one of the most important contemporary writers, not only among Native Americans or women, but also in general. (For more detail, see the Erdrich essay in Part III of this volume.) Karen Louise (Turtle Mountain Ojibwe, 1954–) was born in Little Falls, Minnesota, to Ralph Louis Erdrich (German) and Rita Joanne Gourneau Erdrich (Ojibwe and French). Her parents taught in the Wahpeton Indian Boarding School, Wahpeton, North Dakota, where Erdrich grew up. She was the eldest of seven children, an influence that appears in her novels of extended Native

American families. She frequently visited her maternal grandparents on the Turtle Mountain reservation where she is an enrolled member. In her verse and novels such as *Love Medicine* (1984), *Tracks* (1988), *The Beet Queen* (1986), *The Bingo Palace* (1994), and *Tales of Burning Love* (1996), she draws upon her years in North Dakota and on her heritages to portray the great endurance of women and Native Americans. For example, *Tales of Burning Love* is the story of four wives of Jack Mauser who survive a blizzard by telling their lurid stories of involvement with Mauser.

Like other significant Native American women writers, she is troubled by stereotypes of Native women. At least one early reviewer of her work responded to some of the women in *Love Medicine* as having low moral character. However, Erdrich is known for her strong women characters such as Fleur, who has many medicine powers, half crazy Pauline who becomes Sister Leopolda, Lulu Lamartine whose special skills are loving men too well, and Marie, who cares for abandoned children. With equally complex and sympathetic male characters, she has created a vast North Dakota saga that is akin to William Faulkner's Yoknapatawpha County.

In *The Antelope Wife* (1998), she creates a new set of characters with a central motif of Native spirits representing greed and lust set in Minneapolis. In *The Last Report on the Miracles at Little No Horse* (2001), her female protagonist takes the role of a priest to serve the reservation. *The Master Butchers Singing Club* (2003) continues the exploration of the German side of her heritage she began in *The Beet Queen*. The non-fiction *Blue Jay's Dance* (1995) covers being pregnant and the birth of her three daughters. Throughout her writing, Erdrich displays such unapologetic love and humor that her readers cannot help but be charmed, all the while she is tackling the issues that matter – love, death, abandonment, community, passion, addiction, greed, aging, and parenting. A consummate storyteller, she represents the flowering of Native American literature.

The important contributions of Native women writers, then, can be summed up in four overlapping areas. They fought against stereotypical popular culture representations of Native women; they attempted to reinstate the importance of women to Native American cultures, and they contributed to the continuity and preservation of Native culture, not only by extending Native American values and materials into their writings and advocating for their people, but also by showing their belief in Native culture as something strong and vital. In addition, by extending Native American elements such as the oral tradition into their work, they created new forms of literature. From Jane Johnston Schoolcraft to Louise Erdrich, Native American women writers have left an immense legacy, not only to Native literature and culture, but also to American literature and culture in general.

Notes

1. See Rayna Green, *Women in American Indian Society*, New York: Chelsea, 1992, p. 51.
2. Paula Gunn Allen, *The Sacred Hoop: Recovering the Feminine in American Indian Traditions*, Boston: Beacon, 1986, p. 263.
3. Ibid., p. 265.
4. See Karen Kilcup's introduction to *Native American Women's Writing, 1800–1924, an Anthology*, Karen Kilcup, ed., Oxford: Blackwell, 2000, p. 6.
5. See A. Lavonne Brown Ruoff, "Early Native American Women Authors: Jane Johnston Schoolcraft, Sarah Winnemucca, S. Alice Callahan, E. Pauline Johnson, and Zitkala-Ša," *Nineteenth-Century American Women Writers: a Critical Reader*, Karen L. Kilcup, ed., Malden, MA: Blackwell, 1988, pp. 81–111.
6. Some of this material is taken from my "S. Alice Callahan," in Sharon M. Harris, Heidi Jacobs, and Jennifer Putzi, eds. *American Prose Writers, 1870–1920, Dictionary of Literary Biography*, CCI. Detroit: Gale Research, 2000.
7. Shagganappi is a Cree word for buckskin pony. See Donald A. Pecosky, "Pauline Johnson," in W. H. New, ed., *Canadian Writers, 1890–1920, Dictionary of Literary Biography*, p. 92, Detroit: Gale Research, 1990, p. 163.
8. See Allana Kathleen Brown, "Mourning Dove (Humishuma)," in Kenneth M. Roemer, ed., *Native American Writers of the United States, Dictionary of Literary Biography*, p. 175, Detroit: Gale Research, 1997, p. 194.
9. Some of this material is from my "Leslie Marmon Silko," in Sharon Malinowski, ed., *Notable Native Americans*. Detroit: Gale Research, 1994.
10. Some of this material can be found in my "Paula Gunn Allen" in Malinowski, *Notable Native Americans*.
11. See Laura Coltelli, "Joy Harjo," in *Winged Words: American Indian Writers Speak*, Lincoln: University of Nebraska Press, 1990, p. 130.
12. See Bruchac, "The Story of All Our Survival: an Interview with Joy Harjo," in *Survival This Way, Interviews with American Indian Poets*, Tucson: Sun Tracks and the University of Arizona Press, 1987, p. 97.
13. See Kathryn W. Shanley, "Linda Hogan," in Kenneth M. Roemer, ed., *Native American Writers of the United States, Dictionary of Literary Biography*, p. 175, Detroit: Gale Research, 1977, p. 128.
14. See "Two Dresses," in Brian Swann and Arnold Krupat, eds., *I Tell You Now: Autobiographical Essays by Native Writers*. Lincoln: University of Nebraska Press, 1989, p. 172.
15. Ibid., p. 183.

Major secondary sources

Allen, Paula Gunn, *The Sacred Hoop: Recovering the Feminine in American Indian Traditions*. Boston: Beacon, 1986.
  ed., *Spider Woman's Granddaughters: Traditional Tales and Contemporary Writing by Native American Women*. Boston: Beacon Press, 1989.
Bataille, Gretchen M. and Kathleen Mullen Sands, *American Indian Women: Telling Their Lives*. Lincoln: University of Nebraska Press, 1984.

eds., *American Indian Women: a Guide to Research*. New York: Garland, 1991.

Bataille, Gretchen M. and Laurie Lisa, *Native American Women: a Biographical Dictionary*, 2nd. edn. New York: Routledge, 2001.

Bloom, Harold, ed., *Native American Woman Writers*. Philadelphia: Chelsea House, 1998.

Erdrich, Heid and Laura Tohe, eds., *Sister Nations: Native American Women Writers on Community*. St. Paul: Minnesota Historical Society Press, 2002.

Green, Rayna, ed., *That's What She Said: Contemporary Poetry and Fiction by Native American Women*. Bloomington: Indiana University Press, 1984.

Women in American Indian Society. New York: Chelsea House, 1991.

Harjo, Joy and Gloria Bird, eds., *Reinventing the Enemy's Language: Contemporary Native Women's Writings of North America*. New York: Norton, 1997.

Kilcup, Karen, ed., *Native American Women's Writing, c. 1800–1924: an Anthology*. Oxford: Blackwell, 2000.

Mihesuah, Devon Abbott, *Indigenous American Women: Decolonization, Empowerment, Activism*. Lincoln: University of Nebraska Press, 2003.

PART II
GENRE CONTEXTS

4

BERND PEYER

Non-fiction prose

Much of what has been written about American Indian literature so far generates the false impression that its beginnings date back to the 1960s and that poetry and fiction are its predominant genres. The literary potential of American Indian "legendary materials" has been recognized since the publication of Henry Rowe Schoolcraft's *Algic Researches* (1839) and Longfellow's *Hiawatha* (1855). Consequently, Euro-American readers have been more inclined to welcome the fusion of traditional storytelling and creative writing than to give up the common belief that there is an unbridgeable gap between expository writing and orally transmitted knowledge. English non-fiction prose produced by American Indians has received relatively little critical attention so far because "the keeping of written records" (*Webster's*) continues to be regarded as the essential distinction between civilization and primal oral societies. We are obviously much more familiar with the farewell orations attributed to Logan and Seattle than the countless letters, petitions, and tracts penned by acculturated Indian leaders seeking to affirm native rights to a prosperous future in America. Nonetheless, non-fiction prose has fully dominated American Indian letters since at least the second half of the eighteenth century. If one is also prepared to accept newspapers as a legitimate forum for literary production, then it continues to do so today. This essay focuses on the following fluid categories of non-fiction prose literature: evangelist, council, periodical, political, humorous, historical, and contemplative (see also the separate section on autobiographies in this book).

Evangelist literature

American Indian literature has its antecedents in seventeenth-century New England, where Protestant missionaries composed religious texts in the Massachusett language. John Eliot's famous "Indian library," the first major colonial publishing venture, would never have materialized without the indispensable assistance of bilingual Indian translators like Cockenoe-de-Long Island (Montauk), Job Nesuton (Massachusett), and James Printer (Nipmuck). Some of these "Praying Indians" also left behind a few contracts and letters, usually written in unconventional English. Bona fide publications by North American Indians, however, did not appear until the second half of the eighteenth century, when Protestant missionaries affiliated with the series of religious revivals that swept through American colonies known as the Great Awakening (c. 1730–40), began to instruct their native charges in English. The writings produced by these mission-trained authors, notably sermons and spiritual autobiographies, obviously reflect the Protestant Ethic propagated by their mentors.

The foremost publication from this period is Samson Occom's *A Sermon Preached at the Execution of Moses Paul* ..., printed by the press of Thomas and Samuel Green at New Haven on 31 October 1772. At least 19 subsequent editions appeared in various towns in New England and in London, including a Welsh translation in 1789. Occom (Mohegan, 1723–92), an ordained Presbyterian minister and hymn writer, was the most acclaimed Indian convert of his day. His sermon, originally delivered at the public hanging of a fellow Mohegan for drunken homicide, is a particularly successful example of a unique New England literary creation known as the "execution sermon." More than sixty such tracts, authored in part by celebrities like Increase and Cotton Mather and read as widely as captivity narratives, were published between 1639 and 1800. What makes Occom's fairly standard execution sermon stand out from the others is that it directly addresses his "poor kindred" on the problem of intemperance. The "Pious Mohegan," as Occom was widely known, overtly berates his fellow tribesman in order to appease Puritan moral self-righteousness, while at the same time making a covert appeal to his peers to resist one of colonialism's most effective agents. A drunkard, he warns, is an irrational being who may "be cheated out of all he has." Occom's execution sermon, reprinted as recently as 1992, thus introduces one of the most crucial and prevailing topics in American Indian literature.

A similar execution sermon in epistolary form titled *Letter from J—h J——n* ... was also printed by the press of Timothy Greene in 1772. The author, Joseph Johnson (Mohegan, 1751–76), Occom's son-in-law and a licensed Presbyterian minister, was the most prolific of the New England Christian Indian writers. He produced a great number of sermons, letters, petitions, and council speeches that were recently published collectively as *To Do Good to My Indian Brethren* (2001).

The Christian tradition in American and Canadian Indian literature is still evident today in works like James Treat's (Creek) *Native and Christian*

(1996), a collection of essays in which contemporary Christian Indians argue that religious, cultural, and racial contradictions are socially constructed rationalizations rather than self-evident facts.

Council literature

A somewhat different work is Hendrick Aupaumut's "A Narrative of an Embassy to the Western Indians," originally written around 1793 and published posthumously among the *Memoirs of the Pennsylvania Historical Society* in 1827. Aupaumut (Mahican, 1757–1830), a mission-educated sachem and veteran of the American Revolution known as "Captain Hendrick," acted as official US emissary of peace at several council meetings with leaders of the Iroquois and various Ohio Valley tribes between 1791 and 1793. "A Narrative" is a detailed account of Aupaumut's diplomatic mission to the Ohio Valley in 1792–93, and thus a unique contribution to a popular eighteenth-century American genre typically referred to as "treaty literature." It begins with a prefatory outline of traditional kinship-based relations in the Northeast in which each tribe is accorded its proper status as a higher- or lower-ranked relative. This is followed by several of his own speeches recommending peaceful relations with the Americans and the responses elicited from representatives of the "hostile" tribes. Although Aupaumut recorded them in English, the speeches still retain a certain distinctiveness in style as a result of the frequent infusion of native syntax and the author's careful reproduction of traditional council oratory conventions. Aupaumut's "A Narrative" is thus a genuine manual for Northeastern Indian diplomatic etiquette.

Joseph Johnson, who co-founded an independent community of Christian Indians in Oneida territory in New York known as Brothertown with Occom, transcribed his official exchange with the Oneidas in January of 1774. His request for land, reproduced in James D. McCallum's *Letters of Eleazar Wheelock's Indians* (1932), distinguishes itself from most other treaty literature in that it was originally delivered in English, which served the delegates of mutually unintelligible Algonquian and Iroquoian speech communities as lingua franca. Johnson's speech, which includes a caustic denunciation of the English treatment of New England Indians, follows the same strict council conventions outlined in Aupaumut's narrative.

What the execution sermons and council records mentioned above have in common is that each exemplifies the confluence of native oratory and European literacy. "Indian monologues" have fascinated European-American readers since the second half of the seventeenth century, and it is no coincidence that most of the early Indian authors were also accomplished public speakers.

Transcriptions of public addresses consequently make up a substantial portion of American Indian nonfiction prose up until the beginning of the twentieth century.

Periodical literature

In the first quarter of the nineteenth century missionaries, affiliated with the widespread flowering of religious sentiment and unprecedented expansion of church membership throughout the United States known as the Second Great Awakening (c. 1790–1830), concentrated their efforts on the populous tribes of the Southeast, especially the Cherokees. Their reformist ideas were readily adopted by a small but highly influential group of mixed-bloods, who in less than three decades managed to transform a loosely organized coalition of villages into a constitutional government patterned after the United States. As a means of promoting their own progressive politics and challenging the novel policy of removal, Cherokee administrators established an independent bilingual press and launched the *Cherokee Phoenix* or *Tsa-la-ge-Tsi-le-hi-sa-ni-hi* on 21 February 1828. This tribally owned newspaper initiated a rich journalistic tradition that was carried on by the Cherokees west of the Mississippi with the establishment of the *Cherokee Advocate* in 1844. In *American Indian and Alaska Native Newspapers and Periodicals, 1826–1924* (1984), Daniel Littlefield, Jr., and James Parins estimate that over fifty tribal, nontribal, or intertribal newspapers and periodicals were either founded, edited, or maintained by American Indians and Alaskan Natives in the decades that followed. During the second half of the nineteenth century, journalism blossomed in Indian Territory, where several tribal and nontribal newspapers existed alongside a much larger number of periodicals that were neither owned nor edited by Indians but dealt intensively with local Indian issues. Fanned primarily by partisan politics, this flourishing newspaper business transformed Indian Territory into a veritable literary center.

Tribally run newspapers like the *Cherokee Phoenix* (1828–34), *Cherokee Advocate* (1844–53, 1870–75, 1876–1906), or the short-lived *Indian Champion* (Choctaw Nation, 1884–85) obviously transmitted the official views of the tribal administration. Under the able editorship of Elias Boudinot (Cherokee, 1804–39), the *Cherokee Phoenix* developed into a formidable organ for upper-class Cherokee notions of "civilization" and anti-removal sentiment – that is, until he suddenly reversed his stand and tendered his resignation on 1 August 1832. Convinced that further resistance to removal was futile, Boudinot joined a small pro-removal faction, later known as the Treaty Party or Ridge Party, in opposition to the official Cherokee administration under Principal Chief John Ross (1790–1866) and his supporters (National Party or Ross Party). This dissenting minority signed the illegal Treaty of New Echota in 1835 accepting the federal government's conditions for removal without official authorization, an act of treason that cost Boudinot his life four years later. The *Cherokee Advocate*, which was founded after the Ross administration resumed power in the Cherokee Nation West in 1839, faithfully adhered to the National Party's platform and mounted a relentless campaign against the surviving members of the Treaty Party. Illustrative for the factionalism among the Cherokees then is the fact that one of Boudinot's sons, William Penn Boudinot (1830–98), an uncompromising advocate of Indian rights, and his own grandson, Elias Cornelius Boudinot, Jr. (1854–96), a supporter of the National Party, both edited the pro-Ross Party *Advocate* temporarily.

Political partisanship in turn motivated many ambitious individuals to establish independent nontribal newspapers to give voice to their own views concerning vital issues such as granting rights-of-way to railroads, opening Indian lands for white settlement, or acquiring territorial status. During one of the interims when the *Cherokee Advocate* ceased publication, for instance, Elias Cornelius Boudinot (1839–90), another one of Elias Boudinot's sons, co-owned and edited the *Indian Progress* (Muskogee and Vinita, 1875–76), a paper advocating white settlement in Indian Territory. In response to Boudinot's booster paper, the Indian International Printing Company, an organization made up of several important citizens from the Five Civilized Tribes, established *The Indian Journal* (Muskogee and Eufaula, 1876–present), an intertribal newspaper that was temporarily chartered by the Creek Nation. Other notable nontribal newspapers include the *Choctaw Telegraph* (1848–49) and *The Choctaw Intelligencer* (1850–51), edited by the Choctaws Daniel Folsom (nd) and Jonathan Edwards Dwight (nd) respectively; the *Chickasaw and Choctaw Herald* (1858–60?), published by Henry McKinney (Chickasaw, nd); and the *Indian Chieftain* (1882–1902), edited temporarily by the Cherokees William Potter Ross (1820–91) and future US Senator Robert L. Owen (1856–1947). With the abolition of the Indian governments in 1906 and the incorporation of Indian Territory into the state of Oklahoma in 1907, this regional journalistic tradition began to ebb.

The propagandist campaign initiated by the coercive reform movement of the last quarter of the nineteenth century further promoted the development of American Indian journalism. Eastern secular publications like the Women's National Indian Association's *The Indian's Friend* (1888–1951) and the Indian Rights Association's *Indian Truth* (1924–86), or religious periodicals like the Roman Catholic *The Indian Sentinel: the Magazine of the Indian Missions* (1916–62), all of which focused on both national and regional topics, frequently included material written by Indians. Equally important were the newsletters, newspapers, and magazines published by off-reservation boarding schools, such as Hampton Institute's *Talks and Thoughts of the Hampton Indian Students* (1886–1907) and *The Southern Workman* (1872–1939); Carlisle Indian Industrial School's *The Indian Helper* (1885–1900), *The Red Man and Helper* (1880–1904), *The Carlisle Arrow and Red Man* (1904–18); Haskell Institute's *The Indian Leader* (1897–1964); or Chilocco School's *The Indian School Journal* (1900–80). Each of these educational institutions promoted the skill of printing as part of their vocational training programs.

The first two decades of the twentieth century saw the rise of national Indian newspapers and periodicals in major American cities, a trend fore-shadowed to some extent by *Copway's American Indian*, a weekly that George Copway (Ojibwe, 1818–69) published single-handedly in New York City from 10 July to 4 October 1851. In terms of Indian literary production, the closing decades of the Progressive Era were dominated by a group of highly educated urban professionals who formed an intellectual network that embraced a pronounced nationalistic ideology. In 1911 they founded the first major intertribal political organization, the Society of American Indians (SAI), which, among other objectives, set out to educate (rather than implicate) the white audience about "the true history of the race." The SAI began to publish its own periodical in Washington, DC, as of January 1913: *The Quarterly Journal of the Society of American Indians* (1913–15), later renamed *The American Indian Magazine* (1915–1920) and transferred to Cooperstown, New York, in 1917. The SAI journal covered a wide array of topics from editorial comments on current national political issues to personal communications about local reservation problems. In general, it promoted the basic precepts of the allotment era: improved education, concrete legal status, and citizenship for Indians. It was partly in response to the prevailing moderate stand of the SAI journal that Carlos Montezuma (Yavapai, c. 1867–1923), a member of the organization who advocated the immediate abolishment of the Bureau of Indian Affairs (BIA) and the reservation system, decided to disseminate his radical ideas in a private monthly newsletter, the *Wassaja* (1916–22).

American Indian journalism has experienced an unprecedented expansion as of the late 1960s, a reflection of the general upsurge in Indian literary production often referred to as the "Native American Renaissance." Today hundreds of tribal, nontribal, and intertribal newspapers are being published on a regular basis along with scholarly and literary periodicals. This boom was initiated in part by widely read newspapers like the tribal *Akwesasne Notes* (1968–92), published by the Mohawk Nation Council and revived in 1995 as a magazine; and the intertribal *Wassaja: a National Newspaper of Indian America* (later *Wassaja: a National Newsmagazine of Indian America*, 1973–82), brought out by the Indian Historian Press in San Francisco. These have been succeeded by very successful internationally circulating newspapers like the tribally owned *Navajo Times* (1959) and the intertribal weekly *Indian Country Today* (formerly *The Lakota Times*, 1981).

Political literature

American Indian writers also expressed their political views in countless memorials, petitions, tracts, pamphlets, and books. On 26 May 1826, Elias Boudinot delivered a speech at the First Presbyterian Church in Philadelphia that was printed that same year under the title *An Address to the Whites*. This widely read promotional tract highlights the exceptionally successful implementation of the federal civilization program among the Cherokees and concludes that the establishment of a Cherokee press and newspaper would greatly speed up their advancement. His call for the establishment of "a vehicle of Indian intelligence, altogether different from those which have heretofore been employed" helped to generate the funds that launched American Indian journalism in the Southeast and Indian Territory.

Boudinot's and the Treaty Party's subsequent campaign in favor of removal was censured by Principal Chief John Ross in a number of widely circulating letters, resolutions, and petitions to Congress that have been published collectively as *The Papers of Chief John Ross* (1985). Boudinot in turn attempted to vindicate his turnabout in a polemic tract titled *Letters and Other Papers Relating to Cherokee Affairs* (1837), arguing that since removal was inevitable the Treaty of New Echota represented the most intelligent compromise that could be reached with the federal government at the time. Not surprisingly, Governor Lumpkin of Georgia had several hundred copies reprinted under the title *Documents in Relation to the Validity of the Cherokee Treaty of 1835* and distributed to members of the Senate in 1838. The bulk of Boudinot's tract, however, is composed of vicious slander against Ross and the National Party. This "literary feud" was carried on by future generations of Cherokees in Indian Territory.

Boudinot's son Elias Cornelius, for instance, called for the division of the Cherokee Nation West into a southern and a northern sector in a tract titled *Comments on the Objections of Certain Cherokee Delegates to the Propositions of the Government to Separate the Hostile Parties of the Cherokee Nation* (1865). In *Remarks of Elias C. Boudinot* (1874), he demanded that Indian Territory be incorporated as a territory of the United States. Furthermore, E. C. Boudinot ardently, and at times unscrupulously, promoted the privatization of Cherokee lands, rights-of-way for railroads, the opening of Indian Territory to white settlers, and universal citizenship for Indians. His own brother, W. P. Boudinot, in turn applied his talents as editor of the *Advocate* and Cherokee administrator to maintain the sovereignty of the Cherokee Nation West. He thus shared the views propagated by some of his brother's staunchest opponents, such as Princeton graduate and fellow *Advocate* editor W. P. Ross, who was a nephew of John Ross and served as principal chief in 1873–75.

A similar literary dispute occurred among the Senecas in New York, who were also confronted with a fraudulent removal treaty in 1838. The ensuing ten-year controversy issued in a thorough reformation of the Seneca government as well as the genesis of Seneca literature in English. On 28 August 1838, Maris Bryant Pierce (1811–74), a Dartmouth scholar and active "Young Chief" of the Senecas, delivered an anti-removal speech at the Baptist Church in Buffalo on 28 August 1838, that was published under the title *Address on the Present Condition and Prospects of the Aboriginal Inhabitants of North America* that same year. Pierce maintained that the Senecas were as capable of adopting civilized ways as the Cherokees and that this could best be accomplished if they remained in New York. Three years later, Nathaniel Thayer Strong (1810–72), a US interpreter and "Young Chief" like Pierce, challenged this view in his *Appeal to the Christian Community on the Condition and Prospects of the New York Indians*. Echoing the reasoning of the Jackson administration, he argued that removal from the corrupting influences of whites was a benevolent policy. Foreshadowing the General Allotment Act of 1887, he suggested that private ownership of land in the West held the most promising future for his people. In contrast to the Cherokees, the Senecas managed to work out a compromise in 1842 whereby they retained their reservations at Cattaraugus and Allegany at the cost of Buffalo Creek and Tonawanda. However, with the able assistance of Ely Samuel Parker (Seneca, 1828–95), who served as commissioner of Indian affairs in 1869 until 1871, the Tonawanda Senecas also managed to save their reservation by 1857. Parker, who was Lewis H. Morgan's principal informant, wrote a number of essays, speeches, and historical pieces, some of which were published posthumously in the *Proceedings of the Buffalo Historical Society* in 1905. In a report addressed to Ulysses S. Grant in 1867, who was Secretary of War at the time, Parker also presented a four-point plan proposing to return the BIA to the War Department, abolish private trade with Indians, consolidate tribes in a number of districts under a territorial government, and create a permanent commission composed of respectable whites and educated Indians to monitor Indian affairs.

William Apess's (Pequot 1798–1839) earlier *Indian Nullification of the Unconstitutional Laws of Massachusetts Relative to the Marshpee Tribe* (1835) and *Eulogy on King Philip* (1836) are two of the most extraordinary examples of Indian political prose ever published. Both texts have recently been reproduced along with Apess's other writings under the title *On Our Own Ground* (1992). Apess, an ordained minister of the Methodist Protestant Church and an intellectual offshoot of the Second Great Awakening, was particularly influenced by radical abolitionism and African American liberation theology. *Indian Nullification* offers detailed documentation of his decisive involvement in a minor but uncommonly successful Indian insurrection of the removal era known as the "Woodland Revolt." The Mashpee, a heterogeneous Praying Indian community established in Cape Cod in 1665, managed to obtain the temporary status of a semi-autonomous district from the Massachusetts legislature in 1834. Apess's chronological account of this event, written in the spirit of American revolutionary rhetoric and the polemic style of Jeremiah Evarts's anti-removal "William Penn" essays, is a complex collage of primary and secondary texts that presents the controversy from several points of view (pro and contra) and places it within the relevant context of recent American history. He concludes that white treatment of Indians has been "one continued system of robbery."

Eulogy on King Philip is the published version of an emancipationist address Apess delivered in Boston on 8 January 1836. His rendition of King Philip's War actually serves as a rhetorical platform from which to denounce the Puritans' treatment of Indians in general. As far as Apess was concerned, American racism actually had its roots in the "sins" perpetrated by the select Pilgrim Fathers. Reviewing Indian policy up until his own day, he surmises that the long trail of broken treaties leading up to the infamous removal policy actually began at Plymouth Rock.

In 1850 George Copway or Kah-ge-ga-gah-bowh, an expelled Wesleyan Methodist minister turned author and public speaker, outlined his rather lofty plan for the creation of a Northwestern Indian Territory in a pamphlet addressed to the 31st Congress of the United States under the title *Organization of a New Indian Territory*. It was to be located in the "unsettled" lands between the territories of Nebraska and Minnesota, or smack in the hunting grounds of the unsuspecting Sioux. This scheme was hardly original – an almost identical plan had been formulated by Secretary of War John Bell as recently as 1841 – but Copway still managed to present his case convincingly enough to garner the pecuniary support of numerous members of the Eastern literary and political elite.

In protest against the representation of Indians as primitive savages in the ethnological exhibits at the World Columbian Exposition in Chicago in 1893, author and lecturer Simon Pokagon (Potawatomi, 1830–99) wrote a bitter resume of Indian–white relations titled *The Red Man's Rebuke* (later changed to *The Red Man's Greeting*), which he had printed up in a 16-page (24×50 mm) booklet composed of manifold native birch bark. "In behalf of my people, the American Indians," the preface proclaims, "I hereby declare to you, the pale-faced race that has usurped our lands and homes, that we have no spirit to celebrate with you the great Columbian Fair now being held in this Chicago city, the wonder of the world."[1] One of the more striking aspects of Pokagon's miniature manifesto is its denunciation of the wanton destruction of nature by the colonists, thus anticipating one of the central concerns in contemporary American Indian literature. In its highly critical review of Indian–white relations, *The Red Man's Rebuke* is somewhat reminiscent of Apess's work, only that Pokagon occasionally lapses into the hackneyed lamentations of "vanishing Indian" literature.

This moribund style of language was also adopted in part by Andrew J. Blackbird (c. 1810–1900), an Odawa historian who produced a very similar emotional indictment of white Indian policy titled *The Indian Problem, from an Indian's Standpoint* (1900), which closes with a pathetic "Lamentation of the Overflowing Heart of the Red Man of the Forest." On a more practical side, Blackbird suggests that Indian children should be transferred from denominational institutions to regular public schools, an educational policy that the federal government began to implement with increasing regularity at the close of the nineteenth century.

Among the most important Indian political monographs to appear during the Progressive Era are the *Report of the Executive Council on the Proceedings of the First Annual Conference of the Society of American Indians* (1912); Charles A. Eastman's *The Indian To-day* (1916); Carlos Montezuma's *Let My People Go* (1915); and Laura Cornelius Kellogg's *Our Democracy and the American Indian* (1920).

The SAI's *Report* contains the minutes of the first "epoch-making Indian convention" that took place on the campus of the Ohio State University in Columbus on 12–16 October 1911. It also reproduces a series of lectures by notable Indian professionals on the industrial, educational, legal, political, moral, and religious aspects of the "Indian Problem," followed by panel discussions on each topic. Particularly noteworthy are the talks given by Laura Cornelius Kellogg (Oneida, 1880–1947), an activist with modern corporate ideals who had studied sporadically at Stanford, Barnard College, Columbia, Cornell, and the University of Wisconsin and was one of the original founders of the SAI; Marie L. B. Baldwin (Ojibwe, b. c. 1864), a graduate of the Washington School of Law and suffragette; and Angel De Cora Dietz (Winnebago, 1871–1919), an artist who studied at the Smith

College Art Department and the Boston Museum of Fine Arts School. Much more so than their male colleagues, these Indian women stressed the need to maintain unique Indian cultural traits, especially in the field of art, rather than to imitate the ways of whites which, as Cornelius points out with reference to the phenomena of proletarianization and ghettoization in American society, were far from perfect.

In *The Indian To-day*, Charles A. Eastman (Santee Sioux, 1858–1939) takes a critical look at contemporary Indian–white relations in the United States. Eastman concedes that successful adaptation to the dominant society inevitably entails the abandonment of a former way of life, regardless of how satisfactory it may once have been. In his opinion, the solution to this dilemma lies in an enlightened reform policy aimed at the total "emancipation" of the Indian. As far as Eastman is concerned, Grant's Peace Policy, the Board of Indian Commissioners, Carlisle Indian Industrial School, the Lake Mohonk Conference of the Friends of the Indian, and the General Allotment Act all pointed in the right direction.

Let My People Go is Montezuma's most widely read plea for the immediate abolishment of the Indian Service. Originally an address delivered at the SAI conference at Lawrence, Kansas, on 30 September 1915, Montezuma had it published as a tract that served as a guideline for the radical faction of the organization and was subsequently read during the first session of the Sixty-Fourth Congress in 1916.

Kellogg's *Our Democracy and the American Indian* is a little-known work that diverges markedly from the usual productions of the Progressive Era. Instead of allotment, the author proposes the establishment of what she terms the "Lolomi Program of Self-Government," which involves the incorporation of the remaining Indian land base into independent industrial communities working on a cooperative basis.

Two noteworthy publications appeared in 1944: Ella Cara Deloria's (Yankton Nakota, 1889–1971) *Speaking of Indians* and Ruth Muskrat Bronson's (Cherokee, 1897–1982) *Indians Are People Too*. Although still markedly influenced by progressive ideas and their own Christian backgrounds, both authors condemn the deterministic politics of coercive assimilation and call for a more enlightened policy that would allow Indians to accommodate voluntarily at their own chosen pace and still retain some of their ancient ways. In part, their recommendations reflect the more assertive ideology of the National Congress of American Indians (1944), of which Bronson was an active member.

American Indian political literature attains its highest standard with the writings of lawyer–philosopher Vine Deloria, Jr. (Yankton - Standing Rock Sioux). His first book, *Custer Died For Your Sins* (1969), is as significant a work for the genesis of the "Native American Renaissance" as N. Scott Momaday's novel *House Made of Dawn* (1968). With mordant irony and humor, Deloria critiques Western institutions like the Church, the federal government, and anthropology departments with the end in view of dismantling sundry white misconceptions of Indian–white relations. Here and in most of his ensuing work, Deloria takes criticism of dominant society one step further to express the firm conviction that Indian ways of life and thought are actually superior in terms of a more humane and ecologically sound choice of existence. One of his main political arguments, as formulated in *We Talk, You Listen* (1970) and *Behind the Trail of Broken Treaties* (1974), is the need to recognize the legality and practicality of Indian sovereignty. In his more recent political works published in cooperation with other authors, such as *American Indians, American Justice* (1983), *The Nations Within* (1984), *The Aggression of Civilization* (1984), and *American Indian Policy in the Twentieth Century* (1985), Deloria takes a more formal scholarly approach to the analysis of the historical and legal complications behind the "Indian Problem."

Humorous literature

Although humor has been present in American Indian writings since the days of Samson Occom, this aspect has only recently received the attention it merits from literary critics. One probable reason why is that mirth obviously does not fit in with the still widely accepted stereotype of the stoic Indian. A very distinctive school of American Indian literary humor developed in association with the newspaper boom in Indian Territory during the second half of the nineteenth century. From the 1870s on, writers who were predominantly citizens of the Cherokee Nation produced a large number of Indian-English dialect letters to the editor with sardonic comments on a great variety of local events.

One of the most prominent and talented exponents of Indian Territory humor is the Muskogee poet and journalist Alexander Lawrence Posey (1873–1908). Between 1902 and 1908 he produced just over seventy "Fus Fixico Letters," brief humorous sketches in Creek-English dialect that were published collectively in 1993. Using a partly imaginary and partly historical set of conservative and seemingly naive Creek characters (Fus Fixico, Hotgun, Tookpafka Micco, Wolf Warrior, Kono Harjo) who regularly discuss contemporary issues as a literary mask, Posey was in the position to mock, criticize, or promote practically every facet of Indian Territory politics with editorial impunity. Most of his letters revolve around the activities of the conservative Snake faction of Creeks, separate statehood for Indian Territory, allotment of Creek lands, and local elections. Regionalism is a main characteristic of Indian Territory humor, which makes it as difficult for the modern-day audience to comprehend as Old Southwest humor. Only occasionally do Hotgun and Tookpafka Micco, the main speakers whose heated conversations are reported by Fus Fixico, also discuss national topics. For instance, in a letter that first appeared in the *Muskogee Daily Phoenix* (16 April 1905), Teddy Roosevelt's foreign policy is taken to task:

> And Hotgun he look wise, like the supreme court, and explain it, "Well so the Big Stick was the symbol of power, like a policeman's billy. In the jungles of Afriky it was called a war club; and in the islands a the sea, like Australia, it was called a boomer-rang; and among us fullblood Injins we call it a ball-stick; and if it was fall in the hands a the women folks, it was called a rollin-pin, or maybe so, a broom-handle. It was had lots a different names, like a breakfast food. Over in Europe a king was had precious stones put in it, to make it more ornamental than useful, and call it scepter. The brass-knucks was the latest improvement on it. In olden time Samson was had a Big Stick made out of a jaw-bone of an ass, and was made a great hit with it among the Philistines. Same way the Great White Father was want to show his influence all he had to do was flourish the Big Stick and everybody was get out from under it."[2]

As the example above shows, one of the most outstanding qualities of Posey's "Fus Fixico Letters" is their language. Of course, he made abundant use of conventional Old Southwest techniques such as comic similes, puns, metaphors, and irregular grammar, as well as frequent allusions to the Bible, classical history, and Euro-American literature in keeping with the tradition of the "literary comedians." Unlike the so-called "phunny phellows" and their numerous Indian Territory imitators, however, Posey never tortured the English language for a cheap laugh. On the contrary, it is obvious that he took great care to recapture the rhythm and style of the Creek-English dialect, so that the letters have a distinct lyrical tenor that becomes particularly evident when they are read out loud. In terms of both style and content, the comic dialogues in the Fus Fixico letters are so constructed that the reader laughs with the ostensibly naive Creek characters rather than at them.

National and world politics, rather than regionalism, is at the heart of the work of the most illustrious offshoot of Indian Territory humor, William Penn Adair Rogers (Cherokee, 1879–1935). This is undoubtedly why "Will" Rogers is seldom studied within the context of American Indian literature. Nevertheless, he did address Indian issues occasionally. In one of his regular weekly articles for the *Tulsa Daily World* titled "Story of a Misspent Boyhood" (29 September 1929), America's famous "cowboy philosopher" jokingly referred to himself as a part-Cherokee with "enough white in me to make my honesty questionable." Like most Cherokees, he had a marked dislike for Andrew Jackson. "Well, to tell you the truth, I am not so sweet on old Andy," Rogers admits in "Writes on Feeding Democrats Raw Oratory at

Jackson Dinner" (*Tulsa Daily World*, 5 February 1928). "He is the one that run us Cherokees out of Georgia and North Carolina." Then, in his characteristic guise of the wise innocent, Rogers reasons that Jackson "had unconsciously done us a favor" because contemporary Georgia, North Carolina, and Alabama could hardly keep up with oil-rich Oklahoma, where Indians were now being despoiled by the Standard Oil Company.[3] The Puritans fared no better in his estimation than in Apess's *Eulogy*. "They were very religious people that come over here from the old country," he opines in "Where Wallace Learned Economics" (*Tulsa Daily World*, 10 June 1934). "They were very human. They would shoot a couple of Indians on the way to every prayer meeting."[4] In yet another piece for the same daily titled "Red Men Got Big Laugh" (16 March 1930), in which he describes the dedication ceremonies for Coolidge Dam in Arizona, Rogers surmises that "we were out there on Indian land dedicating a Dam to get water for white people to come out and use and gradually take more Indian land away."[5] Other topical Indian issues he commented on in Oklahoma-based newspapers include Custer's avoidable debacle at the Little Big Horn ("Will Rogers Says We're Yokels If We Don't Boost Air Traffic," *Tulsa Daily World*, 17 April 1927); the groundless defamation of Indian religious ceremonies ("All About the Big Snake Dance," *Tulsa Daily World*, 9 September 1928); the discrimination against persons of Indian descent in the General Federation of Women's Clubs and the unjustified recall of Jim Thorpe's Olympic medals ("The Indians Are Coming," *Daily Oklahoman*, 23 June 1935). Although his Indian-related articles are few and far between, Rogers's overall philosophy – racial tolerance, anti-denominationalism, self-determination of nations – fits in seamlessly with the ideas propagated by his contemporaries. In addition, his obvious penchant for hyperbole, puns, misspellings, or irregular application of the past tense ties him linguistically to the humorous conventions of the Old Southwest and Indian Territory. Will Rogers's famous opening line – "All I know is what I read in the papers" – is thus a befitting salutation to the fruitful union between native wit and the blossoming of Indian Territory journalism.

The remarkable success of contemporary authors like Vine Deloria, Gerald Vizenor, Sherman Alexie, Thomas King, or William S. Penn, whose works are permeated with humor, has finally given this much-neglected aspect of Indian creativity the public exposure it deserves.

Historical literature

If one disqualifies Samson Occom's "An Account of the Montauk Indians, on Long Island" (written 1761, published among the *Massachusetts Historical*

Society Collections in 1809) on account of his tribal background, the earliest example of an "insider" tribal history is Hendrick Aupaumut's "History of the Muh-he-con-nuk Indians" (written 1790, published in Electa Jones, *Stockbridge, Past and Present*, 1854). In both cases, the authors are at pains to demonstrate to a non-Indian audience that the tribes they were describing already had the inherent tenets of a Christian democracy and were thus fully capable of further "advancement." Although deferential to occidental civilization, they still made a conscious effort to revise the one-sided interpretation of frontier history. This form of politically motivated historiography continued to dominate tribal histories well into the twentieth century.

The earliest full-length tribal history to be published in the United States is David Cusick's *Sketches of Ancient History of the Six Nations* (c. 1826–27). Even though Cusick (Tuscarora, c. 1780–c. 1840) belies his own intent by describing his work as a "history involved with fables" in the preface, he nevertheless focuses exclusively on the oral traditions about the origin, migration, warfare, and alliance of the pre-contact Iroquois. Cusick's booklet, which is not considered to be a faithful rendition of Iroquois oral traditions because of its obvious Christian influence, attracted the notice of Henry Rowe Schoolcraft and Francis Parkman, both of whom rejected it as an "absurdity." This pronounced skepticism toward narrated history as a legitimate source of information is still shared by inflexible adherents of Western historiography.

Tribal histories began to appear more regularly in the Great Lakes region as of the 1850s, when a number of Anishinaabeg converts north and south of the Canadian–American border turned to writing. These include George Copway's *The Traditional History and Characteristic Sketches of the Ojibway Nation* (1850), William Whipple Warren's (Ojibwe, 1825–53) *History of the Ojibways* (written 1851–54, published 1885); Peter Jones's (Ojibwe, 1802–56) *History of the Ojebway Indians* (1861); and Andrew J. Blackbird's *History of the Ottawa and Chippewa Indians of Michigan* (1887). With the exception of the thoroughly converted Jones, these native historians acknowledge their debt to narrated history and the elders who, as Warren recognizes, are the repositories of the traditions of the tribe. Whereas Warren focuses on the oral accounts of the long-drawn Ojibwe wars with the Iroquois and Sioux, his fellow Anishinaabeg historians present a more typical potpourri of autobiographical, historical, ethnographical, linguistic, mythological, and polemical information. All four also perform a precarious balancing act between a sincere show of deference toward mainstream notions of social advancement and an equally candid manifestation of pride in traditional ways, especially their native languages.

At least three other orally based tribal histories were produced during the last quarter of the nineteenth century: Peter Dooyentate Clarke's (Wyandot, nd) *Origin and Traditional History of the Wyandots* (1870), a string of warrior narratives ending up with Tecumseh's ill-fated confederacy; Elias Johnson's (Tuscarora, nd) *Legends, Traditions, and Laws of the Iroquois, or Six Nations* (1881), a revisionist account of the post-contact Iroquois that redresses some common misconceptions of Indian ways; and Joseph Nicolar's (Penobscot, 1827–94) *The Life and Traditions of the Red Man* (1893), a collection of stories about a Penobscot culture hero. In each case, the declared purpose for writing a "traditional" history was to salvage information for posterity.

As cultural pluralism gradually displaced social evolutionary thought after the turn of the twentieth century, Indian intellectuals discarded the sometimes patronizing and often deferential stand of their mission-trained predecessors in favor of a more balanced scholarly approach. Highly educated historians like Emmett Starr (Cherokee, 1870–1930), who was also a dedicated genealogist, and professional anthropologists such as Arthur C. Parker (Seneca, 1881–1955), Francis La Flesche (Omaha, 1857–1932), John Napoleon Brinton Hewitt (Tuscarora, 1859–1937), and William Jones (Sac-Fox, 1871–1909) produced a voluminous body of historical and ethnographic writings about their respective tribes. Particularly noteworthy among these are La Flesche's *The Omaha Tribe* (1911), a classic Omaha ethnography written in cooperation with Alice C. Fletcher; and Parker's *The Code of Handsome Lake, the Seneca Prophet* (1913), a translation and interpretation of the philosophy of the founder of the Longhouse Religion of the Iroquois. Two historical publications from the Progressive Era deserve mention as well: Emmett Starr's *History of the Cherokee Indians and their Legends and Folk Lore* (1921), a meticulously detailed and well-documented account that brings the tradition of the layman tribal history up to par with Western standards for historiography; and Charles Eastman's *Indian Heroes and Great Chieftains* (1918), a collection of fifteen biographical sketches of prominent nineteenth-century Indian leaders that clearly anticipates Alvin Josephy's popular *Patriot Chiefs* (1961) in its creation of a gallery of historical American Indian heroes. Both authors relied heavily on orally transmitted information.

The conventional tribal history has since been displaced by revisionist ethnohistory and literary history. Revisionist ethnohistory views the role of dominant society in Indian–white relations critically, but treats Indians as active participants in the historical process rather than victims of a predetermined contest. The late novelist, short-story-writer, and scholar, D'Arcy McNickle (Métis Cree / Salish, 1904–77), who actively promoted the restoration of tribal sovereignty, is one of the first native authors to interpret Indian history broadly as an ongoing process of adaptation and resilience. In *They Came Here First* (1949) McNickle condenses some 25,000 years of Indian history into a single volume addressed to the lay audience. This book continues to be a standard introductory text along with similarly structured books by Edward H. Spicer and William T. Hagan. *Indians & Other Americans* (1959, with Harold E. Fey) makes a critical appraisal of federal Indian policy, much like Vine Deloria's later publications on the development of Indian law. *The Indian Tribes of the United States* (1962), which was revised and reissued as *Native American Tribalism* (1973), is a historical tribute to Indian survival in the face of well-intended but hopelessly misguided federal Indian policy. In all of his works, McNickle refrained from casting Indian–white relations in terms of malefactors and victims. Instead, he situated the roots of the "Indian Problem" in the lack of adequate cross-cultural communication.

Literary history attempts to bond facts with creativity. One example is John Joseph Mathews's (Osage, 1894–1979) voluminous publication, *The Osages: Children of the Middle Waters* (1961), in which gaps in the documentary evidence are filled with information gathered by word of mouth and the author's own imagination. This and the overly ornate narrative style of Mathews's book, which is very reminiscent of his earlier and much more successful historical novel *Wah'kon-tah* (1932), induced some reviewers to recognize its merits as a work of "art" rather than "history." Mathews may have been slightly ahead of his time, as only a few years later N. Scott Momaday finally found a rather ingenious way to close the imposed breach between narrative and written history in his immensely popular work titled *The Way to Rainy Mountain* (1969). By keeping oral traditions, historical data, and personal impressions graphically and spatially separate in the layout of the book, Momaday manages to relate a multifocal and yet harmonious account of the three-hundred-year journey of the Kiowas from the headwaters of the Yellowstone River in present-day Montana to Rainy Mountain in what is now the state of Oklahoma.

Contemplative literature

Contemplative literature explores the meaning of tribal and national Indian identity, often in juxtaposition with contemporary European-American society. The first significant publication of this nature is Charles Eastman's *The Soul of the Indian* (1911). In this somewhat eccentric interpretation of Sioux spirituality, Eastman creates the earliest literary expression of an Indian environmental ethic, or "Mother Earth" philosophy. Even though the historical origins of this term have been subjected to debate, the perception of a kinship-based bond between humans and all of creation has since become the elemental doctrine of modern-day Indian thought and literature. The persuasion that respect for "Mother Earth" is a characteristic principle of an "indigenist" *weltanschauung* is reasserted in Luther Standing Bear's (Sichangu Sioux, c. 1868–1939) popular autobiography *Land of the Spotted Eagle* (1933) and has since been philosophically refined in Vine Deloria, Jr.'s *God Is Red* (1973) and *The Metaphysics of Modern Existence* (1979). Like Eastman and Standing Bear before him, Deloria also believes that traditional American Indian ethical codes provide the only logical key to human survival. Deloria's philosophical vindication of Indian ideals and simultaneous dispute with the basic tenets of Christianity and Western scientific thought have been carried on in his recent collections of essays titled *Red Earth, White Lies* (1995), *Spirit and Reason* (1999) and *Evolution, Creationism, and Other Modern Myths* (2002). Connectedness with the earth and its creatures is also one of the fundamental feminist concepts in Paula Gunn Allen's (Laguna / Métis) *The Sacred Hoop* (1986), who argues that traditional Indian culture and society essentially promoted a woman-centered worldview. Finally, the "Mother Earth" land ethic is evident as well in recent works dealing with concrete ecological problems threatening Indian communities such as Jace Weaver's (Cherokee) *Defending Mother Earth* (1996) and Green Party vice-presidential candidate Winona LaDuke's (Ojibwe), *All Our Relations* (1999).

The study of tribal Indian identity is best exemplified by Alfonso Ortiz's (San Juan Pueblo, 1939–97) acclaimed *The Tewa World* (1967). Employing complex structural theory, "insider-anthropologist" Ortiz provides a sophisticated analysis of the traditional Tewa worldview and how it is still reflected in current tribal institutions and customs.

During the final decade of the twentieth century, scholars claiming American Indian descent have set about developing a tribally oriented methodology for the analysis of Indian-related topics, which they consider to be excessively dominated by non-Indians. At the same time, they have opened a critical literary forum for discussions revolving around their own roles as authors and mediators. In her collection of essays titled *Talking Indian* (1992), novelist and short-story-writer Anna Lee Walters (Pawnee-Otoe) asserts that tribal people have an inherent right to interpret history according to their own aesthetics and values, even if it contradicts mainstream conventions. Robert Warrior (Osage) points out that a sustained discourse between American Indian writers is an essential step toward intellectual sovereignty in *Tribal Secrets* (1995), a comparative interpretation of the works of John Joseph Mathews and Vine Deloria, Jr. In his in-depth study of the American Indian novel, *Other Destinies* (1992), the late novelist and scholar Louis Owens (Cherokee / Choctaw, 1948–2002) focuses on the transcultural experiences of the predominantly mixed-blood authors and the fragmented sense of self reflected in the protagonists they created. In *That the People May Live* (1997), Cherokee literary critic Jace Weaver proposes that proactive commitment toward the Indian community, or what he terms communitism, should be the essential characteristic looked for in the reading of American Indian literature. In his examination of Creek writings in English titled *Red on Red* (1999), Craig Womack (Creek-Cherokee) advocates a kind of "Red Stick" literary criticism that emphasizes native resistance against colonialism and racism, does not hesitate to broach the subject of native sovereignty and nationalism, and roots American Indian literature in native landscapes and cultures. In *Fugitive Poses* (1998) and *Postindian Conversations* (1999, with A. Robert Lee) Ojibwe poet, novelist, and postmodernist critic Gerald Vizenor heralds in the "post-Indian" era when intellectual "victimry" is finally discarded along with all the other ideological burdens he associates with the colonialist misnomer "Indian." In *Feathering Custer* (2001), Nez Perce novelist and essayist William S. Penn detects severe deficiencies in the application of mainstream critical theory to native literatures and announces the advent of an alternative bilateral "Nuestra American" theory that finds its identity in the oral storytelling traditions of the Western hemisphere. Past and present appropriation and misrepresentation of American Indian cultures by European-Americans are also exposed in Elizabeth Cook-Lynn's (Dakota-Crow Creek Sioux) *Why I Can't Read Wallace Stegner and Other Essays* (1996) and *Anti-Indianism in Modern America* (2001), as well as in Philip J. Deloria's (Sioux) *Playing Indian* (1998).

American Indian non-fiction prose is significant for several reasons other than its obvious relevance as "written records": it is the earliest genre used by Indians; it has been and probably still is the most widely read form of Indian literature; it is both multi-genre (humor–journalism) and mixed genre (histories and council records that combine written and oral conventions); it has continually challenged stereotypical notions about Indians; and it has regularly confronted existential issues like federal policy, sovereignty, identity, spirituality, ecology, and nationalism.

Notes

1. Simon Pokagon, *The Red Man's Rebuke*, Hartford, MI: C. H. Engle, 1893.
2. Daniel F. Littlefield, Jr., and Carola A. Petty, eds., *The Fus Fixico Letters*, Lincoln: University of Nebraska Press, 1993, p. 203.
3. James M. Smallwood, ed., *Will Roger's Weekly Articles*, vol. III, Stillwater: Oklahoma State University Press, 1981, pp. 128, 129.

4. Steven K. Gragert, ed., *Will Roger's Weekly Articles*, vol. VI, Stillwater: Oklahoma State University Press, 1982, p. 126.
5. Ibid. vol. IV, p. 126.

Major secondary sources

Brooks, J., *American Lazarus: Religion and the Rise of African American and Native American Literatures*. New York: Oxford University Press, 2003.

Jaskoski, H., ed., *Early Native American Writing: New Critical Essays*. New York: Cambridge University Press, 1996.

Konkle, M., *Writing Indian Nations: Native Intellectuals and the Politics of Historiography, 1827–1863*. Chapel Hill: University of North Carolina Press, 2004.

Littlefield, Jr., D. F. and James W. Parins, *A Biobibliography of Native American Writers, 1772–1924*. Metuchen, NJ: Scarecrow Press, 1981.

American Indian and Alaska Native Newspapers and Periodicals, 1826–1924. Westport, CT: Greenwood Press, 1984.

A Biobibliography of Native American Writers, 1772–1924: A Supplement. Metuchen, NJ: Scarecrow Press, 1985.

Murphy, James E. and Sharon M. Murphy, *Let My People Know: American Indian Journalism, 1818–1978*. Norman: University of Oklahoma Press, 1981.

Murray, D., *Forked Tongues: Speech, Writing & Representation in North American Indian Texts*. Bloomington: Indiana University Press, 1991.

Peyer, B. C., *The Tutor'd Mind: Indian Missionary-Writers in Antebellum America*. Amherst: University of Massachusetts Press, 1997.

Ruoff, A. L. B., *American Indian Literatures: an Introduction, Bibliographic Review & Selected Bibliography*. New York: MLA, 1990.

Wiget, A., ed., *Dictionary of Native American Literature*. New York/London: Garland Publishing Co., Inc., 1994.

Wyss, H. E., *Writing Indians: Literacy, Christianity and Native Community in Early America*. Amherst: University of Massachusetts Press, 2000.

5

HERTHA D. SWEET WONG

Native American life writing

Autobiography understood as a literary genre only came into being in what is now the United States in the 1960s, beginning with publications by Georg Misch, Georges Gusdorf, William Spengemann, and Roy Pascal. Up until that time, autobiography, like biography, was simply considered history – another mode of recording experiences of the past. But while scholars such as James Olney were laying the foundation for the field of autobiography studies (outlining its parameters and characteristics), other scholars, particularly those focused on feminist and ethnic American self-narrations, countered with alternative definitions of the form and its subjects.

While the debates about how to define the emergent field of autobiography raged (and they continue to do so), in the 1970s deconstructionists proclaimed the death of "the subject" (the biographical person and/or the self) and, as a natural consequence, the demise of autobiography. But the lively debates about whose lives should be included in autobiography and in what forms could not be stopped by a theoretical pronouncement. Instead, acknowledging or ignoring the deconstruction of the subject, scholars began to articulate the many selves (women, people of color, working class and poor people) disallowed by the founding formulations of autobiography theorists who had focused primarily on the literary productions of elite Western men.

Autobiography – most often defined concisely and canonically as "the story of one's life written by oneself" – is widely understood to be a Western form arising during the Enlightenment. Associated with the term was a pronounced belief in the idea of the autonomous, unified, universal self, a concept that, beginning in the 1970s, was historicized by scholars interested in including the self-narrations of women and people of color who often did not share such a self-conception. Since then the essentialist formulation of an autonomous, unified, and universal self (revealed to be Western and male) has been reformulated as relational, multiple, and localized – historically, socially, and culturally constructed. It is within this historical academic framework that Native American self-narrations began to be discussed as "autobiography." Prior to this period, Native American self-narrations, if read at all, were considered part of cultural anthropology, usually in the form of ethnographic life histories. But considering Native American autobiography demanded a reconsideration of all three of its roots – self, life, and writing. Native American notions of self, while varied, tend to share an emphasis on interrelatedness (not only among people, but between humans and the natural world) and community, rather than individuality; indigenous ideas of what kind of life is worth narrating are inclusive of the partial, everyday experiences of ordinary people, rather than focused on the complete lives of important public people; and while Native people have and do write autobiographies, historically, they spoke, drew, and performed aspects of their life stories.

Two groups of scholars have claimed that there is no such thing as Native American autobiography: the first were those who were ethnocentric enough to assume that indigenous people were "primitive" and therefore had no sense of self and no writing with which to record; the second were cultural relativists who claim that autobiography is a Western form not practiced by Native people who shared their personal stories orally. For the ethnocentric scholars, Native autobiography was an impossibility because indigenous people were incapable of the concepts and means necessary to produce it; for the cultural relativists autobiography by a Native person was still a Western form that erased even a trace of Native subjectivity and culture. At the same time, a third set of scholars – Gretchen Bataille and Kathleen Mullen Sands, H. David Brumble III, Arnold Krupat, David Murray, and myself, among them – while recognizing autobiography as a Western form, researched indigenous modes of self-narration and examined the interaction of the two in historical and cultural contexts.

Native American autobiography can be organized into three basic historical periods: the *early period* (from pre-Columbian times to the nineteenth century), the nineteenth- early twentieth-century *transitional period* and the *contemporary period* (beginning in the twentieth century, but really burgeoning with what has been called the Native American Renaissance, the outpouring of Native publications associated with N. Scott Momaday's Pulitzer Prize as well as, perhaps, the Second Wounded Knee protest in 1973, held at the same site as the notorious massacre of 1890). The long (and difficult to document) early period includes oral, dramatic, and pictographic forms of self-narration; the transitional period includes numerous "as-told-to" life histories (which were solicited, translated, and edited by Euro-Americans), a few autobiographies written in English or syllabary by Native Americans and numerous pictographic art and ledger books; the contemporary period includes the continuation of collaboratively produced oral life histories as well as autobiographies written in English (and a few bilingual ones) by Native American writers who combine Native and European American forms and themes. This way of organizing the field acknowledges the historical transformations from orality to literacy as well as from pre-colonial times to reservation and urban life. The field could also be organized in many other ways: according to the variety of forms such as oral self-narrations, pictographic life stories, ethnographic life histories, written autobiographies; by tribe/nation or culture group such as Diné self-narration, Cheyenne life story or Chickasaw autobiography; or geographically – Southwest, Northeast, Upper Plains or reservation- or non-reservation-based life narratives. Krupat has noted two basic types of Native life writing: "autobiographies by Indians," those written by Native people, and "Indian autobiographies," those not self-written by Natives, but produced in collaboration with an amanuensis.[1]

The early period

Even before Europeans arrived in North America Native people were telling, producing, and enacting their personal narratives through stories, pictographs, and performances. While William Smith defines Native American autobiography as "verbal expressions, whether oral or written" and Lynne Woods O'Brien notes the existence of Native "oral, dramatic, and artistic expressions" of one's life, H. David Brumble III and myself develop the discussion of such forms. Brumble presents a history of Native American autobiography, comparing "preliterate" Native life narratives to the classical oral traditions of Greeks and Romans and plotting the development of Native American autobiography in general. He delineates "six fairly distinct kinds of preliterate autobiographical narratives": coup tales, informal autobiographical tales, self-examinations, self-vindications, educational narratives, and stories of quests for visions and power. As well as examining indigenous oral self-narrations, Wong discusses forms of literacy such as narrative wampum belts, quillwork, and pictographic life narratives.[2]

These forms of autobiographical story do not conform to European American notions about autobiography that emphasize autonomous individuality and writing. Instead, the self-narrations in this period emphasize a communal or relational self; they often narrate a series of anecdotal moments rather than a unified, chronological life story; and they may be spoken, performed, painted, or crafted, rather than written. But even these earliest forms have been mediated by non-Natives who were often responsible for translating, collecting, and preserving them.

One type of oral autobiographical narrative is "the coup tale" (derived from the French word "to touch," to "count coup" was to touch an enemy with a hand or a coup stick and escape unharmed) told by Plains Indian men. A man's status was determined, in part, by his martial achievements, which were ranked. Counting coup, rescuing a wounded comrade, and stealing an enemy's horses were considered commendable deeds. Returning from battle with fellow warrior-witnesses to attest to his actions, the man would narrate his accomplishments to his community. The basic form of the coup tale is to announce one's name, identify one's associates, locate oneself geographically and strategically, list one's achievements, and conclude with an ending formula. Telling coup stories was a way for the community to be informed about its warriors and for the narrator to articulate his personal experience and rank, perhaps even his right to be heard.

Plains Indian men not only told the stories of their personal exploits, they painted them as well. Pictographs (picture-writings) were often painted on hides, tipis, shields or, later, cloth. Before 1830 pictographic narratives were concise ways to record and communicate. According to John Ewers, key characteristics of this artistic mode included "little interest in anatomical details," "relative scale," or "perspective."[3] Basic conventions of the form include: horse and warrior in action; horse depicted with elongated neck, small head and legs outspread; warrior "shown in profile but shoulders broadside"; stylized detail of costume; no perspective; no landscape or background; outlined figures "filled in with bright, flat colors" and right-to-left flow of action.[4] Using such conventions and relying on synecdoche (a part standing for the whole – for example, a few horse hoof prints representing numerous horses), pictography portrayed visual personal narratives vividly and concisely. A few examples of surviving pictographic self-narrations will be discussed in the next section.

The transitional period

Pictographic self-narratives

In the 1830s, as a result of George Catlin's 1832 visit to the Upper Missouri and Karl Bodmer's 1833/34 visit to the Plains, during which they introduced realistic drawing, paper, pencils and watercolors, a few Native pictographers began to paint and draw on paper. By the 1870s painted buffalo hide robes had been replaced by trade blankets. Throughout this period pictographers' materials changed dramatically as paper and cloth replaced hides and commercial paints and pens replaced plant dyes. Native pictographers often sought out books upon which to record. One group of well-preserved pictographic narratives are those produced by the men imprisoned at Fort Marion in St. Augustine, Florida from 1875 to 1878. With art books and supplies provided by Euro-American patrons, the Fort Marion artists used new materials, addressed a new audience, and depicted cultural documents more than personal stories. Two examples of Fort Marion pictographic art depict the shift from early nineteenth-century hide-painting conventions to late nineteenth-century innovations. In "On the War Path" (figure 5.1), Making Medicine (Cheyenne) provides a good example of early artistic conventions: right-to-left flow-of-action, side view, elongated horses, absence of landscape, details of warriors' ornamentation to illustrate identity and rank (the title was added by a Euro-American patron). In contrast, in "Indian Between Two Cultures" (figure 5.2), Wohaw (Kiowa) addresses a new subject (a Native torn between two worlds) in an innovative style (symmetrical image, not read from left-to-right). Wohaw stands in the center, positioned between two worlds. On his right is the Native way of life depicted by the buffalo, the tipi, and the woods; on his left is the Euro-American way represented by the cow, the house, and the cultivated field. He offers a pipe to both, but his left foot is positioned on the farmland of the Euro-American world, suggesting his cultural conversion. The name-symbol has been replaced by his name written in the English alphabet.

Yet another transformation occurred later with the addition of English and/or syllabary (a Native language written phonetically using the English alphabet) to supplement the drawings. Zo-Tom's (Kiowa) pictographic art book depicts his temporary cultural conversation (figure 5.3 –"A Class of Indians in Fort Marion") in which his Kiowa clothes and long hair have been replaced by Euro-American suits and short hair and the Kiowa name-symbols have been replaced by English-language autographs.

Because the pictographic self-narrations produced at Fort Marion were purchased by curious Euro-Americans as examples of Indian art, they have been well preserved. There are fewer surviving pictographic life stories produced by Native men in freedom. One example (figure 5.4) is a page from a pictographic diary composed by one or more Cheyenne men. They have sketched on scraps of paper gathered from the refuse of the US Cavalry (envelopes, letters, grocery lists, and sick lists) and stitched them together to form a book. Here the autobiographers have depicted a courtship scene on an envelope addressed to "Commanding Officer, Company "G." 2nd Cavalry." In the top scene the lovers' meeting is illustrated. In the more fully developed narrative of the bottom scene, the lovers leave the tipi (the broken lines indicate their tracks) to meet near the river depicted by the wavy line and shrubbery along the bottom. Such forms were carried on well into the twentieth century.

Figure 5.1. "On the War Path" by Making Medicine, Cheyenne, August 1875. (Courtesy of the National Anthropological Archives, Smithsonian Institution.)

Collaborative life histories

In *An Annotated Bibliography of American Indian and Eskimo Autobiographies* (1981), Brumble lists almost 600 Native self-narrations. With more produced and discovered annually, the exact number is difficult

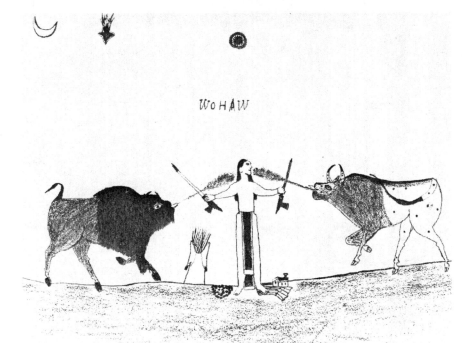

Figure 5.2. "Indian Between Two Cultures" by Wohaw, Kiowa, January 1877. (Courtesy of Missouri Historical Society.)

Figure 5.3. "A Class of Indians in Fort Marion with their Teacher, Mrs. Gibbs" by Zo-Tom, Kiowa, 1877. (Courtesy of the Southwest Museum, Los Angeles, California, Neg. No. 34, 649.)

Figure 5.4. "Courtship Scene Drawn on Envelope dated 1877" by unknown Cheyenne artist/s, post 1877. (Courtesy of the Southwest Museum, Los Angeles, California, Neg. No. 37, 103.)

to calculate, but the numbers are substantial. Because the majority of early life stories of Native people were solicited, collected, translated, and edited by Euro-American traders, missionaries, military officials, and travelers, later followed by ethnologists and anthropologists, a significant collection of Native American self-narrations are collaboratively authored. This has led scholars to conclude that one of the most dominant features of Native American autobiography of this period is characterized by "bicultural composite composition," a "collaboration of the narrator and recorder/editor."[5] Usually addressed to non-Native readers, these types of life narratives have key characteristics: collaborative authorship, blending of personal and cultural narratives, belief in the power of language, and a focus on action rather than reflection. Brumble makes a useful distinction between two types of editors: "Absent Editors" who pretend that the narrative is the Native informant's and "Self-Conscious Editors" who acknowledge their own shaping of the story, but try to preserve the Native's perspective and narrative style (1988, 82–83).

The Life of Black Hawk is the earliest example cited as a fully developed collaborative autobiography. In 1833 Black Hawk or Makataimeshekiakiak (Sauk) told his story through interpreter mixed-blood Antoine LeClaire. Newspaperman John B. Patterson then edited it. Primarily addressing Euro-Americans, the imprisoned Black Hawk defends his participation in the 1832 Black Hawk War. Not long after, a far different collaborative life story was produced. Traveling musician and former slave Okah Tubbee (self-identified as Choctaw, most likely to erase his slave history) told his story to his wife, Laah Ciel (Delaware and Mohawk), who wrote it down. It was edited by Reverend Lewis Leonidas Allen and published in 1848, followed by an expanded version that included Ciel's story. In the late nineteenth century with "the closing of the frontier" and the so-called "vanishing Indian," interest in Native peoples and cultures surged, resulting in the increased production and circulation of collaborative life histories.

Written autobiographical narratives

The earliest written (using alphabetic literacy) "autobiography" is still thought to be the 1768 execution sermon of Samson Occum (Mohegan), though it was not published until 1982. The next was William Apess's (Pequot) Son of the Forest (1829). This was followed by George Copway's (Ojibwe) Life, History, and Travels of Kah-ge-ga-gah-bowh (1847). Both Methodist ministers, Apess and Copway used narrative structures adapted from Christian conversion narratives and focused on spiritual confessions and testimonials. Copway, in particular, wrote in a form that would be repeated often by Native writers – an interweaving of myth, history, and contemporary incidents as well as an intertwining of personal experience with tribal history and culture.

Sarah Winnemucca Hopkins (Paiute) wrote one of the more detailed personal histories, outspokenly critical of the American misdealings with her people, and one of perhaps only two or three autobiographies written by a Native woman during the nineteenth century. In *Life Among the Piutes: their Wrongs and Claims* (1883), Winnemucca narrates the arrival of the whites, who came into Paiute country "like a roaring lion"[6] (5), for whom she served as interpreter and guide during the Bannock War. As a child her grandfather brought home a collection of gifts he had acquired from his travels among white people: "a more wonderful thing than all the others ... was a paper, which he said could talk to him" (18). Not surprisingly, Winnemucca grows up to use the talking paper (writing) to communicate her people's experiences and grievances to Euro-American readers. Using recreated dialogue, speeches, direct addresses to the Reader, and abundant description, she creates scenes of dramatic intensity as well as of domestic detail. Later, she went on national tours to lecture about the conditions and concerns of Native people.

The highly educated writer and political activist Gertrude Simmons Bonnin (Yankton-Dakota), whose pen name was Zitkala-Ša, is best remembered for her collections of Lakota legends, her lifelong political activism, and her then controversial essay "Why I am a Pagan" (1900) – a dramatically defiant statement countering the Christian conversion narratives Euro-American readers expected from Natives. In addition, she wrote autobiographical essays about growing up on the Yankton Reservation: idyllic scenes of play, work, family gatherings, and storytelling occur amidst the loss of land, the arrival of missionaries, the removal of children from their families, and the ongoing suffering of her people at the hands of whites. In "Impressions of an Indian Childhood," Bonnin describes how her father, sibling, and uncle died from illnesses (directly related to contact with Euro-Americans), how her mother was in perpetual mourning and warned her to distrust the "paleface," how as an eight-year-old a missionary told her of orchards of red apples in the East that would be available to her should she decide to go to boarding school there. Alluding to the Biblical temptation of Eve in the Garden of Eden, Bonnin suggests that she was tempted by the missionary; and her own eagerness to go to school to become "civilized" was not an ascent, but a fall. In "An Indian Teacher Among Indians," Bonnin reverses the usual story of a Euro-American schoolteacher heading West to teach Native children and tells of how she (a young Native teacher) travels East to teach other Natives. When she returns to visit her mother, she sees her home through the distorted lens of a missionary school education. And when she returns East, she compares herself to an uprooted tree, ripped from its native soil, but not yet rooted in the new white world. Hers is a critical, articulate, and literary voice for Native rights.

Some autobiographical writings, such as those by G. W. Grayson (Creek) who documented Creek experiences during the Civil War, were never published until the twentieth century. Grayson's autobiography was edited by historian W. David Baird and published in 1988.

The contemporary period

A key focus in twentieth-century Native American autobiography, as in fiction, has been Native identity. Is a Native American defined by blood quantum, cultural involvement, community recognition, self-identification, or residence? What does it mean to have survived a treacherous history that suppressed, destroyed, reformulated indigenous cultures and languages? Throughout this period such questions are addressed in Native American life stories that continue to be spoken, written, and performed. Collaborative life histories continue, although re-envisioned in the late twentieth century by the "crisis of representation" that particularly challenged cultural anthropology and its ethnographic fieldwork practices that had previously assumed the possibility of pure linguistic and cultural translation by an "objective" practitioner, but now were accused of intellectually colonizing Native speakers. The examples that follow illustrate a range of editorial practices, from the "Absent Editor" to the "Self-Conscious Editor."

Collaborative life stories

Collaborative life stories have been produced by both academically trained scholars (primarily, anthropologists, historians, and linguists) and a host of others interested in Native cultures (often writers, journalists, clergy). While there are many important collaborative life histories the most famous and popular is still *Black Elk Speaks*. Nicholas Black Elk (Lakota) told his story to John G. Neihardt. The Black Elk–Neihardt collaboration is more complex than most such autobiographical processes. Sitting on the South Dakota plains with a gathering of family and friends, Black Elk spoke in Lakota, which his son, Benjamin, translated into English. Neihardt would interrupt the process to ask questions. Neihardt's rewording of Ben's English translations of Black Elk's Lakota words was transcribed by Neihardt's daughter, Enid, who later typed the transcript. As Raymond DeMallie points out, Enid's stenographic notes were not "a verbatim record of Black Elk's words, but a rephrasing in comprehensible English."[7] From these translations, Neihardt organized and edited what would become *Black Elk Speaks*, accompanied by pictographic drawings by Standing Bear (Lakota). Like the "Absent Editor," Neihardt made certain choices that he did not share with his readers. Among other things, he emphasized Black Elk's sense of communal identity, spoken voice, and Lakota spirituality and de-emphasized Black Elk's accounts of hunting and warfare and, perhaps more importantly, Black Elk's Catholicism. Clearly, Neihardt's aim was to present a Lakota poetic and spiritual autobiography, rather than a culturally hybrid, secular self-narration. Scholars have assessed the collaborative relationship variously, from claiming that Black Elk–Neihardt's was an exceptionally good one to denouncing it as "an act of ventriloquism"[8] – in which the white editor speaks, not the Native informant.

No Turning Back: a Hopi Indian Woman's Struggle to Live in Two Worlds (1964) by Polingaysi Qoyawayma or Elizabeth Q. White (Hopi) as told to Vada F. Carlson (a newspaper journalist) is a boarding-school story. Qoyawayma tells of her eager acculturation to Euro-American culture (and her consequent denunciation by the Hopi). By the end, however, she advises Hopi young people to evaluate and retain the best of both cultures.

Lame Deer: Seeker of Visions (1972) by John (Fire) Lame Deer (Lakota) and Richard Erdoes is a good example of a popular collaborative autobiography with an "Absent Editor" who offers no commentary about the collaborative editorial process. Lame Deer conveys aspects of Lakota cultural and spiritual practices and comes across as a humorously irreverent, politically outspoken, Tricksterish Holy man. Still an "Absent Editor" eighteen years later, Erdoes published *Lakota Woman* (1990), the life story of Mary Brave Bird (Lakota) who married activist and spiritual leader Leonard Crow Dog and became active in the American Indian Movement in the 1970s.

Other popular collaborative life histories include those told by Plenty-Coups (Crow) and Pretty-Shield (Crow) to Frank Linderman in 1928 and 1930, Wooden Leg (Cheyenne) with Thomas B. Marquis, Fools Crow (Teton Sioux) to Thomas E. Mails, Two Leggings (Crow) to William Wildschut (edited by Peter Nabokov), Albert Yava (Hopi and Tewa) with Harold Courlander, and Thomas Yellowtail (Crow) to Michael Oren Fitzgerald.

With the rise of anthropology in the early twentieth century came an increase in the production of ethnographic life histories within academic circles. Newly Boas-trained anthropologists sought out the least documented tribes. Ruth Underhill, wanting a woman's story, produced *Papago Woman* (1936), the story of Maria Chona (Tohono O'odham). Translated, interpreted, and edited by Underhill, Chona's autobiography tells of her marriages and her healing powers. As the title suggests, Underhill was interested in recording the life of a "representative" woman from this relatively unknown desert people. She also brought along her own feminist agenda. Among the many academic collaborative life histories to note are those by Crows Heart (Mandan) and Alfred E. Bowers, Sam Blowsnake (Winnebago) and Paul Radin, Left-Handed (Diné) and Walter Dyk, Mountain Wolf Woman (Winnebago) and Nancy O. Lurie, Don Talayesva (Hopi) and Leo W. Simmons, John Stands in Timber (Cheyenne) and Margo Liberty, Moses Cruikshank (Athabaskan from Alaska) and William Schneider, and Mabel McKay (Pomo) and Greg Sarris.

One of the best examples of an ethically edited, scholarly, informed, community-based collaborative life story is *Life Lived Like a Story: Life Stories of Three Yukon Native Elders* (1990) by Julie Cruikshank in collaboration with Angela Sidney (Tagish/Tlingit), Kitty Smith (S. Tutchone/Tlingit) and Annie Ned (S. Tutchone/Tlingit). Cruikshank includes a comprehensive description of her fieldwork, detailing her editorial practices and emphasizing the reciprocity of the collaborations. It is especially important that the three women initiated the project and decided its uses – primarily to educate the next generation of children in their community. Sidney, Smith, and Ned talk about their lives using oral traditions grounded in the local idiom and a shared body of knowledge. The stories of the women and the history of the Yukon are mapped onto the land so that what seems like travelogue is actually clan history. Their life stories focus on the land, myth, history, travel, kinship, and continuity between generations.

More recently, in a dramatic departure from editors claiming a privileged relationship with their informants, Kathleen Sands makes "no claim to rapport" with Theodore Rios (Tohono O'odham).[9] In fact, she explains that as much as she wishes to have attained a "dialogic mode" of talking across cultures (2000, 79), she has not. Instead, she documents not Rios's life story, but the story of her process of coming to consciousness about the political, literary, and cultural aspects of cross-cultural mediation.

Written autobiographies

While Native speakers and Euro-American editors collaboratively produced Native life stories, Natives also wrote their own life narratives, what Krupat refers to as "autobiographies by Indians." Born in 1853 into an "aristocratic" family, Lucy Thompson (Yurok) wrote *To the American Indian: Reminiscences of a Yurok Woman*, which was published originally in 1916, but soon disappeared until its resurrection and republication in 1991. The "first California Indian woman to be published,"[10] she writes to present a Native perspective, particularly to counter the "fairy tales" that "lower-class" Yuroks have told to anthropologists. Her writing retains the shape of oral storytelling mingled with Biblical and literary allusions as she describes Yurok cultural practices and the history of Native/white interactions.

One of the most prolific Native writers at the turn of the twentieth century was Charles Alexander Eastman (Santee Sioux) who, with the help of his wife Elaine Goodale Eastman, wrote companion autobiographies: *Indian Boyhood* (1902) and *From the Deep Woods to Civilization* (1916). Adapting the conversion narrative, Eastman tells the story of how he moves from a traditional Sioux training as a child to the Euro-American education from which he earned an MD. Internalizing the roles of Native informant and editor, Eastman critiques "civilization" and Christianity as manifested in American society, yet seeks membership in both. Eight years before Native people were granted US citizenship, Eastman insists that he can be both "Indian" and "American." This theme of trying to reconcile two worlds, Native American and Euro-American, becomes central to twentieth-century Native American fiction. Others who wrote their autobiographies include Luther Standing Bear (Sioux) and John Joseph Mathews (Osage), both adapting Western narrative conventions to tell their stories. Native Americans also occasionally wrote in syllabary, as Sam Blowsnake (Winnebago) did in 1920.

The publication history of Mourning Dove's autobiography echoes Grayson's mentioned earlier. When she died in 1936, Mourning Dove, whose real name was Christine Quintasket (Salishan), left parts of an unfinished autobiographical manuscript. These were not published until 1990 when Jay Miller shaped them into an autobiography entitled *Mourning Dove: a Salishan Autobiography*. Organized into three sections, Mourning Dove's autoethnography is both a tribal and personal history. In particular, she focuses on "female activities, seasonal activities, and incidents from recent history."[11] In one especially vivid story, she recounts her paternal grandmother, "a brave, mean woman,"[12] who battled with a grizzly bear for a patch of berries – and won, a suitable precursor to the young Mourning Dove who would refuse dolls, preferring instead bows and arrows. She recounts also her spiritual education, mission-school experience, introduction to womanhood, experiments with love charms, as well as numerous anecdotes about fishing, hunting, dancing, seancing, and participating in sweat lodge ceremonies. She concludes with a concise Okanogan history, from the pre-contact legend of Nicola and the migration of the people to interactions with the Pacific Fur Company and Catholic priests to farming and "the invasions of miners and settlers" (1990, 177).

With the deconstruction of the subject and the complexities of contemporary Native identities in the late twentieth century, there are many writers who have turned to autobiographical writing as one mode of grappling with vexed questions about the instability of identity and perhaps as a way to articulate or fashion a coherent Native subjectivity. Foremost among these is N. Scott Momaday (Kiowa) who has written *The Way to Rainy Mountain* (1969) and *The Names: a Memoir* (1976). Storytelling unites Momaday's concerns for the land, the Kiowa, and the imagination and memory necessary to articulate them. The first of his two autobiographies, *The Way to Rainy Mountain*, is the more experimental. In it he constructs and narrates a Kiowa personal identity that is imagined in relation to Kiowa myth and history. Momaday's writing here is also a reconstruction of the spoken word. The four-part structure reflects three narrative voices – the mythical, the historical, and the personal, each distinguished by different fonts and all permeated by a visual narrative (eleven illustrations drawn by Al Momaday) and linked by an elaborate process of association. The twenty-four three-part narrative units are divided into three larger chapters: "The Setting Out," "The Going On," and "The Closing In," reflecting the historical Kiowa migration as well as Momaday's journey in their footsteps.

Seven years after *The Way to Rainy Mountain*, Momaday published *The Names*, a more conventional autobiography based on Western forms. He continues to address how language, land, and history shape individuality. But whereas the first autobiography focuses on Kiowa history and culture, the second concentrates more strictly on Momaday himself.

Leslie Marmon Silko's (Laguna) primary autobiographical work is *Storyteller* (1981), a collection of previously published poems, short stories, myths, letters, essays, anecdotes, and photographs. In these varied forms, Silko tells her mythical, community, and personal narratives, continuing the Laguna Pueblo practice of articulating personal identity from communal stories. Especially concerned with recreating the voice on the page, Silko offers multiple retellings of the same story, including as well the stories that arise from photographic images. In 1993 she published *Sacred Water*, a collection of autobiographical musings and vignettes, juxtaposed with photographs of the land around her home in Arizona. Her autobiographical writings continue in some of the essays in *Yellow Woman and a Beauty of the Spirit: Essays on Native American Life Today* (1996) in which she discusses Laguna Pueblo concepts of place, how stories are embedded in the land, political opinions and literary influences.

In *Interior Landscapes* (1990) Gerald Vizenor (White Earth Anishinaabeg), alternating between first- and third-person narration, strikes Trickster poses and underscores the inevitably fictive/imaginative nature of any autobiographical representation. Claiming, "Autobiographies are imaginative histories,"[13] he narrates his miraculous survival of violence, poverty, and racism. Interwoven with tales of his father's murder in the streets of Minneapolis when Vizenor was still a toddler and a series of abusive foster parents and stepfathers are darkly comic scenes about other abuses of power: the memorable Boy Scout Camp experience at White Earth reservation on "land ... stolen from tribal people by the federal government" (1990, 62) and the infamous Army initiation that sends him on a zany quest to locate his "masturbation papers" (82). He documents also his career as social worker, activist, and writer.

Diane Glancy's (Cherokee) *Claiming Breath* (1992) contains autobiographical poems about mixed-blood identity and the power of language to unify the cultural divide. Throughout her anecdotes and reflections on a failed marriage and a difficult relationship with her mother, she weaves advice about writing and pronouncements about poetry. Experimenting with language in English peppered with Gaelic and Cherokee, she explores "that empty space, that place between-2-places"[14] (4) in order to construct a solid ground upon which to stand as a mixed-blood Cherokee, Christian woman.

The following year Janet Campbell Hale (Coeur d'Alene) published *Bloodlines: Odyssey of a Native Daughter* – a collection of autobiographical essays in which she moves "back along [her] bloodlines to imagine the people [she] came from in the context of their own lives and times."[15] She imagines her parents and other relatives and speculates about how "dysfunction begets dysfunction" (xxxii), about the legacy of her alcoholic Coeur d'Alene father and verbally abusive mixed-blood mother and about the abiding strain of poverty. Like many Native writers, Hale attempts to go home (in this case, back to the Coeur d'Alene Reservation in northern Idaho) only to discover that she will always be estranged from her land, her people, and her past.

In 1994 Simon Ortiz (Acoma) published *After and Before the Lightning*, a collection of personal essays and poems about his residence on the Lakota Rosebud Reservation one South Dakota winter (November 1985 to March 1986) – reflections on history, politics, and cold weather.

Using a similar seasonal structure (Winter, Spring, Summer, Fall), Louise Erdrich's (Ojibwe) *The Blue Jay's Dance: a Birth Year* (1995) is a gathering of reflections about one year of a child's life, from being carried in her mother's womb to birth to weaning, walking, and talking. Rather than focus on Native identity, Erdrich muses about herself as a woman writer. "This book," she begins, "is a set of thoughts from one self to the other – writer to parent, artist to mother."[16] Such an internal split is reflected in the thematic set of binary oppositions throughout the work: birth/death, individual/communal, body/spirit, wild/domesticated, among them. With an acute awareness of loss, she struggles against depression as she interweaves history, recipes, and observations about the natural world. The autobiography is permeated with images of home – mother's body, houses, nests, earth, all womb-like places of both containment and emergence, highlighting the central paradox of the work.

At the turn of the twentieth into the twenty-first century, Linda Hogan (Chickasaw) and Anita Endrezze (Yaqui-Romanian/German/Italian/Slovenian) suggest both the continuities of and departures from past Native American life writing. Like Silko's *Storyteller*, Endrezze's *Throwing Fire at the Sun, Water at the Moon* (2000) is a multiform collection. In the service of self-narration, she retells not only family stories, but also Yaqui history. Throughout the two sections – "Mexico" and "Family" – she combines short fiction, poetry, historical retellings, first-person narratives, letters, diaries, journal-like musings, retold myths, and paintings.

Linda Hogan (Chickasaw) continues the interweaving of myth, history, and personal experience in *The Woman Who Watches Over the World: a Native Memoir* (2001). Linking the body and the earth, as she did in *Dwellings: a Spiritual History of the Living World* (1995), Hogan devotes her memoir to healing "the wounds of history (15)".[17] Throughout the autobiography, history is an illness that recurs in the blood of Native (and, to a certain extent, all) people so that what the earth needs is a good cure. Hogan begins with an anecdote about a trip to Mexico where she purchases a clay figure of "The Bruja Who Watches Over the Earth." But when the clay Woman arrived in the mail a few weeks later, "she wasn't whole ... The woman who watches over the world was broken ... as broken as the land, as hurt as the flesh people" (18). For Hogan, self-writing is about exposing personal and historical abuses and healing from both.

This overview has not considered the many autobiographical poems by Native poets such as Luci Tapahonso (Diné) who writes in English and Navajo, Joy Harjo (Muscogee/Cherokee), Wendy Rose (Hopi/Miwok), Janice Gould (Maidu), Ofelia Zepeda (Tohono O'odham), Ray A. Young Bear (Mesquakie), and many others. It has not examined the few bilingual autobiographical writings, a trend that is on the rise as efforts to recuperate or save indigenous languages continue, by writers like Luci Tapahonso, Ofelia Zepeda, and Peter Kalifornsky (Kenai Dena'ina). It has not addressed the autobiographical dimensions found in films such as Sherman Alexie's (Spokane/Coeur d'Alene) *Smoke Signals* and Valerie Redhorse's *Naturally Native*. Neither has it considered the autobiographical essays by writers like Paula Gunn Allen (Laguna/Métis) nor the popular autobiographies by public figures such as former Cherokee tribal chairperson Wilma Mankiller

(Cherokee). There are numerous and varied autobiographical voices and forms being produced today, each articulating the diversity and creativity of Native America.

Prior to the arrival of European colonists Native North America was multicultural and multilingual (well over 250 culture and language groups in what is now the United States and Canada). It still is. To make any generalizations about Native American life writing, then, is reductive at best. Even so there are key changes in practices of self-narration that reflect historical transitions. Native American self-narration began with storytelling – oral accounts of personal experience shared with family and community. Some people portrayed their life achievements and dreams in pictography (picture writing) or in symbols fashioned into animal hide shields or into quillwork or, later, beadwork as well as various other artistic forms. By the nineteenth century, bicultural, collaborative life histories (life stories solicited, translated, and edited by Euro-American amanuenses), both popular and academic, began to be published. Just as ethnographic life histories continue to be produced, the early forms of self-narration continue, in modified forms. Life writing (in English) by Natives began as early as 1768, but only in the late twentieth century did it become common. Most contemporary Native autobiographers interweave their personal stories with cultural myths and histories, emphasizing a specific subjectivity and the continuity of oral traditions. The movement from life storytellers to life historians to life writers (although these three modes often occur simultaneously) reflects the transformation from orality to alphabetic literacy, from pre-colonized times to the (post)colonial present. The attempt to translate Native verbal art onto the page insists on its survival and continuance through the memory and imagination of contemporary writers.

Since time immemorial, as the elders say, Native Americans have shared stories about their lives and dreams, articulating achievements and strivings. But those who write autobiographically often do so as a form of testimony, bearing witness not only to a history of genocide, but to survival and continuance and the possibility of healing from the "wounds of history."

Notes

1. Arnold Krupat, *Native American Autobiography: an Anthology*, Madison: University of Wisconsin Press, 1994, pp. 3–4.
2. William F. Smith, Jr., "American Indian Autobiographies," *American Indian Quarterly* 2.3 (1975) p. 237; Lynne Woods O'Brien, *Plains Indian Autobiographies*, Boise, Idaho: Boise State College, 1973 p. 5; H. David Brumble, III, *American Indian Autobiography*, Berkeley: University of California Press, 1988, p. 11; Hertha D. Sweet Wong, *Sending My Heart Back*

Across the Years: Tradition and Innovation in Native American Autobiography, New York: Oxford University Press, 1992.

3. John C. Ewers, Introduction, *Howling Wolf: a Cheyenne Warrior's Graphic Interpretation of His People*, ed. Karen Peterson, Palo Alto, CA: American West, 1968, pp. 7–8.

4. Karen Daniels Petersen, *Plains Indian Art from Fort Marion*, Norman, OK: University of Oklahoma Press, 1973, p. 57.

5. Arnold Krupat, *For Those Who Come After: a Study of Native American Autobiography*, Berkeley: University of California Press, 1985, p. xi; Kathleen Sands, *Studies in American Indian Literature*, ed. Paula Gunn Allen, New York: Modern Language Association, 1982, p. 5.

6. Sarah Winnemucca Hopkins, *Life Among the Piutes: their Wrongs and Claims*, ed., Mrs. Horace Mann 1883, Bishop, CA: Sierra Media, Inc., 1969, p. 5.

7. Raymond J. DeMallie, Introduction, *The Sixth Grandfather: Black Elk's Teachings Given to John G. Neihardt*, ed. Raymond J. DeMallie, Lincoln: University of Nebraska Press, 1984, p. 32.

8. Thomas Couser, "*Black Elk Speaks* with Forked Tongue," *Studies in Autobiography*, ed. James Olney, New York: Oxford University Press, 1988, p. 84.

9. Theodore Rios and Kathleen Mullen Sands, *Telling a Good One: the Process of a Native American Collaborative Biography*, Lincoln: University of Nebraska Press, 2000, p. 36.

10. Julian Lang, Introduction, *To the American Indian: Reminiscences of a Yurok Woman*, Berkeley, CA: Heyday Books, 1991, p. xvii.

11. Jay Miller, Introduction, *Mourning Dove: a Salishan Autobiography*, ed. Jay Miller, Lincoln: University of Nebraska Press, 1990, p. xxxiii.

12. Mourning Dove, *Mourning Dove: a Salishan Autobiography*, ed. Jay Miller, Lincoln: University of Nebraska Press, 1990, p. 23.

13. Gerald Vizenor, *Interior Landscapes: Autobiographical Myths and Metaphors*, Minneapolis: University of Minnesota Press, 1990, p. 262.

14. Diane Glancy, *Claiming Breath*, Lincoln: University of Nebraska Press, 1990, p. 4.

15. Janet Campbell Hale, *Bloodlines: Odyssey of a Native Daughter*, New York: Random House, 1993, p. xxii.

16. Louise Erdrich, *The Blue Jay's Dance: a Birth Year*, New York: Harper Collins, 1995, p. 4.

17. Linda Hogan, *The Woman Who Watches Over the World: a Native Memoir*, New York: Norton, 2001, p. 15.

Major secondary sources

Bataille, Gretchen M. and Kathleen Mullen Sands, *American Indian Women: Telling their Lives*. Lincoln: University of Nebraska Press, 1984.

Brumble, H. David, III, *An Annotated Bibliography of American Indian and Eskimo Autobiographies*. Lincoln: University of Nebraska Press, 1981.

American Indian Autobiography. Berkeley: University of California Press, 1988.

Katz, Jane, ed., *Messengers of the Wind: Native American Women Tell their Life Stories*. New York: Ballantine Books, 1995.

Krupat, Arnold, *For Those Who Come After: a Study of Native American Autobiography*. Berkeley: University of California Press, 1985.

The Voice in the Margin: Native American Literature and the Canon. Berkeley: University of California Press, 1989.

Native American Autobiography: an Anthology. Madison: University of Wisconsin Press, 1994.

Krupat, Arnold and Brian Swann, eds., *Here First: Autobiographical Essays of Native American Writers*. New York: Modern Library Association, 2000.

Mallery, Garrick, "Picture-Writing of the American Indians," in J. Powell, ed., director, *Tenth Annual Report of the Bureau of Ethnology to the Secretary of the Smithsonian Institution, 1888–1889*, 2 vols. 1892, 1893. New York: Dover, 1972.

O'Brien, Lynne Woods, *Plains Indian Autobiographies*. Western Writers Series No. 10. Boise, ID: Boise State College Press, 1973.

Owens, Louis, *Mixedblood Messages: Literature, Film, Family, Place*. Norman: University of Oklahoma Press, 1998.

Ruoff, A. LaVonne Brown, *American Indian Literatures: an Introduction, Bibliographic Review, and Selected Bibliography*. New York: Modern Language Association, 1990.

Sands, Kathleen, "American Indian Autobiography," in Paula Gunn Allen, ed., *Studies in American Indian Literature: Critical Essays and Course Designs*. New York: Modern Language Association, 1983, pp. 55–65.

Sioui, Georges E., *For an Amerindian Autohistory: an Essay on the Foundations of a Social Ethic*, Trans. Sheila Fischman. Montreal and Kingston: McGill-Queen's University Press, 1992.

Swann, Brian and Arnold Krupat, eds., '*I Tell You Now*': *Autobiographical Essays by Native American Writers*. Lincoln: University of Nebraska Press, 1987.

Vizenor, Gerald and A. Robert Lee, *Postindian Conversations*. Lincoln: University of Nebraska Press, 1999.

Wong, Hertha D. [Sweet], *Sending my Heart Back across the Year: Tradition and Innovation in Native American Autobiography*. New York: Oxford University Press, 1992.

Wong, Hertha D. Sweet, "First-Person Plural: Subjectivity and Community in Native American Women's Autobiography," in Sidonie Smith and Julia Watson, eds., *Women, Autobiography, Theory: a Reader*. Madison: University of Wisconsin Press, 1998, pp. 168–178.

6

NORMA C. WILSON

America's indigenous poetry

Casting light on ancient philosophies, demonstrating their survivance (to use Gerald Vizenor's term), American Indian poets had come into their own by the late twentieth century. Like Native singers and storytellers, indigenous poets writing in English or tribal languages transmit ancient mythologies and migratory and settlement histories spanning thousands of years.

Rooted in oral traditions, including tribal stories and songs, Native poetry has also been nurtured by a century and a half of American Indian poetry written in English, by American and English poetics, and by international literary traditions and forms. Yet, despite five centuries of colonial efforts to reshape or silence indigenous voices, Native poets continue to speak from a tribal perspective. As Craig Womack states in *Red on Red: Native American Literary Separatism* (1999), "tribal literatures are not some branch waiting to be grafted onto the main trunk. Tribal literatures are the *tree*, the oldest literatures in the Americas, the most American of American literatures."[1]

John Rollin Ridge, Jane Johnston Schoolcraft, E. Pauline Johnson, Alexander Posey, and Zitkala-Ša are predecessors, but they have had less influence on Native poetics than have indigenous stories and songs. Taught in the Euro-American tradition, these five adopted formal English verse, often alluding to classical Greek and Roman mythology. Nevertheless, while their style is European, they all advocated respect for American Indians in poems that reflect their cultures' lives before and after colonization.

Jane Johnston Schoolcraft, or Bame-wa-wa-ge-zhik-a-quay or Woman of the Stars Rushing Through the Sky, was the first Native American woman to publish, but she was known less as a writer than as the wife of Henry Rowe Schoolcraft, Indian agent and author. Her poems appeared in 1826 and 1827 issues of *The Literary Voyager or Muzzeniegun*. Schoolcraft's poems, published under pen names Rosa and Leelinau, "reflect a love of nature, gentle piety, and fondness for English pre-Romantic and Romantic poetry," as LaVonne Ruoff points out.[2] While her style is imitative, to Schoolcraft's credit, she insists on accurate representation of Ojibwe culture in poems such as "Invocation to My Maternal Grandfather On Hearing His Descent from Chippewa Ancestors Misrepresented." But it is Johnston's prose and not her poetry that distinguishes her as a writer.

John Rollin Ridge, the best-known American Indian poet of the nineteenth century, was born into a prominent Cherokee family 19 March 1827. Though better known for his novel, *The Life and Adventures of Joaquín Murieta, the Celebrated California Bandit* (1854), Ridge began writing poetry in the 1840s. His early verse was influenced by the English Romantics. Critic James Parins points out that Ridge's best known poem, "Mount Shasta," "closely resembles Shelley's 'Mont Blanc' (1853) in its theme, use of natural description, diction and even meter."[3]

Ridge's later poems, expressing faith in human progress, are unique. The best of these, "The Atlantic Cable," appears in Ridge's only book of poetry, *Poems* (1868). Ridge traces the evolution of human cultures, finally asserting that once human beings could communicate from nation to nation across the wide ocean they would be "Together brought in knitted unity."[4] Despite the early trauma of witnessing his father's assassination, Ridge thought the cable would "vibrate to the voice of Peace, and be / A throbbing heartstring of Humanity!" His faith that improved communications would bring peace indicates that Ridge had bought into his assimilationist education. But Ridge's outlook could also be an extension of the Cherokee worldview, that people should live responsibly in relationship to community, which Ridge increasingly saw as global.

E. Pauline Johnson or Tekahionwake, a Mohawk, produced a large body of poetry, which she performed in her native Canada, as well as in England and the United States, beginning in 1892 at a Toronto reading with other Canadian authors. After the audience heard Johnson recite "A Cry from an Indian Wife," they called for an encore. Toronto newspapers said Johnson should be on the platform as a professional reader. Two weeks later she presented a reading in Toronto's Association Hall.[5]

Born on her father's estate, "Chiefswood," Johnson memorized and composed verses before she learned to write. An avid reader of Scott, Longfellow, Byron, Shakespeare, Addison, Foster, and Meredith, Johnson was influenced by the popular literature of her time to use terms like "Brave" and "Red Skin," and much of her verse is extremely sentimental. Although her "Cry from an Indian Wife" asserts, "By right, by birth we Indians own these lands," the poem's ending undercuts this call for justice, stating, "Perhaps the white man's God has willed it so."[6] Such concessions no doubt increased Johnson's popularity with a white audience. Along with thirty-five other poems, "Cry" was included in Johnson's first book *The White Wampum*, simultaneously published in London and Boston in 1895. Two more books of poetry followed: *Canadian Born* in 1903 and *Flint and Feather* in 1912. Generations of Canadian schoolchildren memorized Johnson's most famous poem "The Song My Paddle Sings." Ruoff points out that Johnson "wrote as a mediator between the Indian – particularly the Iroquois – and non-Indian worlds."[7]

Alexander Lawrence Posey was born 3 August 1873 in the Creek Nation in Indian Territory to a Scots-Irish and Creek father and a full-blood Creek mother. His father spoke fluently both Creek and English. Posey's mother, a devout Baptist, spoke only the Creek language and passed along to her son the ancient Creek stories and customs. At seventeen, Posey entered the Indian University at Bacone where he set type and wrote for *The Instructor* newspaper. Posey delivered the commencement address for his graduation ceremony in 1895. After graduation, he entered Creek politics, taught school, and served in tribal administrative positions. Posey wrote his best poetry after 1897 when he moved to a farm near Stidham. He died of drowning in the North Canadian River in 1908.

After his death, Posey's wife edited a book of his work, *Poems of Alexander Lawrence Posey: Creek Indian Bard* (1910). Chickasaw poet Linda Hogan says that in mixing Greek with Creek mythology, Posey illustrated that his "own sense of himself is committed to recognizing and combining the two cultures."[8] This is certainly true of his poem "The Flower of Tulledega" in which Posey compares Stechupco, a legendary Creek flute player who dwells in the forest, to the Greek god Pan. Pan is also mentioned in Posey's "The Call of the Wild."

But not all of Posey's poems reflect mixed loyalties. "On the Capture and Imprisonment of Crazy Snake January, 1900" praises Chitto Harjo, leader of a band of Creeks who fought for their tribe. Harjo was imprisoned several times for defying the United States government. Posey calls Harjo, "The one true Creek, perhaps the last / To dare declare, 'You have wronged me!'."[9] To those who say, "Condemn him and his kind to shame," Posey answers, "I bow to him, exalt his name!"

Another turn of the century Native poet, Zitkala-Ša or Gertrude Simmons Bonnin, was born in 1876 in Dakota Territory. She left the Yankton Reservation at the age of eight to attend White's Indian Manual Labor Institute, a Quaker school in Wabash, Indiana. After three years she returned to the reservation, but found she was no longer happy there. She returned to the East, eventually completing a college education at Earlham. Although she would never again live among the Yankton people, Zitkala-Ša spent her life building a pan-Indian community to assist Natives of all tribes. Hogan says that among the nineteenth-century Native poets, Zitkala-Ša had the most "realistic attitude toward assimilation."[10] In "The Indian's Awakening," Zitkala-Ša described her situation in these lines: "I've lost my long hair, my eagle plumes too. / For you my own people, I've gone astray. / A wanderer now, with no place to stay."[11] The only hope expressed in this poem is for a spiritual escape from America. She embraced the philosophy of her deceased "loved ones" at home in the stars: "Direct from the Spirit-world came my steed. / The phantom has place in what was all planned. / He carried me back to God and the land / Where all harmony, peace and love are the creed."[12]

The best-known Native poet of the next generation was Frank James Prewett, an Iroquois born in 1893 near Mount Forest, Ontario, and educated at the University of Toronto. Prewett met Siegfried Sassoon at Craiglockhart Hospital in Scotland, while recovering from a war injury during the First World War. Sassoon sent Prewett's work to Virginia Woolf, who published Prewett's first book, *Poems*, in 1917. After Prewett died in 1962, a collection of his work was edited by Robert Graves and published in 1964. Some of these poems are included in *Harper's Anthology of Twentieth Century Native American Poetry* (1988).

Prewett's poems are not overtly expressive of an indigenous consciousness; yet, within his rhymed and stanzaed lyric verse, one finds an intense love and respect for the creation. In "I Shall Take You in Rough Weather," he wrote, "We shall warm each other in the lee of trees / [. . .] where no obstinate wall / Angers the gale, where elemental enmities / For small creatures and lovers are musical."[13] His reflective poetry sings of love, accentuating the peace and quiet of nature. Although most later Native poets would write free verse, some of the poetry of Jim Barnes, N. Scott Momaday, and Elizabeth Cook-Lynn is similar in tone and style to that of Prewett.

When he first began to write poetry, Creek writer Louis, or Little Coon, Oliver, a contemporary of Prewett, modeled his poems after Posey's. Born in 1904 in Oklahoma, Oliver began to experiment with new forms consistent with his tribal traditions in the 1980s after meeting Joseph Bruchac and other contemporary poets.[14] Once introduced to poetry in what he called "the contemporary idiom," Oliver exhibited a facility with form and image and a creative tribal perspective on modern life that have been seldom matched, for he was a repository of Creek history and philosophy.[15] His poem "Empty Kettle" about hungry children inspiring a hunter begins, "I do not waste what is wild / I only take what my cup / can hold."[16] Oliver illustrates this philosophical statement with the story of a hunter seeing a buck, then singing the deer chant – "He-hebah-Ah-kay-kee-no!" – then killing a deer so the children can eat. After paying his "debt" to sustain his people, the hunter sings "a different song," in celebration. The poem, which ends, "I sing. / I sing," incorporates chant-like repetition, as well as Creek philosophy, language, and experience.

By the time Oliver began writing, younger poets had been drawing upon their Native oral traditions and contemporary experience and writing free verse for more than a decade. In his introduction to an early Native poetry anthology, *Voices from Wah'Kon-Tah* (1974), Vine Deloria, Jr., called the new poets a "bridge" linking the "glorious past with which we all agree and the desperate present which Indians know and which the white man refuses to admit."[17]

The "desperate present" formed the background and setting for the new Native literature that appeared in the late 60s. N. Scott Momaday's 1969 Pulitzer Prize encouraged other Native writers, including Linda Hogan, who was inspired by Momaday's use of the ceremonial power of words to effect positive change. Momaday used the conventional Jemez invocation and ending for his text, which according to Louis Owens, "signals a transformative act, a subtly subversive process that runs counter to the internationalist orientation of modernism with modernism's emphasis on a placeless iconography."[18] Also, by placing at the center of his novel a prayer-chant from the Navajo Night Way and using its opening line as his title, Momaday acknowledged and affirmed the centrality of oral tradition. Momaday's early poem "Earth and I Gave You Turquoise" appeared in the *New Mexico Quarterly* in 1958. The poem's Navajo persona defines his existence by the landscape around him – Black Mountain, Chinle, Red Rock, places associated with his beloved wife, who has died. The poem's short statements, forming five six-line stanzas, and its rhythm and syllabic regularity make this elegy sound like an oral chant.

While pursuing a PhD in English at Stanford University, Momaday's mentor was Post-Symbolist Yvor Winters. Winters's emphasis on the sound of verse no doubt reinforced what Momaday had learned through the spoken literature of the Kiowa, Pueblo, and Navajo people. By emphasizing the power of words as a means of survival and by insisting that contemporary human beings should maintain an ethical relationship to nature, Momaday accentuated two guiding principles for contemporary American Indian literature. Like Momaday, all the other poets featured later in this volume adhere to these principles. I would devote more attention in this introduction to the poetry of Momaday, Ortiz, Welch, Silko, Vizenor, Erdrich, and Harjo if each were not being highlighted with a separate chapter.

Unlike Momaday's first novel, most poetry by Native writers in the late 60s and early 70s was published by small presses and in small-circulation magazines. "Coyote," which Osage writer Carter Revard considers his "ars poetica," appeared in a 1960 issue of *The Massachusetts Review*. Revard, who completed a PhD in English at Yale in 1959, taught medieval English literature at Washington University in St. Louis from 1961 to 1997.

Meanwhile, he wrote poetry. Revard's poems are rich with stories, remembered images and spoken words from the eastern Oklahoma landscape and Osage culture that formed him, but influenced by many literary traditions. Osage cosmology is conveyed through Old English, Italian, English Renaissance, sprung rhythm, and free verse forms.

Anishinaabeg writer Gerald Vizenor, who began writing haiku in the early 1950s while serving in the army in Japan, has compared the haiku form and content to Ojibwe dream songs, which he began translating in the early sixties. His collection, *Summer in the Spring: Lyric Poems of the Ojibway*, was published in 1965. Vizenor went on to write longer, imagistic poetry and more haiku, but his later work is primarily prose.

Like Revard and Momaday, Vizenor grew up in the thirties. Each of these poets looks to his indigenous tradition for insight and identity. Vizenor pays attention to the butterfly, sparrow, and squirrel. Momaday gives voice to his residing spirit, Bear, while Revard looks to the eagle to bring him closer "to Wakonda's ways."[19] Their tribal languages, structures, and ceremonies inspire them.

Like Revard, Cheyenne poet Lance Henson was raised in Oklahoma, close to his Native culture. Point Riders Press of Norman, Oklahoma, published Henson's *Naming the Dark: Poems for the Cheyenne* in 1976 and Revard's *Ponca War Dancers* in 1980. These poets, from different parts of Oklahoma and different tribes, developed very different styles. Revard's poems are full of motion, description, and conversation; Henson's poems are sparse and minimalist, like the traditional Cheyenne songs he has translated. Yet both poets reflect their tribal cultures and histories, their life experiences, and the politics of their time. Both condemn America's exploitation of tribal lands, resources, and cultures, and identify with oppressed peoples throughout the world.

By the mid-70s, there could be little doubt that American Indians were writing some of the most creative and engaged literature. Although she has devoted most of her writing to fiction, Leslie Marmon Silko's first book, *Laguna Woman* (1974), was poetry. Many of its poems, including "Prayer to the Pacific," and "Toe'Osh: a Laguna Coyote Story," were included in Kenneth Rosen's anthology, *Voices of the Rainbow* (1975), along with the work of twenty other poets. Silko's poems were also featured in Duane Niatum's *Carriers of the Dream Wheel* (1977), which included poetry by sixteen writers, including Jim Barnes, Joseph Bruchac, Lance Henson, Roberta Hill, N. Scott Momaday, Duane Niatum, Simon J. Ortiz, Anita Endrezze Probst, Wendy Rose, and Ray A. Young Bear. Niatum's title, from a poem by Momaday, connects the new poets with their ancient oral traditions.

In 1976 Harper and Row published books of poetry by James Welch and Simon J. Ortiz. Welch's *Riding the Earthboy 40* and Ortiz's *Going for the Rain* both offer Native perspectives on America's bicentennial. Welch's poems, such as "The Man from Washington," speak with bitter irony of the United States government's false promises that robbed his people of a future. Portraying the federal agent as a "slouching dwarf," the poem allows readers to see the disrespect and injustice of colonization from a Blackfeet perspective. Latin American poets influenced Welch's style, which includes the wild juxtapositions of dreams. Though he did not publish another book of poems, similar thematic and stylistic elements are found in Welch's novels.

Having grown up among working Acoma people, many of whom were displaced in the 1950s by the relocation programs of the Eisenhower administration, Simon J. Ortiz gave voice in his first book to the pain of separation many indigenous people suffered in cities. The journey format allowed Ortiz to relate both the loneliness of urban Indians dislocated from their land and the long journey of his Acoma people over the millennia. For Ortiz, language itself is a journey from inside to outside oneself and back. As he states it, "Language is life."

Ortiz described the history and meaning of the indigenous journey, combining prose and poetry, in his later work. *Fight Back: For the Sake of the People, For the Sake of the Land* (1980) commemorates the successful Pueblo Revolt of 1680, relating it to Pueblo resistance two centuries later. *From Sand Creek* (1990) considers the massacre of Cheyennes on 29 November 1864 by Fort Lyons troops and Colorado volunteers within the entire context of the Euro-American empire. A veteran of the United States army and inheritor of thousands of years of Acoma life, Ortiz shows that violence to the land and to the people is one and the same. Yet, though blood is the central image in *From Sand Creek*, Ortiz writes with vision, not despair: "The blood poured unto the plains, steaming like breath on winter mornings; the breath rose into the clouds and became the rain and replenishment."[20]

In 1980 Harper and Row published Ray Young Bear's *Winter of the Salamander*. Young Bear, a resident of the Meskwaki Tribal Settlement near Tama, Iowa, began thinking the poems in Meskwaki, then wrote them in English. Within the stream of consciousness evident in poems like "the moon and the stars, the stone and the fire," Young Bear recorded the ongoing life of his people, bound to one another through their respect for the natural elements and also by their love.

Three Iroquois poets – Maurice Kenny (Mohawk), Joseph Bruchac (Abenaki) and Roberta Hill Whiteman (Oneida) – were featured in

Carriers of the Dream Wheel. Like Niatum, Kenny and Bruchac helped other Native writers through editing and publishing their work. Kenny's Strawberry Press and Bruchac's Greenfield Review Press nurtured Native poetry. At the same time, both Kenny and Bruchac were writing their own poems, which were featured in *The Blue Cloud Quarterly*, published each season by The Blue Cloud Abbey in Marvin, South Dakota. For two decades, the *Quarterly* featured a diversity of American Indian poets, including Robert J. Conley, Wendy Rose, Mary TallMountain, Lance Henson, Elizabeth Cook-Lynn, Tony Long Wolf, Jr., and many others.

Bruchac, Kenny, and Whiteman also published their own books. Poems from six of Kenny's books are collected in *On Second Thought* (1995). Roberta Hill Whiteman wrote two books of poetry, *Star Quilt* (1984) and *Philadelphia Flowers* (1996). Bruchac's most recent books are *Ndakinna (Our Land): New and Selected Poems* and *Above the Line: New Poems*, both published in 2002.

As her work developed, the message of Whiteman's poetry became increasingly political. Memories of traditional Oneida culture that helped her people survive in *Star Quilt* gave way in *Philadelphia Flowers* to warnings of humanity's tenuous existence at the turn of the twenty-first century. "Some of you bluster and do not believe / we have cut out the heart of the sky. / You give gasoline to the lords / of your death, / spoon out the sugar, / ignoring its tears," she concludes in "Acknowledgement."[21]

Many issues raised in the seventies by *Akwesasne Notes*, a Mohawk Nation newspaper, remain important topics for poetry. A member of the Turtle Clan of the Mohawk Nation, Peter Blue Cloud often wrote for the newspaper, and served as poetry editor in 1975 and 1976. The traditional ways of his people and the movement politics of the late sixties and beyond inspired poems like "When's the Last Boat to Alcatraz?" written, this poem says, "ten seconds to America" in 1976 and "Crazy Horse Monument" written the same year. Both appear in a recent anthology, *Native Poetry in Canada* (2001), coedited by Jeannette C. Armstrong and Lally Grauer. Like the Native poets of the United States, Blue Cloud considers the entire spectrum of history – from the Mohawk ceremonial dancing bear, to the transition period when Mohawks like his father constructed high steel buildings, to the political movements of the mid-twentieth century, to the transgender and border politics at the turn of the twenty-first century.

In her introduction Armstrong says that "Peter Blue Cloud's refrain, 'a tribe is an island' symbolically identifies Native protestors converging on Alcatraz from all over North America as one tribe" and suggests the " 'turtle island' " of North America.[22] The 1969 sovereignty action at Alcatraz came to represent the beginning of the modern pan-Indian movement, which had many antecedents.[23]

Blue Cloud's "Crazy Horse Monument," looks quite different from the one still being blasted and chiseled in the Black Hills:

> To capture in stone the essence of a man's spirit,
> to portray the love and respect of children and elders,
> fashion instead the point of a hunting arrow sharp,
> and leave to the elements the wearing-down of time.[24]

In the final stanza of Blue Cloud's poem, "Crazy Horse rides the circle of his people's sleep," suggesting that his spirit remains alive in Lakota people. No doubt, people gathered in the spirit of Indian sovereignty at Alcatraz and at Wounded Knee inspired the first generation of contemporary Native authors to assert a stronger voice.

Geary Hobson's anthology *The Remembered Earth* (1979), which introduced more than fifty Native writers of poetry, fiction, and non-fiction prose, placed the poems of Native Canadian Peter Blue Cloud and Native Hawaiian Dana Naone, alongside poems from the mainland United States. Although Hawaii became a state in 1959, Hawaiian literature is rarely studied on the mainland. Yet, Native Hawaiians share many of the same tribal concerns as Natives of North America – land theft, exploitation, pollution, and destruction, loss of language and culture, and the need for cultural autonomy and sovereignty. Dana Naone Hall is actively involved in Native sovereignty issues at her home on the island of Maui. Her poetry was also included in *Carriers of the Dream Wheel* and more recently in Joy Harjo and Gloria Bird's anthology, *Reinventing the Enemy's Language: Contemporary Native Women's Writings of North America* (1997), as was the work of younger Hawaiian poet, Haunani-Kay Trask. Naone and Trask identify with their islands, lamenting their exploitation, while also accentuating responsible ways of living.

The loss of a home has been a persistent theme among Alaskan poets who identify with their wilder animal relatives who have also been displaced. Koyukon Athabaskan poet Mary TallMountain's poem "The Last Wolf" envisions this endangered species entering her hospital room in the "ruined city": "he laid his long gray muzzle / on the spare white spread / and his eyes burned yellow." The poem's last two lines speak to the wolf of the shameful destruction, "Yes, I said. / I know what they have done."[25]

In offering a critical perspective on history and politics, Native poets distinguish themselves from the self-consciously introverted mainstream of contemporary poetry in the United States. While Native poetry evolves from individual experience, indigenous poets rarely stop with psychoanalysis. Rather, like Ginsberg and the Beats, they look outside themselves, considering the impact of their social and political environment. Hopi / Miwok poet

Wendy Rose's *Academic Squaw* (1977), included in *Lost Copper* (1980), and Chickasaw poet Linda Hogan's *Daughters, I Love You* (1981), included in *Eclipse* (1983), emphasized issues of great importance to American Indians, from intimate, personal perspectives. Rose condemned the cataloguing and theft of indigenous bones and sacred objects in "Three Thousand Dollar Death Song." Writing from the perspective of indigenous bones that were advertised for sale, she asks, "At what cost then / our sweet-grass-smelling / having-been? Is it to be paid / in clam shell beads or steatite, / dentalia shells or turquoise, / or blood?"[26]

Hogan's poems, from *Calling Myself Home* (1978) to *The Book of Medicines* (1993), have given voice to women, to the animals, and to the working class. *Daughters, I Love You* laments the injuries and threats posed by the development of nuclear weapons and nuclear energy. The mother grieves that she cannot protect her daughters, their unborn or the planet from being poisoned by nuclear radiation. But like Silko, Hogan speaks against nuclear development.

Duane Niatum's collection, *Harper's Anthology of Twentieth Century Native American Poetry* (1988), included thirty-six poets, most of those mentioned earlier as well as younger poets, such as Louise Erdrich, whose first book *Jacklight: Poems* was published in 1984. These poems consider the entire colonial history of America, from the perspectives of both Indian and Euro-American women and through the eyes of the deer. The strong images of poems like "Indian Boarding School: the Runaways" evoke the often painful experience: "All runaways wear dresses, long green ones / the color you would think shame was. We scrub / the sidewalks down because it's shameful work."[27]

Erdrich, Vizenor, and younger poet Kimberly Blaeser draw upon the rich resources of their Anishinabe and European heritages as well as the realities of mobility and urban life, to present a modern view of their mixed culture, and of the realities of history. Mirrored in their poetry is the amazing survival of the generations, as illustrated in Blaeser's stanza of "Shadow Sisters," dated 1992: "Indians everywhere are coming out, celebrating five hundred years of survival. These women have been out their whole lives, know survival like a long hangover."[28]

Few critical works have been devoted to contemporary Native poetry. However at the turn of the twenty-first century, three books appeared – Robin Riley Fast's *The Heart as a Drum: Continuance and Resistance in American Indian Poetry* (1999), Kenneth Lincoln's *Sing with the Heart of a Bear: Fusions of Native and American Poetry 1890–1999* (2000) and my book *The Nature of Native American Poetry* (2001). Referring to the "vibrant borderland poetics" of Native authors, Fast shows that contested spaces are a main impetus for American Indian poetry.[29] Lincoln "cross refers Anglo-American and American Indian literatures, as they have evolved over a century."[30] I consider the poetry of Revard, Momaday, Ortiz, Henson, Hill, Hogan, Rose, and Harjo within its cultural and literary contexts, ending with a chapter on the younger poets.

Craig Womack notes that Muskogee culture has been the "cornerstone" for poet Joy Harjo. "Placed in a historical context," Womack says, "Creeks have always experienced powerful cultural growth as a result of pan-tribal influence."[31] Influenced by Simon Ortiz (Acoma) and Leslie Marmon Silko (Laguna) as well as her Muskogee and Cherokee heritage, Joy Harjo published her first book of poetry *The Last Song* in 1975. An adventurous improvization sets her apart as perhaps the most creative and prolific of contemporary Native poets. Harjo constantly tries new forms. Her interest in jazz and playing saxophone led her in 1992 to form a band, Poetic Justice, which set to music many of her poems. Her book *A Map to the Next World* (2000) indicates the pattern of her life in the final line of its title poem: "You must make your own map."[32] Recalling her entire experience in prose and poetry, Harjo spirals backward from her life in Honolulu at the beginning of the twenty-first century, affirming that the world is held together with the passionate intensity of love. Harjo and other Native writers suggest that through a spiritual communion with the earth it may still be possible for human beings to enter a reciprocal relationship with the cosmos, similar to that of their ancestors.

Yet, industrialization has disrupted this relationship, as Huron / Tsalagi poet Allison Hedge Coke notes in "The Change." She recalls raising tobacco when "tobacco was sacred to all of us and we / prayed whenever we smoked and / did not smoke for pleasure."[33] But when "automated farming" took over the landscape, she knew it was time to leave Willow Springs, North Carolina. Approximating with spaces between her words the caesuras of speech, Hedge Coke recalls

> I rolled up my bedroll, remembering before,
> when the fields were like waves on a green ocean,
> and turned away, away from the change
> and corruption of big business on small farms
> of traditional agricultural people, and sharecroppers.
> Away, so that I could always hold this concise image
> of before that time and it
> floods my memory.[34]

Influenced by the breath units of beat poetry, Hedge Coke, whose book *Dog Road Woman* won the 1998 American Book Award, studied with Ginsberg at the Naropa Institute in Boulder.

Since the late sixties, the number of published Native American poets has more than doubled. Many have completed graduate work in English and have become teachers. One of the new generation of poets, Janet McAdams, a professor of English at Kenyon College, won the American Book Award for *The Island of Lost Luggage* (2001). She grew up in Alabama, the traditional homeland of her Muskogee grandfather, who "stayed and took / the one name Moses, that most conjures up / the laws by which they could not live."[35] McAdams attempts to reconstruct her family history from the fragments of paper and stone that remain. Her poems span the colonial history of the Americas, beginning with the arrival of Columbus. In "The Hands of the Taino," "The severed hands of the Taino / wave in clear salt water, / in pink-tinted water. / They wave as the gold mines dry up, / as the Governor leaves Hispaniola in chains."[36] Oddly, yet not surprisingly, the dismemberment that began the colonization, remained a fact of life for America's tribal people five hundred years later.

Anita Endrezze, who is of Yaqui ancestry, was inspired in a different way by the history of Latin America. Earlier included in Niatum's first anthology, she produced *Throwing Fire at the Sun, Water at the Moon* (2000) after travelling to Sonora, Mexico. The journey enabled her to express the meaning of the sacred myths of the Aztec figures in poems such as "Coatlicue" and "Mother of Near and Far." Endrezze's focus on her Mexican heritage further broadens the geographical and cultural scope of American Indian poetry.

The gender balance in indigenous cultures and the powerful roles of women in communities have been reflected in poetry produced by many contemporary Native poets. The poems of Paula Gunn Allen, Wendy Rose, Linda Hogan, Joy Harjo, Beth Brant, and Crystos pointed the way for a younger generation of women, including Heid Erdrich and Laura Tohe, whose anthology *Sister Nations: Native American Women Writers on Community* (2002) features the work of thirty-six writers. "The Big Rectangle" and "Tsoodzil, Mountain to the South," by Tohe, a Navajo, are beautiful love poems, much like Silko's early poetry. Also included in this anthology is Cherokee poet Diane Glancy's poem "The Abandoned Wife Gives Herself to the Lord." Glancy imagines the perspective of a nineteenth-century Warm Springs woman, who was put away by her husband at the insistence of the US government. Like Welch, Glancy uses masterful irony to expose the injustice and inhumanity of historical government policy:

> She felt dizzy with hunger. The spirits began to speak. She saw the Holy One on his cloud spearing something. He fished as if he had a claw and the salmon jumped to him. She sat on the rock waiting for him to see her. She'd heard his believers called the Bride of Christ. She knew he was a man who took more than one wife.[37]

In the work of Spokane poet Sherman Alexie, one finds a similar use of irony. Alexie is sometimes starkly serious, at others, wildly hilarious. Best known for his film *Smoke Signals*, Alexie is an accomplished poet, as well as a writer of lively stories. In the title poem from his book *The Summer of Black Widows* (1996), Alexie acknowledges spiders as the source of stories. Like his ancestors and the contemporary Native poets who influenced him, Alexie spins stories as an act of creation and a means of survival: "The elders know the spiders / had left behind bundles of stories. / Up in the corners of our old houses / we still find those small, white bundles / and nothing, neither fire / nor water, neither rock nor wind, / can bring them down."[38]

By the end of the twentieth century, the cross-pollination of Native poetry was obvious, as the younger poets mentioned older ones who influenced their work. Native poets Leslie Marmon Silko, Adrian C. Louis, Simon J. Ortiz, and Luci Tapahonso have all influenced Alexie's poetry, which also sometimes alludes to Walt Whitman and Allen Ginsberg. In turn, Alexie has inspired and encouraged a younger generation of poets, including Tiffany Midge, who also grew up on the northwest coast and whose book *Outlaws, Renegades and Saints: Diary of a Mixed-Up Halfbreed* won the 1994 Diane Decorah Award, established in conjunction with the Returning the Gift Festival. Like Alexie, Midge entertains with her wit and humor, but also reminds readers of the horrors of contemporary life, which are not spiders or the ghosts of Indians murdered in the late nineteenth century, but rather a hollow consumerism:

> The bones of the dead
> are excavated, scattered, sold.
> *Shrines* are blasted from sacred
> rock in the name of patriotism.
>
> Lakota religion is stolen by goofy mystics
> peddling crystals and incense.
> Cherokee becomes just another brand
> for affordable clothing and 4x4s.
>
> A magnificent past is reduced to hallmark
> cards postmarked galaxies away.[39]

Another young poet from the Northwest, Elizabeth Woody, who is Navajo and Warm Springs Wasco, illustrated Alexie's book *Old Shirts and New Skins* (1993). Her book *Luminaries of the Humble* was published by Sun Tracks in 1994. These poems are stylistically and thematically similar to the poetry in Ray Young Bear's second book of poetry *The Invisible Musician* (1990). Both poets emphasize the insignificance of human beings in relation to the cosmos. Unlike Alexie and Midge, whose poetry is colloquial, Woody and Young Bear utilize a high level of abstract diction.

An impressive diversity of poetic subjects, styles, and themes is evident at the outset of the twenty-first century. In April of 2002, the Native American Literature Symposium held at the Mystic Lake Casino near Prior Lake, Minnesota, featured a variety of established Native poets, including Carter Revard, Laura Tohe, Kimberly Blaeser, Diane Glancy, and Heid Erdrich, as well as younger and lesser known poets. Revard gave a luncheon speech in which he cited Marjorie Perloff's review in *Symploke* of Cary Nelson's *Anthology of Modern American Poetry* (2000) as an example of critical ethnocentrism. He pointed out that Perloff's dismissal of Adrian Louis's work as inferior was due to her ignorance of Louis's poetry's literary and cultural contexts. Revard noted that Perloff also failed to recognize Louis's allusions to European classics, concluding that she did not give serious attention to Louis's poems.[40]

Revard suggested in this address that scholars should engage in comparative studies of Native and European or Euro-American poetry. In his book *Family Matters, Tribal Affairs* (1998), Revard contrasts Wallace Stevens's "Anecdote of the Jar" with Simon J. Ortiz's "Speaking." Writing like a tourist, Stevens views the jar as superior to the "slovenly wilderness" of Tennessee, the place, where he "placed" it. In contrast, Ortiz takes his son "outside / under the trees" and both "listen to the crickets, / cicadas, million years old sound." Together, father and son engage in a conversation with the nature surrounding them. Revard explains: "the idea of America in Ortiz's poem is truly a healing reminder of what is amiss in the remarkable poem by Stevens, where abstraction disdainfully dominates nature."[41] As Revard illustrates, it is the understanding that nature is family that gives life to Native poetry. This enduring, comprehensive vision distinguishes American Indian poetry, sets it apart and ensures its endurance as long as there are ears to hear, eyes to read, hearts to care.

Notes

1. Craig S. Womack, *Red on Red: Native American Literary Separatism*, Minneapolis: University of Minnesota Press, 1999, pp. 6–7.
2. A. LaVonne Brown Ruoff, "Early Native American Women Authors: Jane Johnston Schoolcraft, Sarah Winnemucca, S. Alice Callahan, E. Pauline Johnson and Zitkala-Ša," *Nineteenth-Century American Women Writers: a Critical Reader*, ed. Karen L. Kilcup, Malden, MA and Oxford: Blackwell, 1998, pp. 81–111.
3. James W. Parins, "John Rollin Ridge," in Kenneth Roemer, ed. *Native American Writers of the United States: Dictionary of Literary Biography*, Vol. 175. Detroit: Gale Research, 1997, p. 245.
4. John Rollin Ridge, *Poems*, San Francisco: Henry Payot and Co., 1868, p. 21.
5. E. Pauline Johnson (Tekahionwake), *Flint and Feather*, Toronto: Musson Book Company, Ltd., 1912, p. xvi.

6. E. Pauline Johnson, *The White Wampum*, Boston: Lamson, Wolffe, 1895, p. 19.
7. Ruoff, "Early Native American Women Writers," p. 97.
8. Linda Hogan, "The Nineteenth Century Native American Poets," *Wassaja* 13.4 (November 1980), p. 25.
9. Minnie H. Posey ed., *Poems of Alexander Lawrence Posey: Creek Nation Bard*, Muskogee: Hoffman Printing Co., 1910, p. 207.
10. Hogan, "Nineteenth Century Native American Poets," p. 28.
11. Zitkala-Ša, *Dreams and Thunder: Stories, Poems and the Sun Dance Opera*, ed., P. Jane Hafen, Lincoln: University of Nebraska Press, 2001, p. 115.
12. Ibid., p. 118.
13. Duane Niatum, *Harper's Anthology of Twentieth-Century Native American Poetry*, New York: Harper and Row, 1988, p. 2.
14. Womack, *Red on Red*, p. 188.
15. Ibid., pp. 187–211.
16. Niatum, *Anthology*, p. 5.
17. Robert Dodge and Joseph B. McCullough, eds., *Voices from Wah'Kon-Tah: Contemporary Poetry of Native Americans*, New York: International Publishers, 1974, p. 12.
18. Louis Owens, *Other Destinies: Understanding the American Indian Novel*, Norman: University of Oklahoma Press, 1992, p. 93.
19. Carter Revard, *An Eagle Nation*, Tucson: University of Arizona Press, 1993, p. 35.
20. Simon J. Ortiz, *From Sand Creek*, New York: Thunder's Mouth Press, 1981; 2nd edn., Tucson: University of Arizona Press, 1999, p. 66.
21. Roberta Hill Whiteman, *Philadelphia Flowers: Poems*, Duluth, MN.: Holy Cow! Press, 1996, pp. 23, 24.
22. Jeannette C. Armstrong and Lally Grauer, eds, *Native Poetry in Canada: a Contemporary Anthology*, Peterborough, Ontario: Broadview Press, 2001, p. xxiii.
23. See Hazel W. Hertzberg, *The Search for an American Indian Identity: Modern Pan-Indian Movements*, Syracuse: Syracuse University Press, 1971.
24. Armstrong and Grauer, *Native Poetry in Canada*, p. 33.
25. Geary Hobson, ed., *The Remembered Earth: an Anthology of Contemporary Native American Literature*, Albuquerque: University of New Mexico Press, 1981, p. 45.
26. Wendy Rose, *Academic Squaw*, Marvin, S D: Blue Cloud Abbey, 1977, n. p.
27. Niatum, *Anthology*, p. 335.
28. Heid E. Erdrich and Laura Tohe, eds., *Sister Nations: Native American Women Writers on Community*, St. Paul: Minnesota Historical Society Press, 2002, p. 12.
29. Robin Riley Fast, *The Heart as a Drum: Continuance and Resistance in American Indian Poetry*, Ann Arbor: University of Michigan Press, 1999, p. 215.
30. Kenneth Lincoln, *Sing with the Heart of a Bear: Fusions of Native and American Poetry 1890–1999*, Berkeley: University of California Press, 2000, p. xi.
31. Womack, *Red on Red*, p. 260.
32. Joy Harjo, *A Map to the Next World: Poetry and Tales*, New York: W. W. Norton and Co., 2000, p. 21.
33. Allison Adelle Hedge Coke, *Dog Road Woman*, Minneapolis: Coffee House Press, 1997, p. 6.

34. Ibid., p. 7.
35. Janet McAdams, *The Island of Lost Luggage*, Tucson: University of Arizona Press, p. 43.
36. Ibid., p. 7.
37. Erdrich and Tohe, *Sister Nations*, p. 161.
38. Sherman Alexie, *The Summer of Black Widows*, Brooklyn: Hanging Loose Press, 1996, p. 13.
39. Tiffany Midge, *Outlaws, Renegades and Saints: Diary of a Mixed-Up Halfbreed*, Greenfield Center, NY: Greenfield Review Press, 1996, p. 102.
40. Carter Revard, "Teaching: Anthologies." Luncheon address, Native American Literature Symposium, Mystic Lake Casino, Prior Lake, Minnesota, 10 April 2002.
41. Carter Revard, *Family Matters: Tribal Affairs*, Tucson: University of Arizona Press, 1998, pp. 163–66.

Major secondary sources

Bruchac, Joseph, *Survival this Way: Interviews with American Indian Poets*. Tucson: Sun Tracks and University of Arizona Press, 1987.

Fast, Robin Riley, *The Heart as a Drum: Continuance and Resistance in American Indian Poetry*. Ann Arbor: University of Michigan Press, 1999.

Hogan, Linda, "The Nineteenth Century Native American Poets," *Wassaja* 13(4) (November 1980), pp. 24–29.

Lincoln, Kenneth, *Sing with the Heart of a Bear: Fusions of Native and American Poetry 1890–1999*. Berkeley: University of California Press, 2000.

Wilson, Norma C, *The Nature of Native American Poetry*. Albuquerque: University of New Mexico Press, 2001.

7

A. LAVONNE BROWN RUOFF

Pre-1968 fiction

Native authors did not begin publishing fiction until the mid-nineteenth century. Although her writing has long been neglected, Betsey Guppy Chamberlain (1797–1886) was also one of the first people to protest in fiction the injustices the dominant society inflicted on Native people. Born in Brookfield, New Hampshire, Chamberlain was of Flemish / English and Native ancestry from a tribe of the Algonkian Confederacy, possibly Abenakie and Narragansett. Chamberlain married Colonel Josiah Chamberlain in 1820. After his death, Chamberlain married and was widowed three more times in Massachusetts and in Du Page County, near Chicago.

Chamberlain published thirty-three prose works in *Lowell Offering* 1 (1841), and *Lowell Offering* 2 (1842). Four more appeared in *The New England Offering* 1 (1848). All were collections of writing by women working in the Lowell mills. One of the most interesting and bizarre is "A Fire Side Scene," a brief story of how the settlers burned the Miami Indians in the battle of Fallen Timbers in 1794. "The Indian Pledge" tells of a Connecticut settler who cruelly refuses to give an Indian food and water; later he depends on that Indian to keep him from starving. Many of Chamberlain's stories about women record village life and legends, told from a woman's point of view. Throughout, she demonstrates keen observation and the storytelling power to create memorable portraits and to capture local dialects. Despite her talent as a writer, Chamberlain ceased publishing after she left Lowell.

John Rollin Ridge (Cherokee, 1827–1867) was the first Native author to publish a novel: *The Life and Adventures of Joaquín Murieta* (1854). Ridge was the half-Cherokee grandson of Major Ridge, one of the most influential leaders of the tribe before Removal (Indian Removal Act of 1830) and he was only twelve at the time of the forced march to Indian Territory, now Oklahoma. Both Major Ridge and his son, John, the father of John Rollin Ridge, were assassinated for their role in bringing about the sale of Cherokee lands. In 1849, John Rollin Ridge shot a man, probably in self-defense, and fled in 1850 to the California gold fields, where he worked as a clerk.

Writing under the name Yellow Bird, a literal translation of his Cherokee name Cheesquatalawny, Ridge contributed regularly to such San Francisco periodicals as *Gold Era, Hesperian,* and *Pioneer.* One of the first Native authors to earn his living as a writer, Ridge later became owner and editor of various California newspapers.

The Life and Adventures of Joaquín Murieta was widely copied and was even made into film versions. Ridge combines the exploits of several famous bandits and echoes the experiences of the Cherokees in his description of how greedy settlers drive the hard-working, ambitious Murieta off his land. Like the Byronic hero, Murieta is a good man driven to violent deeds by injustice, a gallant gentleman to women, a courageous leader to his men, and an unrelenting enemy to his foes. Narrated at a break-neck pace, the novel is filled with dangerous exploits and frequent gunfire. In its emphasis on regionalism in California, the romance also reflects the local-color tradition.

S. Alice Callahan (Muscogee-Creek, 1868–1894) is the first Native American woman to publish a novel, *Wynema* (1891). Callahan's father was Samuel Benton Callahan, who was one eighth Muscogee-Creek. He held various positions with that nation, edited the *Indian Journal,* and supervised the Wealaka Boarding School for Muscogee-Creek Children. After she attended the Wesleyan Female Institute in Staunton, Virginia for ten months in 1888, Callahan taught at Muskogee's Harrell International Institute, a Methodist high school. In 1892 and 1893, she taught at the Wealaka School, before moving back to Harrell in 1893. In December 1893, she contracted pleurisy and died on 7 January 1894.

Wynema was her only book. The plot describes the acculturation and romances of two heroines, Genevieve Weir, a non-Indian Methodist teacher from a genteel Southern family, and Wynema Harjo, a full-blood Muscogee-Creek child who becomes her best student and dear friend. Part One chronicles Genevieve's adjustments to life as a Methodist teacher in the Muscogee-Creek Nation, aided by Wynema and the Reverend Gerald Keithly. Both Parts One and Two describe the "civilizing" of Wynema. The latter chronicles the Creek girl's acculturation while visiting Genevieve's family in the South. By the end of the novel, Genevieve marries Keithly and Wynema weds Robin, Genevieve's brother. Because Callahan was writing the novel during the hostilities of late 1890 that led to the massacre at Wounded Knee on 29 December, she incorporates into the novel an episode in which a Methodist missionary and Robin dash off to the Sioux Nation to help friends there. Although the novel is primarily a sentimental romance, Callahan does include discussions of Creek culture, politics, and women's rights. Like other women writers of the period, Callahan uses the tradition of the sentimental romance for political purposes.

At the turn of the century, Simon Pokagon (1830–99) published *O-gi-mäw-kwe Mit-I-gwä-ki (Queen of the Woods)* (1899). He was the son of Leopold, chief of the Pokagon Band of Potawatomi. Simon's collaborator on the novel was probably Mrs. C. H. Engle, wife of his close friend and lawyer. The novel combines nostalgic reminiscence for the lost golden age of the Potawatomi with fiery attacks on alcohol, which had destroyed Indian families. It chronicles the experiences of Simon, who has just returned from a white-run school, and Lonidaw, the name of Pokagon's own wife. At one with nature, Lonidaw is always accompanied by a jealous albino deer, which departs after Pokagon and Lonidaw marry. After his marriage, Simon abandons the "civilized" society for a forest life, living with his wife and two children in solitude. Their Edenic life ends in tragedy. Their son, who has been away at school, returns as an adolescent drunk, and their daughter is drowned when her canoe is struck by two drunken settlers. Almost drowned while trying to save her daughter, Lonidaw succumbs two weeks later.

Emily Pauline Johnson (Canadian Mohawk, 1861–1913) achieved great public and critical acclaim as a poet and performer of her poetry in Canada, United States, and England. Many of her short stories appeared in *Mother's Magazine* and *Boy's World*, journals published in the Chicago suburb of Elgin, Illinois. In 1910, when Johnson was writing for *Mother's Magazine* it had a circulation of over 600,000. Johnson's parents were George Henry Martin, a Mohawk chief, and Emily Susanna Howells, an English-born cousin of William Dean Howells, the renowned American writer. Chiefswood, the family's home in Brantford, Ontario, was a gathering spot for Indian and non-Indian visitors. Johnson was educated primarily at home by her mother, who introduced her to the classics of English and American literature. She briefly attended Brantford Collegiate Institute. The family left Chiefswood after the death of her father in 1884. Her career as a poet and performer began in January 1892, when she electrified her Toronto audience with her recitation of "A Cry from an Indian Wife," based on the first mixed-blood rebellion (1869–70), led by Louis Riel, against the Canadian government.

Most of Johnson's fiction is collected in *The Moccasin Maker* (1913) and *The Shagganappi* (1913), both published posthumously. *The Moccasin Maker*, the better of the two volumes, includes stories about Indian and non-Indian women as well as the essay "A Pagan in St. Paul's Cathedral." Like the heroines of most women's nineteenth-century fiction, the female protagonists of Johnson's stories inevitably triumph over great difficulty. Like other women writers of the period, Johnson uses the sentimental tradition for political purposes. Her heroines and their lovers or husbands recognize that genuine love between men and women reflects shared values. Johnson combines the domestic romance with protest literature as she describes the experiences of women and Indians in "Red Girl's Reasoning" and "As It Was in the Beginning," two of the best stories in the collection. In both she combines the plot of the mixed-blood woman betrayed by a weak white lover with a forceful attack on non-Indian hypocrisy. "The Legend of Lillooet Falls," "Tenas Klootchman," and "Catherine of the 'Crow's Nest'" portray the deep love Indian women felt for their natural and adopted children, as well as the roles they play as guardians of tribal traditions. Mother love is also a powerful force in Johnson's stories about non-Indian frontier women and in her romanticized account of her parents' courtship and marriage, entitled "My Mother."

Johnson was also a prolific writer of juvenile boy's fiction. Between 1906 and 1913, she published more than thirty stories in *Boy's World*, most of which appear in *The Shagganappi* (1913). Containing Native, mixed-race, and non-Native protagonists, the stories were filled with adventure and important moral lessons.

The most widely read Native author in the early twentieth century was Charles Eastman or Ohiyesa, (Santee Sioux, 1858–1939), who was one of the first Indian doctors. In his lifetime, Eastman moved from the nomadic tribal life of the Santee Dakota to the drawing rooms and lecture halls of America and England. After his father, Jacob or Many Lightnings, returned from imprisonment for his role in the Minnesota Sioux uprising in 1862, he enrolled his son in school in Flandreau, Dakota Territory. For the next seventeen years, he attended such schools as Beloit College in Wisconsin, Knox College in Illinois and graduated from Dartmouth College (Class of 1887) and Boston College Medical School (1890). While an agency physician at Pine Ridge, he met and married Elaine Goodale Eastman, a Massachusetts writer and teacher on the Great Sioux Reservation. As a result of policy disputes with Pine Ridge agents, the Eastmans moved to St. Paul, where Eastman was unable to establish a medical practice. For the next two decades, Eastman held a variety of positions in Indian affairs and the YMCA; he was also active in Indian reform movements, such as the Society of American Indians.

During this period, the Eastmans collaborated in writing many books, most of which were non-fiction. Two collections of short stories, primarily written for young people, portray Dakota or Sioux worldviews and history. *Red Hunters and the Animal People* (1904) reflect Dakota respect for animals. In *Old Indian Days* (1907), the Eastmans primarily emphasize plot and ethnography, although they include some stories that focus on character. Divided into "The Warrior" and "The Woman," the book focuses on individuals whose actions illustrate Sioux history, customs, and values. "The Warrior" section depicts the code of behavior, rituals, and challenges that warriors experience from adolescence through adulthood. "The Woman" section represents one of the few examples of contemporary ethnographic fiction on American Indians to deal with women. The Eastmans also reinterpreted traditional stories for children in *Wigwam Evenings: Sioux Folktales Retold* (1909), reissued in 1910 under the title *Smoky Day's Wigwam Evenings: Indian Stories Retold*.

Gertrude Simmons Bonnin or Zitkala-Ša (1876–1938) is another Sioux writer whose importance as a writer has gained increasing recognition. Born on the Yankton Nakota Reservation in South Dakota, she attended two Indiana schools: White's Manual Labor Institute and Earlham College, both Quaker. In 1899, she taught at Carlisle Indian School. A talented violinist, she studied at the New England Conservatory, Boston, from 1900 to 1901. As a young adult, Bonnin gave herself the Lakota name Zitkala-Ša or Red Bird, which she used in her writing. Her creative career essentially ended when she married Raymond Talefease Bonnin (Yankton Nakota) and moved with him to the Uintah Ouray Ute Agency in Duchesne, Utah, where their only child was born in 1903. The Bonnins remained at the Agency until 1916.

For much of her life, she was a political activist, who worked for the Society for the American Indian and later was founder and president of the National Council of American Indians. Although she was Yankton Nakota, she worked with the Dakota language and oral traditions. Her most important book is *American Indian Stories* (1921). In addition to her three autobiographical essays and an essay on "America's Indian Problem," the volume contains her powerful and vivid short stories. One of her most interesting is "A Warrior's Daughter," which portrays the courage and determination of Tusee, a beautiful daughter of a chief. Disguised as an old woman, Tusee sneaks into the enemy camp to rescue her lover. "The Trial Path," published originally in *Harper's Magazine*, March 1901, is a complex story of Dakota justice. Here a grandmother tells her granddaughter about how her husband, when he was young, killed his closest friend and rival for the grandmother's hand. After her husband successfully rides a wild pony to the center of a circle, as the victim's father demands, the family of his victim accepts him as their son and harmony is maintained within the camp circle. The melodramatic "The Soft Hearted Sioux," also published in *Harper's*, October 1901, expresses Zitkala-Ša's disillusionment with missionary schools. The story describes the cultural conflict faced by a young Sioux who has returned to his tribe after years at a mission school. Convinced he can save his dying father with Christian prayers, the son sends away the medicine man. Because his father is starving, the young man kills a cow and then murders the settler who catches him. He subsequently turns himself in and accepts his death sentence. Other collections of Zitkala-Ša's works include *Dreams and*

Thunder: Stories, Poems, and The Sun Dance Opera (2001), edited by P. Jane Hafen. This volume contains traditional and creative stories. It also includes *The Sun Dance Opera,* on which she and William F. Hanson collaborated in 1913.

In the early twentieth century, Mourning Dove or Christine Quintasket, (Colville, 1888–1936), published the second novel by an American Indian woman: *Cogewea, the Half-Blood* (1927). Mourning Dove, who completed only the third grade and briefly attended business school, worked most of her life as a migrant worker in Washington State. Written in collaboration with Lucullus Virgil McWhorter, Mourning Dove's novel focuses on issues of tribal cultural and political sovereignty, identity issues of a mixed-blood, and the importance of oral tradition. Mourning Dove combines these elements with plot elements from popular westerns. Proud of her Carlisle education and full of ambition, Cogewea initially rejects a mixed-blood, cowboy suitor for a "crafty Easterner," because accepting the cowboy would mean living Indian. By the end of the novel, she recognizes the importance of the value that the cowboy and her Indian grandmother represent. Particularly interesting is her creation of a strong-willed, independent heroine who is as capable of doing ranch work as any cowboy.

The most controversial Native writer of the 1920s was Sylvester Clark Long, a Lumbee (1890–1932). The child of ex-slaves, Long was a mixed-blood. His mother was Caucasian and Lumbee. His father was at least partially African American and claimed Caucasian and Indian ancestry. In Winston-Salem, North Carolina, where the family lived, they were described as "colored," a designation applied to both African Americans and Indians in the South at that time. At thirteen, Long joined a Wild West Show, where a Cherokee taught him some of the language. In order to be admitted into Carlisle Indian School, Long persuaded his father to certify that his son was Cherokee. When Carlisle Cherokee students failed to accept him, Long gave himself the name Long Lance. He was later appointed as a Cherokee to West Point, which then excluded African Americans. After serving in the Canadian army during World War I, Long became a journalist in Alberta, where he met members of the Blackfeet tribe. In *Long Lance* (1928) he describes himself as a Blackfeet chief named Buffalo Child Long Lance. Although he calls the book an autobiography, it is actually fiction. Set in the 1890s and after, the book describes growing up on the far western Canadian Plains. Based on Long's interviews with Canadian Blackfeet and Blood Indians, the book was highly praised by such authorities as Ernest Thompson Seton and Paul Radin. Long became a popular lecturer on Indian topics, performing in full regalia. He also costarred in the 1930 Indian film *Silent Enemy*. After his family, whom he had avoided for over twenty years, reestablished contact, he moved from New York to Los Angeles. Overwhelmed by depression, he fatally shot himself in 1932.

Perhaps the most prolific Native writer of the early twentieth century was John Milton Oskison (1874–1947). One-eighth Cherokee, Oskison was raised in Oklahoma, graduated from Stanford and attended Harvard. He was an editor and feature writer for *Collier's Magazine* and a freelance writer on finance and Indian affairs. Oskison's *Wild Harvest* (1925) and *Black Jack Davy* (1926) are "southwesterns" set in Indian Territory just before statehood and deal with the surge of settlers into Cherokee land near a fictional town called Big Grove. In *Brothers Three* (1935), Oskison correctly describes these two novels when Henry Odell, the fictional version of the author, calls his first novel "a mess, misty, sentimental, badly knit, with impossible situations and caricatures of human beings" and the second as "amateurish" but containing "the people and the country I knew" (343–44). Oskison's best novel is *Brothers Three*, which chronicles the efforts of three sons to hold on to the farm established by their father, Francis, and quarter-Cherokee mother, Janet. At the end of the novel, the third son returns from his New York life as a writer and investor to help reestablish the farm. Although the major characters are part Indian, the novel focuses not on Indian life but rather on the importance of honesty, loyalty, hard work, and thrift and on the economic and social history of Oklahoma. A good example of regionalism, *Brothers Three* demonstrates Oskison's ability to create believable characters and realistic dialogue.

When he died, Oskison had completed much of "Singing Bird," possibly the first historical novel written by a Native American author. The novel, which Timothy Powell and Melinda Smith have now co-edited, has a provisional publication date of 2006 with the University of Oklahoma Press. It deals with Cherokee history in Arkansas and Indian Territory from the 1820s through the beginnings of the War Between the States. It particularly focuses on the 1840s and 50s and includes the Cherokee Removal and conflicts between the Eastern and Western Cherokee after they settled in Indian Territory. It recounts the adventures of a group of New England missionaries who establish a mission among the Arkansas Cherokee and move with them to Indian Territory. In addition to narrating Cherokee history, the novel records the tangled relations of the family of the Reverend Daniel Wear, who is torn between his commitment to the Cherokee and his passion for his tempestuous, amorous, and selfish wife, Ellen. Here Oskison demonstrates his ability to create vivid characters, effectively using dialect and storytelling to particularize minor characters.

During the 1930s, the most sophisticated Native American novelists were John Joseph Mathews, (Osage, 1894–1979), and D'Arcy McNickle (Métis Cree/Salish, 1904–77). Unlike other American writers of the 1930s who emphasized economic and social issues, Mathews and McNickle stressed the importance of tribalism, community, and the devastating impact on tribes of the federal government's assimilationist policies. One-eighth Osage, Mathews grew up in Pawhuska, the Osage Agency. During World War I, he served in the aviation branch of the Signal Corps in France. He subsequently received his BS from the University of Oklahoma in 1920 and his BA in natural science from Oxford University in 1923. Mathews also attended the School of International Relations in Geneva and traveled widely in Western Europe, Britain, and North Africa. After his divorce in 1929, he returned to Pawhuska, where he built a cabin in the blackjack oaks region and lived the next ten years.

Mathews's first book was *Wah'Kon-Tah* (1932). Based on the journal of Major Laban J. Miles, the first government agent for the Osage, this fictional account portrays the tribe's determination to retain its traditional ways as Laban attempts to lead them down the "white" world's road. The last chapter introduces the prototype of the hero of *Sundown* (1934) a young, jazz-age Osage, ashamed of his backward parents but dependent on them for money. Both in this book and in the novel *Sundown,* Mathews vividly portrays how Osage culture was affected by life on the reservation, by allotment, and by the Oklahoma oil boom of the 1920s. After allotment, the Osage retained their mineral rights, which provided income when oil was discovered. In both *Wah'Kon-Tah* and *Sundown,* Mathews deals with Osage sovereignty issues.

The parents of the protagonist of *Sundown,* Challenge Windzer, are Osage. The traditionalist mother is a full-blood, while the father, who is one-quarter white, is an assimilationist and a strong advocate of allotment. Windzer is a passive hero who rejects his ancestral past without feeling at home in the non-Indian world. His education in the schools in that world has cut him off from his Indian roots; his cultural separation is completed by a brief stint at the University of Oklahoma and service with the armed forces during World War I. Dreaming of glory, Windzer lives in an alcoholic haze, unable to cope with either the Osage or the non-Indian world. Nevertheless, the Osage landscape and natural world recall for Chal the worldviews and customs of his people.

The best-written and most polished novel published by a Native American in the 1930s is McNickle's *The Surrounded* (1936). By blood, McNickle was Métis of Cree extraction on his mother's side and white on his father's. His mother's family had settled on the Flathead, now called the Salish-Koutenai, Reservation. Her children were added to the Flathead or Salish rolls by tribal vote, making them eligible for land allotments. After his parents separated, McNickle was sent to Indian boarding school in Chemawa Oregon. He attended the University of Montana but left short of graduation; he also briefly attended Oxford and Grenoble. One of the strongest influences on McNickle's writing was his experience with federal Indian policy gained as an employee of the Bureau of Indian Affairs from 1936 to 1952. McNickle began his career in the BIA under the enlightened leadership of John Collier, a staunch advocate of the Wheeler–Howard Indian Reorganization Act of 1934, which supported tribal autonomy. After the government embarked on a policy of terminating the reservations and eliminating Indian influence in the BIA, McNickle resigned. During the next few years, he worked for American Indian Development, conducting community improvement workshops and directing a health education program for the Navajos in New Mexico. In 1965, he became chair of the Division of Social Sciences of the University of Saskatchewan, Regina, a position he retained until 1971. In addition, McNickle co-founded the National Congress of American Indians and served as the director of the Center for American Indian History, Newberry Library, Chicago.

McNickle's novel *The Surrounded* chronicles a mixed-blood's search for his place and emphasizes the importance of oral traditions to the cultural survival of the tribe. It also stresses Native sovereignty over culture and land as well as the destructive role of the Catholic Church in its attempts to acculturate the Salish. Published two years after the Indian Reorganization Act, the work movingly describes the disintegration of a tribe as a result of the destruction of its religion and values and the loss of Indian lands to settlers. The protagonist, Archilde Leon, is the son of a Flathead (Salish) woman, renowned for her Catholic piety and for her refusal to abandon Indian ways, and a Spanish father, who, after forty years of living among Indians, has no insight into their worldviews. The couple has been separated for many years. Returning home for a last visit to his parents, Archilde is inadvertently caught up in unpremeditated murders that his mother and girlfriend commit. His strongly traditional mother and a tribal elder lead him back to the Salish culture he had rejected. Through its emphasis on the role of tribal religion and culture in restoring the tribe, *The Surrounded* offers more hope for the survival of American Indian culture than does Mathews's *Sundown*.

McNickle's *Runner in the Sun* (1954), written for middle-school readers, is one of the few novels published by an Indian author between the 1930s and 1968. Set in the pre-contact Southwest, this taut novel evokes the life, customs, and beliefs of the ancient cliff dwellers of Chaco Canyon, in what is now northwestern New Mexico, as they battle the forces of nature and society that threaten to destroy them. Central to the plot are the adventures of Salt, a teenager being trained to lead his people. He survives the efforts of his archenemy, Dark Dealer, to control the village and destroy the young boy. After a hazardous journey to Mexico, Salt brings back a hardy strain of corn that his people can grow to save themselves from starvation. McNickle incorporates the hero twins motif, common in pueblo oral literature, through the character, Star Child, who is Salt's age but is more passive than his friend.

McNickle's next novel, *Wind from an Enemy Sky,* was published post-humously in 1978. Here McNickle moves from the clash of two cultures within the individual to a conflict between groups. The plot contrasts the values of non-Indian culture, symbolized by a dam that cuts off the Indians' water and violates a holy place, with the values of Indian culture, symbolized by the tribe's sacred Feather-Boy medicine bundle. The plot also contrasts the responses by two brothers, one a traditionalist and the other an assimilationist, to government efforts to alter Native life-style. A young Indian's murder of a dam engineer sets off a chain of tragic events. As in *The Surrounded,* the cultural clash ends in the death of the participants. McNickle's forty years of experience in Indian affairs since the publication of his first novel strengthened his belief in the continuing inability of the representatives of the two cultures to communicate their vastly different worldviews to one another. McNickle also wrote and published some short stories in his youth, which Birgit Hans collected and edited in *The Hawk is Hungry and Other Stories* (1992). Most of his other books have been histories.

One of the few Indian authors of mystery and detective fiction is [George] Todd Downing (Choctaw, 1902–74). Raised in Atoka, Oklahoma, Downing received his BA and MA from the University of Oklahoma. He also studied at the National University of Mexico City and conducted tours of Mexico. Downing taught Spanish at the University of Oklahoma and worked in the bilingual program at Southwestern College (now University) in Durant, Oklahoma. His novels, most of which were set in Mexico, include *The Cat Screams* (1934), *Murder on Tour* (1935), *Vultures in the Sky* (1935), *Murder on the Tropic* (1935), *The Case of the Unconquered Sisters* (1936), *The Last Trumpet* (1937), *Night over Mexico* (1937), *Death under the Moonflower* (1938), *The Mexican Earth* (1940), and *The Lazy Lawrence Murders* (1941). Although his novels have long been out of print, his best book, *Night over Mexico* was reprinted in 1996 by the University of Oklahoma Press, with an introduction by Wolfgang Hochbruck. Here Downing uses the form of the travelogue to tell Mexican history from a Native point of view.

Few Indians published fiction in the 1940s and 1950s. Much of their writing during this period appeared in newspapers and journals. One of the few to publish a novel was Ella Deloria (1889–1971), who is primarily known as an anthropologist and linguist. Born on the Yankton Nakota Reservation, she was raised on the Standing Rock Reservation, both located in South Dakota. She grew up speaking Dakota, Lakota, and Nakota. Deloria attended Oberlin College and Columbia University, from which she graduated in 1914. While at Columbia, she worked with the anthropologist Franz Boas, collecting material on South Dakota Indian languages and ethnography. She is best known for *Dakota Texts,* 1932. During the 1940s, she completed the ethnographic novel, *Waterlily,* not published until 1988. Told from a woman's perspective, *Waterlily* vividly portrays the lives of a Dakota mother and daughter in the late nineteenth century. Deloria incorporates her detailed knowledge of Dakota history, kinship customs, social rules, religion, and culture and depicts the impact on that society of growing encroachment from settlers.

Nineteenth- and early twentieth-century Native authors used their fiction to introduce readers to the major issues of sovereignty, culture, community, and identity. With insight and power, they describe how Native people survived while their traditional lifestyle was altered during the reservation and allotment periods. These books attest to the power of the creative imaginations of American Indian authors who continue to educate, enlighten, and delight us.

Major secondary sources

Owens, Louis, *Other Destinies: Understanding the American Indian Novel.* Norman: University of Oklahoma Press, 1992, pp. 3–89.

Parins, James W., *John Rollin Ridge: his Life and Works.* American Indian Lives Series. Lincoln: University of Nebraska Press, 1991.

Parker, Dorothy Ragon, *Singing an Indian Song: a Biography of D'Arcy McNickle.* American Indian Lives Series. Lincoln: University of Nebraska Press, 1992.

Purdy, John, *Word Ways: the Novels of D'Arcy McNickle.* Tucson: University of Arizona Press, 1990.

Ranta, Judith A., *The Life and Writings of Betsey Chamberlain: Native American Mill Worker.* Boston: Northeastern University Press, 2003.

Ruoff, A. LaVonne Brown, *American Indian Literatures: an Introduction, Bibliographic Review, and Selected Bibliography.* New York: Modern Language Association, 1990, pp. 62–76.

Strong-Boag Veronica and Carole Gerson, *Paddling her own Canoe: the Times and Texts of E. Pauline Johnson, Tekahionwake.* Studies in Gender and History. Toronto: University of Toronto Press, 2000.

Warrior, Robert Allen, *Tribal Secrets: Recovering American Indian Intellectual Traditions.* Minneapolis: University of Minnesota Press, 1995, pp. xiii–86.

Weaver, Jace, *That the People Might Live: Native American Literatures and Native American Community.* New York, Oxford: Oxford University Press, 1997, pp. 75–120.

Wilson, Raymond. *Ohiyesa: Charles Eastman, Santee Sioux.* Urbana: University of Illinois Press, 1983.

8

JAMES RUPPERT

Fiction: 1968 to the present

1968 marks the publication of N. Scott Momaday's Pulitzer Prize winning novel, *House Made of Dawn* and as such, it is usually considered to mark the beginning of a steady rise in literary production by Native American writers often termed "The Native American Renaissance." Some scholars hesitate to use the phrase because it might imply that Native writers were not producing significant work before that time or that these writers sprang up without longstanding community and tribal roots. Indeed, if this was a rebirth, what was the original birth? However, the term is useful in pointing out that between the publication of *House Made of Dawn* in 1968 and *Ceremony* in 1977, there was an unprecedented increase in the printing of work by Native American writers. There is no question but at this time, the landscape of Native American literature changed. Not only was there increased public interest in writing by Native Americans, but also Native writers felt inspired and encouraged. Suddenly it seemed possible that they could be successful with their writing and still remain true to their unique experience.

One can easily identify a few proximate causes. First of all, the counter-cultural perspective of the youth movement encouraged readers to explore the experiences of minority people and of those marginalized by mainstream American society. Many of these readers sought expressions of community, spirit, ecology, and egalitarianism that they could not find in mainstream society. The civil rights movement had turned many people's attention to questions of social justice and naturally Native American claims, having always formed a pole in the development of American self, came to the fore. The reissue of *Black Elk Speaks* in 1961 sparked an interest in Native values and philosophy that culminated with the publications of Carlos Castaneda's *The Teachings of Don Juan: a Yaqui Way of Knowledge* (1968) and its increasingly fantastic sequels. This interest with Native experience was coupled with a desire to explore Native perspectives as social criticism. The Indian "takeovers" at the BIA in Washington and at Wounded Knee in 1973 highlighted the activism of the American Indian

Movement (AIM) and brought Native social criticism to the television. Many people wanted to understand Native perspectives on American values and the dominant society while they hoped to encounter Native values. Native authors were not always obliging, but this broad interest created the groundwork for a probing and engaging literature.

Concurrently, the National Endowment for the Arts began a program of support for literary magazines, small presses, and individual artistic fellowships. Editors began to publish special issues of magazines dedicated to Native writers. Some even began to publish small books by Native writers. Native writers won grants to focus their energies on writing. This extraordinary level of support encouraged and enlivened Native people, making it possible to create and publish literature at a level unseen before. Some years later mature Native writers conceded that there was work published during the hectic heyday of small-press production that was not really ready to stand alone before the ages, but what is more important, many new voices were heard and encouraged to join the cultural conversation.

Less apparent but equally important, a community of Native writers emerged, began to get published and to read each other's work. The development of this pan-tribal intellectual community created a network of writers who shared some similar values, responded to some similar history and had some similar things to say. They responded to each other, shared stories and manuscripts, visited and lectured with each other. In other words, a Native and a non-Native audience developed when none had existed previously.

Geary Hobson and Vine Deloria, Jr. have both suggested that this rise of interest comes about periodically in the American public. They have commented that while things Indian may come in vogue, eventually the interest dwindles until the next cycle. This allows a few Native writers to rise in popularity while Euro-American society tries to assimilate the token of the "Otherness." While one can see some evidence of this on the historical level, the lack of public interest in Native experience during the 1930s, 40s, and 50s does not exactly parallel the sustained interest in Native American literature during the 1980s and 90s, though much of the federal and financial support that existed during the Native American Renaissance has disappeared.

This period between 1968 and 1977 is marked by three powerful and formative novels that pattern the substructures of contemporary Native American literature: *House Made of Dawn* by N. Scott Momaday, *Winter in The Blood* (1974), by James Welch, and *Ceremony* (1977) by Leslie Marmon Silko. While each of these novels is discussed in length in other essays, I will briefly characterize them here. *House Made of Dawn* was a marvelous achievement. It merged elements from contemporary novels with

Navajo and Pueblo perspectives on life. Momaday was able to draw on a variety of sources from Pueblo religious chants to historical documents as he created a lyrical and compelling story of an alienated and disaffiliated young World War II veteran and his inability to bring himself back to health and harmony. Set in the 1950s period of relocation and termination, Momaday's veteran Abel moves from pueblo to prison to Los Angeles back to the pueblo. At the end of the novel, as Abel listens to his grandfather's life stories, he sees that there might be a place for him in the community and in the universe. He joins the Pueblo dawn runners and begins to find some connections.

In 1969 Momaday continued to hold center stage with the publication of *The Way to Rainy Mountain*. The small but popular book combined historical accounts with Kiowa oral narratives and personal observation. Momaday's skillful blend of various sources, artwork, and lyrical perception continues to win over readers as he celebrates the evolution and accomplishment of the Kiowa spirit. The book was also influential for Native writers as one can see the mixture of personal observation with retellings of oral tradition in many works by contemporary Native writers.

Welch's narrator in *Winter in the Blood* is another alienated young man who finds little meaning in his life and in the loves of those around him. He shuts out a painful past that includes the death of a brother and father and insulates himself from emotions and connections. A series of revelations about his family and their history helps rebuild bridges that were previously destroyed. As the novel ends, the narrator takes some tentative steps to regain his connections with family and tradition. He begins to thaw the winter in his blood.

Welch followed the critical success of *Winter in the Blood* with an even darker view of life on the northern plains, *The Death of Jim Loney* (1979). His mixed-blood protagonist struggles to find meaningful connections to family and community, but seems unable to overcome the social forces that marginalize him. Loney is haunted by his past and mired in a meaninglessness that he has trouble understanding. The novel ends with Loney's death at the hands of an Indian policeman, an event that Loney himself has orchestrated.

In *Ceremony*, Silko revisits the condition of the returned war veteran. Her protagonist Tayo has been shattered by the experience of World War II and has withdrawn from the world. Always the outsider, Tayo must come to understand the forces behind the destructive patterns of his experience. Using oral tradition and an unorthodox ceremony, the novel binds the fate of the reader with the fate of Tayo and humankind in a struggle that holds off mass destruction and brings renewal to the Pueblo traditions. For Silko, his integration into society, culture, and myth represent revitalization of tradition by those marginalized by both traditional Native societies and mainstream American society.

Both *Winter in the Blood* and *Ceremony* illustrate the interest that New York City publishers were expressing in Native authors. Harper & Row became the best known of these with the series of publications it started in the early 1970s. Without a climate like this, the publication of *The Man to Send Rain Clouds: Contemporary Stories by American Indians* in 1974 would not have been possible. Edited by Kenneth Rosen, the book brought together the short fiction of seven unknown Southwestern Indian writers, propelling the work of Leslie Silko and Simon Ortiz into national attention. Silko and Ortiz created rich stories layered with myth, witchcraft, and spirituality. Their narrative stances articulated a Native worldview, one critical of non-Native ignorance and cultural assumptions and centered on the intelligence of a Native perspective. Rather than dwell on historical oppression, their stories such as "The Man to Send Rain Clouds," and "The San Francisco Indians," reinforced a belief in the continuance and continuity of Native cultures and values. Both Silko and Ortiz deliberately incorporated oral narratives as subject matter and oral storytelling techniques into their fiction. Both wanted their narrative standpoints to represent authentically Native perception because, for the first time, Native fiction writers recognized the existence of a Native literary audience.

During this period other books were published that were influential. With colorful pictures, mandala-like shields, and a fantastic storyline, Hyemeyohsts Storm's *Seven Arrows* (1972) was both controversial and successful. While some debated the authenticity of the author and the book, readers from the counter-culture added it to their bookshelves, next to *Black Elk Speaks*. In 1981, Storm published *The Song of Heyoehkah,* a similar book, but it was not oriented toward medicine wheels. It was not well received and Storm never became a major voice in Native American literature.

Shortly after his death in 1977, two of D'Arcy McNickle's novels were published. *The Surrounded* originally published in 1936 was reissued in 1978 and *Wind from an Enemy Sky* (1978) was published posthumously. The influence on the field was immense as both writers and readers began to perceive the work of contemporary writers in a larger historical scope.

In 1978, Peter Blue Cloud published his first collection of short stories. Blue Cloud took for his inspiration the Coyote tales common among many western tribes to create the stories in *Back Then Tomorrow*. In his retellings, he fictionalizes and restructures the tales so they read like short fiction. He also takes the Native trickster and places him in contemporary situations to give a material presence to Native mythic reality. This volume was expanded and revised in 1982 and published as *Elderberry Flute Song*. He also published *The Other Side of Nowhere: Contemporary Coyote Tales* (1990).

The 1970s closed with the introduction of two new voices, two fiction writers, essayists, and editors who would continue to develop and influence Native writing over the next twenty years. Joseph Bruchac, noted as a poet and publisher of the *Greenfield Review*, brought out a novel, *The Dreams of Jesse Brown* (1978). His magazine and the press associated with it have published many Native writers and Bruchac has emerged as a major storyteller.

Gerald Vizenor had published poetry and journalism, but in 1978 he published a collection of short fiction *Wordarrows: Indians and Whites in the New Fur Trade* and a novel *Darkness in Saint Louis Bearheart* (later reissued and retitled *Bearheart: the Heirship Chronicles* in 1990). In *Wordarrows*, Vizenor's stories grow out of the urban reservation of the Twin Cities. His characters battle racism, poverty, misconceptions, and self-delusions as they cut out a path for survival. The fabulist elements of the narratives marked Vizenor as a unique voice on the scene and his amazing and outlandish stories revealed humor and a keen wit. While tricksters appear in *Wordarrows*, they are at the heart of *Darkness in Saint Louis Bear Heart*. Set in a fantastic post-apocalypse America, it follows a group of tricksters and pilgrims on the way from the Great Lakes woodlands to Chaco Canyon. Myth and reality become fused in the novel, allowing Vizenor to take on the traditions of violence and linguistic manipulation that underpin modern America while creating "mythic verism."

One might think of the next phase (1978–89) as kicked off by the publication of *The Remembered Earth: an Anthology of Contemporary Native American Literature* edited by Geary Hobson in 1979. This was the first thorough and representative collection of contemporary Native American poetry and fiction. While other smaller and more local anthologies had been published, Hobson's book was organized around regions and included a wide variety of poets and fiction writers, some who were seasoned veterans, some who were publishing for the first time. One might see this as heralding the kind of diversity that would develop in the 1980s as Native American Literature began a sustained and varied development.

This volume was followed by another Southwest editor's work. In 1983, Ortiz edited one of the best collections of contemporary Native American short fiction, *Earth Power Coming*. In it Ortiz brought together the fiction of Silko and Louise Erdrich with that of many other writers previously noted for their poetry, for example, Maurice Kenny, Paula Gunn Allen, Carter Revard, Ralph Salisbury, and Linda Hogan. Striking stories by Anna Walters, Elizabeth Cook-Lynn, and Peter Blue Cloud combined with work from less well-known writers to create a powerful anthology, one still used in many classrooms today.

Well known as a poet, Simon Ortiz has been acclaimed and influential as a fiction writer. His stories have been widely anthologized. His reputation as a writer of short fiction chiefly rests on two small press collections, *Howbah Indians* (1978) and *Fightin': New and Collected Stories* (1983). *Howbah Indians* consists of four short stories and *Fightin'* includes nineteen, three of which were published in earlier volumes. The stories in *Howbah Indians* present the everyday life of Indian people struggling with common problems but they also present moments of humor and poignant juxtaposition of Native values and modern society. Many of the stories in *Fightin'* develop a sophisticated view of cultural politics, yet in a way that respects any individual's potential to move past the problems that divide us and seek a common ground of humanity. Ortiz's skillful use of the storyteller's persona places the reader as an insider aligned with the Pueblo perspective on America.

The 1980s were a decade of the growth and development of Native American fiction. Many of the writers who gained notice during the Native American Renaissance continued to build their careers and their readership with new work. Many were branching out, cultivating new approaches and new subject matter. Moreover, many new writers encouraged by the sustained creative activity of other writers and the growth of local interest in Native voices started to bring their work to a national audience.

James Welch opened new ground with his historical novel *Fools Crow* (1986). Welch still remains one of the few Native writers willing to take on the risks inherent in writing historical novels. Here Welch tries to place the reader in the world of the Blackfeet before white settlers disrupted their culture in the 1870s. Welch focuses on the growth and development of one young man, Fools Crow, as he moves from a young man with little distinction to a leader of his group, one whose visions will help guide his band. Through the use of Blackfeet words translated into English phrases and first-person visions, he tries to make his reader participate in a more Native perception of the invasion by the white world and the disruption it brought to Native peoples.

N. Scott Momaday brought out his long awaited second novel, *The Ancient Child* (1989) to mixed reviews. In it, a mixed-blood artist is separated from his Kiowa past, but lured back to Oklahoma by the power of myth and tradition. As he searches for his true identity, he is aided by a young Navajo girl with strong spirit power. Eventually he merges with the Bear Boy of Kiowa myth to find his most authentic self.

Leslie Silko published a collection of stories, poems, and photographs called *Storyteller* (1981). In the book she places her poems and fiction in the context of the Laguna oral tradition especially as it becomes intertwined with the experiences of her family and ancestors. Each item resonates with those that precede it and Silko builds an intimate picture of connectedness and community. Silko's use of myth and oral tradition was highlighted and the volume included a number of her popular short stories, such as "Storyteller" and "Yellow Woman." Many of the noteworthy elements of her short fiction such as the use of oral narrative and the evocation of mythic reality are reminiscent of *Ceremony*.

In 1984 with the publication of *Love Medicine*, a new voice began to be heard among Native writers. Louise Erdrich's novel won the National Book Critics Circle Award for Fiction and immediately she became the most popular Native American novelist. Erdrich brought to the forefront a humor that was lacking in many of the other popular Native writers. Her mixture of first person narration, oral tradition, and colorful images brought life to the imaginary reservation on the northern prairie, but has also proven to be a useful model for Native writers in the 1990s. Her work appeals to a broad audience of Native and non-Native readers partly because she explores themes so common to all her readers. Generational conflicts revolve around family history and individual obsessions. Religious expression merges ancestral and contemporary beliefs and the worlds of her novels are ripe with contemporary references and reminders of a confluence of traditional values and contemporary experience.

Erdrich followed up the success of *Love Medicine* with *The Beet Queen* (1986) and *Tracks* (1988) making three of a projected quartet of novels exploring the lives of Chippewa people on a reservation in North Dakota. Erdrich's fiction is noted for its striking symbolic episodes, its use of oral tradition, its unique characterization, and its humor. While *Love Medicine* examines the intricacies of the connections between a few families, *The Beet Queen* is set in a bordertown and follows the lives of Mary and Karl Adair. Erdrich chronicles the difficulties and despair of making lasting interpersonal connections and deep meaningful relationships. Hope and redemption always seem just out of the reach of the people in this novel. *Tracks* functions as a prequel to *Love Medicine* exploring the early lives of some of its characters. Readers are immersed in the changes shaping the Chippewa reservation and society in the years from 1912 to 1924: the old growth forests are being felled, white schools are making inroads as are Christian missionaries, and the federal bureaucracy is being felt as a palpable entity. The characters in the novel illustrate a variety of community responses to these changes, but the first-person narration of the novel gives it the feel of a storytelling session.

Michael Dorris, emerging from his collaborative efforts with his wife, Louise Erdrich, published his first novel in 1987. *A Yellow Raft in Blue*

Water presents the characters Christine, a Native from Montana living in the Seattle area, and her daughter Rayona, the result of a brief marriage with a black man. The two attempt to balance their needs for independence, love, and connection with their conflicting cultural, racial, and personal values. The novel moves from Seattle to the reservation in Montana as both try to reconnect with family, tradition, and community.

Vizenor continued to publish at an amazing rate. During the decade he published poetry, tribal history, literary criticism, novels, and family histories. In 1981, he published *Earthdivers: Tribal Narratives on Mixed Descent* and extended the urban mixed-blood characters of *Wordarrows*. Puns, word play, and wild imagination in the tradition of the tribal trickster create stylistic and fantastic views of the intersection of modern American experience and tribal consciousness. He explored the film medium with his screenplay "Harold of Orange" (1984). It won the Film in the Cities award and was fine-tuned at the Sundance Institute. Here the compassionate urban trickster comes to life in the person of Oneida comedian Charlie Hill as he tries to play the foundation game and secure funds for his warriors of orange. Vizenor published two more books, *Griever: an American Monkey King in China* (1987) and *The Trickster of Liberty: Tribal Heirs to a Wild Baronage at Patronia* (1988). *Griever* won the 1988 Fiction Collective Prize and incorporated some of his 1983 experiences as a university English teacher in China. Vizenor likens the Monkey King from the Chinese classic, *Journey to the West* to the Native American trickster. In the novel, Griever, a reservation trickster turned university professor works for the liberation of all people and animals from the narrow, life-denying thinking (which he calls terminal creeds) of official China. *The Trickster of Liberty* is a collection of short fiction that reads like a novel. It presents the stories of a family of reservation tricksters who infiltrate contemporary America with the goal of freeing themselves of convention and hypocrisy, and of liberating people from repressive images of identity, especially images of Indians.

One of the exciting voices to emerge in the 1980s was Anna Lee Walters, whose work had seen limited publication. In 1985 she published a collection of short fiction *The Sun is Not Merciful* that won the American Book Award in 1986. This collection of eight short stories contains vivid portraits of people carved out of Walter's past in Oklahoma. In these stories of a struggle with the delegitimizing influence of contemporary life, Walters's characters draw on cultural values and the oral tradition to redefine identity and establish community. Especially memorable is her story "Warriors," where a Korean War veteran and his nieces struggle to retain the beauty and integrity of their lives while they balance personal and communal needs and demands. She followed this up with the novel, *Ghost Singer* (1988). In this work, Walters draws on her experience working at the Smithsonian Institution in Washington, DC. The story follows the lives of a number of characters who inquire into the mysterious deaths of museum officials working in the archives. Walters bring two medicine men together in the halls of the Smithsonian to deal with this supernatural threat, but their abilities are limited by museum attitudes toward grave artifacts and the spirit world. History and spiritual perception inform the novel as it examines some specific aspects of cross-cultural misunderstanding and the strength of the human spirit.

Many new voices were heard on the literary front in the 1980s, though some had published in related areas or in small and local publications previously. Paula Gunn Allen noted for her poetry and critical work published a novel in 1983. *The Woman Who Owned the Shadows* follows the growth and development of Ephanie from the sense of alienation she feels as a mixed-blood Hispanic/Indian to an expanding sense of self and identity through her female relatives ultimately to a larger connection with a spiritual realm and her own spirit power.

Janet Campbell Hale's second novel *The Jailing of Cecilia Capture* came out in 1985. Her first novel, published for the juvenile fiction market, was *The Owl Song* (1974) which told the story of Billy White Hawk, a fourteen-year-old reservation Indian who moves to the city and must find a way to come to grips with racism, cultural dissolution, and death. The protagonist of *The Jailing of Cecilia Capture* is a university law student who is arrested for drunk driving. Much of the novel is an interior monologue as Cecilia reviews her life and experience of alienation, death, alcoholism, and racism. She leaves the city to return to the reservation to find identity and community.

1990 not only marked the beginning of a new decade, but it was a banner year for Native American Literature. Welch published *Indian Lawyer*, Linda Hogan published *Mean Spirit*, Tom King published *Medicine River*, and Elizabeth Cook-Lynn unveiled *The Power of Horses and Other Stories*. During the decade the best-known writers continued to expand and deepen their works, writers noted for work in other fields turned to fiction, new writers emerged, and the body of published fiction got richer and more complex as it dealt with changes in mainstream America, reservation life, urban experience, and new ways of looking at old relationships.

N. Scott Momaday broadened his body of work with *In the Presence of the Sun: Stories and Poems 1961–1991* (1992), *Circle of Wonder: a Native American Christmas Story* (1994), *The Man Made of Words: Essays, Stories, Passages* (1997), and *In the Bear's House* (1999). Though he produced no novels in the 1990s, Momaday did create some hauntingly lyrical pieces of short fiction reinforcing his close connection to land and spirit.

After a hiatus of fourteen years, Leslie Silko returned to the novel with *Almanac of the Dead* in 1991 and then *Gardens in the Dunes* (1999). *Almanac* is a massive novel that tries to pull together the history of the domination of the Americas, the evolution of political revolutions, the mythic legacy of the two continents, and forge a unity from diverse Native traditions. As the novel progresses, a set of notebooks presaging the apocalyptic movement of people and traditions is revealed and they become central to the growing Native revolt against the dominant culture's theft of land and culture. The novel is a prophecy of the reassertion of Native values as Native people take back the land. *Garden in the Dunes* is Silko's foray into the historical novel. Following the life of a Native girl whose tribe is hidden in the desert, Silko also explores late nineteenth-century/early twentieth-century botanical and financial entrepreneurship, religious discussions of paganism and early Christianity, and Women's positions in the Native and white worlds. Myth is again central to Silko's work, but much of her interest seems to lie in mythic commonalties between cultures, and the dominant culture's lack of understanding of that reality.

James Welch's *Indian Lawyer* moved to new ground as he presents a Native character who is flourishing and in the process of being groomed for unparalleled success in his local community. His secure life is shaken by a run-in with a convict and he realizes that there is something missing in this world of accomplishment. He has lost his connection with community and with his Indianness, but what that should mean to the protagonist and how he should redefine himself is left open. Welch seems to see many possibilities that are genuine.

Gerald Vizenor continued to produce books at an amazing rate. His fiction included *Heirs of Columbus* (1991), *Landfill Meditations: Crossblood Stories* (1991), *Dead Voices: Natural Agonies in the New World* (1992), and *Hotline Healers: an Almost Browne Novel* (1997). He continued to evolve fantastic mixed-blood characters who rewrite the codes of the world with mythic imagination. Compassionate urban tricksters shock, stimulate, confuse, and transform the reader. In *Heirs of Columbus*, a Native descendent of Columbus discovers that his DNA contains healing genes and the novel proceeds to satirize notions of discovery, the romanticism of Native people, and the hallowed representations of Columbus. *Landfill Meditations* brings together some previously published work with new tales of mixed-blood liberations and tricksteresque deconstructions of accepted representations of Indians. *Dead Voices* moves the struggle between imagination and stultification into an exclusively urban environment as the mythic reality focuses on a mind game where the stories of animals underpin the reality of the city. *Hotline Healers* is a series of linked stories centering around the antics of

Almost Browne as he maneuvers through the university and publishing circles liberating all intellectuals from one-dimensional and dead-end thinking.

The decade was also a prolific time for Louise Erdrich. She released *The Bingo Palace* (1994), *Tales of Burning Love* (1996), and *The Antelope Wife* (1998). With her husband Michael Dorris, Erdrich published *The Crown of Columbus* (1991) written for the 500th anniversary of the arrival of Columbus on the shores of America. The couple was the subject of much interest because of their discussions of collaborations in writing and the reputed one million dollar advance they received. The story revolves around two professors who seem mismatched in all but love. The female protagonist comes across a lost Columbus diary that leads them on a treasure hunt into the Caribbean. *The Bingo Palace* returns to the characters and reservation made popular in her earlier books and explores their relationship to the new tribal entrepreneurial focus, the casino. *Tales of Burning Love* spins off from Erdrich's already developed characters as one of the minor characters in *Love Medicine* now becomes central to this collection of stories of women's lives and loves. *The Antelope Wife* leaves behind her much explored characters for a new set. The novel spans a number of generations of twins and weaves together beading, animals, human connections, and naming practices into the stories of two powerful and possessive love affairs, neither of which are untainted by sorrow. The lives of her Native and non-Native characters are intricately bound together in and around the city of Minneapolis.

Linda Hogan, long noted as an influential poet, blossomed into fiction with *Mean Spirit* (1990), *Solar Storms* (1995), and *Power* (1998). *Mean Spirit,* set in the Oklahoma oil fields of the 1920s, centers on the domination and killing of Native people to obtain their oil wealth. Hogan creates a vivid picture of the lives of Native communities and the interplay of tradition and change. *Solar Storms* is set in northern Canada and uses a local struggle by Native people against a dam to tell the story of a young girl separated from her family and her past as she journeys to regain her sense of harmony and balance. *Power* deals with similar themes though it is located in Florida and involves a forbidden killing of the endangered Florida panther. The young female protagonist bonds with a local woman who is disliked by her parents but who was raised in Native tradition and is closely attuned to the natural world.

Elizabeth Cook-Lynn had a reputation as a poet, essayist, and editor of *Wicaso Sa Review* before she published volumes of fiction. In 1990 she produced *The Power of Horses and Other Stories* and, in 1991, *From the River's Edge.* Her short story collection presents portraits of contemporary and traditional Sioux people surviving and responding to the challenges of the twentieth century from World War I to Indian activism, but responding in a way that confirms Dakotah values. The protagonist of *From the River's*

Edge is engaged for much of the novel with a trial over stolen cows but through the trial he realizes the extent to which Dakotah values have been compromised.

Ray Young Bear, an accomplished poet, also published fiction in the 1990s. *Black Eagle Child: the Facepaint Narratives* (1992) follows the life of Edgar Bearchild as he grows in artistic ability and insight into the community around him, the Black Eagle Nation. Young Bear's mixture of voices, writing techniques and autobiographical information creates a stylistic and engaging exploration of contemporary Native experience and contemporary Native communities. *Remnants of the First Earth* (1996) continues the fictionalized autobiographical writings of Bearchild as he comes of age in his rural Native community, but this time Young Bear ties it into a murder mystery.

A number of new writers who published their first works of fiction in the 1990s have garnered a great deal of attention, foremost of which is Sherman Alexie. Alexie's first published work was poetry but during the decade he published a collection of short stories, *The Lone Ranger and Tonto Fistfight in Heaven* (1993) and two novels, *Reservation Blues* (1995) and *Indian Killer* (1996). Alexie's fiction is characterized by a decidedly anti-romantic view of Native life and of the everyday struggles to survive. His reservation dwellers do not contemplate myth or pronounce wisdom about nature. *Reservation Blues* follows the lives of some of the characters from his other short stories as they form an ill-fated rock band. Obsession and self-destruction haunt the members as the reader tries to decide if their lack of success is failure or redemption. *Indian Killer* is a murder mystery where Alexie turns a self-conscious eye on the genre as well as on the popular images of Indians and the complexities of cross-cultural interaction. Alexie's attention has also been focused on writing for the cinema. He turned one of his short stories into the film "Smoke Signals."

Scholar Louis Owens turned his attention to fiction and published a series of well-liked novels, *Wolfsong* (1991), *The Sharpest Sight* (1992), *The Bone Game* (1994), *Nightland* (1996), and *Dark River* (1999). The protagonist of *Wolfsong* is a young Native who returns home for the funeral of his uncle. The story involves the exploitation of sacred land by a logging company. *The Bone Game* is a metaphysical murder mystery where a mixed-blood university professor must solve the crime with the help of dreams, Choctaw traditions, and Native American history. *Nightland* tells the story of two mixed-blood brothers estranged from their ancestral homeland who find a huge amount of drug money and then must decide what they want with their lives and how to keep the drug lords and police from killing or arresting them. *Dark River* tells of a mixed-blood Choctaw tribal ranger living on Apache land and married into the tribe. He struggles against his own demons and against the corrupt tribal politicians that want to sell the beauty of the land.

In the 1990s, Thomas King burst on the writing scene with his Canadian First Nations inspired fiction. *Medicine River* (1990) tells the story of a Native photographer who returns to the town of his youth only to find a lost commitment to family, friends, and community. *Green Grass, Running Water* (1993) is a sparkling novel that merges a narrator talking with Coyote, contemporary Blackfoot people, four old Indians that may be characters in Native and/or Western creation stories. Much of King's humor comes from busting stereotypes about Indians and satirizing modern Western culture. *Truth and Bright Water* (1999) is a *bildungsroman* set on the Canadian–American border between the two towns of Truth and Bright Water. He also has published a collection of short stories entitled *One Good Story, That One* (1993).

Scholar Greg Sarris also made his debut into fiction with the publication of *Grand Avenue* (1994). The novel is comprised of a series of short stories that link the lives of Pomo Indians living in the town of Santa Rosa, California. Sarris weaves history, spiritual belief, and contemporary survival into the stories of an extended family living in a multicultural world. Sarris worked on a screenplay for the novel and it was eventually produced as a Home Box Office movie. *Watermelon Nights* (1998) returns to the world of Santa Rosa and follows the lives of its Pomo and mixed-blood characters as they struggle to maintain tradition and integrity against poverty, racism, and the indifference of the federal government.

Throughout the 1990s, Joseph Bruchac has continued to publish fiction such as his collections of short stories, *Turtle Meat* (1992) and retellings of traditional Native American tales. He has published many pieces of juvenile fiction with Native themes. In his role as publisher and editor, Bruchac had made a lasting contribution to the development of Native American literature. Simon Ortiz also gathered his fiction and published *Men on the Moon: Collected Short Stories* (1999). Cook-Lynn continued her work in fiction with *Aurelia: a Crow Creek Trilogy* (1999) and in the same year, Jane Campbell Hale published *Women on the Run*.

During the 1990s, Diane Glancy has emerged as a very prolific and versatile writer. She has published poetry, plays, short stories, and novels. Her list of publications includes *Trigger Dance* (1990), *Firesticks: a Collection of Stories* (1993), *Monkey Secret* (1995), *The Only Piece of Furniture in the House* (1996), *Pushing the Bear: a Novel of the Trail of Tears* (1996), *Flutie* (1998), *Fuller Man* (1999), *The Voice That Was in Travel: Stories* (1999), *The Man Who Heard the Land* (2001), *The Mask*

Maker (2002), *Designs of the Night Sky* (2002), and *Stone Heart: a Novel of Sacajawea* (2003). Much of her work focuses on contemporary Native characters and the new myths and adaptations by which they survive.

The twenty-first century opened up with strong contributions for noted writers. James Welch produced *The Heartsong of Charging Elk* (2000). In the novel Welch returns to historical fiction as he tells the story of a nineteenth-century Sioux man who is left behind in Marseilles by Buffalo Bill's Wild West Show and lives his life in France. Gerald Vizenor offered readers *Chancers* (2000) where he satirically depicts academic culture and neo-cultist Indians. Sherman Alexie's collection of short stories *The Toughest Indian in the World* (2000) explores the contemporary urban experience of middle-class and professional Native people with humor, irony, and sympathy. Louise Erdrich returns to the reservation people of *Love Medicine* and *Tracks*, to Father Damien, Sister Leopolda, the Kashpaws and the Nanpushes in *The Last Report on the Miracles at Little No Horse* (2001) in order to tell a tale of sexual and spiritual transformation. In 2003, she brought out *The Master Butchers Singing Club*.

One can observe a number of changes in the fiction of Native writers after 1990. There are more urban characters, more middle-class and professional Native protagonists with stories set in the city as often as on the reservations. It might reflect the simple fact that more Native people live in cities than on reservations, or that most university education takes place in an urban setting. Or it may indicate a shift in perspectives as the dominant culture and Native cultures change.

In her introduction to *Song of the Turtle*, Paula Gunn Allen imagined the field of Native American fiction as separating itself out into three distinct waves. The first wave from 1870 to 1970 reacted to the loss of land and culture with fiction that was predominately derived from characters, settings, and themes popular in America and Europe. She sees the second wave of writers beginning in 1974 and lasting until the early 1990s. She sees this wave of writers as defined by "a sense of renewal and hope, reasserted often deeply angry, Native identity; and incorporation of ritual elements in both structure and content drawn from the ceremonial traditions" (8). The stories were concerned with cultural conflict that reflected an internal conflict. The tone was of an exotic and alien world where victimization was unrelenting. Allen felt the goal here was to create an "authentic" Indian that would resonate with the expectations of the non-Native world while exploring a Native perspective. She sees the third-wave writers as creating a more authentic picture of modern Native American experience while recasting American and Native traditions or the "transformation of alien elements into elements of ceremonial significance" (13). "Their focus shifts from history and traditional culture unalterably opposed to Anglo-European culture to urbanity and a more comprehensive, global perspective" (14).

One might also see this shift as registering the influence of postmodernism. Much of the fiction published before the 1990s was based on a modernist paradigm that set up as unalterable opposites the city and the reservation, the white man and the Indian, community and estrangement. Many protagonists are mired in alienation from the modern world, from community, and from self. Identity is fragmented and the only path to balance, harmony, and identity is a return to the reservation and to connect with ritual and tradition. One might see *House Made of Dawn* as a perfect expression of the native perception of modernism. The city was a wasteland of modern culture. People in the cities were alienated from their surroundings, their communities, and their cultures. The reservations held connection to nature, spirit, culture, and community. The modernist protagonist must return to his roots and seek reintegration into the community and tradition to make himself whole and to dissolve alienation.

It seems to me that contemporary Native American writers have approached the world of the 1990s and the paradigm of experience that it presents, in at least three significant ways, two of which appear, at first, to be decidedly non-postmodern, but might also be seen as moving beyond the limitations of the postmodern in a direction only Native writers lead. Some writers like Sarris want to redefine contemporary experience in terms that rise only out of that experience itself. Some like Silko in *Almanac of the Dead* or Erdrich in *The Antelope Wife* try to recreate a mythological framework that engenders new significations for older patterns. And yet others like Vizenor in *Dead Voices* seek to reimagine the modernist oppositions in radically new ways that call into question all presuppositions.

Native writers in the 1990s and the twenty-first century seek to renegotiate the dualisms of modernism. They mediate the opposition between urban and rural, between Native and non-Native readers. For them, oral tradition is not opposed to alienation, community is not always racially or culturally defined, and self-definitions are not exclusively constructed of history and culture. The values of modernism are disrupted so that they may be renegotiated. Irony is key to their literary productions.

Major secondary sources

Allen, Paula Gunn, *Song of the Turtle: American Indian Literature, 1974–1994*. New York: Ballantine, 1996.

Cheyfitz, Eric, ed., *The Columbia History of Native American Literature Since 1945*. New York: Columbia University Press, 2005.

Larson, Charles R., *American Indian Fiction*. Albuquerque: University of New Mexico Press, 1978.

Owens, Louis, *Other Destinies: Understanding the American Indian Novel*. Norman: University of Oklahoma Press, 1992.

Ruppert, James, *Mediation in Contemporary Native American Fiction*. Norman: University of Oklahoma Press, 1995.

Velie, Allan R., *Four American Indian Literary Masters: N. Scott Momaday, James Welch, Leslie Marmon Silko, and Gerald Vizenor*. Norman: University of Oklahoma Press, 1982.

9

ANN HAUGO

American Indian theatre

Like the Native American Literary Renaissance, the Native Theatre Movement is a relatively recent phenomenon. With the formation of several Native American theatre companies in the 1970s, many Native playwrights began finding audiences for their work, yet publications of their plays or scholarship on Native theatre was rare. In the first years of the twenty-first century, while more published plays are available, Native theatre productions in the US are still limited in number, a point of frustration for playwrights, actors, and other artists. This chapter provides an overview of the Native Theatre Movement both in print and on the stage and notes in particular some of the challenges and difficulties that Native theatre artists face and overcome. Because the film industry has parallel issues, the article also references – though sparingly – recent developments in film.

The Native Theatre Movement

Native people were by no means new to the performing arts in the late twentieth century. One of the more successful playwrights of the 1930s, in fact, was Cherokee. Born in Indian Territory in 1899, Lynn Riggs wrote over twenty-five plays, and most of them were published during his lifetime. He is best known now for his play *Green Grow the Lilacs* (1929/1931), which was adapted by Richard Rodgers and Oscar Hammerstein II to become *Oklahoma!* While writing *Green Grow the Lilacs*, Riggs wrote to a friend that he had an idea for a new American play, "one I have contemplated for some time, a dramatic study of the descendants of the Cherokee Indians in Oklahoma, to be called *The Cherokee Night*."[1] *Cherokee Night* (1930/1932) would be Riggs's only play with Indian themes. His writing had not been included often in discussions about Native literature until Jace Weaver offered a new reading of three of Riggs's plays in *That the People Might Live: Native American Literatures and Native American Community* (1997).

Before the 1970s, Native theatre artists were rarely in control of their medium, however. Early attempts to write for the theatre or to form companies mark important moves by Native artists to gain some control over public representation of their cultures or art. Whether on stage or on the screen, the beginning of a discernible movement is marked by the shift from an industry in which Native artists' creativity is controlled or directed by others, to an industry in which an increasing number of Native artists exert creative control. In theatre, that change began in 1972, when Hanay Geiogamah (Kiowa / Delaware) launched the first successful long-running Native theatre company, the American Indian Theater Ensemble, later known as the Native American Theatre Ensemble (NATE). Then, in 1975, Muriel Miguel and a handful of other women created a multiracial, radical feminist performance group known as Spiderwoman Theater, a company that would become the longest continually running women's theatre and the longest continually running professional Native theatre in the US. The decade following NATE's premiere saw the formation of several other Native theatres, among them At-Tu-Mai/Southern Ute Performing Arts Company (1974), Red Earth Performing Arts Company (1974), Echo Hawk (1976), Indian Time Theatre (1981), Tulsa American Indian Theatre Company (1976), and Washington's First American Theatre/Free Spirit Players (1982).[2]

In NATE, Geiogamah envisioned a theatre that would relate to the lives of the Native artists and their audience, a theatre much like the theatre produced by the Black Arts Movement, which Geiogamah describes as work "about social issues, cultural issues, identity issues."[3] Some of this work would grow from oral traditions; other work would examine issues and situations from daily life. For NATE's premiere performance in October of 1972, they presented a double bill. *Na Haaz Zaan* was an adaptation of the Diné Creation Story; *Body Indian* was a two-act play Geiogamah wrote for the company.

During NATE's nine-month training schedule at La Mama in New York City, company members Geraldine Keams, Robert Shorty, and Timothy Clashin, all Navajo, worked with Lee Breuer, a founder of the performance collective Mabou Mines, to develop *Na Haaz Zaan*. Keams's grandmother had told the story, and Keams and Clashin worked together to translate it into English. The performance used the original language, with English translation provided for the audience. Shorty worked with Breuer on the staging of the piece, which followed the Diné emergence using a multi-level playing area and stylized movement and choreography to give visual form to the story. Keams later commented that the experience of "weaving words and visuals together" with Breuer increased her interest in this type of creative process.[4]

The second piece presented that evening was Geiogamah's *Body Indian*. As a dramatic work, *Body Indian* is somewhat conventional in form, reflecting Geiogamah's formal writing training. A short play, it takes place in five scenes set in an urban Oklahoma apartment. Bobby Lee, the primary character, wears an artificial leg, having lost his leg after passing out on a track and being hit by the train. Bobby's physical malady and the train accident both become metaphor in the play. Physically damaged, Bobby Lee also leads a spiritually damaged life, and in this sense he can be understood as a sort of Indian Everyman, insofar as the Everyman character lives metaphor onstage in order to lead the true everyman – the audience or general citizenry – toward enlightenment.

Bobby Lee has received his allotment money and arrives at the apartment in part to tie one on, but he announces that he hopes to use the allotment money to check into rehab. The others persuade Bobby to keep drinking, and once he passes out, his "friends" repeatedly roll him for his money, rifling through his clothes and eventually even taking his artificial leg to hock it. As more and more of Bobby Lee's money disappears, we witness the gradual disintegration of hope for his future, though at first Bobby himself seems unaware of this. At each violation of Bobby Lee's body, we hear and see the train rolling down the tracks. A familiar symbol in Native literature of destruction and colonization, the train in this play signals the characters' destruction of each other. In the final moments of the play, Bobby seems to recognize some of the import, as he raises himself up on the bed where he has passed out and repeats the greeting he received on entering the apartment. Yet he ends the story even more damaged than when he started it.

Geiogamah still describes the play as an examination of social problems in Indian country, and it remains a daring exploration of the seedier side of life, or what *New York Times* critic Clive Barnes recognized as a "nastily accurate" portrait of people – not just Indian people – "without work, or hope."[5] An oft-repeated anecdote about the play describes how the audience, much to the company's surprise, laughed during the performance, finding the action, however tragic, also at times humorous and poignant. Yet the fact remains that one of the first successful Native-authored and Native-directed portraits of Native people on the stage repeats an image that many would rather not see again. Is another image of Indian alcoholism really necessary? Does non-Native America already focus too much attention on this "problem" in Indian country? Need Native writers echo this fascination?[6]

Jeffrey Huntsman remarks that the play's central theme is not alcoholism but "the way people – Indian people in particular – abuse, degrade, and cripple each other and themselves."[7] If Bobby Lee can be seen as Everyman, the play's resolution leaves little resolution for Bobby Lee or the people he might represent. Instead, it leaves questions, and they are questions directed at Native audiences more than non-Native audiences. At what point, Geiogamah seems to ask, does the cycle of self-destruction and victimization end? When will "Bobby Lee" recognize when he is being preyed upon or doing the preying? In this light, the play is not "about" alcoholism; alcohol is just one dysfunctional element circulating through Bobby Lee's life.

The two pieces that began NATE's tenure illustrate a diversity still true of Native theatre, as playwrights and companies tackle a wide range of perform-ance styles and topics. While many Native playwrights share some common themes and purposes, there are undoubtedly more differences among artists, between how they write, whether they perform their own work, and what subject matter they choose. Some playwrights' work is as politically charged as *Body Indian* – perhaps even more so. Other plays have purposes that are not so vividly political – such as a desire to teach or share stories or to use indigenous languages and work toward their preservation. Some theatre straddles the lines altogether, creating characters from traditional stories but dropping them into conventionally structured dramas.

Spiderwoman Theatre's plays draw on oral tradition for form and auto-biography for content and often launch political commentaries. In the 1970s, Spiderwoman was not a Native theatre exclusively but a multiracial feminist company; by 1980, the core members of Spiderwoman were Miguel and her two sisters, founding members Lisa Mayo and Gloria Miguel. Early on, the company developed a process they call "storyweaving." Although story-weaving has many roots, including the feminist emphasis on non-hierarchical organization and creation, the company names as their inspiration the Hopi deity Spiderwoman, who taught her people to weave. Because the sisters maintain a firm connection with their Native identity and cultures, story-weaving combines the philosophy and style of radical feminist theatre with traditional storytelling. Spiderwoman describes the process as "creating designs and weaving stories with words and movement."

> We translate our personal stories, dreams and images into movement, and refine them into the essential threads of human experience. In seeking out, exploring, and weaving our own patterns, we reflect the human tapestry, the web of our common humanity. Finding, loving and transcending our own flaws, as in the flaw in the goddess's tapestry, provide the means for our spirits to find their way out, to be free.[8]

In practice, Spiderwoman's method involved each member telling her own stories in the rehearsal space and finding connections between stories, fig-uratively "weaving" the connections into an episodic, alternately serious and comic, and sometimes deliberately zany, performance piece.

Like *Na Haaz Zaan*, these pieces have a structure different from plays authored within western dramaturgical principles. Playwright Drew Hayden Taylor notes that while Native storytelling might progress rather naturally to the stage, Native stories – creation stories, trickster tales, or others – may not contain the element of conflict considered elemental in Western theatre.[9] Whether the conflict is absent because the form of the story is essentially narrative or because, as Taylor states, the cultures themselves attempt to avoid conflict, the resulting adaptation process can be complicated. Does a theatre company adapt the story to fit the Western paradigm, emphasizing conflict where it might be latent? Does the company use the story's structure to create a fluid, episodic storytelling event? When that event is staged, how does an audience that might expect a conventional work react to its episodic, narrative form?

Still other work combines conventional Western form with traditional cultural elements. Bruce King's *Evening at the Warbonnet* (1990) sets two trickster characters, Ki and Ducky, in a contemporary urban Indian bar as human barkeepers – so human, in fact, that they aren't immediately recognizable as tricksters. As the evening clientele arrives, and we learn more details of Ki and Ducky's past, it becomes clear that something is not right. Ki remembers events in the nineteenth century, for example, though this is a contemporary bar. And they both tease the bargoers about their names, their pasts, or anything else that strikes their fancy. In the second act, it becomes clear that this is not really a bar. It is limbo, a place where troubled souls land before it is determined when or if they can get to the "other side." Ki and Ducky are here as a punishment, forced to be guides to the other side, forced to do something slightly out of the trickster's character. King describes the germination of the play:

> I wanted to … ask, "What if coyote is one of the pivotal characters? What if he's a person, with the sensitivities of a real person, and if so, where has he been? Where did he go?" And all of sudden, this whole Beckett/Ionesco thing started happening about well, there are these places, these pockets of purgatory everywhere. All the great writers attest to this, and I thought, why not?

Fusing tribal content with dramatic form, or tribal performative modes like storytelling with dramatic performance, playwrights like King and companies like Spiderwoman make Native theatre one of the most innovative sites of American theatre today.

Native theatre in publication

In the last five years the number of published Native-authored plays has grown exponentially, but as late as 1995, only Hanay Geiogamah's *New*

Native American Drama: Three Plays (1980) and a few individual titles had been published. Canadian publications were somewhat more successful. By 1995, several Native Canadian playwrights including Tomson Highway, Monique Mojica, Daniel David Moses, and Drew Hayden Taylor had been published, and one collection was available, *The Land Called Morning: Three Plays,* edited by Caroline Heath (1986).

Between 1999 and 2003, four multi-author collections of Native plays were published in the US: *Keepers of the Morning Star: an Anthology of Native Women's Theater,* edited by Jaye T. Darby and Stephanie Fitzgerald (Cree) (2003); *Seventh Generation: an Anthology of Native American Plays,* edited by Mimi D'Aponte (1999); *Stories of Our Way: an Anthology of American Indian Plays,* edited by Darby and Geiogamah (1999); and a collection of children's plays, *Pushing Up the Sky: Seven Native American Plays for Children* (2000), adapted and edited by Joseph Bruchac (Abenaki).

Both *Seventh Generation* and *Stories of Our Way* include playwrights of historical importance in the Native Theatre Movement and playwrights relatively new to the field. *Stories of Our Way* gives some historical context for Native theatre by including Lynn Riggs's *The Cherokee Night,* the first time that the play has been published since 1936. Among its many plays, this collection prints King's *Evening at the Warbonnet,* mentioned above. King's long career in the theatre deserves more notice, as along with Geiogamah, Yellow Robe, and Spiderwoman, he is one of the artists with the longest tenure in theatre. He started writing for the theatre in the late 1960s and founded the company Indian Time Theatre in 1981 after working with several Native theatre companies. Despite his contribution to Native theatre, *Evening at the Warbonnet* is his first play to be widely available.

D'Aponte's collection, *Seventh Generation,* publishes works by American Indian playwrights in the United States as well as Native Canadian author Drew Hayden Taylor's (Ojibway) *Only Drunks and Children Tell the Truth* and Hawaiian playwright Victoria Nalani Kneubuhl's *The Story of Susanna.* In the US and Canada, much cross-fertilization occurs in Native theatre, with actors, directors, and other artists frequently crossing the border to work on projects. Taylor's work is produced often in the States; Spiderwoman Theatre actors have worked several times for Toronto's Native Earth Performing Arts. Politically, national borders divided indigenous groups, so that Ojibway people, for example, live on both sides of the US/Canada border. While they are subject to different sets of federal laws, culturally some such divided groups might share important qualities and histories. The national borders, then, were rather random in their application for indigenous groups, and some activists and artists find it valuable to identify with fellow indigenous people across those borders.

Darby and Fitzgerald's *Keepers of the Morning Star* includes eight plays by Native women in a nicely balanced collection of well-established names like Spiderwoman Theatre, Diane Glancy, and artists newer to the field. Darby notes each play examines serious contemporary issues in Native America, yet all the playwrights "celebrate the healing power of story and performance" (xv). Their differences in form and subject matter reflect the diversity of form and style that characterizes contemporary Native theatre. Marie Clements's (Métis) *Urban Tattoo*, for example, is a multi-media one-woman piece, while Daystar/Rosalie Jones's (Pembina Chippewa) contribution to the volume is a dance drama, a form she herself has created. Spiderwoman Theatre's *Winnetou's Snake Oil Show from Wigwam City* also appears here. Using German novelist Karl May's Noble Savage character Winnetou as a starting point, the company examined American Indian stereotypes and appropriations and misrepresentations of Native spiritual traditions, ending the piece with emphatic declarations of their own identities as contemporary Native women.

In *Pushing Up the Sky*, Bruchac adapts stories from several tribal traditions. Native stories are popular source material for Theatre for Youth, and Bruchac's anthology offers a collection of stories that retain their tribal specificity. Many children's plays on Native topics generalize across cultures: They may include a handful of characters from several cultures' oral traditions in the same story or create a non-tribally specific trickster character. Bruchac introduces each tribally specific story with a short explanation about the culture, outlining their history and where their homeland is. Each explanation ends with information about who the people are today and avoids historicizing Native people. In the introduction to *The Cannibal Monster*, Bruchac writes, "The Tlingit are still great fishermen to this day and tell many stories of how things came to be. The Tlingit people also continue to make very tall totem poles that tell stories" (67). Such explanations encourage the adults to use the plays as an educational exercise for children/students to learn more about each culture.

Several playwrights have published volumes of their own plays. Cherokee playwright Diane Glancy has two collections in publication. *American Gypsy: Six Native American Plays* (2002) is the most recent; *War Cries* was published in 1997. An accomplished poet, essayist, short story writer, and novelist, Glancy is also one of the most prolific Native playwrights today. Her work often challenges conventional dramatic structure, exploring how storytelling and mythic time, for example, affect scene and dialogue structure. *The Woman Who Was a Red Deer Dressed for the Red Deer Dance* is a short play structured as a conversation between a grandmother and granddaughter punctuated by occasional short monologues. In her introductory notes, Glancy writes,

In this I try. Well, I try. To combine the overlapping realities of myth, imagination, & memory with spaces for the silences. To make a story. The voice speaking
in different agencies. Well, I try to move on with the voice in its guises ... Not
with the linear construct of conflict-resolution, but with story moving like rain
on a windshield. Between differing and unreliable experiences.   (4)

William S. Yellow Robe's (Assiniboine) five-play collection *Where the
Pavement Ends* and E. Donald Two-Rivers's (Anishinabe) *Briefcase
Warriors: Stories for the Stage* both appeared in 2001. Yellow Robe's long
career in the theatre includes working as an actor, director, producer, and
teacher, as well as a playwright, and most recently founding his own company, Wakiknabe, in Albuquerque. Yellow Robe's anthology publishes five
of the more than thirty plays that he has written and seen produced: *The Star
Quilter*, *The Body Guards*, *Rez Politics*, *The Council*, and *Sneaky*. The plays
examine contemporary social issues through honest and realistically
troubled character relationships. *Star Quilter* introduces Mona, a maker of
beautiful star quilts, and Luanne, a white woman who can recognize neither
her exploitation of Mona's talents nor the effects that that has had on Mona
personally. *Rez Politics* examines the effects of internalized racism on children, as it stages an identity tug-of-war between two ten-year-old boys
fighting violently over who is "more Indian."

Two-Rivers's collection contains six plays, many of which were produced
by Chicago's Red Path Theater Company, where Two-Rivers served as
Artistic Director for several years. Some of Two-Rivers's usually comic,
witty plays are decidedly urban in flavor. The one-act *Coyote Sits in
Judgment* opens with a character description that is nothing if not urban:
"A grumpy Coyote addicted to Starbuck's coffee and Whitman poetry. Also
likes to surf the Internet. Sometimes visits the porno pages, but doesn't know
why – there are so many of them. Irrelevant to this tale" (146). Coyote must
decide a court conflict between characters Technology and Business, each
suing the other for environmental destruction. Carrying elements of the
hapless trickster into this tale, Coyote irreverently distracts himself from
serious commentary on the environment to appease his stomach: "Mankind
is violently extracting natural resources faster than they can be replaced. Life
cannot be sustained without limits and moderation. (*Pause.*) Does anybody
have some pizza?" (151).[10]

Scholarship and criticism of American Indian theatre

Theatre Studies is among many academic areas that have capitalized, for
better or worse, on interest in American Indian cultures.[11] In the 1970s,
theatre scholars began asking questions about cultural rituals, identifying

performative patterns in them. At first, scholars were interested in cultures outside of mainstream Euro-America, including Native American cultures. The result was a first wave of Native American theatre scholarship that identified theatrical elements in social and religious ceremonies. One of the most influential of these studies was a dissertation by Linda Walsh Jenkins entitled "The Performances of Native Americans as American Theatre: Reconnaissance and Recommendations."[12]

Like Jenkins's dissertation, some studies of this period did make reference to regular theatre. In Jenkins's case, she included in her final chapter an examination of NATE's work. These studies provided a bridge from American Indian ceremony as object of study to newer developments on the theatrical horizon. In the 1990s, that interest continued, as several graduate students, Native and non-Native, began dissertation projects on Native theatre topics. One of those graduate students, Paul Rathbun, began circulating *The Native Playwrights' Newsletter* (*NPN*) while still completing his doctoral coursework at the University of Wisconsin-Madison. For the first time since the beginning of the movement, a periodical was available that allowed Native artists and others to share information. Each issue of *NPN* carried at least one interview with a Native playwright, often published a script, and also reproduced information about recent performances or shared archival information. Regrettably, *NPN* no longer circulates, and another publication has yet to take its place.

Critical works about Native theatre have also begun to appear. Per Brask and William Morgan collaborated on the text *Aboriginal Voices: Amerindian, Inuit, and Sami Theater* (1992), which contained articles, interviews, and three scripts. The Amerindian work examined in this book is First Nations (Native Canadian) theatre, but some of the articles are useful because the issues they introduce are applicable to Native theatre in the States. Essays in this volume were among the first publications to begin a dialogue about Native theatre within Theatre Studies. They introduce some of the issues that remain central in understanding the production and reception of Native theatre.

Geiogamah and Darby collaborated on a companion volume to *Stories of Our Way*. Geared toward faculty and students, their edited volume *American Indian Theater in Performance: a Reader* (1999) contains articles, interviews, and a resource section that includes a bibliography of critical resources and published plays. Interviews with Geiogamah, Lisa Mayo of Spiderwoman Theatre, Bruce King, and William Yellow Robe, Jr., provide windows into the writers' processes and purposes. Essays by some of these playwrights and by other Native theatre artists further the dialogue, and the text also offers historical and critical readings that provide a framework for understanding the plays' contexts.

Challenges and rewards

These publications present evidence of growing interest in Native theatre, as more playwrights are seeing their work published and more people are reading their work. But in theatre, the frame must be a bit wider than this. Theatre requires not just the playwright, his or her work, and individual readers to be fully realized. Theatre must be *performed* to be truly theatre. To understand the nature of Native theatre today, we need to grapple not just with playwrights and their published work, but – and some would argue more importantly – the production and reception of their plays as live theatre. The picture here is not quite so positive, as Native playwrights' work tends to not be produced as readily as it is published. In a discussion at a conference sponsored by the Native American Women Playwrights' Archive in 1999, JudyLee Oliva (Chickasaw) commented, "It seems to me like everyone wants to print our plays in anthologies, but no one wants to do them … They want to read and they want to study them, but no one wants to do them on stage." Oliva connected this interest in studying and publishing to a broader tendency among non-Native people to study, define, and analyze Native cultures, a tendency that other writers such as Vine Deloria, Jr., have described. Oliva continued, "There is this interest in trying to define [Native theatre] … in that kind of academic way. But there doesn't seem to me to be an equal interest in coming to see our work and experience it."[13] Oliva is not alone in this observation. At gatherings of Native theatre artists, the topic of how to get plays produced inevitably arises.

As artists, Native people face industries – theatre, film, television – in which the expectations of non-Native and some Native artists and audiences have been nurtured by centuries of misrepresentations of Native people and cultures. The nineteenth-century stereotypes popularized on stages translated too easily to the screens of early cinema and then to television. They are still with us today: the Noble Savage, the Red Villain, the Indian Princess, and the Squaw. The artists themselves are often faced with a catch-22: take the role that they find a bit questionable and have work, or refuse the role and not work. Many playwrights comment that they began writing to see realistic portrayals of Native people in the theatre. Métis playwright/actor Marie Humber Clements comments:

> I never really thought of being a "writer," or a playwright, until I started acting, … As a First Nations actor in Canada I found … that I just didn't know the people, the characters. I'd never met any Indian people like that. I didn't want to keep perpetuating stereotypes that as a Native person and as a woman I don't appreciate to see.[14]

As a Native woman, the import is doubled: not only are the characters stereotypical "Indian" figures, but also they are stereotypical "female" figures. Clements describes a parallel situation in film.

> Native women aren't silent. We might be quiet at times, but I'm sure a Native person … would attest to the fact that we don't just point, you know? "Go Big Brave." So, we have big mouths, and we have a good time and laugh a lot. And I never saw that in a lot of scripts[15]

Few of the common Indian roles written by non-Native writers for stage, film, or television represent a contemporary traditional elder, or especially a younger Native man or woman who has a vested interest in the survival of Native traditions. Images of active cultural life are usually historified, and often, even in news programs that intend to present the information objectively, traditions are spoken of in the past tense.

The tide may be turning in the film industry. In the late 1990s, author Sherman Alexie (Spokane / Coeur d'Alene) and director Chris Eyre (Cheyenne / Arapaho) joined forces on a short film adapted from one of Alexie's short stories. It would become "Smoke Signals" – the first major motion picture written, directed, and co-produced by Native artists. A rez road film, *Smoke Signals* follows Victor Joseph and Thomas Builds-the-Fire (played by Adam Beach [Salteaux] and Evan Adams [Coast Salish], respectively), two young men from the Coeur d'Alene Reservation in Idaho, as they venture off the rez bound for Arizona, where Victor hopes to recover the ashes of his recently deceased but long absent father. True to the road film genre, Victor discovers more about himself than he anticipated and comes to terms with his troubled memory of his father.

The film's quirky, less-than-perfect, and therefore highly believable characters are not only a refreshing change from the typical Hollywood Indian fare; they also challenge that Hollywood fare. On the journey, Alexie takes the audience through a quick analysis of Indian representation, as Victor tries to "teach" Thomas how to be Indian, revealing in the process that both characters' ideas of how to be Indian have been affected by misrepresentations. Victor jokingly accuses Thomas of learning to be Indian from *Dances with Wolves* and begins to teach Thomas how to be a "real Indian." Yet Victor's advice to Thomas rolls through several more Hollywood stereotypes, as unreal as the heady spiritualism that Thomas had gleaned from *Dances with Wolves*. "Get stoic," Victor advises. "White people will run all over you if you don't look mean." The good look is the warrior look: "You got to look like you just got back from killing a buffalo." Even when Thomas guilelessly points out that their people were never buffalo hunters, but salmon fishermen, Victor insists on the viability of the stereotype: "What? You want to look like you just came back from catching a fish?" In the subtext of the scene lies the question left to the audience. How exactly do these two young men learn what it means to be "really" an Indian, in a world, even on the reservation, that is replete with misrepresentations and falsehoods? What is a "real Indian?"[16]

Valerie Red Horse's film *Naturally Native* was also released in 1999. While it did not have as wide a national release as *Smoke Signals*, it is as significant as *Smoke Signals* for several reasons. *Naturally Native* tells women's stories, following three Native sisters as they battle to start their own business and regain their tribal identity, lost when they were adopted out of their tribal family to a white home. The film's director, producers, writer, and actors were all Native women – a first for a major film. And finally, *Naturally Native* is the first film to be entirely financed by a Native nation. Red Horse received full support for the project from the Mashantucket Pequot Nation. In an industry where artists often feel that they first must convince backers of the validity of their stories, the turn to tribal financing is hopeful.[17]

Native filmmakers have been making independent films for several decades. "Art" films generally do not reach the same audiences that a major motion picture release might reach, however. This point is not meant to undermine the work of filmmakers such as Victor Masayesva (Hopi), Annie Frazier Henry (Blackfeet / Sioux), Sandra Sunrising Osawa (Makah) and many others, but to clarify that the audiences and conditions are different. Yet with the success of *Smoke Signals* more and more artists are considering film as a vehicle, and producers might be more inclined to back a Native project. In 2003, the Sundance Film Festival's Native Project received 50 percent more submissions than in 2002, 150 submissions for 11 spots in the Festival lineup.[18]

When Native artists take creative control and attempt to create positive or accurate portrayals of themselves, their efforts are sometimes greeted with puzzled wonder. Playwright Bruce King writes,

> Those of us practicing theater constantly confront preconceived notions of what Native American people should perform on stage. Most of the time these notions reinforce what others believe Indians should be – sharing, demonstrating, creating, understanding, quaint, colorful, and, ... safe. If, on the other hand, a story, structured in the play form, deals with an issue that indicts and holds certain individuals or peoples responsible for our contemporary situations, that is not considered native theater. It's called controversial, political, and biased. It is not entertainment.[19]

King's comments describe a condition that many playwrights have noted. In some cases, the concern is over how audiences will receive a Native piece.

In other cases the concern is about how to get Native theatre produced. When the people choosing plays for seasons have preconceived notions about Native theatre, they might not appreciate the Native scripts that land on their desks. When directors have preconceived notions about Native theatre or Native people in general, the quality of the production can be affected. One way that playwrights have tried to circumvent or solve such problems has been to found their own companies, as mentioned previously. Yellow Robe founded the Wakiknabe Theatre Company in Albuquerque after growing disillusioned with the treatment of his plays in regional theatres. Borrowing its name from the Assiniboine word "wakikna," or "we return home," Wakiknabe was conceived as a space where the talents of Native playwrights from many backgrounds could be nurtured and developed.[20]

In addition to theatre companies, some organizations with broader goals have been created in order to foster the growth of Native theatre. In 1994, Illinois State University faculty Randy Reinholz and Jean Bruce Scott created Native Voices: A Festival of Native Plays. The week-long festival brought five Native playwrights to campus to workshop their pieces with directors, dramaturgs, and actors. The 1995 festival repeated the routine, this time with a full production of one of the previous year's workshopped plays, Marie Humber Clements's *Now look what you made me do.* Toronto's Native Earth Performing Arts had held their annual Weesageechak Begins to Dance festival for many years by this time, and Native Voices brought to the US a similar opportunity. Native Voices followed Reinholz and Bruce Scott to the West Coast, where it took residency at the Autry Museum of Western Heritage, albeit in slightly altered form, producing one work at a time though always with the goal of fostering the development of Native playwrights.

In 1996, Miami University of Ohio established the Native American Women Playwrights' Archive (NAWPA), marking the opening with a one-day conference in February of 1997 entitled "Women's Voices in Native American Theatre" and an exhibit of correspondence, photos, posters, programs, reviews, and script fragments donated by Spiderwoman Theater. Miami University representatives hope that the archive can promote both scholarly recognition and professional productions of the plays of Native women. In addition to the standard archival collection of scripts, reviews, programs, audio-visual recordings, and other source documents, the archive maintains a directory of Native women playwrights accessible through a website.

In 1997, Hanay Geiogamah with Jaye T. Darby initiated Project HOOP – Honoring Our Origins and People through Native Theatre, Education, and Community Development. By this time, Geiogamah was a Full Professor in the Theatre Department at UCLA, and Project HOOP was initiated in part through UCLA's American Indian Studies Center. With NATE, Geiogamah had sought in part to bring theatre to reservation communities and to foster the growth of Native theatre companies around the country. Twenty-five years later, Project HOOP continues that effort. It seeks

> ... to establish Native theater as an integrated subject of study and creative development in tribal colleges, Native communities, and all other interested institutions, based on native perspectives, traditions, view of spirituality, histories, cultures, languages, communities, and lands.

Whether working with institutions new to Native theatre, like its first partner Sinte Gleska University (Rosebud Reservation, South Dakota), or with organizations with longer histories like its latest collaborator, Thunderbird Theatre at Haskell Indian Nations University, HOOP's emphasis on curriculum development and training reaps immediate rewards in the young artists emerging into the field. Bringing theatre to communities has its own rewards, as communities begin to use theatre to address their own needs. Following the tornadoes on the Pine Ridge Reservation, for example, Jeff Kellogg, the theatre instructor at Sinte Gleska, hired there through Project HOOP support, worked with elders and children to develop a theatre piece that could help children recover from their fears of the storms. Using traditional stories of the Wakinyan (Thunder Beings) and incorporating traditional dance, Kellogg and community members created a piece that re-embraced the people's connection to the weather, in a medium easily understood and enjoyed by children, that emerged directly out of their cultural heritage.

As playwrights and companies experiment with dramatic form and performance style, they bring their own stories to the stage, making Native theatre one of the most exciting and innovative areas of American theatre. Writing for their own communities, those involved in Native theatre take part in and often lead efforts to retain cultural belief systems and intellectual systems. Occasionally, they launch searing and sometimes comical revisions of Native stereotypes, challenging audiences to rethink their ideas about Native America. From the handful of companies formed in the 1970s, Native theatre has become a multi-faceted movement that promises to continue challenging the limits of western dramaturgy and contributing new energy to the American theatre.

Notes

1. Quoted in Phyllis Cole Braunlich, *Haunted by Home: the Life and Letters of Lynn Riggs*, University of Oklahoma Press, 1988, p. 77.
2. Sally Ann Heath, "The Development of Native American Theatre Companies in the Continental United States," PhD diss., University of Colorado, 1995, pp. 148–59.

3. Interview with Hanay Geiogamah, 14 March 2003.
4. Gretchen M. Bataille, "An Interview with Geraldine Keams," *Explorations in Ethnic Studies* 10.1 (January 1987), pp. 1–7.
5. Clive Barnes, "Stage: the American Indian Theater Ensemble," *The New York Times*, (30 October 1972), n.p., Spiderwoman Theatre Collection. Native American Women Playwrights' Archive. Miami University King Library.
6. See Elizabeth Cook-Lynn's rejoinder in *Why I Can't Read Wallace Stegner and Other Essays: a Tribal Voice*, Madison: University of Wisconsin Press, 1996, to Michael Dorris's exposé on alcoholism among Indian women of child-bearing age in *The Broken Cord*, Scranton, PA: Perennial, 1992.
7. Jeffrey F. Huntsman, Introduction, *New Native American Drama:Three Plays*, Norman: University of Oklahoma Press, 1980, p. xiv.
8. Printed in *Women in American Theatre*, eds. Helen Krich Chinoy and Linda Walsh Jenkins, 1981, New York: Theatre Communications Group, 1987, pp. 303–04.
9. Drew Hayden Taylor, "Alive and Well: Native Theatre in Canada," *American Indian Theater in Performance: a Reader*, eds. Hanay Geiogamah and Jaye T. Darby, Los Angeles: UCLA American Indian Studies Center Press, 2000, pp. 256–64.
10. For more complete lists of plays in publication, see my "Contemporary Native Theater: Bibliography and Resource Materials," in Hanay Geiogamah and Jaye T. Darby, eds., *American Indian Theater in Performance: a Reader*, UCLA: American Indian Studies Center Press, 2000, pp. 367–90, and "Published Plays by Native Women Playwrights in the United States and Canada" in eds. Jaye T. Darby and Stephanie Fitzgerald, eds., *Keepers of the Morning Star: an Anthology of Native Women's Theater*, UCLA: American Indian Studies Center Press, 2002, pp. 375–78.
11. For a detailed discussion of the critiques made of scholarship on Native cultures, see David Murray's essay in this volume. The articles in Devon Mihesuah's *Natives and Academics: Researching and Writing about American Indians*, University of Nebraska Press, 1998, offer a solid foundation in the controversies.
12. Linda Carol Walsh Jenkins, "The Performance of Native Americans as American Theatre: Reconnaissance and Recommendations." PhD diss., University of Minnesota, 1975.
13. "Authors' Roundtable Discussion," *Native American Women Playwrights' Archive*, 19 March 1999, http://staff.lib.muohio.edu/nawpa/roundtable.html.
14. *Native Playwrights' Newsletter* 7 (Spring 1995) p. 80
15. Ibid.
16. Sherman Alexie, *Smoke Signals: A Screenplay*. Hyperion, 1998, pp. 62–63.
17. "About the Production," *Naturally Native*, http://www.naturallynative.com/fframe.html, 14 November 2002.
18. Reed Martin, "Native American Films Attempt to Cross Over," *USA Today*, 27 January 2003 (http://www.usatoday.com/life/movies/2003-01-27-native-usat_x.htm, accessed 29 July 2003).
19. "Emergence and Discovery: Native American Theater Comes of Age," *American Indian Theater in Performance: a Reader*, UCLA: American Indian Studies Center Press, 2000, p. 167.
20. "The Wakiknabe Theatre Company," *American Theater Web* http://www. americantheaterweb.com/TheaterDetail.asp?ID = 1486, 15 September 2003.

Major secondary sources

Brask, Per, and William Morgan, eds., *Aboriginal Voices: Amerindian, Inuit, and Sami Theater*. Baltimore: Johns Hopkins University Press, 1992.

Canadian Theatre Review 68 (Fall 1991). (Special issue on Native theatre.)

Geiogamah, Hanay, and Jaye T. Darby, eds., *American Indian Theater in Performance: a Reader*. Los Angeles: University of California, Los Angeles Press, 2000.

Huntsman, Jeffrey F., "Native American Theatre," In eds. Maxine Schwartz Seller, *Ethnic Theatre in the United States*. Westport, CT: Greenwood Press, 1983, pp. 355–86.

Johnson, Sue M., "Hanay Geiogamah," in Kenneth M. Roemer, ed., *Native American Writers of the United States*, Detroit: Gale, 1997, pp. 101–4.

Theobald, Elizabeth, "Beyond the Images: Native Voices and Visions in New York Theater." *Akwe:kon Journal: Native American Expressive Culture* 11 (3–4) (Fall/Winter 1994), pp. 160–64.

PART III
INDIVIDUAL AUTHORS

10

CHADWICK ALLEN

N. Scott Momaday: becoming the bear

Beginning in the mid-1960s and throughout the 1970s, a new generation of American Indian writers surprised the mainstream literary establishment by publishing an unprecedented range of innovative poetry, autobiography, fiction, non-fiction, journalism, and mixed-genre works of undeniably high quality. Neither "American literature" nor "American Indian literature" would ever mean quite what they had in the past, and the assumed distinctions between these categories – written vs. oral or transcribed, sophisticated vs. primitive, familiar vs. exotic – were increasingly questioned by gifted and diverse Indian writers who not only published in all genres but, importantly, began to produce their own body of relevant scholarship. Although many individuals participated in this explosion of Native writing, it is the Kiowa and Cherokee author N. Scott Momaday who is credited with inaugurating this period as the beginning of a contemporary "renaissance" for American Indian literature.

Momaday's reputation was secured in 1969, when his provocative debut novel, *House Made of Dawn* (1968), won the Pulitzer Prize for fiction and captured the attention of critics. For the first time, the dominant culture in the United States formally acknowledged that twentieth-century American Indians could produce a written literature that was intellectually demanding and "serious." Early critics noted the novel's sophisticated techniques of narration and they were intrigued by the novel's depiction of social alienation in its Indian protagonist and his desperate need to recover a viable identity within his community. These themes resonated with non-Indian audiences of the time, and they could be labeled as "modern" and "universal" rather than exclusively "Indian." The novel's striking ambiguities, however, are clearly anchored in its Native contexts, and the difficulty of resolving these ambiguities has insured a steady stream of response by two generations of readers and scholars. This critical work has focused on clarifying the functions of the novel's cyclical narrative structure and complex sets of flashbacks; and it has worked to explicate the novel's complicated imagery, which integrates Navajo, Jemez Pueblo, Kiowa, and Euro-American symbolic traditions into a dense matrix of associations and allusions.

Momaday's position in the so-called American Indian literary renaissance is also the result of timing and circumstance. The first decade of his publishing career, between 1967 and 1976, coincided with dramatic events of Indian political activism and a period of increased attention to American Indian issues in the popular press. Inevitably, after winning the Pulitzer Prize, Momaday was looked to as a spokesperson for all of Native America, whether or not he embraced that role. Commentators have noted that Momaday's major works from this period do not carry overtly activist messages and that in most published interviews Momaday has refused the label of political activist. Nonetheless, his writing participated in 1960s and 1970s activism by providing emblematic representations of Indian identities that challenge the simplistic stereotypes of Indians as either frozen in the nineteenth century or completely severed from their indigenous cultures. For Native audiences, especially, Momaday's writing affirmed a vital and contemporary indigenous identity that is both *multi-tribal* – in Momaday's case, drawing predominantly from Kiowa, Navajo, and Jemez Pueblo traditions – and *multicultural* – drawing not only from Native sources but also from European and Euro-American sources. In this way, his work reflects the mixed and often multiply hybrid experiences of American Indians in the post-World War II era. At the same time, Momaday investigates a set of core questions about his specific tribal identity as Kiowa. Like other Indians of his generation, in the 1960s and 1970s he felt compelled to learn all that he could of and from his elders and ancestors, who represented the fragile link to the Kiowa past. Moreover, he has dedicated over three decades of his working life to the contemplation of his personal stake in the oral, pictographic, and written narratives that are his familial and tribal inheritance and that articulate his potential relationships to specific lands.

Momaday's Kiowa father grew up securely in his Native culture and speaking his Native language. Momaday's mother, who was of mixed Scottish, French, and Cherokee descent, was raised within the dominant culture, but she decided, as a young woman, to actively reclaim her Indian identity. Momaday writes in his memoir *The Names* (1976) that his mother's example of reimagining herself as an Indian greatly influenced his own sense of self and his conviction that all of us discover our most essential being and identity in acts of the imagination. Momaday spent his own formative years moving between the Kiowa country of his father's native western Oklahoma, where Momaday was born in 1934, and Indian reservations located in Arizona and New Mexico. During his childhood and adolescence, Momaday's parents, both of whom had earned college degrees, worked as teachers in several communities on the Navajo reservation (between 1936 and 1943) and at Jemez Pueblo (beginning in 1946); after graduating with a BA in political science from the University of New Mexico in 1958, Momaday himself worked for a year as a teacher on the Jicarilla Apache reservation. Matthias Schubnell argues in his excellent biographical work *N. Scott Momaday: the Cultural and Literary Background* (1985) that, contrary to the negative images of Indians "caught between two worlds," Momaday appears to have benefited from his multi-tribal and multicultural upbringing. He was exposed to his particular Native heritage as well as to other Indian cultures and languages, but his parents also emphasized their strong belief in the importance of a broad education that included literature and the arts. His father, Al Momaday, was a well-known Kiowa visual artist; his mother, Natachee Scott Momaday, published short stories and three books of her own. Encouraged by family and friends, who felt he had a gift for writing, Momaday pursued graduate study in California. Under the guidance of the poet Yvor Winters, who became Momaday's principal mentor, Momaday completed a Master's degree in creative writing at Stanford University in 1960, and then earned a PhD in literature in 1963. Since the mid-1960s, as he developed his body of creative work in all genres, Momaday has held professorships at several major universities, including Stanford University, where he has taught courses on both American and American Indian written literatures and on the oral tradition. Currently, he is Regent's Professor at the University of Arizona.

Momaday's literary accomplishments include two novels, *House Made of Dawn* (1968) and *The Ancient Child* (1989); several collections of poetry, *Angle of Geese and Other Poems* (1974), *The Gourd Dancer* (1976), *In the Presence of the Sun: Stories and Poems, 1961–1991* (1992), and *In the Bear's House* (1999); a memoir, *The Names* (1976); a mixed-genre work that combines memoir with transcribed stories from the Kiowa oral tradition and historical accounts of the Kiowa, *The Way to Rainy Mountain* (1969, with illustrations by Al Momaday); a book for children, *Circle of Wonder: a Native American Christmas Story* (1994); and a large number of personal, persuasive, and critical essays, thirty-eight of which are collected together as *The Man Made of Words: Essays, Stories, Passages* (1997). Momaday's most famous essay, also titled "The Man Made of Words," is included in the book *Indian Voices: the First Convocation of American Indian Scholars* (1970) and has been reprinted in numerous anthologies. In the mid-1970s, following in his father's footsteps, Momaday began to work in the visual arts. Early examples of his drawings illustrate his 1976 memoir and 1976 collection of poems; in more recent works, Momaday has increasingly integrated drawings and paintings with his written texts.

Other works by Momaday are less readily available than those listed above. These include a scholarly edition, *The Complete Poems of Frederick Goddard Tuckerman* (1965); an early collection of transcribed Kiowa oral narratives, *The Journey of Tai-me* (1967), which was a precursor to *The Way to Rainy Mountain*; the book *Colorado: Summer, Fall, Winter, Spring* (1973, with photographs by David Muench); and the series of weekly newspaper columns Momaday wrote for *Viva: Northern New Mexico's Sunday Magazine* between April 1972 and December 1973. Momaday has also written a play, *The Indolent Boys* (first performed in 1994), and he co-wrote the screenplay for a film version of *House Made of Dawn* (1996, with Richardson Morse).

Scholarship on Momaday's work has tended to focus on one or more of his early major texts, rather than on the persistent ideas, symbols, and themes that repeat and develop across the entire body of Momaday's literary and artistic production. Understandably, Momaday's highly complex and Pulitzer Prize winning first novel has generated the greatest volume and widest range of critical responses. *House Made of Dawn*, which takes its title from the language of Navajo ceremonial, is most often described as a novel about spiritual and psychological illness and the process of healing. Abel, the novel's protagonist, is ill because he is separated from his community at Jemez Pueblo in northern New Mexico (which Momaday refers to by its local name, Walatowa) and because he is alienated from the land that gives his community its identity.

The brief Prologue is actually the end of the novel, and its scene of Abel running in the dawn is suggestive of his eventual healing. As is often the case in the oral tradition, the audience is aware of the ending before the story begins; what is important is the telling itself. Part 1 is set in 1945, when Abel returns from military service in World War II. As the novel progresses, readers learn that Abel's traumatic experience of a foreign war is only one aspect of his alienation from his people. In a series of flashbacks to his childhood, we learn that Abel never knew the identity of his father and that he lost his mother and brother to early death, leaving him with only his grandfather as a link to family and community; that Abel violated local spiritual traditions by killing an eagle; and that he was cursed by a witch. Abel's alienation continues in his post-war experiences at Jemez, culminating in his ritualized murder of an albino Indian. Parts 2 and 3 of the novel are set seven years later, in 1952, after Abel has served time in prison and has been relocated to Los Angeles. He experiences further alienation and violence in California, but with the help of his Navajo friend Ben, he also begins his process of healing. In Part 4, also set in 1952, Abel returns to Jemez, where he attends to his dying grandfather and begins his own rebirth.

While most readers have appreciated the beauty of the novel's poetic prose and the provocative strangeness of its settings and themes, many have found its fragmented plot difficult to follow and its multicultural and multi-tribal symbolism difficult to grasp fully. Critics have stressed two concepts at work in Momaday's novel that are central to American Indian cultural traditions: a communal understanding of human relationships to land and a high regard for the power of language. Landscape functions in *House Made of Dawn* not only as setting, but also as an essential character; and, as Robert Nelson argues, Abel's identity ultimately derives *from* the land itself.[1] Momaday opens and closes the novel with formulaic words spoken at Jemez Pueblo to begin and end formal storytelling, placing his contemporary written narrative within the conventions of the oral tradition. Other markers of orality are the novel's circular structure and its development by parallelism and repetition of characters and scenes.

The cyclical nature of the novel's overall structure is readily apparent – the narrative begins where it ends, with the ceremonial running at Jemez. Its organization as a ritual journey, however, is more subtle and requires specialized knowledge to fully elucidate. Attentive readers notice, for instance, the recurrence of the number four (the novel is divided into four major parts, and, as part of Abel's healing process, four characters tell significant stories about bears and bear power from four cultural perspectives) as well as several significant "pairs" or sets of "twins" (most notably Abel and his brother Vidal in the flashbacks to their childhood at Jemez, and Abel and Ben in contemporary Los Angeles, but also the snake-like albino at Jemez and the "culebra"/snake Martinez in Los Angeles). Four is associated with the sacred in many American Indian traditions and indicates balance, completion, and harmony; twinning is also an important Native concept, and many oral traditions, including Navajo, Pueblo, and Kiowa, figure their primary culture heroes as twins. More precisely, Susan Scarberry-Garcia demonstrates, the plot of *House Made of Dawn* mimics Navajo chantways or healing ceremonials in its general movement from discord to harmony (or, following a Navajo conception of disease, from the damaging fragmentation of Abel's sense of self to its positive reassemblage) as well as in many of its specific details.[2] Lawrence Evers points out, further, that the plot of the novel mimics both Kiowa and Navajo storytelling traditions in its patterning as a journey of re-emergence.[3]

Although Abel, his illness, and his ritual healing are the unifying force of *House Made of Dawn*, the novel also can be read as driven by an ensemble of central Indian characters rather than by a single protagonist. Key passages in the Los Angeles sections are narrated from the perspectives of Ben Benally, a Navajo, and John Big Bluff Tosamah, a Kiowa. Their voices broaden the novel's representation of post-war Indian experience: Ben, who displays attributes of a traditional healer, is in many ways still naive about the realities of living in the dominant culture, while Tosamah, who is an intellectual, a peyote priest, and something of a trickster, is overly cynical.

All three characters, Abel, Ben, and Tosamah, narrate memories of a grandparent figure who is central to their sense of Indian identity. The bond between grandparent and grandchild becomes a running theme in the novel, emblematic of the increasingly tenuous link between generations that are separated not only by time but also by dramatic demographic and socio-cultural changes, including those specific changes brought by World War II and the era of Indian Relocation that followed in its immediate aftermath. Surprisingly, memories of these grandparent figures reveal not a static indigenous past but rather a long history of indigenous change and adaptation. Abel's grandfather Francisco recalls the story of his Bahkyush ancestors, immigrants who integrated themselves into Jemez Pueblo after the decimation of their own community, while Tosamah's grandmother recalls the migration of her ancestors from the mountain wilderness in what is now Montana down into the southern plains and, along the way, the complete cultural and spiritual transformation of the Kiowa. The bond between grandparent and grandchild thus recalls the power of change as well as the power of tradition and continuity. Ben's memories of his grandfather recall the Navajo Night Chant, a healing ceremonial, which is also a narrative of transformation and continuance. This theme of memory enabling a persistent bond between indigenous ancestors and contemporary American Indians also can be traced in Momaday's mixed-genre work *The Way to Rainy Mountain* (1969), his memoir *The Names* (1976), and his second novel *The Ancient Child* (1989).

From the vantage point of the new century, we can trace a number of persistent connections among Momaday's works in all genres over the more than thirty-year period of his publishing career. A striking feature of Momaday's work as a whole is its multiple representations of specific characters, landscapes, stories, and concepts. One of these is an attention to issues of environmentalism and a consistent call for Americans to develop a contemporary "land ethic" that is environmentally sound and spiritually meaningful. Another is Momaday's signature phrase "blood memory" or "memory in the blood," which appears in all of his major texts. Momaday's provocative juxtaposition of "blood" and "memory" is highly suggestive, foremost, as an activist response to the federal government's attempts since 1887 to quantify Indian identity through a fractional system of "blood quantum" or "degree of Indian blood." A system of racial identification, blood quantum requirements, have enabled the US government to limit the number of individuals and communities who are eligible for federal Indian services and, historically, to facilitate the large-scale expropriation of Indian land. In response, Momaday's "blood memory" asserts the power of Native oral traditions to instill vital and distinctive cultural knowledge into contemporary individuals, whatever their official status.

Perhaps the most compelling autobiographical strand that runs through all of Momaday's work is an ongoing negotiation of his personal relationship to sacred geography. In his essay "A First American Views His Land" (1976), Momaday describes the acts of imagination through which one might "invest" oneself in a particular landscape and at the same time "incorporate" that landscape into one's "fundamental experience" and thus into one's sense of self. For Momaday, this relationship proceeds from "ethical imperatives" he sees operating in American Indian worldviews, including a sense that the earth is "vital" and possesses a "spiritual dimension."[4] Further, according to Momaday, as an American Indian, these processes for establishing a meaningful place-identity involve a generational perception of American landscapes, preserved in what he calls the "racial memory," passed down in the oral tradition. Memories of ancestors and their stories become vehicles for connecting Momaday to particular landscapes and their dense histories; in turn, landscapes "cured in blood" become vehicles for connecting Momaday to ancestors and their authenticating stories. Ultimately, Momaday says that he is interested in how individuals and peoples – specifically, himself and other American Indians, but potentially all of us – can be "translated" into landscape through processes of imaginative investment and appropriation (36).

Strikingly, Momaday's discussion of place-identity here and elsewhere is focused *not* on an individual's or a people's inherent racial or even cultural qualities, but rather on what he calls "acts of the imagination." Repeating a line from his celebrated essay "The Man Made of Words" (1970), Momaday asserts, "We are what we imagine ... The Native American is someone who thinks of himself, imagines himself in a particular way" (39). He continues, "By virtue of his experience, his idea of himself comprehends his relationship to the land." What *is* affected by the individual's "racial and cultural experience," Momaday argues, is the "quality of this imagining" (39). Momaday's ideas on this topic have made some readers uncomfortable, for he argues that it is American Indians' long tenure in the land and, importantly, their ongoing narratives of that long tenure in the land, that distinguishes their imaginative and spiritual relationships to the American soil and thus their sense of place-identity. Theirs is, Momaday writes, "a perception that is acquired only in the course of many generations" (38). In a related essay, titled "Sacred Places" (1993), Momaday refines this view further by arguing that "Sacred ground is in some way earned. It is consecrated, made holy with offerings – song and ceremony, joy and sorrow, the dedication of the mind and heart, offerings of life and death."[5]

Reading across Momaday's texts, we encounter numerous attempts to "earn" a place-identity as a contemporary Kiowa. One example is Momaday's multiple inscriptions of his relationship to ceremonial grounds near Carnegie, Oklahoma that are used by the Kiowa gourd dancers. Momaday's grandfather, Mammedaty, was honored in a ritual giveaway during a gourd dance held at these grounds in 1919, when Momaday's father was a small boy. Remembering his father's stories of that auspicious event is central to Momaday's poems "The Gourd Dancer" (1976) and "Carnegie, Oklahoma, 1919" (1992); that memory also figures significantly in his memoir *The Names* (1976) and in his essay "Sacred Places" (1993). Read together, these four versions demonstrate Momaday's method for incorporating his father's memory into his own, and they show how that incorporated memory "translates" him into a particular sacred landscape. Momaday imagines himself into the story of how his grandfather was honored on the "red earth" of the gourd-dancing grounds by focusing his attention, in particular, on two details: first, that his father was a young boy when he witnessed the giveaway ceremony and, second, that another young Kiowa boy was in charge of presenting the gift – a beautiful horse – to his grandfather. In retelling his father's memories, Momaday imagines himself as both boys, as a key witness and as a vital participant. These shifts in narrative perspective enable Momaday to effect a collapse of distance in time and space. The concluding lines of his 1992 poem present this collapse in the apparent paradox of "not here"/"am here," in which the repeated term, "here," denotes both space and time: "and I am not here [at the sacred grounds in 1919] / but, grandfather, father, I am here."[6] Momaday's 1993 essay states the same theme more directly: "The brilliant image of that moment [of the giveaway] remained in my father's mind all his life, as it remains in mine. It is a thing that related him and relates me to the sacred earth" (113).

Another prominent example of these acts of translation is Momaday's multiple inscriptions of his personal, familial, and larger cultural relationships to the monolith Tsoai, the "Rock Tree," also known as Devils Tower, which is located in northeastern Wyoming. Momaday's evolving textual relationship with Tsoai can be traced across four of his major works, which span the thirty-year period of his career. The titles of these works indicate the trajectory of Momaday's representations of his relationship to Tsoai and the monolith's role in forming his sense of self in relation to the Kiowa landscape. *The Way to Rainy Mountain* (1969) emphasizes

Momaday's attempt to situate himself within the larger story of the Kiowa people's historic migration out of the mountains and down into the plains and the resulting transformation of their culture and sense of who they were – and are – as a community.[7] In contrast, *The Names* (1976) emphasizes Momaday's attempts to situate himself within narratives of his particular family's genealogies. Although it is a work of fiction, *The Ancient Child* (1989), with its powerful oxymoron, emphasizes Momaday's attempts to synthesize the historic and the communual with the contemporary and the individual. And finally, *In the Bear's House* (1999), with its implicit reference to Tsoai, asserts the achievement of that hard-won synthesis.

One of the projects of *The Way to Rainy Mountain* is to recount Momaday's physical pilgrimage across the Kiowa's ancestral landscape, his retracing of their migration route from the Yellowstone down into western Oklahoma. That route passes by the monolith Tsoai. Momaday asserts that, struck by the awesome strangeness of Devils Tower, "because they could not do otherwise, the Kiowas made a legend at the base of the rock."[8] To convey his own sense of awe at seeing the Rock Tree during his contemporary journey, Momaday recalls and retells a version of the Kiowa story of the monolith's creation, the story of a boy who transformed into a bear and his seven sisters who became the stars of the Big Dipper. Significantly, he tells that story not in his own contemporary voice but in the remembered voice of his Kiowa grandmother, Aho. Momaday offers limited commentary on the story itself. He writes, "From that moment, and so long as the legend lives, the Kiowa have kinsmen in the night sky" (8). In the act of retelling the story in his own text, Momaday aligns his voice with the voice of his ancestors, affirms his identity as Kiowa, and reaffirms the connection to sacred landscape entailed in that identity. The alignment of his own voice with the voice of his grandmother is particularly interesting: Momaday embeds an oral narrative within his written text, marked off by italics to indicate its difference, and he shifts his narrative perspective to that of an elder, who represents connection to the Kiowa past. The framing of the inner narrative, however, is that it represents a *memory* of the grandmother's storytelling. The italicized narrative is not a quotation from the past but, similar to his versions of the story of how his grandfather was honored during the giveaway, a contemporary act of Momaday's imagination. In the representation of encounter with sacred geography, Momaday incorporates the voice of the ancestor and the significant past that voice represents. Momaday's own voice continues to speak, but his narrative perspective shifts to a different temporal dimension and to a different register of authority.

In his powerful memoir *The Names*, Momaday adds depth to his account of his relationship to Tsoai. Here he reveals an earlier childhood encounter with the monolith that reframes the adult encounter he describes in *The Way to Rainy Mountain* and gives it additional meaning as a return to the site of multiple origins. He writes, "When I was six months old my parents took me to Devils Tower, Wyoming, which is called in Kiowa Tsoai, 'rock tree.' Here are stories within stories; I want to imagine a day in the life of a man, Pohd-lohk, who gave me a name."[9] Momaday then again retells the story of Tsoai's creation, but now in the imagined voice of his great-grandmother, Keahdinekeah, aligning his contemporary voice with an even older Kiowa voice than in *Rainy Mountain*. After this retelling, through his great-grandmother's imagined thoughts, Momaday reveals the significance of his parents' decision to take him to visit Tsoai: "And her grandson Huan-toa [Momaday's father] had taken his child to be in Tsoai's presence even before the child could understand what it was, so that by means of the child the memory of Tsoai should be renewed in the blood of the coming-out people [the Kiowa]" (55). One of Momaday's Kiowa names, Tsoai-talee, "Rock-tree Boy," given to him by the elder Pohd-lohk to commemorate the journey, binds him to landscape significant in the Kiowa memory and to the stories associated with that landscape. In contrast to *Rainy Mountain*, where Momaday uses an encounter with Tsoai to assert the Kiowa's relationship to sacred geography as a community, here Momaday uses the encounter with sacred geography to assert a defining aspect of his personal identity. In Momaday's imagined account of the naming ceremony, the authenticating Kiowa elder, who represents the link to the past, positions the boy and his contemporary encounter with Tsoai within a larger tradition of Kiowa narratives stretching back to the period of creation. Both the recent event and the newly named boy, Tsoai-talee, are made integral parts of this ongoing Kiowa narrative of defining themselves as a people in the American landscape. Finally, Momaday writes, "Pohd-lohk affirmed the whole life of the child in a name, saying: Now you are, Tsoai-talee" (57). This formula for identity, which equates the self with the auspicious name, underpins the entire project of the memoir, and it helps to explain the meaning of the Cartesian-sounding formula that opens the book: "My name is Tsoai-talee. I am, therefore, Tsoai-talee; therefore I am" (n.p.).

On the very last page of *The Names*, Momaday tells part of the story of his adult encounter with Tsoai that is left out of his account in *Rainy Mountain*, his interpretation of his response – in other words, the reason he responded with storytelling. "This strange thing," he writes, "this Tsoai, I saw with my own eyes and with the eyes of my own mind" (167). It is the act of the imagination – seeing with the mind – that gives the landscape its communal and personal significance. But this act of imagination is no flight of idiosyncratic fancy. Rather, it is the far more difficult act of entering into a highly developed system of narratives that are inextricably tied to a particular landscape that has itself been made sacred by a particular community.

Momaday's second novel, *The Ancient Child*, has been described as both semi-autobiographical and as an exercise in myth making. Like Momaday, the novel's protagonist is part-Kiowa and a successful artist, and he is related to the story of Tsoai and the boy who transformed into a bear through a personal name: Set, which translates from Kiowa as "bear." Like Abel in Momaday's first novel *House Made of Dawn*, Set is alienated from his family, tribal community, and ancestral land. Adopted into a white family as a child, he has grown up with only a vague sense of his identity as a Kiowa or American Indian. The novel charts his difficult discovery of these identities. Like Abel, Set is assisted in his ritual journey of healing by several helpers, most prominently by Grey, a young Kiowa and Navajo medicine woman who eventually becomes his wife. The novel ends with a climactic scene of transformation. During a pilgrimage to Tsoai, Set has a vision in which he becomes the bear in the Kiowa story of the monolith's creation.

The novel does not end with this powerful vision, however. In an italicized epilogue, Momaday retells another "traditional" Kiowa story to suggest in yet more detail the role the imagination plays in the relationship between sacred landscape and personal identity. Momaday writes: "Koi-ehm-toya's great-great-grandson became a renowned maker of shields. He never saw Tsoai, but he knew Tsoai in himself, its definition in his mind's eye, its powerful silence in the current of his blood."[10] This is perhaps the clearest example of Momaday's attempt, in all three texts, to create a narrative perspective that is transgenerational, both contemporary and ancient, what we might call the "self-in-genealogy" or, more broadly, the "self-in-narrative." For Momaday, what makes such a narrative perspective viable is not simply the land itself but, more importantly, the story of the human relationship to sacred geography. As Momaday presents it for the Kiowa, that story is both communal and transhistorical.

Finally, in his introduction to *In the Bear's House*, his collection of poems, passages, and paintings that center on the figure of the bear and on bear power, Momaday writes, "Bear and I are one, in one and the same story. My Indian name is *Tsoai-talee*, which in Kiowa means 'Rock-tree boy.' *Tsoai*, 'Rock tree,' is Devils Tower in Wyoming. That is where, long ago, a Kiowa boy turned into a bear and where his sisters were borne into the sky and became the stars of the Big Dipper. Through the power of stories and names, I am the reincarnation of that boy."[11] Such a bold statement may strike readers who are unfamiliar with Momaday's earlier works as odd, pretentious, or overly mystical. Situated in the context of Momaday's other publications, however, this statement represents the culmination of a more than thirty-year exploration of his personal, familial, and communal relationships to American Indian sacred geographies and oral traditions. And as in many Native traditions of storytelling and ritual, his bold assertion of identity with the bear is simultaneously serious and playful. Unlike in the previous examples, here Momaday speaks in his own contemporary voice, rather than in the ancestral voice of a specific elder or the Kiowa oral tradition. Read as the culmination of Momaday's exploration of his relationship to Kiowa sacred geography, that is, as a compressed statement of the project begun in *The Way to Rainy Mountain*, *The Names*, and *The Ancient Child*, Momaday's statement can be seen not as a mystification of contemporary American Indian identity (as some critics have suggested) but as a humble statement that subsumes the story of the particular self within the story of the community. In other words, Momaday's seemingly odd and mystical statement is actually highly conservative: it represents the contemporary self as a continuation of ancestral traditions.

Momaday's emphasis on the enduring connection between indigenous ancestors and contemporary American Indians, despite change, is indicative of the activist potential of his work, and Momaday has influenced at least two generations of Indian writers in this regard. More than winning the Pulitzer Prize, Momaday's most important contribution to an American Indian renaissance has been this example of fusing politically charged representations of vital indigenous identities with writing in all genres that is of undeniably high aesthetic quality. During his literary journey of becoming the bear, Momaday's models have helped other American Indians to represent the complexity and seeming contradictions of their contemporary lives fully and well.

Notes

1. Robert Nelson, "The Function of Landscape in *House Made of Dawn*," *Place and Vision: the Function of Landscape in Native American Fiction*, New York: Peter Lang, 1993, pp. 41–89.
2. Susan Scarberry-Garcia, *Landmarks of Healing: a Study of "House Made of Dawn*," Albuquerque: University of New Mexico Press, 1990.
3. Lawrence Evers, "Words and Place: a Reading of *House Made of Dawn*," 1977, rpt. in Richard F. Fleck, ed., *Critical Perspectives on Native American Fiction*, Washington, DC: Three Continents Press, 1993, pp. 114–33.
4. N. Scott Momaday, "A First American Views His Land," 1976, rpt. in *The Man Made of Words: Essays, Stories, Passages*, New York: St. Martin's, 1997, p. 39. Further references appear in parentheses in the text.
5. N. Scott Momaday, "Sacred Places," 1993, rpt. in *The Man Made of Words: Essays, Stories, Passages*, New York: St. Martin's, 1997, p. 114. Further references appear in parentheses in the text.

6. N. Scott Momaday, "Carnegie, Oklahoma, 1919, " *In The Presence of the Sun: Stories and Poems, 1961–1991*, New York: St. Martin's, 1992, p. 136.
7. The Introduction to *Rainy Mountain* repeats Tosamah's speech about his Kiowa grandmother from *House Made of Dawn*, New York: Harper and Row, 1968. The story first appeared as a separate essay titled "The Way to Rainy Mountain" in *The Reporter* 26 January 1967, pp. 41–43.
8. N. Scott Momaday, *The Way to Rainy Mountain*, Albuquerque: University of New Mexico Press, 1969, p. 8. Further references appear in parentheses in the text.
9. N. Scott Momaday, *The Names: a Memoir*, New York: Harper and Row, 1976, p. 42. Further references appear in parentheses in the text.
10. N. Scott Momaday, *The Ancient Child*, New York: Doubleday, 1989, p. 315.
11. N. Scott Momaday, *In The Bear's House*, New York: St. Martin's, 1999, p. 9.

Major secondary sources

Allen, Chadwick, "Blood (and) Memory," *American Literature* 71.1 (March 1999), pp. 93–116.

Evers, Lawrence, "Words and Place: a Reading of *House Made of Dawn*," 1977. Rpt. in Richard F. Fleck, ed., *Critical Perspectives on Native American Fiction*. Washington, DC: Three Continents Press, 1993, pp. 114–33.

Nelson, Robert, "The Function of Landscape in *House Made of Dawn*," in *Place and Vision: the Function of Landscape in Native American Fiction*. New York: Peter Lang, 1993, pp. 41–89.

Owens, Louis, "Acts of Imagination: the Novels of N. Scott Momaday," in *Other Destinies: Understanding the American Indian Novel*. Norman: University of Oklahoma Press, 1992, pp. 90–127.

Roemer, Kenneth M., "Ancient Children at Play – Lyric, Petroglyphic, and Ceremonial," in Richard F. Fleck, ed., *Critical Perspectives on Native American Fiction*. Washington, DC: Three Continents Press, 1993, pp. 99–113.

Roemer, Kenneth M., ed., *Approaches to Teaching Momaday's "The Way to Rainy Mountain."* New York: Modern Language Association, 1988.

Scarberry-Garcia, Susan, *Landmarks of Healing: a Study of "House Made of Dawn."* Albuquerque: University of New Mexico Press, 1990.

Schubnell, Matthias, *N. Scott Momaday: the Cultural and Literary Background*. Norman: University of Oklahoma Press, 1985.

11

PATRICIA CLARK SMITH

Simon Ortiz: writing home

Simon Joseph Ortiz, born in 1941 and raised for the most part near his home pueblo of Acoma, New Mexico, is an internationally known Native American poet, short-story writer, essayist, editor, social activist, and educator. In all these roles, he is a teacher, an elder.

Ortiz's parents were both fluent in English, but his first language was the Keres spoken at Acoma and several other New Mexican pueblos. Some of his poetry follows Keresan oral tradition, incorporating song, chant, and storytelling structures – a good source to consult on this is Robin Riley Fast's chapter "Telling Stories" in *The Heart as a Drum* (1999). Even though Ortiz recounts many old-time stories and songs, and is a lyric poet of the natural world, he is at the same time a realistic chronicler of the recent history of ordinary people, Indian and Non-Indian alike, living on and off reservations, and their struggles concerning labor, health, environment, class, race, and the politics that often pass them by. He reproduces flawlessly the rhythms and nuances of talk overheard around the United States in bus depots, bars, street corners, rehab centers, and other deeply American locales. As he says,

> ... the language of our struggle
> just sounds and reads like an Indian,
> Okie, Cajun, Black, Mexican hero story—
> (*Fight Back* in *Woven Stone*, 328–29)[1]

Ortiz has many stories, but as he writes in *A Good Journey* (1977), his second full-length book of poems, his home is the source of his narratives. Though most readers find his work accessible, it may help to know something about Acoma Pueblo's history and environs. Old Acoma Pueblo, nicknamed by Anglo tourism promoters "Sky City," is a town of two- and three-story stone and mortar houses built atop a pale 350-foot mesa. It rises from a high desert plain strewn with smaller monolithic formations. Archeologists date Acoma back at least to the thirteenth century, making it probably the oldest continuously inhabited site in the United States, but the people them-selves date their presence there further back than that.

In the old days, most Acomas lived atop the mesa for protection from enemies, descending to the fields below to farm, tend their livestock, and haul water. Today only a few families take turns dwelling in the old village year-round, as a ceremonial obligation. By the tribe's choice, at Old Acoma there is no running water and no electricity except from a generator. The majority of people live on the plain below in the small communities of Acomita and McCartys, which have utilities; McCartys is the village where Ortiz himself grew up. Many Acoma people live even further afield, in the cities of Albuquerque, Grants, or Gallup. Like the Ortiz family, most still keep a house in the old pueblo, returning to the mesa top for feasts and occasions like Christmas, Epiphany, and Easter. On those days when the plaza is thronged with Acoma families and visitors who gather to eat together and watch the dances, the high desert air fills with the smells of piñon wood smoke, oven bread, roasting chile, and the sound of the heart-beat drum.

But at Acoma, as in most Native American communities, the contradictory conditions Shoshone / Paiute writer nila northSun calls "The Way" and "The Way Things Are" are both present; that is, strong traditional behaviors and beliefs coexist with poverty, substance abuse, violence, and other ills. Ortiz writes about all with insight, balance, and compassion.

In the Introduction to his anthology *Speaking for the Generations: Native Writers on Writing* (1998), Ortiz discusses eloquently the primal connection between Native Americans and the land, a belief that is shared by traditional people of all tribes:

> The young are frequently reminded by their elders: these lands and waters and all parts of Creation are a part of you, and you are a part of them; you have a reciprocal relationship with them. (xiv)[2]

This concept is repeated again and again through Native oratory and literature, and often gets expressed in rather general terms. But Ortiz backs up his assertion with wonderful particulars. For example, in both the *Generations* Introduction and in "A River is More than Just a River," a long poem in his collection *Out There Somewhere* (2002),[3] he recounts his many connections to the *chunah*, the San José River that flows past his home village of McCarty's. (The same river curves around Leslie Marmon Silko's neighboring home pueblo of Laguna, and plays an important part in her work as well.)

Today, the San José's flow is severely diminished by misuses of land and water, and by the drought that has frequently visited the Southwest for years now. But when Ortiz was growing up, this small river was the life-giving source of water for Acoma and Laguna people, their crops, and their livestock. It was where his mother demonstrated her level-headed strength by scooping him to safety when he fell from the plank bridge as a toddler, where Ortiz learned to swim and fish for trout and read animal tracks in the mud, and where he found a place to dream, as documented often in poems like "The Boy and the Coyote," *Going For the Rain*, (*Woven Stone*, 124–25); and especially in "More Than Just A River" (*Out There*, 107–10).

And indeed, there *is* much more to this river. As Ortiz goes on to say in the *Generations* Introduction, "Believing the *chunah* is more than just a water source is an integral feature of an Acoma Pueblo belief that absolutely accepts – and therefore insists on the maintenance and continuance of – the reciprocal relationship that we as a human culture have with the natural environment in which we live" (xv).

Though he does not go into the sort of detail that would violate tribal privacies respecting that belief, Ortiz suggests how in its very being the *chunah* makes connections between the Acoma people and the spiritual world. The Rio San José arises in the Zuni Mountains, west of Acoma, and its course marks the way home for the Shiwaana, the western-dwelling ancestor spirits of the Acoma. The moist breath and spirit of people's lives, expelled at the moment of death, forms the big weather-bearing clouds. The Shiwaana travel back to the Pueblo by the same route the river follows in order to bless their old home and replenish the *chunah* with their gift of rain. Religious officials journey to shrines where they honor the Shiwaana and ask them to return; hence, the title of Ortiz's first book of poems, *Going For the Rain* (1976).[4]

At Acoma, many sorts of rituals are connected with the *chunah*. For instance, when a hunter kills a deer, as Ortiz remembers doing when he was about sixteen, in one part of the ceremony for thanking the deer, an elder prays by the waters of the *chunah* while offering up the slain deer's eyes, " ... so the deer would return always to the source / of continuing life; so the river would always help us to return life to / continuing life" (*Speaking*, xiv–xvii; "A River Is More Than Just A River," *Out There*, 108).

Ortiz's work speaks of other natural and man-made features around his home. The monoliths rising from the plain surrounding Acoma all have stories attached to them. Here a giant pair of stone lovers yearn toward one another for an embrace; there is the rock where Grandmother Spider let Coyote Woman fall to her death, where she might have lain forever if Skeleton-Fixer had not come along in time to rearrange her scattered bones and sing her back to life. "And there is always one more story ... " (*A Good Journey*, in *Woven Stone*, 177–81).

> To the north of Acoma arises a woman-mountain:
> a white scarf
> tied to her head
> the lines on her face are strong
>
> ("A Snowy Mountain Song," *Going*, 136)

She is the blue height prosaically labeled Mount Taylor on maps, in honor of Zachary Taylor, the military foe of Indians and Mexicans alike, the lackluster twelfth president of the United States. But in the Keres language this beautiful extinct volcano is Kaweshtima ("Snow-Peaked"), and her slopes are the site of many old-time and contemporary adventures:

> On all days of Creation's seasons
> there is always clarity.
> ... wherever I have been
> I have never seen another Mountain
> which has stood more clearly
> in my mind and heart.
> ...
> ... when loneliness for myself
> has overcome me
> the Mountain has occurred.
>
> ("Kaweshtima Sharing Its Existence With Me And Me
> Sharing My Existence With Kaweshtima," *Out There*, 86)

Not only impressive features like monoliths and mountains inspire storytelling throughout Simon Ortiz's work; the land around for many miles is storied, even though some of those places might seem rather ordinary. There are the back-to-the-beginning tales of the Acoma people's emergence from the lower worlds into the light of this earth, somewhere in the vicinity of Mesa Verde in present-day Colorado. Like many Native people, Ortiz dismisses the land-bridge theory of a Pan-Indian ice-age immigration from Asia, a white scholars' notion which denies Indians their accounts of themselves as being truly native to the Americas. His own version of Acoma origins is clear and strong, and he speaks with the authority of the elders:

> You were born when you came
> from that body, the earth;
> your black head burst from granite,
> the ashes cooling.
>
> ("The Creation According to Coyote," *Going* in *Woven Stone*, 41)

Then there is the story of his people's slow and difficult migration from points north southward to Acoma, or *Aacqu,* "that which is prepared," the place ordained for them after many exciting and colorful and tragic adventures (*Fight Back* in *Woven Stone,* 338). And there's the story telling how the rough country the newcomer Spaniards would name the *malpais,* and the Anglos the badlands, the black lava flow that surrounds Kaweshtima, came into being: it is the congealed blood of a monster whose whole pleasure was to kill human beings. His monster-blood spewed afar when the Hero Twins slaughtered him back in the dawn of time – "It must have been a tumultuous event" muses Ortiz (ibid., 346).

Many places in Ortiz's work are connected with more recent New Mexican history as well, such as the early sixteenth-century arrival of the Spanish at Acoma, their occupation of the Pueblo, and the Pueblo Revolt of 1680, when united Indian forces drove the conquistadors back to Mexico for twelve years. There followed the brutal retaking of Acoma by Spain in 1692. Ortiz helped to chronicle this history in *Surviving Columbus,* a 1992 KUNM television documentary distributed widely to Public Broadcasting Stations, marking both the five-hundredth anniversary of Columbus's landfall, the Pueblo revolt, the three-hundredth anniversary of the Spanish reconquest, and the continuance of the people.

At Old Acoma, there still stands the imposing mission church, whose pine *vigas* – massive roof timbers – were hauled overland by Acoma slaves from the slopes of Kaweshtima to their own mesa, some thirty miles to the south. And in the wall surrounding the mission cemetery, there remains the small opening secretly left by the enslaved masons as a portal to home for the souls of their children, whom the Spanish stole in 1598 and sent to Mexico to be concubines and slaves, children who may yet one day return: "The round hole is small but it is big enough / for a little boy or a little girl to climb through" ("For the Children," *Out There,* 70). People still tell about that hole in the wall, and as Ortiz says, "That's a long time for a story to be held on to and remembered."[5]

Ortiz also tells stories of latter-day captives and runaways, like determined escapees from Indian boarding schools, as in "Pennstuwehniyaahtse: Quuti's Story," the saga of a boy, recounted in *Men of the Moon* (1999), who flees Carlisle Indian school, taking refuge for a while with a kind Amish family before he makes his way back on foot to Acoma.[6] Other works chronicle the difficulties of draft-dodgers and veterans of Korea and Vietnam trying to re-enter the world where they were raised (see "Kaiser and the War," *Men,* 23–38, "Crazy Gook Indians," *Fight Back* in *Woven Stone,* 304, and numerous poems elsewhere, especially in *From Sand Creek* [1981], poems written out of Ortiz's experiences undergoing treatment for alcoholism at Fort Lyons Veterans Hospital in Colorado).

Acoma, as Ortiz often notes, lies surrounded by mines, both open-pit and underground, where from the early 1950s through the late 1980s much of the uranium for the Cold War arsenal was extracted, mining done at great risk by low-wage workers – Pueblo and Navajo, Hispanic and white alike. As a young man, Ortiz himself drew pay there, and he does not omit these grim places from his writing (see *Fight Back* in *Woven Stone*, especially "To Change in a Good Way", 308–17 and "What I Mean," 326–29).

Sometimes the places in Ortiz's work are connected with stories that are dramatic indeed, such as the isolated spot off Old Route 66 where in 1952 two Acoma brothers, Louis and Willie Felipe, lured a sadistic state trooper onto a side road on tribal land and murdered him in a ritual manner, a murder that resulted in the first "witchcraft defense" argued before a high court ("The Killing of a State Cop", *Men*, 79–86); he commemorates other places marked by gentler everyday events, such as the stretch of road where a lame elder regularly made his constitutional:

> Whenever people are driving along and stop
> to offer Yuusthiwaa a ride, he refuses
> and says, "I still have my legs,"
> my father says, saying it like the old man,
> a slow careful drawl . . .
>
> ("Yuusthiwaa", *Going* in *Woven Stone*, 137)

Again, Ortiz notes the site of an abandoned gas station where an Acoma man once tried to make a go of free enterprise, with a big sign proclaiming WELCOME HOWBAH INDIANS – "Welcome, All You Indians!" – to the delight and pride of tribal folks passing by on Route 66:

> I mean I guess he owned the gas station, or maybe he was only the manager of it, or maybe he only worked there. I'm sure there was some sort of whiteman trader deal involved with it. But that wasn't important. What was important was that the people believed Eagle owned it. And they would joke with him, "*Gaimuu shtuumu, nuuyuh kudrah* gas station. You don't have to buy gas from Chevron or Conoco or anyone else."   ("Howbah Indians," *Men*, 19–22)

Despite Ortiz's close connection to the land, and to the Keres language and the oral tradition in which he says that relationship is best expressed, he has spent most of his adult life apart from Acoma, called away by his work and by other circumstances, some voluntary, some not. But as he observes in the Preface to his latest book, *Out There Somewhere*, " . . . while I have physically been away from my home area, I have never been away in any absolute way" (Preface, *Out There*, n.p.). For all of his travels, Ortiz returns to New Mexico as often as possible, where most of his family still live. In the late 1980s he served terms as the Acoma Tribal Historian and as Lieutenant Governor, positions of honor and responsibility. Notably, he is one of the few American Indian writers today who is not only a fluent speaker of his native language, but who sometimes writes in it as well.

The land, language, and oral traditions ground Ortiz's writing. So does family. Ortiz was the fourth child and the first son of eight brothers and sisters. His mother Mamie was a gifted potter in a long line of potters. In the poem "My Mother and My Sisters," Ortiz honors his women relatives' art: his eldest sister's "fingers / have to know the texture of clay / and how the pottery is formed from lines / of shale strata and earth movements," and his mother, decorating a pot with a yucca brush, knows deeply "the tensile vibrancy of the yucca stem / and the design that things are supposed to have" (*Going* in *Woven Stone*, 129–30).

Joe Ortiz, his father, worked as a welder for the Atchison, Topeka, and Santa Fe Railroad, and at their home in McCartys the Ortiz family raised chile, corn, squash, chickens, rabbits, and pigs. Ortiz grew up in a hard-working environment rich in his own language and culture, surrounded by members of his mother's Eagle clan – to which, in the matrilineal Acoma way, he principally belongs – and by his father's Antelope Clan, for whom Mr. Ortiz served as a cacique, or religious leader. Joe Ortiz was well known in the Acoma community for composing songs, storytelling, woodcarving, and stonemasonry. Ortiz remembers vividly working beside his father, who explained how walls like the massive four hundred year old walls that shore up the cemetery atop Acoma, are built:

> ... "That's just the part you see,
> the stones which seem to be
> just packed in on the outside,"
> and with his hands he puts the mud and stone
> in place, "Underneath what looks like loose stone,
> there is stone woven together."

The father goes on to demonstrate how carefully the adobe mortar must be mixed, " ... so that, placed between the stones, they hold / together for a long long time" ("The Story of How a Wall Stands," *Going* in *Woven Stone*, 145). Working beside his father, especially with stonemasonry, gave Ortiz a metaphor for some of his own ideas about the surface simplicity and the underlying care and complexity of good writing. It is little wonder that he chose *Woven Stone* (1992) as the title for the University of Arizona's collected edition of his first three books.

Family legend holds that Ortiz was a very late talker until his grandfather gently placed a skeleton key between the little boy's lips and turned it, unlocking the words that then flowed freely. Joe Ortiz remembered his son quietly eavesdropping on grown-up gossip around the kitchen, causing the family to nickname him "The Reporter." When Ortiz entered first grade at the Bureau of Indian Affairs day school at McCartys he knew only the ABCs and a few phrases in English. His introduction to education was luckily much gentler than many Native children of his age experienced at BIA and religious boarding schools. He was a precocious learner, devouring everything from the elementary *Dick and Jane* readers to children's classics, comic books, *The Reader's Digest*, and pulp western and romance magazines. Many of these books described life outside the Pueblo and its close environs, a world Acoma people call *howchaatya dhuuh*, "the world beyond."

Ortiz encountered that world beyond in a tougher way in the fifth grade when his father's work took the family to live for a year in Santa Fe Railroad company housing in Skull Valley, Arizona, where the Ortiz children were the only Native American students at their one-room school house. Here Ortiz first learned to play Cowboys and Indians, swapping roles back and forth with his best friend, the white son of an itinerant ranch hand, a fellow outsider. Ortiz began to learn about the divisions of race and class. Nonetheless, his teacher at Skull Valley recognized his gifts, and with her encouragement he published his first work in the school newspaper, a Mother's Day poem for Mamie Ortiz. He has said the year at Skull Valley taught him he could get along with white people, though he was still "wary of something that drove them willfully, aggressively, powerfully, and arrogantly." Years later, he would understand how that same drive in non-Indian people he observed as a youngster played its role in the history of colonization (*Woven Stone*, 13–14).

Ortiz returned with his family to McCartys for sixth grade, and after a short time as a boarding student at Saint Catherine's Indian School in Santa Fe, where both his parents were educated, he chose to finish at the public high school in Grants, outside of either religious or BIA jurisdiction. He excelled academically and athletically, and started to write in a determined way, but says none of his teenage work would particularly mark him as Native American. Like most beginners, he imitated the authors in the books teachers put before him – Sandburg, McCullers, Saroyan, Steinbeck, Salinger, and especially Hemingway. Always a voracious reader, he was soon discovering Beat writers not in the curriculum – Snyder, Kerouac, Ginsberg, Rexroth – and was fascinated by their colloquial ear, their incantatory style, and the Buddhism he found in their work, which seemed to him to share much with traditional Acoma worldview. From them he began to get the idea that he might become a writer who was both American and from Acoma.

Ortiz did not immediately enter college, but like many of his classmates went to work for the Kerr-McGee mines in order to help support his large family. His job was mostly above ground loading and crushing radioactive raw ore, not in the more immediately hazardous pits and stopes, but the danger of the work and the callousness of the mining corporations were evident even to a youngster. Twenty years later, in 1980, his experience would inform *Fight Back: for the Sake of the People, for the Sake of the Land.*

Ortiz's experience is often hard to track after high school, in part because of the alcoholism he has battled since his late adolescence. He writes openly about his successes and setbacks in that war in his autobiographical accounts and in fiction and poetry. In brief, it has caused him many changes in jobs and residences and relationships. But Ortiz's story is a hero story, for throughout he has continued to write, to edit, to teach, and to empower new writers.

Ortiz made a first stab at higher education at Fort Lewis College in Durango, Colorado, in 1961 and 1962, where he intended to become a chemist. Disillusioned about that career, he left to join the US Army, where he served from 1962 to 1965. He underwent basic training in Louisiana, where he had his first encounters with undisguised racism. An African American sergeant picked up Ortiz and a Chicano buddy hitchhiking and cautioned them, "Dark people get killed around here." The Civil Rights Movement and the courage of its workers were no longer just the subject of articles he read admiringly in the papers, and his Army days in the American South resulted in a series of epistolary poems he called *Dear America*, which remain unpublished.

From 1966 to 1968 Ortiz attended the University of New Mexico in Albuquerque, and in 1968 and 69 was a Fellow in the International Writing Program at the University of Iowa. He had begun to publish here and there, but his first appearance in a well-known periodical came in 1969 when he was included in editor John Milton's unprecedented American Indian issue of the *South Dakota Review* (7.2). Most readers were accustomed to thinking of Native poetry as white writers' romantic "translations" or "renderings" of traditional songs garnered by anthropologists about braves paddling canoes and maidens yearning after lost loves. Suddenly here were the fresh, edgy voices of young Indian writers themselves: "bernstein disc jockey / telling about indians / on ten o'clock news / o they have been screwed ... " wrote Ortiz, and thoughtful people's notions of Native American poetry were forever altered.[7]

Ortiz worked at a number of organizing, public relations, and editing jobs through the early 70s. As his poems continued to appear in journals and anthologies, he resolved to publish a whole book of his own work. A friendly editor told him his 400-page manuscript was too bulky for any publisher, and encouraged him to rework poems and winnow down. The result was two books, *Going For The Rain* in 1976, published by Harper and Row, and

A Good Journey published by Turtle Island Press in 1977. Together, they established Ortiz as a major American writer.

Going For the Rain takes the journey as its dominant note, recounting many sorts of journeys – the ascent of the Acoma people from the lower worlds, and their migrations; the journey of two parents and their daughter toward her birth; the cross-country wanderings of a young man in search of Indian America, and his return to his own roots. *A Good Journey*, the second book culled from the original manuscript, is less formal, angrier, and more exuberant, as befits a book published by an alternative press such as Turtle Island. Here Ortiz is freer to experiment with recapturing in print the experience of oral storytelling, to write lines in untranslated Keres, to replicate the voices of an Acoma audience, to play with typography and the shape of a poem on the page.

In that same year, 1977, Children's Press published his children's book on Native American history, *The People Shall Continue* (revised edition, 1977). Ortiz takes young readers from creation to modern times, giving them a sense of the diversity of Native American peoples. He does not romanticize the past; he describes colonization straightforwardly; he is not bitter about the present. As Ortiz often says, his work is hopeful, in accordance with Pueblo thought, and he offers a vision of a world where "We must take great care with each other. / We must share our concern with each other. / Nothing is separate from us. / We are all one body of people."[8]

Fight Back: for the Sake of the People, for the Sake of the Land appeared in 1980, the three-hundredth anniversary of the Pueblo Revolt. Though this melange of poems, history, and personal essays is focused on the Acoma area, it is a call for all people to fight against oppression in creative ways. "To Change in a Good Way" is one of Ortiz's most moving poems, relating the friendship of two miners' families, Acoma and Okie, as their understanding of one another grows through tough times (*Fight Back* in *Woven Stone*, 308–17).

Ortiz's next book of poetry, *From Sand Creek: Rising in this Heart which is our America* was published by Thunder's Mouth Press in 1981. It is written out of his experiences at Fort Lyons Veterans Hospital in Colorado, his attraction to that landscape, and his sudden realization that in 1864 the cavalry who massacred the Cheyenne and Arapaho rode forth from this very place. On left-facing pages are terse prose observations about Sand Creek, the military, the corporate structure, all of American history; opposite appear reflective lyrical poems on these same matters, but especially upon the veterans who are fellow patients. My Lai and Sand Creek and the damage of all wars are brought together.

After and Before the Lightning (1994) is a book generated by Ortiz's time teaching in 1985 and 1986 at Sinte Gleska College on the Rosebud Lakota Sioux Reservation in South Dakota, far from home. The title is a common Sioux phrase to describe the boundaries of a prairie winter, and the poems are about surviving winter outside and, in James Welch's phrase, "winter in the blood," both the inherited violence of American history and personal dark times.

Ortiz's most recent books were both published by the University of Arizona Press. Ortiz is a powerful fiction writer as well as a poet, and two shorter collections and random pieces have been collected in *Men on the Moon* (1999). Ortiz's most recent work, *Out There Somewhere* (2002) ranges from his childhood memories, such as his long meditation on the *chunah* ("A River is More Than a River") to current diaries kept at Artist in Residency colonies ("Headlands Journal"). There is a great deal of Keres language in this volume, and a special section of poems written in that language ("Acoma Poems," *Out There*, 90–99).

Ortiz has been a Professor of English at the University of Toronto for several years now, often teaching at the University of Arizona in Tucson in the summers. He continues to return regularly to New Mexico and to Acoma. As always, he writes and speaks out for his children and grand-children, and for all people, in the hope of peace, and the survival of all that really matters. Like the woven-stone wall at Acoma, his work endures.

Notes

1. Simon J. Ortiz, *Woven Stone*, Tucson: University of Arizona Press, 1992, com-bines Ortiz's first three collections of poetry: *Going for the Rain* (1976), *A Good Journey* (1977), and *Fight Back: For the Sake of the People, For the Sake of the Land* (1980). The parenthetical pagination references to *Woven Stone* will include a shortened title of the specific collection.
2. Simon J. Ortiz, *Speaking for the Generations: Native Writers on Writing*, Tucson: University of Arizona Press, 1998.
3. Simon J. Ortiz, *Out There Somewhere*, Tucson: University of Arizona Press, 2002.
4. Simon J. Ortiz, *Going for the Rain*, New York: Harper and Row, 1976.
5. Bo Scholer, ed., *Coyote Was Here: Essays on Contemporary Native American Literary and Political Mobilization*, Aarhus, Denmark: SELKOS, 1984, p. 67.
6. Simon J. Ortiz, *Men on the Moon*, Tucson: University of Arizona Press, 1999, pp. 197–203.
7. Simon J. Ortiz, "Ten O'clock News," *South Dakota Review* 7.2 (Summer 1969), p. 5.
8. Simon J. Ortiz, *The People Shall Continue*. San Francisco: Children's Press, 1977, n.p.

Major secondary sources

Brill de Ramirez, Susan, ed., Special Issue on Simon Ortiz, *Studies in American Indian Literatures*, Series. 2, 16.4 (Winter 2004).
Fast, Robin Riley, "Telling Stories," in *The Heart as a Drum: Continuance and Resistance in American Indian Poetry*. Ann Arbor: University of Michigan Press, 1999, pp. 163–82.

Kroeber, Karl, ed., Special Issue on Simon Ortiz, *Studies in American Indian Literature*, 8.3/4 (Summer/Fall 1984).

Lincoln, Kenneth, "The Now Day Indi'ns / Common Walls: the Poetry of Simon Ortiz," in *Native American Renaissance*. Berkeley: University of California Press, 1983, pp. 189–201.

Oandasan, William, "Simon Ortiz: the Poet and His Landscape," *Studies in American Indian Literature* 11.1 (Winter 1987), pp. 26–37.

Scarberry-Garcia, Susan, "Simon J. Ortiz,' in Kenneth M. Roemer, ed., *Native American Writers of the United States*. Detroit: Gale, 1997, pp. 208–21.

Smith, Patricia Clark, "Simon J. Ortiz," in A. W. Litz and Molly Weigel, eds., *American Writers: a Collection of Literary Biographies*, suppl. 4, pt. 2. New York: Scribners, 1996, pp. 497–515.

Wiget, Andrew, *Simon Ortiz*, Western Writers Series, 11. Boise, ID: Boise State University Press, 1986.

Wilson, Norma C., "Language as a Way of Life: the Poetry of Simon J. Ortiz," in *The Nature of Native American Poetry*. Albuquerque: University of New Mexico Press, 2001, pp. 45–63.

12

KATHRYN W. SHANLEY

James Welch: identity, circumstance, and chance

For nothing in the world today is more complex, difficult, disputed, divisive, or so highly charged with dynamic energies as the question of "Indianness."
Louis Owens, *Mixed-blood Messages*

Related to the structures of identity, history, and mythology, the issues of authority, authorship, and authenticity come into play as agents of power. If Indian history since 1492 has been "written" (authored) by white authority, then how can Indians attain or retain authentic identities in the present? The author of history also assumes the power of the author of identity and the arbiter of authenticity.
Scott B. Vickers, *Native American Identities: from Stereotype to Archetype in Art and Literature*

In American Indian communities, elders are the revered, because we recognize them as our culture-bearers. Arguably, they give us the best long view we have of what it means to be human, since they are the ones who mark in memory where we have been and are the ones who most likely possess a collective vision we need to carry forward and the cultural values and truths that give us our identity as a people. "Elders" in that context does not necessarily refer to someone within a tribal culture who has grown to be a certain age, but instead refers to those people to whom we turn for their wisdom. "Elder" stands for influence, mentor, guide, or culture-bearer. James Welch, a writer of Pikuni (Blackfeet) and Atsina (Gros Ventre) descent, has played all of those roles in the tremendous growth period of Native American literature beginning in the 1960s. He has served as what one literary critic calls a "mediator,"[1] because Welch links an older generation of Native writers with a new, links oral traditions with written, and links cultural survival efforts of times passed with continuing efforts.

When we see stories carried by elders such as Welch as continuing tradition – but not as on a continuum from orality to literacy or as moving from "traditional" to postmodern – we can situate the stories as both traditional and innovative. Welch must be seen as someone working in both oral and written traditions, if we are to understand fully his place in the history of Native American literary expression. To place orality on one end of a continuum and literacy/writing on the other is to duplicate the error of seeing

Native peoples the way reformists so often have, as best when moving from "savage" to "civilized." American Indians have been writing in English for many centuries and participating in the oral cultures of their peoples at the same time, and writing out of cultures held together by their collective stories about themselves. Tribal storytellers dream their cultures into being, whether their dreams occur while they are waking or sleeping and whether they write or speak their dreams. The visions may be sweet and clear with promise, or harsh and yellow with sorrow, but they are nevertheless defining.

Building on such ironies and tensions in "postcolonial" Native America, Welch has played a crucial role in dreaming a contemporary written Native American literature into being and has fostered a vision of Pikuni (Blackfeet) and Atsina (Gros Ventre) pasts, presents, and futures at the same time. Like many writers of his generation, Welch found his voice as a writer through attending university, most specifically, the Creative Writing Program at the University of Montana. Like other Native young people for over a century before him, Welch grew up in the American educational system that requires mastery of English; the acquisition of English most often occurs at the expense of preserving the Native language. Hence, Welch spoke only English, though he may have understood something of the Native languages spoken around him. Whatever the case may be, Native cultural influences figure into his life through oral traditions carried on in English. When asked in a recent interview about the shaping influences on his life, Welch replied:

> I consider myself lucky having been born up there on the Blackfeet Reservation and spent time on the Ft. Belknap Reservation. My parents worked for the Indian Service so we lived in Indian communities like Chemawa, Oregon, and Mt. Edgecombe, Alaska, which was an island and had hospitals and boarding schools and a tuberculosis sanitarium. So I just got to meet so many different Indian people and hear so many stories from various tribal groups. So all of that I think is kind of luck of the draw that I was there then and listened to those stories. And later, maybe they didn't exactly enter my writing verbatim but they would have influenced my writing.[2]

Oral traditional literary practices, influences, and cross-pollinations may not always be evident between any given writer and his/her communities of origin; they are there nonetheless, if we as readers/listeners know enough to be tuned for recognizing them.

The proliferation of writing by American Indians from the late 1960s and early 1970s onward has resulted in an unprecedented body of written works, works in one way or another informed by oral traditions. Welch reached the stature of an elder in that tradition of storytelling, being 62 years old at the time of his death, having published seven books and having earned a national and international reputation. In fact, a few years back, the French Minister of Culture honored Welch by giving him the aristocratic title of "Sir," "Sir James Welch," making him a Knight of the Order of Arts and Letters. All of his books have been translated into many European languages.

Welch's life and work have been informed by several basic things: his tribal heritage and experience; his sense of belonging to a place (Montana and the West); his insistence on seeing (and depicting) American Indian people first as human beings, that is, refusing to sentimentalize or romanticize them; and, last, his preoccupation with creating a portraiture of American Indian men's individual lives and struggles, a glimpse into their psyches and their souls. The questions he poses for the protagonists of his five novels entail dilemmas arising from place-centered values and from the political as well as cultural designation of American Indian identity. Tensions between the pursuit of individual happiness and the hope of communal and/or familial well-being grip all five men. A consistent motif in Welch's work, the contested "right to be Indian," pairs off with the idea that Indians are dealt a double injustice when sentimentality deprives them of being seen as whole and, therefore, as capable of erring as any other human being. Being "Indian" inherently involves being some things anathema to Euro-American law (in the case of Charging Elk, French law), and the individual's struggle against being defined by others dovetails with his own foibles. In other words, throughout his works, Welch has sought recognition of a basic humanity for his characters, who, even though they may be seen as somehow illegimate in a particular place, struggle to belong there and to belong with others.

For Montana Indians, recognition of their humanness entails a two-fold dynamic: affirmation of their unique legal status as citizens of tribal nations and acknowledgment of the history that has denied their citizenship within tribal nations and the state, instead, according them second-class status due to non-Native racism and ignorance. William Bryant, Jr., in *Montana Indians*, offers a glimpse of mid-nineteenth-century white attitudes toward Indians, when he quotes Colonel John Mullan, "the Montana road builder" of historical renown: "The Indian is destined to disappear before the white man, and the only question is, how it may best be done and his disappearance from our midst tempered with those elements calculated to produce to himself the least amount of suffering and to us the least amount of cost."[3] While Mullan's attitude, indeed, his belief, in the inevitability and desirability of Indians' demise was not unique to him in his time, his blatant interest in achieving an economical genocidal end is somewhat shocking. Welch's third novel, *Fools Crow*, begins a half dozen years after Mullan's words were written in 1862. But from the beginning of his writing career, Welch produced poems that challenge attitudes such as Mullan's.

Welch began writing poems in the late 1960s, and published his first volume of poetry, *Riding the Earthboy 40*, in 1971 through World Publishing Company. Due to its limited distribution, the edition soon went out of print; it was reissued in expanded form in 1975. Through the encouragement of Richard Hugo, one of Welch's early mentors, Welch set out to write about what he knew best – life along US Highway 2, known as the Hi-line, in northeastern Montana, where his father had leased a forty-acre tract of land from the Earthboy family.[4] The poems' stories speak of life in that part of the country where temperatures range from fifty below zero in the winter to close to one-hundred above in the summer, where Indians and European Americans alike too often drink to excess out of boredom, and where ideas and images of the West as the stage for a drama involving "cowboys and Indians" persist in corrupt form and new racisms. In *Riding*, the narrators often hiss and sneer at such romanticism, while at the same time holding onto a core matrix of vision; elements of that vision include: historical injustice, natural beauty, cultural conflict, American Indian postcolonial malaise and survival.

The title of the collection, *Riding the Earthboy 40* poetically captures a movement back and forth across a landscape that serves as a place of contemplation as well as a home. As the narrator of the title poem states, "I ride / romantic to those words, / those foolish claims that he [Earthboy] / was better than dirt, or rain / that bleached his cabin white as bone" (*Riding*, 32). Divided into four sections, *Riding* circles through emotions ranging from desperation to defeat to feigned triumph. Hopefulness comes seldom to these seventy-some pages, as the four sections roughly span time from precontact with Europeans to a view of the future: "Knives," "The Renegade Wants Words," "Day After Chasing Porcupines," and "The Day the Children Took Over." Often taking surrealism as their poetic mode, the poems reflect an agonistic effort to feel good in the world and to make sense of a life, lives, as the ground shifts beneath us. The last words of the last poem reflect the ambivalence expressed throughout, as the narrator describes his escape from "home" and his ending up drinking with a friend: "We sit now, a steady demolition team, / under one of the oldest bridges in town. / Any day we will crawl out to settle / old scores and create new roles, our masks / glittering in a comic rain" (71).

Historical portrayals in the collection capture, with bitterness and irony, the interrelated betrayal of Indians by policy makers and the results of decades of poverty among the tribes. A "slouching dwarf with rainwater eyes" comes from America's capital with treaties that assure "life will go on as usual ... everyone – / man, woman and child – would be inoculated / against a world in which we had no part, / a world of money, promise and disease"

(*Riding*, 35). We readily surmise that irony abounds where disease and Indians are mentioned in the same sentence, and that American Indian populations are anything but "inoculated" against disease and deception, though promise often eludes them. Moreover, as Dee Brown's *Bury My Heart at Wounded Knee* made clear in 1970, there is a long history of the shallowness of federal promises and the might of dominance in regions where Indian-hating is the norm. In poems such as "There is a Right Way" and "The Versatile Historian" Welch is careful to insist on the survival of Native American people, survival on terms that allow for a modicum of hope. The title poem of the last section, for example, features children running outside in winter to build a snowman, "to create life, in their own image" (57). If nothing else, the poet seems to be saying, we as humans continue to build things to show we are alive, to reflect on our worlds, and to play. "Vision-seeking" in the world of these poems provides a way of envisioning a place of belonging, and from the beginning of the collection to the end, we find the narrator "riding romantic" between the meanings of "earth" and "dirt."

In his 1970 book, aptly titled *The Right To Be Indian*, Ernest L. Schusky describes well the more dismal aspects of reservation life at the time when James Welch's poetry and his first two novels, *Winter in the Blood* (1974) and *The Death of Jim Loney* (1979), were written. Every indicator of social health from the purity of a community's water to the average life span or infant mortality rates showed American Indians as on the bottom.[5] As the Kennedy and Johnson administrations began waging their "War on Poverty," images of the mean aspects of Indian life began entering middle-class homes across America via television. To those Indians who attempted, in the 1950s, to relocate to cities, or who actually stayed in them, "[u]rban life proved a difficult challenge." Not only were Indian people plunged into the sort of culture shock any rural people would be when economically forced to move to the city, they were also "[i]nsulated from the mainstream culture by strong aboriginal traditions," and "ill-prepared for city life, especially full-bloods, illiterates, and non-veterans. The anonymity of the city contrasted sharply with the personalisms so characteristic of the reservation," and the relocated people's collective identity was "at odds with the materialism of city life."[6] Most faced severe economic struggles; thus, many returned to reservation life.

Over a century of bad US policy provides the backdrop for *Winter in the Blood*, but for Welch to foreground those facts might have doomed the novel to the realm of social tract or political polemic. In many respects, to write about such things is to tell an old story, one that every American more or less thinks s/he knows. For the Indian writer, to avoid portraying Indians as only victims requires great care. An author must present his or her material in such a way that the experience of the character comes across; that experience must hark toward an historical past, but situate the character within a contemporary life. Yet the portrayal must sound out a "difference," an "authenticity" of experience, if you will. Telling all may not be the way to achieve that bond between reader and depiction when it comes to American Indian writing. Welch, I would contend, plays tricks on the reader in order to sound "authentic."

In *Winter in the Blood*, he has created a first-person narration in which the philosophical depth apparent in the narrator's musings is seldom borne out in his actions. The narration is situated in a continuous present, and yet the narrator does not account for the difference between his contemplative and experiential selves. While he may subtly articulate his estrangement and alienation from everyone and everything one moment, the next he gets pathetically and passionately caught up in the events around him. He often reflects upon his life at great distance – either circumstantially or temporally – but even then offers little actual interpretation of its meaning. The result is that, while we are led to believe we are getting to know him, we cannot be sure what we ought to believe. This split narrative point-of-view, in fact, makes Welch's novel unique in Indian literature.

Prior to the 1960s and 1970s, with the exception of a relatively small amount of creative writing, when an Indian spoke for himself about himself in literature, it was not in fiction, but rather in autobiography – the "true account" of a "real" Indian's life. With notable exceptions, Indian autobiographies have the odd effect of perpetuating the image of the defeated, (albeit exotic) Noble Savage and of the vanishing race. Such accounts of Indian lives speak more to the Euro-American need to believe that all real Indians are vanishing than to the free expression of their "autobiographers." Thus, having Welch's narrator in *Winter* speak for himself but tell a different story without nostalgia is a significant ploy. This way, the narrator's is the only vantage point we as readers are offered. Any preconceived notions of what we might discover within the text must be suspended, if not abandoned.

The novel can also be seen as postmodern in its abundance of signifiers and scarcity of signifieds. In other words, an indeterminacy of sorts characterizes the work on every level. Moreover, the nameless narrator's ability to crystallize questions in his mind gets muddled by past, unresolved sorrows; he bumbles along, wondering what to do next. He vaguely perceives a need to reconnect with his girlfriend who has run off with his gun and his razor and is consequently driven to search for her, but until the very end of the novel, he is not certain what he will do when he finds her (he actually finds her once in the course of the novel and lamely suggests to her that she go to school and learn shorthand). Along the way, he haphazardly discovers important things about who he is, even though he can hardly be said to have formulated the question of who he is. The novel ends before we have the slightest inkling of what he will do with what he now knows about himself, his family, and his heritage.

Jim Loney does ask himself who he is – his life is riddled with an abundance of questions – but more importantly, he asks himself what he knows that is worth knowing. Who he is floats on the surface of the story, but the essential question that plagues him is how to love and be loved for who he is. The difference between the first two protagonists in Welch's work is significant. For the narrator in *Winter*, the world is "cockeyed," and the most he can do is find ways of "leaning into the wind." For Jim Loney, "the right light [in which] to see the world [is] between dark and dawn"; the world seen that way allows one "the quiet pleasure of deciding whether the things were there or not" (*Loney*, 167). Loney does not perceive the world as being the problem so much as his way of looking at it.

In significant ways Loney resembles *Winter's* narrator, ways that have nothing to do with either character's degree of Indian blood. When *Winter's* narrator says that he "had been beaten" by both whites and Indians, he alludes to his inability to hold his own with either. His problems with the whites and Indians in town have little to do with his being only "part" Indian, as he would be if his grandfather were Doagie – something he believes for most of the narrative. Rather, he does not fit with either whites or Indians because the whites and Indians he associates with abuse or exploit him, and, in the best of times, offer him little more than company while he drinks. *Winter's* narrator curses Indians and whites alike twice in the novel: first, when he refers to the "stalking white men" and "those Indians" down at Gable's Bar being "no bargain either" (120); second, when he begins to struggle to get the wild-eyed cow out of the mud. Then, he curses the hypocrisy and weakness in everyone he knows as a way of displacing his own guilt and grief. Although he feels uncomfortable in "a world of stalking white men," he never actually curses individual whites. Indians and whites are judged by him according to the same criterion – how they behave. Loney feels similarly alienated, but never attributes that alienation to others' perception or treatment of him as a "halfbreed." He does not "fit in" both because some quality he has is lacking in those around him, and because something others possess he lacks. To say he does not fit in because he is a halfbreed simplifies his dilemma erroneously. Loney, unlike *Winter's* narrator, offers little conscious criticism of others. When he does think of others' motivations, their behavior causes him to reflect negatively on himself.

In the end, Loney cannot escape being a man caught between historical epochs and cultures, between "dark and dawn." Through a set of circumstances, many of them beyond his control, he has gone down the path of alcoholism. He has gone so far down that path that when the "other world" beckons to him, he can only respond by orchestrating his own death, an honorable way for an Atsina man to die when he has committed an egregious offense. Significantly, in terms of the criminalization of American Indian men, Jim Loney's choice has to do with his not wanting to go to prison.

From interviews conducted by other scholars and my own personal conversations with James Welch, I have the impression that he received enough complaints about his first two protagonists' involvement with alcohol that he chose to create a "clean-cut" character in *Fools Crow* (1986). In doing so, he created a character who resembles Leslie Marmon Silko's Tayo much more than Welch's two previous protagonists. In a sense, Fools Crow, like Tayo, is a mythopoetic figure, and therefore not particularly complex psychologically. Moreover, unlike Welch's first two protagonists, Fools Crow lives within a world that tells him how to seek the power to make a name for himself, and the powers of the universe are responsive to his quest. The dilemma he faces is how to live in the present – that is after the Marias Massacre of Blackfeet in 1870 – knowing the future, knowing that things will only get worse for his people. His vision enables him to see Pikuni children in boarding schools, losing their cultural ways. A servant to both his vision and to the community for whom his vision stands, Fools Crow must find his peace in loving and having the levity to see things for which to be grateful.

By the time we get to Sylvester Yellow Calf, the protagonist of *Indian Lawyer* (1990), we find a young man who has choices, who has done well for himself in terms of getting an education and earning a comfortable living, and who seems to have, as they say, "everything going for him." Yet, as a character, he is hardly guided by anything within himself. Others push him in the directions they think he ought to go – he should run for public office, they say, and so he does. But he has unfinished business with himself and is not sharp about the ruthlessness of politics. Like the other protagonists, Sylvester has had difficulty with his mother, and as a result, is guided by questions of how to love and be loved, how to belong, even though he does not consciously shape those ideas as questions. The narrator tells us:

> He had tried many times to understand why she had run off and left him with his grandparents. She hadn't even nursed him she was in such a hurry. By then, she and Sylvester's father were not living together. She could have taken him with her, or come for him later if she had to leave in a hurry ... What if she had wanted him [once she was settled] ... He would have gone to her and been her

son. He would never have been his father's son, but he would have been hers if she had only asked. But she never did, and gradually he came to hate her too and imagined that she was dead, wished that she was dead.

(Indian Lawyer, 249–50)

Later, when as a grown man who has seen other people's marriages fail, Sylvester formulates the question: "Why did his father become a bum and his mother go off without her son?" (250). In a sense, that question begs for a historical contextualization that Sylvester does not give it. As it is with young men when they are learning to play basketball, he plays one-on-one with himself in the end, learning how to accept all of who he is, but at the same time he decides to belong to the larger American Indian community and serve that community by working to promote tribal sovereignty.

Between writing his fourth novel, *Indian Lawyer*, and his fifth, *The Heartsong of Charging Elk* (2000), Welch embarked on a film project with Paul Stekler on the American Indian points of view related to the Battle of the Little Bighorn and Custer's mythic proportions in the American mind. After writing the script for a video with Stekler, Welch and Stekler decided to pull their research together into a co-authored book, *Killing Custer* (1994). As Welch states, "One more thing – whites wrote the history of these and all the other conflicts that resulted from the coming together of the two races. Needless to say, this history has been carefully distorted throughout the years to justify the invasion and subjugation of the indigenous people" (*Killing Custer*, 46). Only recently has the name of the site been changed from the Custer Battlefield to Battle of the Little Bighorn to reflect the historical view American Indian people have of the event. Since Lakota people were the primary combatants in the fight with the Seventh Cavalry, Welch's research took him away from his own tribal roots, but prepared him nicely for his next project, a novel that takes up intriguing questions about identity as tied to place, language, and family – all themes in his first four novels as well as in his poetry.

The dilemma Welch's fifth protagonist, Charging Elk, faces as a lone Lakota man stranded in France, may at first seem unique, but ultimately is tied to the difficulties of the other protagonists. Charging Elk finds himself in an absurd, upside-down world not unlike that faced by the narrator of *Winter in the Blood*; his situation mirrors the alienation of a Jim Loney, who is trapped within his consciousness; and like Fools Crow, he is rooting in a world where the ways of being a man are clear, at least up until he leaves for Europe with the Buffalo Bill's Wild West Show. Like Fools Crow, he knows his world is changing unalterably. He understands the rooted, sense of purpose a Fools Crow would feel, and the positive self-esteem of a Sylvester

Yellow Calf. Left with nothing but himself, his single consciousness, to rely on, he lives on with the most deeply culturally specific aspects of himself locked away – his song. When he finally has the opportunity to return to his former home, he decides there is no going back.

The challenges encountered by all five protagonists are also profoundly shaped by the place of law: with *Winter in the Blood* it is the foreign law the airplane man brings down on himself, a mess the narrator almost gets caught up in; with Loney it is the law of an anachronistic West, where the cowboy rules and the Indian is destined to die in the end; with Fools Crow it is the law of treaties, as white encroachment pushes against the Pikuni people; with Sylvester it is two sides of the same law – the Indian and the non-Indian sides; and finally, with Charging Elk, it is the law that punishes him for acting according to the dictates of his own culture.

Notes

1. J. Ruppert, *Mediation in Contemporary Native American Fiction*. Norman: Oklahoma University Press, 1995, p. vii.
2. K. W. Shanley, "Interview with James Welch," in K. W. Shanley, ed., *Native American Literature: Boundaries and Sovereignties*, Vashon Island: Paradoxa, 2001, p. 37.
3. W. L. Bryant, Jr., *Montana Indians, Yesterday and Today*, 2nd edn., Helena: American and World Graphic, 1996, p. 10.
4. P. G. Beidler, Book Review of *Riding the Earthboy 40, American Indian Quarterly* 1.3 (Autumn 1975), p. 201.
5. E. L. Schusky, *The Right To Be Indian*, San Francisco: The Indian Historian Press, 1970, p. v.
6. J. S. Olson and R. Wilson, *Native Americans In the Twentieth Century*, Urbana: Illinois University Press, pp. 153–54.

Major secondary sources

Bevis, W. W., "Native American Novels: Homing In," in B. Swann and A. Krupat, eds., *Recovering the world: Essays on Native American Literatute*, Berkeley: University of California Press, 1987. pp. 580–620.

"James Welch," in J. L. Thomas, ed., *Updating the Literary West*. Fort Worth: Texas Christian University Press, 1997. pp. 808–26.

"Welch's Winters and Bloods," in *Ten Tough Trips: Montana Writers and the West*. Seattle: Washington University Press, 1990. pp. 117–39.

Beidler, P. G., ed., Special Symposium Issue on James Welch's *Winter in the Blood American Indian Quarterly* 4:2 (May 1978).

Cook, B., "A Tapestry of History and Re-imagination: Women's Place in James Welch's *Fools Crow*," American Indian Quarterly 24:3, pp. 441–53.

Lincoln, K., "Blackfeet Winter Blues," in *Native American Renaissance*. Berkeley: California University Press, 1983, pp. 148–82.

"Red Gods, Blue Humors: James Welch," in *Ind'n Humor*. New York: Oxford University Press, 1993, pp. 254–79.

Lupton, Mary Jane, ed., *James Welch: a Critical Companion*. Westport: Greenwood Press, 2004.

McFarland, R., *James Welch*. Lewiston, ID: Confluence, 1986.

Understanding James Welch. Columbia: South Carolina University Press, 2000.

Nelson, R. M., "The Function of the Landscape of *The Death of Jim Loney*," in *Place and Vision: the Function of Landscape in Native American Fiction*. New York: Peter Lang, 1993, pp. 91–131.

O'Connell, N., "James Welch," in *At the Field's End: Interviews with 20 Pacific Northwest Writers*. Seattle: Madrona, 1987, pp. 58–75.

Owens, L., "Earthboy's Return: James Welch's Acts of Recovery," in *Other Destinies: Understanding the American Indian Novel*. Norman: Oklahoma University Press, 1992, pp. 128–66.

Ruppert, J., "That Other Distance: *Winter in the Blood*," in *Mediation in Contemporary Native American Fiction*. Norman: Oklahoma University Press 1995, pp. 56–73.

Stromberg, E., "The Only Real Indian is a Dead Indian: the Desire for Authenticity in the *Death of Jim Loney*," *Studies in American Indian Literatures* 10:4 (Winter 1998), pp. 33–53.

Thackeray, W. W., "Animal Allies and Transformations in *Winter in the Blood*," *MELUS* 12 (Spring 1985), pp. 37–64.

Velie, A. R., "Welch: Blackfoot Surrealism" and "*Winter in the Blood*: Welch and the Comic Novel," in *Four American Indian Literary Masters*. Norman: Oklahoma University Press, 1982, pp. 66–90, 91–103.

Wild, P., *James Welch*, Western Writers Series 57. Boise: Boise State University Press, 1983.

13

ROBERT M. NELSON

Leslie Marmon Silko: storyteller

Novelist, poet, essayist, photographer, cinematographer, and in every case storyteller: Leslie Marmon Silko is perhaps the most familiar and most often anthologized American Indian writer today, and her novel *Ceremony* is as widely recognized as any other contemporary American novel.[1] In *Ceremony* as in all her other work to date, Silko's creative vision has been shaped in nearly equal measure by the land and by the variety of oral and written storytelling performances that were a part of her life growing up at Laguna Pueblo. According to both cultural anthropology and oral tradition, Laguna has always been one of the most adaptive pueblo communities in the Southwest, and many of the stories comprising Laguna oral tradition preserve the complex strategies of resistance and assimilation that have enabled the people to survive and adjust to myriad external pressures. Like her native Laguna, Silko's work is a study in cultural mediation[2] and spirit transformation. Again and again her creative vision celebrates the transformative power of story and place, working together for life in a healing way.

Backgrounds

Leslie Marmon Silko was born in Albuquerque, New Mexico on 5 March 1948. Her mother, Virginia Leslie, was originally from Montana; her father, Lee Howard Marmon, was at the time just out of the Army, beginning his career as a professional photographer and managing the Marmon Trading Post in the village of Old Laguna, about fifty miles west of Albuquerque. Along with her two younger sisters, Wendy and Gigi, Leslie was raised in one of the houses on the southeast edge of Old Laguna village, the part of the village closest to the Rio San José and, just beyond the river, US Route 66, now Interstate 40.

Silko was born into a family environment already rich with story. From its beginnings, the Marmon family had been prominent in Laguna's history of contact with Euro-American social, political, economic, and educational forces, and its story (like Laguna's) has always been one of outsiders who became insiders and of insiders who became outsiders – a story about cultural transformations and the artful merging of Laguna and Anglo influence. The first Laguna Marmons, brothers Walter and Silko's great-grandfather Robert, came from Ohio in the 1880s as surveyors, married Laguna women, and became part of the community, Walter as a school teacher and Robert as a trader; both eventually were elected to serve as Governor of the Pueblo. Great-grandfather Robert's second wife was Silko's full-blooded Laguna great-grandmother Marie Anaya Marmon, younger sister of Robert's deceased first wife. This is the "Grandma A'mooh" lovingly referred to in *Storyteller* and several of the essays in *Yellow Woman*, who in her youth left Laguna for some years to attend the Carlisle Indian School in Pennsylvania and who "spoke and wrote English beautifully,"[3] who passed time with young Leslie and her sisters both telling them stories from Laguna oral tradition and reading aloud to them from *Brownie the Bear* and the Bible. Her husband Robert, who had shelves of books in his house, also became conversant in Laguna oral tradition and in 1919 was the source of two of the traditional storytelling performances collected in Boas's monumental *Keresan Texts*. Their son Henry, Silko's "Grandpa Hank," attended the Sherman Institute, California's version of Carlisle, while "Aunt Susie" (Henry's sister-in-law Susan Reyes, married to his brother Walter) attended both the Carlisle Indian School and Dickinson College (also in Carlisle); upon returning to Laguna she served the community as a schoolteacher and also as a Keresan cultural historian – a "storyteller" like her mother-in-law Grandma A'mooh, in one of the most important senses of that term. When anthropologist and ethnographer Elsie Clews Parsons came to Laguna to collect the stories published in Boas's edition and in several other shorter collections during the years between World Wars I and II, she stayed at the house of a Marmon kinswoman, Henry's cousin Alice (identified by Parsons as "Mrs. E. C. Eckerman"), another of the family storytellers Silko frequently cites as one of her own mentors. In Silko's own time, her father (who served as Tribal Council Treasurer during the time that uranium began to be mined at Laguna) headed a project to republish John Gunn's largely forgotten 1917 collection of Laguna oral traditional tales entitled *Schat-Chen*. Not surprisingly, given such a heritage, Leslie Marmon Silko grew up in a house full of books and stories – Laguna stories, Euro-American books, books about Laguna stories, Laguna stories about Euro-American contact – a legacy of cultural interplay and mediation that has profoundly influenced her own storytelling style and repertoire.

Silko's creative preoccupation with the theme of cultural mediation is often reflected in the Laguna landscape that functions as setting, and sometimes even character, in much of her work. For Silko, one of the most important of all such places is the bend of the river a short distance from the house where she was raised, itself located at the very southeast edge of the village, where the traffic of the main US cross-country interstate highway mirrors the older, quieter motion of water moving on the land. In several of Silko's *Storyteller* pieces, particularly those featuring the Kochinninako / Yellow Woman motif, this part of the river figures as a contact zone,[4] where a female representing Laguna identity "within" meets a male who represents some other cultural or spiritual identity "out there." This place is also the liminal zone in which the spirits of the Katsinas, passing through it from the direction of sunrise into the village in November, take on the corporeal form of the masked dancers, a transformative event recalled in *Ceremony* (82) and also in Auntie's story about Tayo's mother Laura, which positions her at this place at sunrise, returning to Laguna (70). This is also the place that Tayo positions himself at sunrise on the morning following the autumnal equinox (and the Jackpile mine episode) at the end of the novel (255). In the work of many writers, such places take shape as wastelands, deserts, lifeless and/or life-threatening expanses; in Silko's work, as at Laguna, the site of such transformative contact events appears as a place of comfort and regenerative energy, a place characterized by the twin blessings of shade and moving water even throughout the long summer months. Silko's own affinity for this place reflects, perhaps, her own felt "position," occupying as she does a marginal site with respect to both Laguna "within" and the dominant Anglo mainstream "out there" – and as she depicts it, it's not a bad place to be.

In addition to the education she was receiving from the land and the storytellers in her extended family, Leslie attended the BIA school at Laguna through the fifth grade and then parochial schools in Albuquerque during her teenage school years. She then attended the University of New Mexico, where she was enrolled in the general honors program and received her BA in English (with honors) in 1969, the year the Pulitzer Prize for fiction was awarded to Scott Momaday's *House Made of Dawn*. She then enrolled in the American Indian law program at the University of New Mexico Law School, but after a semester transferred into the creative writing MA program there.

Though her interest in writing predated her college years – she was already writing stories in elementary school – that interest blossomed during her years at the University of New Mexico, during which time she took several courses in creative writing and saw her first work published ("The Man to Send Rain Clouds" in *New Mexico Quarterly*, Winter–Spring 1969). By 1971 she had chosen writing, rather than the practice of law, as her vocation, and in 1974 (at the end of a two-year teaching stint at Navajo Community College) her career became effectively established with two publications: her poetry chapbook *Laguna Woman* (Greenfield Review Press) and Kenneth Rosen's *The Man to Send Rain Clouds*, an anthology of nineteen Native American short stories, seven of them (including the title story) by Silko. In that same year, another of Silko's short stories, the oft-anthologized "Lullaby," was published in *Chicago Review*, and Silko was awarded an NEA writing fellowship.

She then moved to Ketchikan, Alaska, where she lived for two years with her husband, John Silko, and her two young sons, the older of the two from a previous short-lived marriage during her college years. There, supported partially by a Rosewater Foundation grant, she wrote most of what was to become the novel *Ceremony* (1977). The time she spent in Alaska at Ketchikan and the small community of Bethel strongly engaged her imagination – "Storyteller," the title story of her major collection of short works and the only piece not set at or near Laguna, is unmistakably Alaskan in setting and character.

Returning to the Southwest from Alaska, Silko continued to write while holding academic appointments first at the University of New Mexico and then at the University of Arizona. The year after *Ceremony* was published, Silko moved from New Mexico to Arizona and acquired a ranch in the mountains a few miles northwest of Tucson, where she continues to live. In 1981, after her marriage to John Silko had been dissolved, Seaver Books published her book *Storyteller*, which brought together much of her previously published poetry and short fiction, re-embedded in a webwork of family narrative accompanied by photographs of the sources of her storytelling identity – photographs, that is, of the people and the places to which those stories attach. In that same year, Silko was awarded a five-year, $176,000 MacArthur Foundation Prize Fellowship, allowing her to devote herself full time to her artistic pursuits, including writing the novel that over the course of the next ten years would become *Almanac of the Dead*.

Ceremony

Many of the oral traditional stories that Silko heard and read came to shape the structure and texture of her first and most famous novel, *Ceremony*. From the very outset of the novel, the narrative persona aligns herself with Keresan oral tradition by claiming to be one of a very long line of storytellers whose role is to preserve and pass along the story set in motion by "Ts'its'tsi'nako, Thought Woman" (also called Spider Grandmother, who in many of the Laguna and Acoma stories figures as the original life-force or

Creatrix); this story is the life of the people, life for the people. Throughout the novel, passages from the old stories, or "hama-ha" stories as they are called at Laguna and neighboring Acoma, serve to orient a reader already familiar with these stories in the otherwise sometimes chronologically and geographically confusing tale of Silko's twentieth-century protagonist, Tayo. These fragments of story, or embedded texts, remind such an audience that the long story of the people contains precedents for everything that happens in the life of any one of the people. As might be expected, most of the hama-ha stories embedded in *Ceremony* – including the story of the family feud between the first sisters, Corn Woman and Reed Woman; the story of the gambler Kaup'a'ta, who once imprisoned the rainclouds; the story of Arrowboy, who disarms the Gunnadeyah witches by seeing what they are up to; and the long nine-part backbone story of the coming of Pa'caya'nyi and Ck'o'yo medicine to the village and the consequent departure and recovery of Our Mother Nau'ts'ity'i – have clear precedents in the published ethnographic records of Laguna oral tradition. But Silko also weaves in material derived from Navajo story and ceremony, particularly in the episode set in the Chuska Mountains in which Betonie, a venerable old Navajo *hataali* (singer or "medicine man"), enacts a healing ritual that aligns Tayo with the Ghostway story of a young hunter whose human identity is recovered after having been stolen by Coyote.

For readers not already familiar with the Laguna and Navajo stories behind the embedded texts in the novel, Silko offers a second, equally illuminating point of reference in the form of the geography and topology – the "landscape" – of the novel. In *Ceremony*, Silko's creative vision is profoundly rooted in the landscape of her native Laguna: "When I was writing *Ceremony*," she wrote to poet James Wright in 1978, a year after the novel was published, "I was so terribly devastated by being away from Laguna country that the writing was my way of re-making that place, the Laguna country, for myself" (*Delicacy* 27–28). In some ways, the novel offers the reader a guided tour of Laguna country, as Tayo eventually re-visits every part of it, from the southwestern corner of the reservation around Patoch Butte to the westside villages of Cubero and Casablanca; from the one-time truckstop and bar at Budville on the west side to the isolated traditionalist village of Mesita on the east side; from Mt. Taylor in the northwest to Alamo Springs and the sand hills to the southeast; from Paguate village to the north, where some stories say the Laguna people originally emerged from the Fourth World into this one, to Dripping Springs to the south, where water springs cold and clear out of the sides of a sandstone mesa. And at the center of the novel's geography lies Old Laguna village, adobe houses clustered about the gleaming white Catholic mission near its highest point but containing also, as we see at the novel's end, the ceremonial kiva, newly whitewashed for the latest autumnal equinox. This is where Tayo must return to tell, for the first time in his life, his story and theirs to the old men of the village who have been awaiting his return, the way the people in the old stories are always awaiting the recovery of whichever protagonist has departed.

Reinforcing the novel's dominant theme of departure and recovery, many of the key episodes are situated in border, and therefore potentially transformational, zones – border towns like Gallup, New Mexico (where Tayo is born) and Villa Cubero (on the western edge of the Laguna reservation, where the Night Swan settles prior to the War); the corner of Mount Taylor called North Top at Laguna, parts of which lie both on and off the reservation; the sheep camp (modeled after the Marmon family ranch) that lies just southwest of Patoch Butte, the formation that marks the southwest corner of the reservation; the two-mile-long open pit Jackpile Mine that lies along Laguna's north border, a monstrous artificial inversion of the lake after which Kawaika (The Beautiful Lake, which the Spanish translated as Laguna) was originally named.

Set in the years following World War II, *Ceremony* is above all about healing, and about the healing power of the stories and the land. The disease that has infected the people, including Silko's protagonist Tayo, is the old bane known at Laguna as Ck'o'yo medicine, which takes several new, but precedented, forms in the novel: World War II and its dreadful fallout, including such new art forms as nuclear fission and the atomic weapons capable of destroying all life; the polarization of the world's populations along both ideological and generational lines, including the emergence of a bitter animosity between "full-bloods" and "halfbreeds" that threatens to destroy twentieth-century Native communities; and the pervasive feeling of separation and isolation, of anomie or existential alienation, that came increasingly to characterize the American experience in the twentieth century. What Tayo must come to understand is that these are indeed not separate diseases but rather symptoms of a single disease made insidious precisely by its ability to disguise itself as separate diseases. Like the other Indian veterans who have returned to the reservation communities, Tayo suffers the effects of this disease most overtly in the form of the "war stories" that haunt his dreaming and waking hours, and like most of the other vets Tayo attempts to self-medicate with yet another version of Ck'o'yo medicine, alcohol. But even early in the novel, Tayo vaguely understands that neither the disease nor the cure is that simple. As Silko puts it, "They all had explanations; the police, the doctors at the psychiatric ward; even Auntie and old Grandma; they blamed liquor and they blamed the war"; but when a doctor offers this diagnosis to Tayo, he replies "'It's more than that. I can feel it. It's been going on for a long time'" (53). Old Betonie later confirms Tayo's suspicion and gives Tayo a story that effectively locates Tayo's personal illness within the context of the timeless struggle between life and the forces of witchery that seek to consume life; using this story as a corrective lens, and assisted by Spider Grandmother's daughters the Night Swan (prior to the War) and Ts'eh (after the War), Tayo becomes able to complete the healing journey of return that Betonie sets in motion with story and song.

Other works

Silko continues and develops the role of Laguna storyteller in her next book, aptly titled *Storyteller* (1981). In critical reviews *Storyteller* has been variously described as a collage, a montage, or even more loosely an assemblage, and indeed the contents of the book may seem bafflingly random and eclectic until the work is treated as a storytelling performance in which the storyteller is depending on visual imagery to do most of the cultural work of an oral tradition. Seen from this perspective, the text is a virtual encyclopedia of storytelling styles and story materials adapted to textual form, all the kinds and ways of traditional story and storytelling – from the grave and formal tone of the old hama-ha stories like "One Time" and "Up North" to the conversational, even chatty, cadences of contemporary anecdotes such as "Uncle Tony's Goat" and "I Just Fed the Rooster." As though to make the point that these are not separate kinds of story but rather varieties or phases of a single, familial life form, Silko includes several pieces like "Toe'osh: A Laguna Coyote Story" and "Storytelling" which clearly contain both kinds of material while showing their family relationship.

Silko also makes a dramatic point in *Storyteller* of challenging the usual distinction that most readers are conditioned to make between words and other kinds of visual imagery, for included in the composition of this text are twenty-six photographs which (as we are told in the opening piece of the collection, "There Is a Tall Hopi Basket") are illustrative of this or that piece of prose and poetry, much as the storyteller's body language may illustrate one point or another of the spoken text in a live oral performance. It is a technique she uses at least once in *Ceremony*: readers will recall the black-and-white star map that appears in the novel near the beginning of the Mt. Taylor episode, an episode that can be read as a re-happening of the older story of Sun Man's showdown with the gambler katsina Kaup'a'ta, which reappears in *Storyteller* under the title "Up North" – a story that in turn features a star riddle as its climactic element. Silko makes this technique the formal basis for *Sacred Water* (1993), subtitled "Narratives and Pictures," a self-published and hand-stitched eighty-pager in which each pair of facing pages shows a photocopied photograph opposite its companion piece of prose. Speaking of this book in a short essay titled "On Nonfiction Prose" she says, "photocopies of my photographs of clouds and dry washes are an integral part of the text; the photocopy images are as much a part of my essay on water as the narrative of the essay ... In the creation of the text itself, I see no reason to separate visual images from written words that are visual images themselves" (*Yellow Woman* 195).

At the same time, the storytelling voice and vision in this book is, like the voice and vision of *Ceremony*, firmly rooted in the land and landscape of Laguna. In fact, the only verbal piece in *Storyteller* not set in the Southwest around Laguna or its geographical and sociological neighbor Acoma is the title story, "Storyteller." Perhaps it is equally telling that the only two photographs in the book not taken at or near Laguna (numbers 23 and 25) are both taken in the Arizona landscape outside Tucson, where Silko herself has lived since leaving Laguna and a principal setting for her three subsequent works – *Almanac of the Dead* (1991), *Sacred Water* (1993), and *Gardens in the Dunes* (1999). Perhaps these two photos are best understood as the author's way of illustrating how the life of a story, like the life of the story-teller who derives from them and cares for them, can bridge the perceived separations not only between moments of time and cultural categories but also between places.

Forays into non-print narrative with which Silko was involved around the time of the composition of *Storyteller* parallel her concerns as a storyteller-in-print. In 1978 Silko was the subject of a documentary film entitled "Running on the Edge of the Rainbow," one of a series of filmings of oral narrative performances produced by Larry Evers at the University of Arizona, in which she played herself as a Laguna storyteller. Around this same time Silko began to develop her own interest in the visual arts, in particular filmmaking, an interest encouraged earlier in several graduate courses as well as by her father's career as a professional photographer. During the late 1970s and early 1980s, even while her written work was relocating itself in a much larger sociopolitical context with Tucson rather than Laguna at its center, Silko's filmmaking efforts remained anchored at Laguna. There, she founded the Laguna Film Project with an eye to creating a trilogy of films, to be collectively entitled *Stolen Rain*. In a 1978 letter to James Wright, Silko speaks of working on "the scripts which attempt to tell the Laguna stories on film using the storyteller's voice with the actual locations where these stories are supposed to have taken place. In a strange sort of way, the film project is an experiment in translation – bringing the land – the hills, the arroyos, the boulders, the cottonwoods in October – to people unfamiliar with it, because after all, the stories grow out of this land as much as we see ourselves as having emerged from the land there" (*Delicacy* 24). In 1980, with support from an NEH grant and anticipating eventual PBS release, she filmed and produced "Arrowboy and the Witches," a sixty-minute video version of an old Laguna story included in *Storyteller* under the title "Estoy-eh-moot and the Kunideeyahs" (*Storyteller* 140–54).[5] She filmed it in the mesa country south and west of Old Laguna, a landscape of cottonwoods and sandstone caves in an area locally known as Dripping Springs, which has been in the care of the Marmon family for several generations. As part of the setting for this film but also partly, perhaps, fulfilling the words she attributes to her father in *Storyteller* – "You could even live / up here in these hills if you wanted" (161) – Silko erected a stone cottage near the base of the Dripping Springs mesa. It burned down shortly thereafter, but its ruins are still there, along with the shell of the Spider Grandmother dwelling that also appears in her film.

As *Storyteller* does mainly in print and "Arrowboy and the Witches" does mainly in motion-picture form, much of the non-fiction work published by Silko since *Storyteller* (most of it collected in her 1996 *Yellow Woman and a Beauty of the Spirit*) continues to integrate the conventional domains of visual and verbal art as well as the conventional categories: life and land. In 1989, for instance, an essay entitled "The Fourth World" appeared in *Artforum*, a journal of the visual arts, and in 1995 her photoessay "An Essay on Rocks" appeared in a special issue of *Aperture* magazine. As in her filmmaking, Silko's creative vision remains grounded in her years growing up at Laguna: in "The Fourth World," Silko speculates about the connections between the high teenage suicide rate around Laguna and the open Jackpile uranium mine, while in "An Essay on Rocks" her story about a boulder in a Tucson arroyo ends with an allusion to the story of a similar rock on Mt. Taylor that first appeared in *Storyteller* (77–78). And in 1996, the Whitney Museum in New York published *Rain*, a selection of photographs of Laguna faces and places taken by her father, Lee Marmon, with accompanying text by Silko.

The concept that printed words themselves are visual images, and thus close relatives of other visual art forms, is also one of the starting points of Silko's most ambitious work to date, *Almanac of the Dead* (1991). The title refers to the Great Calendar of the Mayan tradition, a way of reckoning time that involves creating and preserving a pictorial image (or "glyph") of each of the faces of time in the understanding that time is a life form that periodically renews itself though transformation: "The days, years, and centuries were spirit beings who traveled the universe, returning endlessly" (523). As Silko tells it in the novel, the sisters Zeta and Lecha, the initial twinned female protagonists of the novel, are keepers of a surviving portion of one of these old Mayan codices, inherited from their grandmother Yoeme (the name means "Yaqui" in the Yaqui language). In this fragment, the past five hundred years – that is, the years between the time of the sustained European invasion of the Americas and the present of the novel, published on the eve of the US Columbian quincentenary – is predicted as the epoch of Death-Eye Dog, one of a series of epochs comprising the Long Count; the fragment also contains annotations, made by its various keepers, of historical events that read as fulfillments of the ancient prophecy. Arguably, Silko's novel may be read as yet one more annotation on the epoch of Death-Eye Dog; from this perspective, the novel also may be read as an introduction to the next epoch of human history, a period to be initiated (as in North America's own Ghost Dance prophecies) by "the disappearance of all things European" (*Almanac* frontispiece).

In *Almanac of the Dead*, Silko portrays Tucson, the novel's apparent center of gravity and the setting for much of the story, as a hopelessly corrupt city "home to an assortment of speculators, confidence men, embezzlers, lawyers, judges, police and other criminals, as well as addicts and pushers" (frontispiece), trembling on the edge of apocalyptic redemption thanks to its locus with respect to the Azteca migration motif. But even in *Almanac of the Dead*, Sterling, Silko's on-again-off-again male protagonist, is a native of Laguna, and the novel can end only when the "Exile" of the novel's second chapter returns to Laguna in its final chapter, titled "Home":

> Sterling hiked over the little sand hills across the little valley to the sandstone cliffs where the family sheep camp was. The windmill was pumping lazily in the afternoon breeze, and Sterling washed his face and hands and drank. The taste of the water told him he was home. Even thinking the word made his eyes fill with tears. (757)

Like Tayo's in *Ceremony*, Sterling's personal history is a story of contact with attractive but dangerous non-Laguna forces, departure from Laguna, and eventual return to Laguna with the acquired knowledge of how to live with those forces. Both men's histories recapitulate the "Yellow Woman" motif that Silko so strongly associates with the image of the river that snakes its way along the southeastern corner of Old Laguna. In *Ceremony*, Tayo completes his personal return (and re-enacts the annual return of the Laguna katsina spirits) by crossing this river from the southeast at sunrise (255). In *Almanac*, however, the water-spirit of Kawaika takes the shape of the giant spirit snake Maahastryu, who formerly inhabited the lake after which the Laguna people were originally named. Maahastryu has reappeared in the open pit of the Jackpile uranium mine, "looking south, in the direction from which the twin brothers and the people would come" (763) in fulfillment of a prophecy of which the Laguna story is but a small part.[6]

Silko continues to explore the motif of departure and return in *Gardens in the Dunes* (1999). Set at the turn of the century, this quiet, elegant novel imitates the style of Victorian historical romance in the diction and narrative distance that characterize the telling of the story; ultimately, however, both plot and style work to give voice to Silko's persistently Laguna storytelling persona. Though the protagonist, Indigo, is from Arizona, one of the Sand Lizard clan, the fragile gardens of the title recall Silko's own description of the gardens near the Laguna village of Paguate that were all destroyed by the Jackpile uranium mining operations in the 1950s (*Yellow Woman* 44). From a Victorian perspective, the novel recounts the life and Pyrrhic liberation of protagonist Hattie Abbott, acquired at the cost of the demise of her photographer and botanist husband Edward Palmer. Hattie and Edward are collectors of exotica, and one of their early acquisitions is the child Indigo, a runaway from the Sherman Indian Institute in Riverside, California. From the perspective of the Indian protagonist, the plot of the novel recapitulates the familiar Laguna motif of departure and recovery: Indigo, like her Laguna analog Kochinninako/Yellow Woman, is spirited away from her homeland by an alien force (here, the failing colonial zeitgeist informing the barren couple Hattie and Edward). After surviving this encounter through a complicated process of both resistance and assimilation, Indigo returns carrying new life for the people – in the form of her story; in the form of the child newly born to her older sister Salt; in the form of the new alliance between the sisters of the Sand Lizard people and the Laguna sisters Vedna and Maytha; and in the form of the new seeds (exotic gladiolus tubers, which the women plant next to native datura in the ancient Sand Lizard gardens in the dunes). Like the hybrid calves of the speckled Mexican cattle in *Ceremony*, all these new forms become, by the end of the novel, a part of the long story of the people.

To date, seven books and innumerable critical essays have been published on Silko's work, and most of the criticism has been positive, especially in the case of *Ceremony*.[7] Silko was recently named a Living Cultural Treasure by the New Mexico Humanities Council. In 1994 she also received the third Wordcraft Circle of Native Writers and Storytellers Lifetime Achievement award, an honor she now shares with, among others, N. Scott Momaday (1992), her Acoma neighbor and old friend Simon Ortiz (1993), and longtime Creek friend and co-actress (in "Running on the Edge of the Rainbow") Joy Harjo (1995). Honored by critics and creative writers alike, Leslie Marmon Silko has clearly earned her status as one of America's premiere storytellers.

Notes

1. For a full account of the novel's popularity see Kenneth Roemer, "Silko's Arroyos as Mainstream," in Allan Chavkin, ed., *Leslie Marmon Silko's* Ceremony: *a Casebook*, New York: Oxford University Press, 2002, pp. 223–39.
2. The term is from James Ruppert, *Mediation in Contemporary Native American Fiction*, Norman: University of Oklahoma Press, 1995.
3. Leslie Silko, *Yellow Woman and a Beauty of the Spirit: Essays on Native American Life Today*, New York: Simon and Schuster, 1996, p. 61. Hereafter this and the following works will be cited parenthetically: *Ceremony*, New York: Viking, 1977; *Almanac of the Dead*, New York: Simon and Schuster, 1991; *Storyteller*, New York: Seaver Books, 1981; and Anne Wright, ed., *The Delicacy and Strength of Lace: Letters between Leslie Marmon Silko and James Wright*, Saint Paul, MN: Graywolf, 1986.
4. The term is Mary Louise Pratt's: see Donald Bartholomae and Anthony Petrosky, eds., "Arts of the Contact Zone," *Ways of Reading: an Anthology for Writers*, Boston: St Martin's, 1993; see also Gloria Anzaldúa, *Borderlands/La Frontera: the New Mestiza*, San Francisco: Aunt Lute, 1987.
5. "Arrowboy and the Witches" (alternately entitled "Estoy-muut and the Gunnadeyah") is available from The Video Tape Co., 10545 Burbank Blvd., North Hollywood CA 91601–2280.
6. Silko offers a non-fictional account of the return of "Ma ah shra true ee, the sacred messenger" (= *Almanac*'s "Maahastryu") in her 1989 *Artforum* essay "The Fourth World" (reprinted, with some changes, in *Yellow Woman*, pp. 124–34).
7. For two notable exceptions to this otherwise positive consensus, see Paula Gunn Allen's "Special Problems in Teaching Leslie Marmon Silko's *Ceremony*," reprinted in Chavkin, *Leslie Marmon Silko's* Ceremony, pp. 83–90), and Shamoon Zamir in Arnold Krupat, ed., *New Voices in Native American Literary Criticism*, Washington DC: Smithsonian Institute, 1993, pp. 396–415.

Major secondary works

Arnold, Ellen, ed., *Conversations with Leslie Marmon Silko*. Jackson: University Press of Mississippi, 2000.

Barnett, Louise K., and James L Thorson, eds., *Leslie Marmon Silko: a Collection of Critical Essays*. Albuquerque: University of New Mexico Press, 1999.

Chavkin, Allan, ed., *Leslie Marmon Silko's* Ceremony: *a Casebook*. New York: Oxford University Press, 2002.

Fitz, Brewster. *Silko: Writing Storyteller and Medicine Woman*. Norman, OK: University of Oklahoma Press, 2004.

Graulich, Melody, ed., *"Yellow Woman," Leslie Marmon Silko*. New Brunswick, NJ: Rutgers University Press, 1993.

Jaskoski, Helen. *Leslie Marmon Silko: a Study of the Short Fiction*. New York: Twayne, 1998.

Salyer, Gregory. *Leslie Marmon Silko*. New York: Twayne, 1997.

14

KIMBERLY M. BLAESER

Gerald Vizenor: postindian liberation

Described by Choctaw writer and scholar Louis Owens as "a trickster, contrary, muckraking political journalist and activist, poet, essayist, novelist, and teacher," and by N. Scott Momaday as "the supreme ironist,"[1] Anishinaabeg author Gerald Vizenor has devoted his career to upsetting the status quo, to deconstructing the term "Indian," to re-defining the mixed-blood, and to liberating the contemporary Native people he identifies as postindian. The author of more than thirty books in multiple genres including poetry, short fiction, the novel, autobiography, journalism, the essay, as well as theory and criticism, Gerald Vizenor is at once one of the most prolific and one of the most versatile of contemporary Native writers. Widely recognized as a leading writer and scholar of Native literature, the innovative author who gave trickster narrative a contemporary turn, Vizenor has lectured and taught nationally and internationally and his work has been widely disseminated and translated in several languages including German, Italian, and French. Vizenor, who received a Lifetime Achievement Award from the Native Writers Circle of the Americas in 2002, has also been the recipient of an American Book Award and a Fiction Collective Award for his 1987 novel, *Griever: an American Monkey King in China*, and a PEN Oakland Book Award for his 1990 autobiography *Interior Landscapes: Autobiographical Myths and Metaphors*. In deference to his stature as a scholar, in 1978 Vizenor was named to the James J. Hill Visiting Professorship in American Indian Studies at the University of Minnesota and in 1990 to the David Burr Chair at the University of Oklahoma. Through his writing and teaching Vizenor has had an impact on a new generation of Native writers and scholars, recasting the very vocabulary with which they approach Indigenous Studies. As the founder of two Native Literature series at major university presses – Oklahoma and Nebraska, he has also played a major role in creating opportunities for Native critical and creative works to find a place in print. Vizenor's mark in the arena of Native Studies is indeed indelible.

Born in Minneapolis in 1934 to a mixed-blood Ojibwe father and white mother – Clement William Vizenor and LaVerne Lydia Peterson – Gerald Robert Vizenor traces his descent from the Crane clan of the White Earth Anishinaabeg. The Crane orators figure significantly into Vizenor's fictional and autobiographical metaphors. He writes of the ajijaak, the Crane clan, and of the characteristics of this great bird, such as its "rolling voice" that carries far, from which derives the other term for the clan, the passweweg or "the echo makers." Among the Crane totem ancestors Vizenor identifies in his works are Keeshkemun, "grandson of the first leader of the Crane families", who received a George Washington Peace Medal and kept his followers neutral during the revolutionary war. He also writes of the Hudon Beaulieus – Colonel Clement, Augustus, and Theodore – who together published *The Progress*, the first newspaper on the White Earth Reservation. In several of his works, Vizenor recounts the seizure of the newspaper by federal agents because of its "controversial" stories and stances, and he reprints part of the testimony given by Colonel Clement Beaulieu in an 1887 subcommittee hearing regarding the case. In these and other accounts of his tribal ancestors, Vizenor finds "myth and metaphors" for his own calling as writer, intellectual, and political activist.

Vizenor's father, who had moved to Minneapolis from White Earth as part of the Relocation program, was murdered before young Gerald was yet two years old. In the ensuing years, Gerald would alternately live with his paternal grandmother and the extended family on his father's side, be cared for briefly by his mother, and be moved in and out of foster homes. At the age of eighteen, Vizenor dropped out of high school and joined the army, a move that would bring about his introduction to Asian literature and have a major influence on his career as a writer. Vizenor's army tour included a stint in Japan and an appointment as military entertainment director. In addition to awakening a latent interest in the arts, the Japanese experience brought Vizenor into intimate contact with the haiku tradition. When he was discharged in 1955, Vizenor returned to the United States and, despite the lack of a high school diploma, managed through a convoluted series of switchbacks and delays to attend first New York University and then the University of Minnesota, earning a bachelor's degree from Minnesota in child development in 1960.

Near the end of his undergraduate days he enrolled in a course on Japanese literature with Edward Copeland and encountered again the Japanese haiku masters Matsuo Basho and Kobayashi Issa as well as critical interpretations of the literature and culture. Vizenor remembers Copeland as a sensitive and influential teacher. By 1959, Vizenor had married Judith Horns and their son Robert was born in 1960. So despite beginning a position at Minnesota State

Reformatory as a social worker and taking on the new duties as husband and father, in 1960 Vizenor began graduate work at the University of Minnesota, taking classes in anthropology and library science, and continuing the study of Asian literature with Copeland. His growing interest in haiku led to the publication of his first haiku collection in 1962, *Two Wings the Butterfly*. This first collection was followed by six additional collections over the years: *Raising the Moon Vines* (1964), *Seventeen Chirps* (1964), *Slight Abrasions* with Jerome Downes (1966), *Empty Swings* (1967), *Matsushima: Pine Islands* (1984), and *Cranes Arise* (1999), as well as a new edition of *Raising the Moon Vines*, which includes a new introduction in 1999. Vizenor has been recognized as among the finest American haiku poets; his poems have been included in *The Haiku Anthology* and as examples in *The Pursuit of Poetry*, and he was invited to offer a keynote address to the Haiku North America Conference in 1999.

Vizenor's work with the haiku form includes not only his several collections of original haiku, but numerous eloquent discussions of the form in which he describes haiku thought in *Matsushima* as "intuitive, a manner of meditation at a dreamscape," the best haiku as "imaginative intersections in the natural world," and the haiku turn as involving "internal transformations." Key to the power of haiku in Vizenor's understanding, is the disappearance of the poem itself in the experience. He quotes Roland Barthes's characterization of haiku as the "literary branch of Zen" that it is "destined to halt language." The poem, according to Vizenor, is meant to bring us to "a moment of enlightenment." "The reader," he writes, "creates a dreamscape from haiku; nothing remains in print, words become dream voices, traces on the wind, twists in the snow, a perch high in the bare poplar" (Vizenor, *Matsushima*, n.p.).

Vizenor's own haiku cover a range of subjects and though about two thirds involve a natural scene, the scene is not rendered in a romantic or nostalgic manner. Instead, many of the poems turn on an unusual juxtapositon, a moment of surprise, an unresolved tension, or an ironic trickster twist. Though no single poem could be read as "typical," among those which Vizenor has included in more than one collection (with slight variation) is a playful poem which opens: "fat green flies / square dance across the grapefruit." After creating this seasonal image and invoking the motion of the scene, Vizenor closes with "honor your partner," offering a tease or twist in perspective. Other of his haiku create a kind of visual doubling or what Vizenor calls a moment of "visual transformation." One haiku, for example, begins with these lines: "march moon / shimmers down the sidewalk." Already we have the seasonal sense and the visual image of the moon's reflective motion. The last line, "snail crossing," adds another layer of movement, moisture, and visual reflection in the image of snail traces. The poem itself takes on a life beyond the words, shimmering on the verge of several possibilities – in the realm of multiplicities.

The haiku form holds additional fascinations for Vizenor who discovered there a kinship with the traditional Anishinaabeg dream songs. Both involve a restraint in language – are brief, tightly constructed, imagistic poems or song poems. Both arise out of a moment in nature, and involve a gesture beyond the poem or song toward experience, vision, or what Vizenor calls "dreamscape" or "transformation." Indeed Vizenor has called dream songs "the Ojibway haiku – in song." During the years that he was particularly immersed in writing haiku, Vizenor was also engaged in creating "reexpressions" of traditional songs, working with the translations published by Frances Densmore in 1910. He published these dream songs together with a short introduction in the 1965 *Summer in the Spring: Lyric Poems of the Ojibway*. A fairly typical example, one of the songs opens with one perception – "the sound of a loon" – then overlays another or transforms the image – "i thought / it was my lover / paddling" – creating the kind of multiplicity we saw in Vizenor's haiku.

Vizenor followed his publication of the dream songs with a 1970 volume of Ojibway stories: *anishinaabe adisokan: tales of the people*. The two books were later combined and published together in 1981 under the title *Summer in the Spring: Ojibway Lyric Poems and Tribal Stories*. This collection was reissued in a new edition in 1993.

By 1964, Vizenor was being pulled away from his graduate studies as he became more and more involved with the linked politics and survival strategies of Indian people in the Twin Cities of Minneapolis and St. Paul. For four years, from 1964 through 1968, he worked as a community organizer, holding a position in 1965 as a social worker for the Waite Settlement House in Minneapolis and in 1966 becoming the executive director of the American Indian Employment and Guidance Center. While working during these years to gain Bureau of Indian Affairs (BIA) support for Native people living in urban areas and working with individuals to troubleshoot issues from homelessness to unemployment to legal entanglements, Vizenor began to write freelance articles for the *Twin Citian* magazine and the *Minneapolis Tribune*. This freelance work eventually won Vizenor a position as general assignment reporter at the *Tribune*, a position he held from 1968 to 1969. He worked as an editorial writer for the newspaper in 1974 and continued as a contributing editor from 1974 to 1976. Many of the articles, editorials, and literary journalistic pieces Vizenor wrote during this time were collected in *Tribal Scenes and Ceremonies* in 1976 and then reprinted in an expanded collection, *Crossbloods: Bone Courts, Bingo, and Other Reports* in 1990.

Vizenor's articles and editorials from that era range broadly in subject, but revolve around contemporary Native issues including Indian child welfare, hunting and fishing rights, land claims, and Indian education. He attracted particular attention for his reporting on Thomas James White Hawk, a Lakota premedical student who was convicted of murder. Vizenor examined the details of White Hawk's life and claimed the young man's action stemmed partly from what Vizenor termed "cultural schizophrenia," arising from a schism between "an Indian unconscious" and "a white man's conscious mind," from the stress of being taken out of his Native culture and being pushed to fulfill "a bourgeois expectation" in a "white-dominated society."[2] Through the Minnesota chapter of the American Civil Liberties Union, Vizenor actually worked for the commutation of White Hawk's death sentence and, as late as 1993, continued to maintain contact with the man. In 1968 his long article on the White Hawk case was republished as a book, *Thomas James White Hawk;* it was reworked and included in *Tribal Scenes and Ceremonies*, and the story was later retold in Vizenor's own autobiography.

During these years as a journalist, Vizenor encountered various Anishinaabeg artists, activists, athletes, elders, and teachers. In 1972, he created a series of descriptive sketches of memorable individuals published under the title *The Everlasting Sky: New Voices from the People Named the Chippewa.* In this volume, Vizenor characterizes the new people of the woodlands, the *oshki anishinaabe*, as real and alive, as contemporary survivors, distinguishing them from romantic images invented to fulfill white men's myths of the *indian*. The collection was republished in 2000 with a new introduction.

A series of editorials Vizenor wrote in 1973 on the American Indian Movement (AIM) also took up the idea of romantic inventions and attracted a great deal of attention. Vizenor was among those critical of the tactics of the political organization, calling them a "symbolic confrontation group" and applying to them the epithet "peripatetic mouth warriors."[3] Vizenor critiqued AIM leaders for capitalizing on Indian stereotypes for publicity and for their perceived failure to invest their time in working for long-term changes. In these early editorials, we see Vizenor's theoretical stance begin to take shape in his pointed identification of the "simulation" as distinct from the real, his unmasking of the "invented Indian" as a political pose.

The new struggle for Native survival Vizenor began to characterize as vested in language; liberation, too, would come with a wresting of identity from the colonial entanglements involved in the language of manifest destiny. This move in Indian/White relationships from the literal to the literary battlefield Vizenor termed the "cultural word wars." In 1978, he published a collection of seventeen fiction and creative non-fiction pieces and entitled the collection *Wordarrows: Indians and Whites in the New Fur Trade*. Vizenor alludes in the title to N. Scott Momaday's story of an arrowmaker whose very survival depends upon language, and in the preface, he claims, "Language determines culture and the dimensions of consciousness" (Vizenor, *Wordarrows*, x). In addition to illustrating this thesis through accounts involving Minneapolis Indian politics, Vizenor also introduces in several stories tribal tricksters, characters the like of which will become his trademark in fiction. Here these imaginative figures – who Vizenor likens to the Ojibwe mythic figure of Naanabozho – playfully expose verbal ironies as they try to maintain a balance in the complicated terrain of urban America.

Several of the *Wordarrows* pieces revolve around language itself and they spin a trickster twist as they refer to, summarize, comment on, and excerpt from another of Vizenor's publications from 1978, the novel *Darkness in Saint Louis Bearheart*. The mutual referral between *Wordarrows* and *Bearheart* begins a trend of intertextuality that continues in Vizenor's later works. *Bearheart* begins, if not a series, at least a group of eight sometimes overlapping novels involving trickster figures and employing a trickster dynamic in their narrative structures. Vizenor constructs complicated family and narrative relationships within and between the novels, sometimes repeating or recasting scenes and stories from one book in another. Scholar Alan Velie has described Vizenor's fiction as "one huge Mobius strip" in which "the same characters scuttle in and out" (*Four American Literary Masters*, 144). But the referential texture of Vizenor's fiction involves more than this narrative fluidity; it involves continuous juxtaposition of supposedly separate realms of experience and knowledge. For example, characters and events from myth, from tribal history, and from Vizenor's personal remembrance exist and act together on the page with contemporary situations and personages. And to all of these sources – history, myth, personal experience, and current affairs – Vizenor adds the imaginative.

The plot of *Darkness in Saint Louis Bearheart*, for example, revolves around an oil shortage. When the lack of fuel brings America's consumer culture to an abrupt halt, a group of tribal clowns undertake a cross-country pilgrimage from the Minnesota Red Cedar Reservation to New Mexico in search of the vision window to the fourth world. The acknowledgments to the book attest to the use in the story of "real people with fictional names" and "fictional characters with real names" (Vizenor, *Darkness*, xxi). Figures on one side or another of these equations include Charles Lindbergh, President Jimmy Carter, N. Scott Momaday, Chief Bigfoot, and John Clement Beaulieu. Tribal myth is interwoven with contemporary politics to create a trickster allegory about liberation and survival.

As in most of his novels, the plot in Vizenor's *Bearheart* is episodic, secondary to the ideas, and the perspective is distinctly postmodern. The pilgrims encounter an array of unlikely characters and situations along their journey, and each situation allows for the introduction or expansion of elements of Vizenor's philosophy. Among the central ideas introduced is Vizenor's notion of "terminal creeds." "Terminal creeds" are static beliefs that prevent vital engagement in life and prescribe identity, especially, in the context of the story, Native identity. Through the novel, Vizenor undertakes the deconstruction of the stereotypical Indian identity, the one invented and sustained in the romantic and tragic poses of classic American representations. Among the characters whose actions in the novel clearly demonstrate the confinement involved in living by terminal beliefs is Belledonna Darwin-Winter Catcher whose clichéd definitions of Indian cause one of the other characters to describe her as "speaking as an invention" (191). Ultimately, the terminal creeds of the characters in the novel lead to their deaths and only those who relinquish word prisons wend their way to the fourth world, to symbolic liberation and survival.

Another characteristic Vizenor focus is introduced in *Bearheart* when the pilgrim clowns visit the Bioavaricious Regional Word Hospital. At this government-funded institution scientists attempt to "fix" language – both to repair its perceived breakdown and to freeze meanings and avoid the dangers of nonsense and language play. "In such a 'hospital,'" writes scholar Louis Owens in *Other Destinies* (1992), "the life of language is consumed and destroyed" (237). In stark contrast to the avaricious attempts of the hospital workers to devour the ambiguity of language Vizenor uses language to shake up fixed meanings, to liberate the thinking of his readers. In *Bearheart* and elsewhere he engages in wild word play. For example, he frequently coins words and phrases like "bioavaricious" itself, using these neologisms to suggest new perspectives. The collection of Vizenorese includes such classic phrases as "survivance," "socioacupuncture," "manifest manners," "postindian," "imagic," and "word cinema."

Vizenor's work reached an important turning point during this era of his life as he moved away from haiku and journalism toward fiction and later literary criticism and theory. This shift in literary focus came at the same time that the author made a gradual shift in his career as well, moving into the college classroom. As early as 1966 Vizenor served as a summer instructor for a special program on tribal cultures at Bemidji State University in northwestern Minnesota. In 1970, he took a one-year teaching appointment at Lake Forest College in Illinois. In 1971, he returned to Bemidji State, this time as director of Indian studies. In the next few years, he taught at several Twin Cities' campuses including Hamline, Augsburg, Macalaster, and the

University of Minnesota before accepting an appointment as lecturer in Native American Studies at the University of California at Berkeley in 1976. For several years he split his teaching between Minnesota and Berkeley finally being named the James J. Hill Visiting Professor in American Indian Studies at the University of Minnesota in 1978. By 1989, he was provost at Kresge College at the University of California, Santa Cruz, and, in 1990, held the David Burr Chair at the University of Oklahoma before returning again to the faculty at Berkeley. The new situations and Vizenor's immersion in the academic world lead to new developments in his writing.

The book to follow *Darkness in St. Louis Bearheart* was the 1981 *Earthdivers: Tribal Narratives on Mixed Descent*, a collection of twenty-one narratives which includes a section entitled "Earthdivers in Higher Education." The opening story of the book, "The Chair of Tears," offers a pointed satire of academic politics and an equally damning send up of the posturing and politics involved in Indian blood-quantum debates. Within the story, Chairman Shammer places the Department of American Indian Studies up for sale to the highest bidder, establishes a tribal color wheel, and brings in a skin dip consultant. The protagonist in this opening story is a trickster shaman who teaches through his humor. This, of course, is precisely what the character's creator does throughout the group of narratives – offers a corrective to faulty thinking and the possibility of another perspective through innovative storylines, humorous twists, and word play.

Key among Vizenor's tactics to awaken a new perspective in *Earthdivers* are his revamping of myth and his use of the trickster figure and trickster dynamic. He employs the earthdiver myth in the collection, but gives it a Vizenor twist suggesting the new earthdivers are "mixedbloods" and "tribal tricksters" who "dive into unknown urban places" in order to build a "new urban turtle island" (Vizenor, *Earthdivers*, ix, xi). Throughout the fiction that follows these early works, Vizenor continues to connect the contemporary to traditional myth or to interpret the contemporary by means of the mythic. He continues to develop his trickster theories, often using the trickster liberator as a metaphor for the tribal mixed-blood, and presenting the mixed-blood reality not as an impure or tragic identity, but as a position of power.

The fiction which follows Vizenor's Bearheart novel and the Earthdiver narratives includes seven other novels: *Griever, An American Monkey King in China* (1987), *The Trickster of Liberty: Tribal Heirs to a Wild Baronage* (1988), *The Heirs of Columbus* (1991), *Dead Voices: Natural Agonies in the Word Wars* (1992), *Hotline Healers: an Almost Browne Novel* (1997), *Chancers* (2000), and *Hiroshima Bugi* (2003). In addition to these works of full-length fiction, Vizenor also published a collection of short stories *Landfill Meditations: Crossblood Stories* in 1991. Although each involves an innovative plot or series of episodic plot elements, characters or their kin cross back and forth between the books as Vizenor develops many inter-related thematic elements and gradually evolves a theoretical language for understanding, not only his own work, but the unique situation of Native peoples and Native literatures in the realms of the Americas and the world.

Griever, for example, links the traditions of the Chinese Monkey King and the Native American trickster figure, offers an innovative retelling of the Chinese Journey to the West, and along the way critiques the political and social constraints of the People's Republic of China. *The Trickster of Liberty* weaves the tales of a family of Anishinaabeg tricksters whose fictional biographies link them to Vizenor's own geographical roots at White Earth Reservation. This novel offers one of Vizenor's strongest indictments of the "invented Indian" or "tribal simulation." One section, for instance, draws upon details from a story that has preoccupied Vizenor throughout his career, the true story of the Yahi Indian called Ishi who was captured and then literally museumized and studied as the "last of the Yahi." Another chapter in *The Trickster of Liberty* entitled "The Last Lecture at the Edge" satirizes the first generation of Indian educators and would-be Indians who, Vizenor contends, invent or perpetuate the romantic stereotyped ideal of Indianness to a new generation. The novel, under the new title *The Trickster of Liberty: Native Heirs to a Wild Baronage*, is to be reprinted by the University of Oklahoma Press in 2005.

The Heirs of Columbus, the novel written to coincide with the quincen-tenary observance of the arrival of Columbus in America, demonstrates Vizenor's penchant for challenging historical accounts and the supposed demi-gods of history. In *Heirs*, Vizenor offers alternative scenarios involving Columbus's religion, his lineage, his "heroic" stature, and his actions. The trickster reversals of the novel include the identification of Columbus as a Mayan descendant, the claim that it was the Mayan who "brought civiliza-tion to the savages of the Old World," and the claim that Columbus's misguided adventure to the Americas was actually a return to "his home-land" (9). But a final twist in Vizenor's imaginative story involves a discovery of healing genes in the bones of Columbus (which belong to the Anishinaabeg as his legal "heirs") and thus, the explorer whose appearance in the Americas brought a wave of destruction to Native cultures becomes the source of health and survival.

The action and characters of *Dead Voices* highlight many of Vizenor's theories about language, especially as concerns the difference between the oral and the written, between the dialogic and the monologic. *Hotline*

Healers challenges both the idea of the written and the idea of authorship as the protagonist Almost Browne signs and sells blank books, many with the signatures of other people. (This element of the novel resurrects one of the most popular stories and characters from his short fiction collection *Landfill Meditations*.) The tale also crosses and recrosses the borders between fiction and reality as it incorporates as characters a long list of contemporary writers and scholars, many in the field of Native literature (N. Scott Momaday, Louis Owens, Kimberly Blaeser, LaVonne Ruoff, John Purdy, etc.), and fictionalizes actual public events and private incidents involving these acquaintances of Vizenor to create a surreal Vizenor collage. The story likewise edges back and forth between legal absurdity and invention in a tale of a tribal casino and the political attempts to tax a luxury train, the Naanabazho Express, which serves tribal members on the reservation.

In both *Chancers* and *Hiroshima Bugi* Vizenor uses his fiction to challenge the status quo. In *Chancers*, he targets the display of human remains. By inventing a tale wherein native skulls are replaced with those of academics, he challenges the practice and strikes a blow for repatriation. In *Hiroshima Bugi*, he attempts to upset our comfort in supposed peace, satirizing the contemporary political system wherein peace is maintained by the threat of nuclear power. Like *Griever*, *Hiroshima Bugi* builds its story across cultures, here weaving Japanese culture and history with the Anishinaabeg and using the dropping of the atomic bomb on Hiroshima, the immediate destruction and the continued literary and symbolic fallout, to ground his critique.

During the years that Vizenor published this impressive collection of fiction, he also continued to work in several other genres. His screenplay "Harold of Orange" won the Film in the Cities award in 1983 and was filmed with Oneida comedian Charlie Hill playing the trickster protagonist. A playful story of tribal dealings with charitable foundations, the film confronts various Indian stereotypes, raises issues of repatriation and challenges enshrined historical accounts by suggesting another perspective.

Vizenor continues his examination of the colonization of history in his 1984 collection *The People Named the Chippewa: Narrative Histories*. His text questions not only the facts as conventionally presented, but also the motives and methods of historiography. As a corrective to alleged objective accounts, he offers a collage of voices that overlap and interact with one another to create a more accurate account of events. Included within this collage are not only the classic historical material, but mythic and fictionalized elements, and contributions from various times and perspectives.

In a similar vein, Vizenor's 1990 autobiography *Interior Landscapes: Autobiographical Myths and Metaphors* critiques the genre itself. Vizenor relates his life story – as the subtitle suggests – through the vehicles of myth and metaphor rather than as mere biography. Prior to the publication of this full-length work, Vizenor had written several shorter autobiographical pieces, touching more than once on the same subjects. In *Interior Landscapes*, he not only relates the events of his life, but comments on his own previous tellings of those events and uses theoretical discussions of autobiography to explain his serial constructions of meaning. For example, he quotes Paul John Eakin's claim that in the "autobiographical act" through our "memory and imagination" we shape materials from our past to "serve the needs of present consciousness" (102). Vizenor's account alludes frequently to the myth of the evil gambler and centers around ideas of survival: personal and cultural survival, actual and symbolic. Although the details of his experiences actually provide a wealth of fascinating material, Vizenor's "auto-bio-graphe" or "self life writing" strives to extend itself in important ways beyond the personal, beyond the mere biographical, and beyond the limits of the written.

Vizenor's employment of theory in the telling of his life story seems a natural outgrowth of his engagement with the works of scholars and the theorists such as Jean Baudrillard, Mikhail Bakhtin, and Michel Foucault. Vizenor has incorporated various elements of Reader Response and postmodern theory in his work and has himself been long engaged in the creation of a scholarly and critical language with which to understand Native literatures and Native experiences. In 1989, he edited the collection *Narrative Chance: Postmodern Discourse on Native American Indian Literatures* which included "A Postmodern Introduction" and his essay "Trickster Discourse: Comic Holotropes and Language Games." In 1994, he gathered together a group of his theoretical essays under the title *Manifest Manners: Postindian Warriors of Survivance*, many of which had earlier been published in journals like *boundary 2* and *World Literature Today*. In 1998, he released a second collection of heavily theory-laden essays in *Fugitive Poses: Native American Indian Scenes of Absence and Presence*.

The range of topics addressed in these collections is expansive involving everything from tribal gaming to works of tribal literature and Vizenor includes many intriguing accounts of figures from Ishi to Luther Standing Bear to Anishinaabeg elder George Aubid, but key to the discussions are issues of Native identity and the barter of language. Identities and meaning(s) Vizenor realizes are confined or liberated through the constructions of language and literature. In essays that make important distinctions like that between the simulation "Indian" and the imaginative survivance of the "postindian," Vizenor debates the fates of tribal sovereignties, attesting again and again that tribal survival depends upon the wresting of language from its colonial influences.

This move to liberate language clearly informs the whole of Vizenor's literary assemblage from haiku to novels to theoretical essays. His goals of survival and healing always come through contradiction and humor, often performed through metaphoric trickster figures. A journalist, poet, and fiction writer, a college professor, theorist, and activist, a "passeweweg," an Anishinaabeg "echo maker" like his ancestors, Vizenor's voice has forever marked the study of Native American Indian Literatures, it indeed "resounds over the earth" (*Interior Landscapes* 5).

Notes

1. L. Owens, "Afterward," in G. Vizenor, ed., *Bearheart: the Heirship Chronicles*, Minneapolis: University of Minnesota Press, 1990, p. 252; N. S. Momaday, "The Native Voice," in E. Elliott, ed., *Columbia Literary History of the United States*, New York: Columbia University Press, 1988, p. 15.
2. G. Vizenor, *Indians and Whites in the New Fur Trade*, Minneapolis: University of Minnesota Press, 1978, p. 154; G. Vizenor, *Tribal Scenes and Ceremonies*, Minneapolis: Nodin, 1976, p. 44; G. Vizenor, unpublished interview by K. Blaeser.
3. Vizenor, *Tribal Scenes and Ceremonies*, p. 52; G. Vizenor, *The People Named the Chippewa: Narrative Histories*, Minneapolis: University of Minnesota Press, 1984, p. 138.

Major secondary sources

Blaeser, K. M., *Gerald Vizenor: Writing in the Oral Tradition*. Norman: University of Oklahoma Press, 1996.

Boyarin, J., "Europe's Indian, America's Jew: Modiano and Vizenor," in *Storm from Paradise: the Politics of Jewish Memory*. Minneapolis: University of Minnesota Press, 1992, pp. 9–31.

Isernhagen, H., "Gerald Vizenor," in *Momaday, Vizenor, Armstong: Conversations on American Indian Writing*. Norman: University of Oklahoma Press, 1999, pp. 77–134.

Krupat, A., "Dead Voices, Living Voice: on the Autobiographical Writing of Gerald Vizenor," in *The Turn to the Native: Studies in Criticism and Culture*. Lincoln: University of Nebraska Press, 1996, pp. 70–87.

Lee, A. R., *Postindian Conversations*. University of Nebraska Press, 1999.
   ed., *Loosening the Seams: Interpretations of Gerald Vizenor*. Bowling Green: Bowling Green State University Popular Press, 2000.

Owens, L., "Ecstatic Strategies: Gerald Vizenor's Trickster Narratives," in *Other Destinies: Understanding the American Indian Novel*. Norman: University of Oklahoma Press, 1992, pp. 225–54.
   ed., Special Issue on Gerald Vizenor. *Studies in American Indian Literature* 9.1 (Spring 1997).

Pulitano, Elvira, "Liberative Stories and Strategies of Survivance: Gerald Vizenor's Trickster Hermeneutics," in *Toward a Native American Critical Theory*. Lincoln: University of Nebraska, 2003, pp. 145–86.

Rigal-Cellard, B., "Vizenor's Griever: A Post-Maodernist Little Red Book of Cocks, Tricksters, and Colonists," in A. Krupat, ed., *New Voices in Native American Literary Criticism*. Washington, DC: Smithsonian Institution Press, 1993, pp. 317–43.

Sims, C., "The Rebirth of Indian and Chinese Mythology in Gerald Vizenor's *Griever: an American Monkey King in China*, " in A. Krupat, ed., *New Voices in Native American Literary Criticism*. Washington, DC: Smithsonian Institution Press, 1993, pp. 171–77.

Velie, A., "Beyond the Novel Chippewa-style: Gerald Vizenor's Post-Modern Fiction," in *Four American Literary Masters: N. Scott Momaday, James Welch, Leslie Marmon Silko, and Gerald Vizenor*. Norman: University of Oklahoma Press, 1982, pp. 123–48.

Wilson, T. P. and R. A. Black, eds., A Special Issue on Gerald Vizenor. *American Indian Quarterly* 9.1 (Winter 1985).

15

CATHERINE RAINWATER

Louise Erdrich's storied universe

At her best, Louise Erdrich spins interconnected tales of unforgettable characters; to read her works is to play an active reader-role within an elaborately structured, historically allusive universe that is rich in layered meaning. Erdrich's recurrent themes concern the ties between people and geographical locations, the importance of community among all living beings, the complexities of individual and cultural identity, and the exigencies of marginalization, dispossession, and cultural survival. Family and mother-hood, storytelling, healing, environmental issues, and historical consciousness are likewise central, thematic emphases that thread Erdrich's works into the expanding web of contemporary American Indian literature.

Moreover, a cross-cultural vision registers powerfully in Erdrich's works and originates directly within her personal experience. Erdrich is the daughter of Ojibwe and German parents. She was born 7 June 1954, to Ralph Louis and Rita Joanne (Gourneau) Erdrich in Little Falls, Minnesota. She spent much of her youth in Wahpeton, North Dakota, where her parents taught at the Wahpeton Indian Boarding School. Her maternal grandparents ran a butcher shop in Little Falls, perhaps inspiring her invention of the Kozkas in *The Beet Queen* (1986) and, more recently, Fidelis Waldvogel in *The Master Butchers Singing Club* (2003). Erdrich's grandfather, Patrick Gourneau, was a beader, storyteller, and powwow dancer who also served as tribal chair of the Turtle Mountain Band of the Chippewa. Erdrich and her siblings were raised as Catholics, so the author of *Love Medicine* (1984, 1993) and other works knows firsthand the experiences of her characters whose spiritual worlds blend Ojibwen and Catholic cosmologies.

In 1972, Erdrich entered Dartmouth College in New Hampshire, where she met her future husband Michael Dorris, a mixed-blood Modoc and, at the time, an assistant professor of anthropology. At Dartmouth, she majored in English and creative writing, and published her first poem in *Ms.* magazine before graduating in 1976. After working at several different jobs, she entered Johns Hopkins University where she earned a master of arts degree in creative writing in 1979. Later, Erdrich returned to Dartmouth as writer-in-residence in the Native American Studies Program, where she also renewed her acquaintance with Dorris, whom she married in 1981. Their collaboratively produced works (for a while written under the pseudonym of Milou North) eventually earned them a national reputation as an idealized, glamorous, artistic couple. They raised three adopted children and three of their own; the eldest of the adopted children was the subject of Dorris's *The Broken Cord* (1989), a powerful exposé of the tragedy of fetal alcohol syndrome among American Indian populations. Dorris and Erdrich also co-authored two books, *The Crown of Columbus* (1991) and *Route Two* (1991). Fans were shocked when their marriage failed and Dorris committed suicide in 1997 in the wake of a particularly unpleasant divorce. In subsequent years, Erdrich has continued to write and to run her own store, Birchbark Books in Minneapolis, which also sponsors and supports Native American grassroots political activities.

Erdrich has won numerous literary awards including the National Book Critics Circle Award, and the Nelson Algren Fiction Award in 1982 for "The World's Greatest Fisherman," a short story that together with "The Red Convertible" and "Scales" would become part of the novel, *Love Medicine*. Her major works include *Jacklight* (1984), *Love Medicine* (1984, 1993), *The Beet Queen* (1986), *Tracks* (1988), *Baptism of Desire: Poems* (1989), *The Crown of Columbus* (with Michael Dorris, 1991),*The Bingo Palace* (1994), *The Blue Jay's Dance: a Birth Year* (1995), *Tales of Burning Love* (1996), *The Antelope Wife* (1998), *The Last Report on the Miracles at Little No Horse* (2001), and *The Master Butchers Singing Club* (2003).[1]

The publication in 1984 of *Love Medicine* marks the beginning of what some call the "second wave" of a Native American literary renaissance that commenced in the late 1960s with works by N. Scott Momaday, Gerald Vizenor, James Welch, and Leslie Marmon Silko. Distinguishing *Love Medicine* among the novels of her predecessors, however, and partially explaining its continued popular appeal, may be its comparably greater accessibility to a mass audience. Though the novel is grounded in tribal, particularly Ojibwe, culture and history, readers unacquainted with these contexts may nevertheless quickly engage with the novel, partly owing to Erdrich's audience-accommodating narrative strategies that are adapted from oral to written storytelling. Also enabling a diverse readership is her primary focus on the development of characters who (like non-native readers deciphering texts by native writers) negotiate gaps between cultural realities. Erdrich's adept construction of cross-culturally nuanced symbols and metaphors further aids readers' efforts to decode her interlaced narratives (for example, the fisherman symbol in *Love Medicine* that invites complementary Ojibwen and Christian interpretations).

In other words, Erdrich seems deliberately to cultivate a general readership by crafting multiple points of entry into her texts, then proceeding to educate the audience more specifically in particulars of American Indian history, culture, cosmology, and epistemology. She might have learned some of these narrative techniques from Silko, whose *Ceremony* (1977) and *Storyteller* (1981) offer metatextual instruction, assisting readers in accurate interpretation. Like Momaday, Vizenor, and Welch, however, and despite her studied attempts at inclusiveness, Silko probably poses greater interpretive challenges than Erdrich for non-native readers. Thus, *Love Medicine* – together with *Tracks* (1988) one of the most frequently taught Native American novels – has perhaps played a key role in the introduction of non-native readers to works by indigenous authors.

Love Medicine is the first in a series of novels developing a multi-generational family saga set in both imaginary and actual places in North Dakota. *The Beet Queen, Tracks, The Bingo Palace, Tales of Burning Love, The Last Report on the Miracles at Little No Horse,* and *The Master Butchers Singing Club* are the other works in the set. Erdrich's narrative tactics in these novels are derived from both Eurocentric and tribal storytelling forms. For instance, critics have noted the influence of Faulkner, whose Yoknapatawpha County folk inhabit several of his novels and short stories, and whose characters variously narrate portions of Faulkner's southern epic from their unique points of view. The obvious influence of Faulkner, however, does not eclipse that of tribal raconteurs whose voices have shaped the traditional Ojibwen tales informing Erdrich's prose.

Erdrich's series of novels is best read in the order it was written, starting with the definitive, revised (1993) edition of *Love Medicine* where we meet members of all the families featured throughout the other five volumes: the Kashpaws, the Lazarres, and Lulu Nanapush's extended family, which includes the Morrisseys. Several plots unfold in *Love Medicine*. A few sub-plots are developed in subsequent novels. The peripheral stories unwind from the central one concerning Marie Lazarre and Lulu Nanapush's rivalry for the attentions of Nector Kashpaw, who marries Marie but conducts a lifelong affair with Lulu. He has children with both women, thus forever entangling two of the families in kinship networks even more complicated than the already intricate tribal ones. *Love Medicine* draws its title from the inept efforts of the clownish Lipsha Morrissey – Lulu's grandson and an important character in three of her novels – to unravel a kinship mystery by concocting a love potion for Nector.

Erdrich's second novel, *The Beet Queen*, features new characters while developing in the background some of the storylines introduced in *Love Medicine*. An oral storyteller's improvisational moves are apparent in this text; Erdrich seems at once to be writing according to a tentative plan for a multivolume set of stories without conveying the impression that any part of the plan is set in stone. The resulting factual and temporal inconsistencies that develop over the course of interrelated volumes eventually win Erdrich both chastisement and acclaim, depending on reviewers' and critics' relative tolerance for such an improvisational style. Indeed, some readers laud her techniques either as "postmodern" or as typical of traditional Indian story-tellers, while others rebuke Erdrich for a perceived carelessness of detail.

The Beet Queen is set in the fictional town of Argus, North Dakota. We meet new characters, both Indian and white, as well as mixed-bloods, but the story revolves mainly around individuals from the latter two groups: the Adares, the Kozkas, and Wallace Pfef are white, while Celestine James and her daughter, Dot, are mixed-bloods. The Beet Queen invites readers to see through the perspectives of characters exhibiting more "Indian" than Western consciousness, and to think about Eurocentric interests and values that dominate the lives of people who do not embrace them. Erdrich's characters are isolated and lonely; their families are fragmented. For their existential pain, Erdrich prescribes selfless, motherly love such as Celestine James (the mother of the "beet queen," Dot Adare) and Wallace Pfef (a compassionate gay man) display. With The Beet Queen, Erdrich begins to acquire her reputation as a writer interested in gender politics and the perspectives of female characters.

Erdrich's third novel in the series – the one set earliest in chronological time – is Tracks. Here we learn about the ancestry and the young lives of Marie, Nector, and Lulu, and about the loss of reservation lands to loggers during the opening years of the twentieth century. Erdrich's environmental consciousness registers as she remarks not only the theft of Indian land, but also its tragic commercial and industrial exploitation. Tracks is alternately narrated by the reliable Nanapush, a man of great medicine power who was educated in white society but rejects it to return to his own culture and beloved trees, and by the unreliable Pauline Puyat, a mixed-blood white-Indian girl who, opposite to Nanapush, deplores her native identity. Both Nanapush and Pauline in Tracks acquaint us with one of Erdrich's most compelling female characters, Fleur Pillager, a woman of strong passions and medicine power to match. Nanapush in his chapters speaks directly to his "granddaughter," Lulu, to tell her about Fleur, who is her mother. Interlaced with Nanapush's benevolent perspectives on Fleur, Pauline's neurotic, con-trapuntal narration portrays Fleur as evil and sheds light onto the perverse identity that Pauline assumes as the nun, Sister Leopolda, in Love Medicine.

Picking up a few years following the events of Love Medicine, The Bingo Palace acquaints us more thoroughly with the lovable buffoon,

Lipsha Morrissey; he is heir to the Pillager's healing touch but incompetent to manage the power to "cure or kill" that Nanapush, Lulu, and Fleur adroitly wield. In a memorable episode underscoring the comic dimensions of Erdrich's writing and Lipsha's trickster identity, Lipsha visits great-grandmother Fleur in her cabin in the woods, only to be scared senseless by the powers of the unseen that align themselves with members of his family. Like some Ichabod escaping the Headless Horseman, Lipsha flees the cabin more terrified by his own overwrought imagination than of anything actual. Instead of learning to use the power that flows in his Pillager blood, Lipsha at the end of *The Bingo Palace* sits stranded in a broken-down car in a blizzard, a scene suggesting that he might die as pointlessly as his mother, June Kashpaw, who perishes drunk in the snow in the opening chapters of *Love Medicine*. However, in the next novel we find that in true trickster fashion, Lipsha escapes the fate impending at the end of *The Bingo Palace*.

The fifth novel in the saga, *Tales of Burning Love*, takes place in Fargo, North Dakota, and in the fictional Argus. Like *The Beet Queen*, it focuses primarily on a new set of protagonists, Jack Mauser and his five wives, but their various relationships to characters in *Love Medicine*, *The Beet Queen*, and *The Bingo Palace* form significant intertextual linkages. Like the other novels, *Tales* features several narrators who recount and revise (or inadvertently contradict, depending upon one's critical appraisal of Erdrich's technique) some of the stories told by other characters in the other novels. *The Last Report on the Miracles at Little No Horse* revisits stories of families introduced in *Love Medicine* and refines, deepens, and complicates (or, again, depending on our critical predilections, perhaps confuses) our view of Lamartines, Pillagers, Morrisseys, and Kashpaws whom we have previously met. Erdrich's readers are especially astonished to learn that Father Damien, a benevolent, cross-culturally sensitive Catholic priest, is not after all a man but a woman. In developing Father Damien's character in this way, Erdrich's penchant for deconstructing social conventions and constructions, including gender norms, finds its most simultaneously serious and comic expression. We see her worldview writ large: reality, like serial texts, is always subject to revision.

Revisions also abound in Erdrich's most recent novel, *The Master Butchers Singing Club*, in which new characters inhabit the familiar town of Argus together with the kin of a familiar family, the Lazarres of *Love Medicine*. This latest novel explores the lives of European settlers in the Argus area. It suggests that immigration occasioned by modern European wars continues, even in the twentieth-century, powerfully to affect the land and the indigenous people of North America. Fidelis Waldvogel settles in Argus after fighting in the German army in World War I as a sniper with a deadly aim. He apparently has an equally keen eye for business. Anticipating America's future global dominion – symbolized by the pre-sliced squares of white bread that Fidelis finds on his plate at the end of the war – Fidelis packs up his new wife, his set of master butcher knives and a case full of sausages, and heads for the United States. Soon he becomes an icon of middle-class prosperity and the leader of a singing club noted for its quality and the diversity of its membership. Like the choral group and the rest of Erdrich's novels, *The Master Butchers Singing Club* features an intricate constellation of characters caught up within several intersecting plot lines. It centers around a powerful, magnetic attraction between Fidelis and Delphine Watzka, both of whom loyally and patiently await their freedom from prior commitments in order to fulfill their apparent destiny together. When Fidelis's wife dies and Delphine's homosexual husband leaves, the two come together like the grand forces of nature to which the narrator compares them. Through the character of Cyprian Lazarre, Erdrich continues to pose questions about human sexuality and the identities that different cultures forge around this powerful force. Through Fidelis, who is capable of both vicious butchery of human beings and exalted, soul-shattering love, Erdrich also explores many of the same paradoxical issues of human potentiality that she has found compelling in the past. Like several of her latest novels, *Master Butchers* has received mixed reviews from critics, some of whom find the plot overwrought and the style too florid; others celebrate narrative and stylistic strategies that have won for Erdrich an array of admirers.

Erdrich has written other novels dealing with entirely different characters. Though *The Antelope Wife* (1998) contains material that could develop into a new multivolume family saga, it has been the most harshly criticized of all of Erdrich's works. Indeed, *The Antelope Wife* challenges even the most experienced of Erdrich's readers; it pressures us to weigh the critical pros and cons of Erdrich's apparently escalating tendency toward what some call postmodern discontinuity and heteroglossia, and what others describe less generously. (The fact that *The Antelope Wife* was written during the bitter aftermath of a divorce, a child custody battle, and the death by suicide of her husband possibly complicates our assessment.)

Set in and around Minneapolis, *The Antelope Wife* interweaves stories of the Roy, the Shawano, and the Whiteheart Beads families. Despite Erdrich's use of a central narrating consciousness reminding us of the collective, third-person narrative passages in *The Bingo Palace*, important connections between and among eight generations of characters are sometimes vague, sometimes confusing enough to discourage even the most diligent reader-sleuths among Erdrich's devotees. The use of Ojibwe words throughout the text further limits accessibility for most readers. Irritated reviewers of this novel as well as of *The Last Report on the Miracles at Little No Horse* charge Erdrich not only with having earlier exhausted the narrative strategies that she employs, but also with managing them far less successfully in these works of her mature years. Nevertheless, we may observe in its favor that *The Antelope Wife* marks a new and interesting turn in Erdrich's environmental consciousness, and affords rewarding material for ecocritics intrigued by her representations of animals. For the first time in Erdrich's novels, we hear animals speak; we are urged to drop not only our Eurocentric views of reality, but some of our anthropocentric ones, as well.

To arrive at our own careful judgments of Edrich's art, both early and recent, we must in the end conduct our own investigations. Readers looking for more than entertainment from Erdrich's works may enjoy enhanced first readings of her novels by consulting beforehand Beidler and Barton's *Reader's Guide to the Novels of Louise Erdrich* (2000). This text provides not only excellent plot summaries of individual works, but also a variety of other reader aids, including maps, family trees, and chronologies; such prompts facilitate sophisticated engagement with Erdrich's art and, doubtless, minimize reader frustration.

Even Erdrich's detractors admit that her works, together with those of the growing numbers of Native American and other minority writers, have expanded the definition of American literature. Contemporary Native American literature fills a conspicuous, centuries-deep silence where voices of indigenous Americans might have sounded. Because most written literature by American Indians has been produced during the later twentieth century and has exploited both modernist and postmodernist literary modes, their writing also potentially affects our understanding of postmodernity and postmodern artistic expression. For the first time in American literary history, writers from previously marginalized groups are shaping literary trends; for instance, we might easily argue that contemporary writers from minority groups have, like Erdrich, in their attempts to correct mainstream views of their identity, aligned themselves with postmodern philosophical inquiry to challenge our very notions of historical truth.

Questions about history – not only about *what* happened in the past, but also about *how* different groups of human beings perceive and record experience from diverse, subjective points of view – are fundamental to postmodernist thought; such questions frequently preoccupy creative artists, who devise poems, novels, and other works inviting us to abandon familiar frames of reference for those of the cultural Other. Like so many Native American writers, Erdrich moves beyond the need merely to address familiar injustices; her works call on us to develop a new historical consciousness. This revised awareness might enable us to see how dominant societies have constructed their own versions of history that have passed for objective truth; furthermore, Erdrich implies, a more inclusive vision might help humanity to heal some historical wounds and to avoid repeating mistakes in the future.

The general "reconstruction" of history, including, but not limited to American history, has been underway for over two decades. Culture studies, gender studies, and the New Social History variously address the experiences of socially and economically disfranchised groups whose voices have been silenced or marginalized in mainstream historical narrative. Together with Native American studies in general, American Indian literature plays a profound role in this revisionary movement. In addition to telling the stories of their people from tribal points of view, Indian writers such as Anna Lee Walters, Robert Conley, Leslie Marmon Silko, Linda Hogan, and Louise Erdrich press readers with questions about the impact of the past on the present moment, as well as on the future.

In *Love Medicine* and its sequels, for example, readers learn, usually for the first time from an Ojibwen perspective, the regional history of the Turtle Mountain Ojibwe of North Dakota, a people many times betrayed in their reluctant, but forced, dealings with Euro-Americans. Their collective and individual identities have been affected dramatically in this process. Readers also learn from indigenous points of view how Roman Catholicism, since its arrival in the early nineteenth century, has transformed native culture. Like Momaday, Silko, Hogan, and others, Erdrich explores the lasting effects of the spiritual as well as the material colonization of Native Americans. We hear the voices of people whom both Catholic and Protestant missionaries set out to "save," but who did not then, and do not now, consider themselves "lost." From Erdrich's prose we also learn Ojibwen names of places, animals, and natural and spiritual phenomena; the words suggest how "the enemy's language" (Muskogee / Cherokee poet, Joy Harjo's description of English) obscures Indian reality, particularly the fusion of material and spiritual realms that is implied in tribal languages.

Numerous critics have addressed Erdrich's treatment of history. Their analyses remind us that Euro-Americans and Native Americans often disagree even regarding what counts as historical information, and why such information ought to be preserved. In *Tracks*, for instance, Nanapush shows little interest in the monumental, large-scale events and high-profile national leaders that would concern a typical Western historian; instead, his attention is drawn to local, communal matters. Moreover, he values the past for its morally instructive capacities: stories remind human beings of their immediate responsibilities to community, nature, and self. That Lulu should know her mother and understand her family's place among the people matters more than any material contained in an archive or a textbook, the sort of "history" one learns at school. Only insofar as personal history branches into national or "official" history does it concern Nanapush, who does know, for instance, the national history behind the environmental destruction of his native lands. Nanapush teaches us to learn history first through our hearts, not our minds, in order to understand our individual responsibilities to past, present, and future. Such an educational process can begin only locally, he implies.

One of Erdrich's contemporaries, Anna Lee Walters, likewise underscores the fundamentally different emphases of Eurocentric and Indian accounts of the past in *Ghost Singer* (1988), a novel exploring the frustrations of a white historian who aspires to write a Navajo history, but who dismisses as trivial or irrelevant all information he receives from Navajo sources. Erdrich, Walters, and others among "second wave" Indian writers today insist that all of us throughout the world need to broaden and deepen our historical consciousness of how the errors of the past, unremedied, continue to shape the present and the future, and of how our personal, intimate histories connect us to the larger national and global scenes. Moreover, within a tribal frame of reference such as Nanapush describes for us in *Tracks*, or as Lipsha begins to grasp in *Love Medicine*, we learn to see our responsibility for repairing a damaged world, even if we are not personally the ones who spoiled it.

In addition to challenging readers' ideas about history and its potential for revision, Erdrich is well known for her cross-culturally innovative use of multiple narrators within single texts, and for elaborate, intertextual connections between and among her novels. Her works demand attentive, participatory readers willing to work hard to perceive and recall subtle but mutually reinforcing patterns – temporal sequences, kinship networks, serial repetition of images, metaphors, and symbols. Strands of references to photographs and posters in *The Bingo Palace*, chains of biblical and literary allusions in *Love Medicine*, strings of interrelated water images in *Tracks* – all are complexly interconnected, as are the sometimes contradictory versions of single stories that different narrators subjectively recount. A significant dimension of the reader's task involves philosophical reflection upon Erdrich's representation of reality; for her and her characters, human experience of the world is radically disjunctive. Indeed, the moral and ethical values that Erdrich espouses through her art – compassion, responsibility, respect, caution (especially in the use of language, the most powerful medicine according to Nanapush) – arise from Erdrich's apparent sense of human vulnerability in a world that is beautiful but ultimately beyond our limited comprehension, despite our paradoxical power to affect the world and one another with our words and deeds.

Besides novels, Erdrich has written essays, children's books[2] and short stories. Many of the stories, too numerous to list but including the widely anthologized "The World's Greatest Fisherman," "The Red Convertible," and "Mauser," she has revised and embroidered into her novels. Erdrich is also an accomplished poet. Her poems, like her narratives, are richly nuanced and reward careful reading. The poem lending its title to her first collection of poems, "Jacklight," and "Captivity" (from the same collection) are among her poems most frequently appearing in anthologies. Both clearly reveal the range and depth of her poetic ability.

As the opening epigram in "Jacklight" alerts us, single words often have a variety of meanings, a linguistic phenomenon that makes much poetry possible. Such polysemous qualities of language, exploited by the poet, lead the mind to imaginative territory undiscoverable in other ways. In "Jacklight," Erdrich not only exploits the protean qualities of single words, but she also shows her skill at developing poems interpretable in several different, though complementary, ways. At one level, "Jacklight" concerns hunters and their prey, who are drawn to the edge of the woods by the hunters' "artificial sun." At another level, the aggressors with their "light" are the United States soldiers, Indian killers, pioneers, missionaries, and other Euro-Americans who, for centuries, have hunted native people variously to move them, kill them, educate them, or "save" them. In this poem, Erdrich portrays native people as the denizens of the woods, at home in the "darkness" of nature much like the animals whom they respect as fellow beings on the earth; both Indians and animals alike have been under assault, she suggests, by the various "lights" of Western European civilization. Possibly alluding to pan-Indian prophecies about the end of Eurocentric dominion in the Americas, Erdrich ends her poem with an ambiguous threat or promise of new times to come: the inhabitants of the woods invite their pursuers to join them in the darkness of nature, where entirely different kinds of knowledge are required for survival.

Like Erdrich's novels, "Jacklight" is a work that rewards careful attention to its complexities at both verbal and thematic levels. "Captivity" also appeals to the close reader who appreciates elaborate symbolism and intertextual play. In this poem, Erdrich appropriates the voice of Mary Rowlandson, author of the classic American narrative of Indian captivity during the violent New England war against Puritan encroachment of 1675 to 1676 (King Philip's War) led by the Wampanoag leader Metacomet, or King Philip. Rowlandson's famous narrative reveals the author's psychological difficulties as she struggles to maintain her biblical and Eurocentric point of view toward her captors and her experience. Long after her release, Rowlandson's tale reveals, she remains deeply disturbed; mere food cannot satisfy her eternal hunger, and she cannot sleep peacefully. She can no longer see the world the way she did before her capture, but any revision of her previous view seems apparently too threatening for her to consider.

Erdrich moves into the dark, psychic territory left unexplored by Rowlandson in her own work. With Rowlandson as the speaker, Erdrich develops a short poem implying that captivity humanized the Indians for the captive and, moreover, made her feel slightly less secure in her Western, Calvinist perspective. Erdrich's "Captivity" suggests that Rowlandson's insomnia and hunger result from her brief glimpse beyond her Western, artificial reality into the world of a people more elementally at home in the universe. An awakened, but barely conscious, awareness of a larger reality haunts the speaker's dreams and daytime musings. Similar to the way in which Jean Rhys's *Wide Sargasso Sea* (1966) intertextually connects with Charlotte Brontë's Jane Eyre (1847) and recuperates the untold story of Bertha Mason, the cultural and ethnic Other, Erdrich's "Captivity" reaches back into the American colonial past to locate parts of Rowlandson's story that she was unable to tell; like Rhys, Erdrich explores dimensions of colonial experience that subtly undercut Eurocentric portrayals of the past and of the relationships between dominant and dominated cultures.[3]

Notes

1. *Jacklight*, New York: Holt, Rinehart, and Winston, 1984; *Love Medicine*, New York: Holt, Rinehart and Winston, 1984/1993; *The Beet Queen*, New York: Bantam, 1986; *Tracks*, New York: Holt, 1988; *Baptism of Desire: Poems*, New York: Harper and Row, 1989; *The Crown of Columbus* (with Michael Dorris), New York: Harper Collins, 1991; *The Bingo Palace*, New York: Harper Collins, 1994; *The Blue Jay's Dance: a Birth Year*, New York: Harper Collins, 1995; *Tales of Burning Love*, New York: Harper Collins, 1996; *The Antelope Wife*, New York: Harper Collins, 1998; *The Last Report on the Miracles at Little No Horse*, New York: Harper, 2001; *The Master Butchers Singing Club*, Harper Collins, 2003.
2. *Grandmother's Pigeon*, New York: Hyperion, 1996; *The Birchbark House*, New York: Hyperion, 1999; and *The Range Eternal*, New York: Hyperion, 2002.
3. Louise Erdrich's *Four Souls: A Novel* (Harper Collins, 2004) appeared after *The Cambridge Companion to Native American Literature* went to press.

Major secondary sources

Beidler, Peter G. and Gay Barton, eds., *A Reader's Guide to the Novels of Louise Erdrich: Geography, Genealogy, Chronology, and Dictionary of Characters.* Columbia: University of Missouri Press, 1999.

Castillo, Susan Perez, "Postmodernism, Native American Literature, and the Real: The Silko-Erdrich Controversy," *Massachusetts Review* 32 (1991), 285–94.

Chavkin, Allan, ed., *The Chippewa Landscape of Louise Erdrich*. Tuscaloosa: University of Alabama Press, 1999.

Peterson, Nancy J., "History, Postmodernism, and Louise Erdrich's Tracks, *PMLA* 109 (October 1994), 982–94.

Rainwater, Catherine, *Dreams of Fiery Stars: the Transformations of Native American Fiction*. Philadelphia: University of Pennsylvania Press, 1999.

Ruppert, James, *Mediation in Contemporary Native American Fiction*. Norman: University of Oklahoma Press, 1995.

Sarris, Greg, Connie A. Jacobs, and James R. Giles, eds., *Approaches to Teaching the Works of Louise Erdrich*. New York: MLA, 2004.

Wong, Hertha D. Sweet, ed., *Louise Erdrich's Love Medicine: a Casebook*. New York: Oxford University Press, 2000.

16

LAURA COLTELLI

Joy Harjo's poetry

Joy Harjo assigns a central role to the power of the word – the mythic embodiment and memory of the Native American world – in shaping the remarkable quality of her writing as a living testimony: without evoking folkloristic elements, her work gives life to characters, stories, beliefs of Indian identity; without pompous statements of intent, she gives force to a political vision; without censorious overtones she gives voice to the passions.

Just as her own position is constantly intertwined with the historical path charted by her own tribe, so the urban cityscape also becomes contiguous with the natural landscape and the dialogue of love and thought becomes continuous with the myths of tradition. Thus, far from evoking a world of picturesque Indians or reminiscences of an ethnographic museum, she offers a serene and strong assertion of a complex personal identity, without reticence, but also without exaggerated emphasis on her roots or lifestyle choices.

Born in Tulsa, Oklahoma, in 1951 to a Creek father (the Creek are also known as the Muscogee) and a Cherokee / French mother, Harjo's paternal ancestors feature valiant warriors such as the Menawa Chief who led the "Red Stick War" against General Andrew Jackson in the early 1800s. As she herself mentions in several interviews, during her childhood and adolescence, she felt considerably closer to her father's family than her mother's. She looked to her grandmother Naomi and her great-aunt Lois, both of whom were artists, as role models of emancipated women and precious sources of transmission of a treasured cultural heritage. After a painful family conflict arising from her parents' divorce, at a very early age, she sought refuge in the Southwest, which would play such a crucial role in her cultural development. She enrolled in the Institute of American Indian Arts (IAIA) in Santa Fe, New Mexico, determined to embark on a career in art and painting. This was a period of growing up and becoming more mature, but also a deeply disordered period. Harjo did succeed in completing the course and obtaining her diploma in 1968. At the age of seventeen, after a brief affair with a student, she gave birth to her first child. Meanwhile, she began to study medicine at the University of New Mexico, abandoning the course shortly afterwards in favor of painting and then creative writing.

The climate of the civil rights movements, especially Indian rights activism, and consciousness-raising among ethnic minorities, especially as inspired by Indian authors, prompted Harjo to give voice to her Indianness. The influence of Leslie Marmon Silko and a young poet, Simon Ortiz, proved decisive for Joy Harjo, who began to write at the age of twenty-two. She published her first compositions and obtained a BA in creative writing in 1976 from the University of New Mexico. She then enrolled at the University of Iowa. Meanwhile, she gave birth to her second daughter, Rainy Dawn, springing from a relationship with Simon Ortiz. Her burdensome family commitments as a single mother compelled her to seek work as a waitress, a hospital cleaner, and a gas station attendant. Nevertheless, she managed to complete her MFA in Iowa in 1978. She also studied cinematographic techniques at the Anthropology Film Center of Santa Fe and subsequently taught creative writing at IAIA, the University of Colorado, Boulder, and Arizona State University in Tempe. She developed even more profound ties with the landscape of the Southwest, which would become as significant in its impact on her creative path as that of her native Oklahoma, which she still today regularly visits in order to take part in the ceremonies of her tribe.

Indeed, the history and culture of the Creeks are intermeshed with her personal history as an Indian in contemporary America. The Creeks, one of the most advanced tribes of the Southeast, were progressively forced to emigrate westwards on account of the violent expansion of the white settlers. In 1832 they lost their lands in Alabama and Georgia and were displaced to present-day Oklahoma. During this Trail of Tears thousands of Indians lost their lives. After bravely reestablishing their identity as a people, the Creeks found themselves once again facing severe challenges. The discovery of oil in Oklahoma at the end of the nineteenth century led to tremendous upheavals, including the forced expropriation of the tribal lands. The division of a tiny section of the land into small plots given to individual Indian families totally disrupted Indian principles of collective ownership. In 1907, when Oklahoma became an official state, the Creek Indians together with other tribes were already a severely marginalized tribe.

Thus over a span of about forty years the Creeks were twice deprived of their land, becoming "a stolen people in a stolen land," as Harjo would later say in *In Mad Love and War* (1990). Loss of identity, dissolution of cultural roots, disintegration of the community and the family unit, alcoholism, violence, the tenacious will to survive and breathe new life into one's group, all of these represent the main themes of Harjo's poetry. These themes are charted in *She Had Some Horses* (1983), the collection that marked Harjo as one of the most accomplished Native American women poets of her generation. The themes are emphasized in her poetry, in her teaching at UCLA, where she is a full professor, and in her many popular performances of her poetry, which have included backing music by her former band Poetic Justice. For her new band of accomplished musicians she is writing original music.

Harjo published her first collection of poetry in 1975. *The Last Song* reveals her awareness of the alienated situation of Indians in American society; the "young warriors" transformed into "broken men" as in the poem "3 AM" where "two Indians / at three in the morning / trying to find a way back". Yet it is a world that comes alive through the interplay of opposites. Squalid bar scenes are offset by inspiring views of natural landscapes, which in later collections become mythical places and an important focus of Harjo's poetry. Other elements that foreshadow her later poetry are the trickster, represented here by the crow – a metaphor of freedom and transformational power – and the wind as a purifying element. The female universe is also strongly present in these early poems. There are figures of women who are attempting to deal with harsh family and environmental situations, "angry women" who "are building / houses of stones / they are grinding mortar / between straw-thin teeth / and broken families" ("Conversation Between Here and Home"). One also finds figures, stories, places, images visited with the eye of memory, that "delta in the skin" as Harjo would call it in *She Had Some Horses*, with which she engaged in a close-meshed dialogue to combat or come to terms with painful legacies. Reflecting her artistic background, these are poems that include images hinging on chromatically clear-cut contrasts. Indeed, the drawings accompanying the poems furnish visual commentary. The language of this poetry is linear and not convoluted; it brings into sharp focus certain elements of a scene that she perceives through fragments and half-glimpsed shots.

In 1979 she published *What Moon Drove Me to This?*, which included the ten poems of *The Last Song*. Organized into two sections, "Winter" and "Summer," this collection likewise contained a preview of a number of themes that would be foregrounded in her later collections. "Winter" contains twenty-five poems with images of a devastating whiteness that act as the background to an Indian context of absolute isolation. But one also finds intense underscoring of the passion of love and of bonding with the mother figure as a founding experience of continuity and renewal. In the thirty-two poems of "Summer," on the other hand, there is a predominance of sunlit imagery that springs from contemplation of the landscape with which the poetic self establishes a regenerating connection. The figure of a woman also stands out with increasing intensity, "a dangerous woman," who has come from a hard background but who, at the same time, stretches forcefully toward a rebirth she feels to be possible as she listens to the "voices of mountains ... the forgiveness of blue sky," aware that "she must flow with the elusive bodies / of night wind women / who will take her / into her own self" ("Fire").

Noni Daylight, Harjo's alter ego, makes her first appearance in four poems poised between rage and violence, fear and desire to remember the past, the power of the word and the bondage of silence. "Four Horses Songs" prefigure the horses in *She Had Some Horses*. Here they are identified through four colours. Three of them – white, red, grey – are contaminated by white culture. The yellow horse contains the signs of a rebirth, albeit rendered problematic by the adversities of the present. The relationship with the earth seems to offer the only impulse of life and loyal alliance in a fragmented and divided world.

Equally significant is the last poem, which is only one line long, "That's what she said." The statement highlights the role of storytelling and therefore of oral culture. This line is echoed by the section title "What I Should Have Said" in *She Had Some Horses*; the title implies a critical glance at the past and an uninterrupted dialogue with her own life story.

What Moon Drove Me to This? is built around oppositions expressed in the structural division of the two parts – a fracture that fails to seal even though the desire for a unifying impulse is perceived. These are the dualities that creep into the identity of the "mixed blood" and insinuate themselves between male and female, Indian America and dominant America, frenzied big city life and the silence of the Southwest landscape, swaying between the constant alternation of desperation and hope. Corresponding to these blocks of opposites one finds oppositions suffused through the language and structure. Thus short highly evocative poems of a visionary nature ("Early Morning Woman," "Space," "Rainy's Suns," "Morning Once More") are offset by long compositions exhibiting a prose-writing and narrative tone, with a precise referential apparatus of places and names ("Crossing the Border into Canada," "Ozone," "Obscene Phone Call n. 2," "A Scholder Indian Poem," "Escape").

She Had Some Horses, published in 1983, marks a significant milestone in Harjo's poetic career. The image of a barrier dominates the poem that opens the collection, while the crossing of that barrier concludes the collection. The barrier imprisons the ancestral lands inside reservations and cities, inside tradition and modernity, inside lost native language and language forcibly acquired. The self that speaks in the poems feels that the body is rent asunder by the split between fear and defiance, alienation and creativity.

Recomposing the fragments of such a lacerated space leads Harjo to a lucid and courageous realization of what it is that draws the boundary which constrains, restricts, destroys. The most all-pervading theme of the collection is fear, and the dominant image is that of the horse, an image found in the works of many Indian-American authors. Perhaps no one has developed the semantic potential of the horse image to the extent achieved by Harjo in *She Had Some Horses*.[1]

The collection is strategically divided into four parts; the divisions endow the poems and the themes with a circular structure.[2] The poems of "Survivors" list the various forms of fear, its genesis, and its devastating consequences. In "Call it Fear" the sense of dread is linked to a tribal past of defeats and losses and which, together with the hostility of silence, thwarts any possibility of revival. "Edge" becomes a keyword of much of this developmental path, along which images of boundaries stand out sharply: the boundaries of space, of one's own body, prevent meetings with others, expression, and movement. At this point in this collection the numerous *personae* are stopped in their tracks. There is even a reverse thrust back towards a no man's land: "There is this edge where shadows / and bones of some of us walk / backwards. Talk backwards" ("Call it Fear").

Three poems feature a reappearance of Noni Daylight, who is sometimes Harjo's *alter ego* or imaginary projection of herself closed up within the fear of a woman who has lost her self-awareness ("Heartbeat"), who nevertheless in "Kansas City" and "She Remembers the Future" seems to reach a more meditative state, almost free from the invasive siege of unanswerable questions. Fear can give way to "a fierce anger": the sense of living and being alive is not lost. The definitive farewell by the poetic self to this tormenting *alter ego* forms the prelude to the objectivization of an encirclement that had seemed to be insurmountable. For if "Survivors" indicates a passive floating through life, it also contains the will to set out on an existential path of regeneration.

Emblematic in this context is the poem "For Alva Benson," which weaves a close-knit relation between language, earth, and woman. Contact with the earth is an essential element of regeneration. This is forcefully underlined from as early as the very first line, thanks to the polysyndeton "And" ("And the ground spoke when she was born"). The earth thus becomes a primary poetic subject, linked to the birth event of a woman; this connection is taken up again in various ways right up to the end and is rendered even tighter and more dynamic by the two interconnected actions indicated by the verbs *spoke* and *she was born*: the word and the giving of life establish a connection between expressiveness and procreation. In the subsequent lines the voice of the earth does not go unheeded if "her mother heard it" and "in Navajo she answered as she squatted down against the earth to give birth." The native language is the bearer of this possibility of communicating with the earth as though language itself were imbued with earth, just as the act of giving life declares, anew, that physical contact is established with this earth itself. The temporal antithesis, "It was now," repeated at the beginning of line 5, expresses a cyclic continuity. Throughout the poem, word, creation, and procreation of a generational chain are contained and fertilized by the revitalizing relationship with the earth. This revitalization also means resistance to any attempt at physical and cultural extermination, a resistance underscored by the insistent use of present participles, gerunds, and an alternation of simple past and present verb tenses.

The horses that appear in the first two sections are life-giving forces, but they are often frozen in ice or in the density of stone. They reappear in the section "She Had Some Horses," but now they are accepted or rejected, loved or fought against. In revealing themselves, they enter into a contraposition that traces the lines of a personal and tribal history as well as a recomposition of those who are "loved" and those who are "hated" into a single being, now understood and addressed.

The final section "I Give You Back," composed of one single poem, closes the thematic frame: the fear present at the outset is driven out of life and history. The memory of the genocide of the Creeks no longer arouses terror, but prompts the will to struggle. "You have gutted me, but I gave you the knife" ("I Give You Back") expresses the refusal to take on the identity of a victim and the resolve to transform a personal story into collective history. The backwards thrust caused by fear, which leads toward a "non life" delineated in the opening poem, is transformed and inverted into a challenge: "But come here, fear / I am alive and you are so afraid / of dying" ("I Give You Back").

The tropos of the horses, which are depicted as imprisoned and inarticulate in the previous sections, is assigned a denotative presence in the third and penultimate section. In the title poem they too seem to have burst forth from the earth, dense with the matter of the landscapes they have traversed. But immediately afterwards they also take on human characteristics with unconfessable dreams and terrors. They are vitalizing or destructive forces, sublime with beauty or lost in delirious lies and squalid everyday reality. From them the whole of life – uncontainable – streams forth. The anaphoric enumeration, spell-binding like an incantation, and the presence of the partitive adjective create a map in which the multiplicity of the images lays emphasis on the partial aspect of each of the horses. There emerges a multifaceted picture against which the poetic self measures its motion.

The parallel structure of the lines underscores not so much a selection of elements placed in opposition to one another as, rather, co-presence and equivalence: "She had horses she loved / She had horses she hated. / These were the same horses." This final line, despite its apparent homophony with the preceding lines (*some horses, same horses*), displays two substantial differences: the verb *to be* and the adjective *same*. It is a linguistic choice that indicates reciprocal identification of the horses in spite of their diversity, signalling the acknowledgment and acceptance of divergent and contradictory elements inherent in each one of us. Alienating conflictual mind-sets are thus overcome in a dialectic of co-presence and inclusion.

From a stylistic point of view *She Had Some Horses* represents a truly fundamental stage in Harjo's poetic development, revealing her experiments with the evocative and narrative potential embodied in words. The organizational simplicity of the first compositions, achieved by means of sounds, images, spoken language, is here replaced first and foremost by traditional Indian-American structures designed to recover the tonal effects of ritual chanting. The dominant stylistic feature is iteration, applied to realistic descriptive and/or metaphorical/associative forms of language as, for instance, in "The Woman Hanging from the Thirteenth Floor Window." In contrast to *What Moon Drove Me to This?*, there is a dilation of the lines and verses in a quest for expression that frequently tends to move toward true storytelling. Indeed, the frequent use of *enjambement*, which leaves no marked caesura between one line and the next, contributes to shaping an almost prosodic rhythm.

The process of integration set in motion in *She Had Some Horses* becomes the starting point for *In Mad Love and War* (1990). "Grace," the opening poem, tends toward "a promise of balance" in order to fully attain a new vision of the self and the world. The entire collection broadens out into a more expansive backcloth with a great variety of themes: the very "war" that gives its title to the first part is amplified into a denunciation of conflicts occurring everywhere. To a large extent they spread through "the backbone of these tortuous Americas" ("The Real Revolution is Love"), amid tribal wars or victims of political and racial oppression.

Fury is transformed into a potential for achievement and new modes of expression. With the power of the word, a new image of the self can be deconstructed and reconstructed: "I am an arrow, painted / with lightning / to seek the way to the name of the enemy, / but the arrow has now created / its own language" ("We Must Call a Meeting"). This is a form of incisive and performative power, whose recovery ("Give me back my language") can open up a new voice.

Such a process does not impose divisions, but rather a union between the concretely real world and the mythic space Harjo seeks to conquer afresh, a space that is constantly present even within degrading situations like "Deer

Dancer." It is a totalizing vision that leads her back to the heart and spirit of her culture. "The Real Revolution is Love" places the seal of closure on "The Wars" and constitutes a significant interface with the subsequent poems.

The second part, "Mad Love," indicates the continuation of the journey from fragmentation to completeness. The section is energized by a movement replete with evolutionary potential. Thus "Mad Love" opens with "Deer Dancer," almost as a counterpoint to "Deer Ghost," to underline the fact that interaction between the mythic dimension and the earthly has now been attained. Even the autobiographical approach of several poems ("Javelina," "Rainy Dawn," "Crystal Lake") tends to connect these two worlds. For instance, in "Javelina" myth can insinuate itself into squalid and humdrum everyday life, and in such a case "The mythic world will enter with the subtlety of a snake the color of / earth changing skin." The event of the birth of her daughter Rainy Dawn is experienced as the moment of a present life in the mythic spiral of time: "I had to participate in the dreaming of you into memory ... " The recollection of a boat trip with her grandfather unveils a broad expanse of water where "We skimmed over mythical fish he once caught, over fish who were as / long as rainbows after the coming storm."

Thus an Indian legacy of struggle affirms the interrelatedness of all things. Aware of these multiple strands, Harjo adopts them as the base on which to construct her poetic testimony in *In Mad Love and War*; each element contains the energy of the past and the seed of all future transformations. If in *She Had Some Horses* memory is "a delta in the skin," in *In Mad Love and War* it becomes "a revolutionary fire." And if the key word of the former is "edge," in the latter it is "transformation." Transformation means penetrating even more deeply into the roots of her own culture, in a way. It means opening up to a creative dialogue with the otherness one meets along the way: "Transformation is really about understanding the shape and condition of another with compassion, not about overtaking." This concept is then figuratively identified by Harjo as embodied in "the shape of spiral in which all beings resonate."[3] This image is repeated over and over again in *In Mad Love and War*, together with that of fire; in fact, it provides the dominant motif governing the reciprocal transformative motion of this collection, which is at times reflected in the graphic layout of the texts in the use of *enjambements* that convey the sense of an uninterrupted and undulating flow.

Harjo's increasing interest in jazz enhances and gives shape to her poems at various levels. The resonances sounding through her language are those that often connote the extreme possibilities of a musical instrument, as expressed in the successions of assonance and alliteration, together with the searing blend of intertwined auditory and visual perceptions, "balancing on a tightrope of sound" ("Bleed Through"). The blending of poetry and music guides poetic art back to its performative power. The setting up of the band "Joy Harjo and Poetic Justice" is part and parcel of this project. But there is also the intention to lead the written text back to its oral dimensions of native tradition.

The stylistic variety of the collection reverberates through the alterations between fleeting lyrics (for instance, "Fury of Rain," "Trickster") and poems characterized by the *low rider*. The *low rider* highlights a figurative detail that becomes laden with evocative atmosphere created by the use of metaphors and similes endowed with a powerful distancing force that is detached from the metaphor's familiar contexts. At the phonic level, Harjo turns to a rhythmical structure that intensifies the evocative atmosphere. This very dense metaphorical layering goes far beyond that observed in *She Had Some Horses*. The layering is also present in the poems that follow a storyline and are characterized by the vocative ("you" or identifiable character).[4] Surreal images are overlaid one upon another, dilating their meaning or, in some cases, the external image and inner image ultimately become compenetrated precisely in order to abolish the gap between the two planes of reality: "It is not by accident you watch the sun / become your heart / sink into your belly then reappear in a town / that magnetically attracts you" ("Bleed Through").

In *In Mad Love and War* there is another type of poetic composition – the prose poem. Here, one sometimes finds a division into stanzas, albeit with a perfectly aligned right-hand margin. While in some cases the language has the feel of prosody, with the inclusion of direct speech, at other times it becomes highly visionary ("Deer Dancer," "Santa Fé," "Day of the Dead," "Original Memory"), with words joined in an arresting and thought-provoking manner. The striking arrangement of the accents imparts a rhythmical movement, characteristic of poetry. Thus without abandoning certain devices of poetic composition, Harjo experiments with a form that captures the narrative concreteness of storytelling, yet draws upon powerfully evocative language.

These same peculiarities lie at the heart of the language of *Secrets from the Center of the World* (1989), in which Harjo interprets Stephen Strom's photographs depicting the landscapes of Navajo lands. Harjo and Strom weave a form of dialogue and find a common denominator in the composed yet intensely vibrant force that pervades Strom's images and Harjo's words. Her commentary is not a vaguely poetic word description recounting the content of the pictures, but rather an evocation of the spirit of place. The protagonist is the specific atmosphere and the life the earth encompasses. The grandiose photographic scenarios in which the human presence is absent or tiny are replaced with images and words populated by presences, even though they may not be visible: "A summer storm reveals the dreaming place of bears. But you cannot see their shaggy dreams of fish and berries, any land signs supporting evidence of bears, or any bears at all. What is revealed in the soaked earth, forked waters, and fence line shared with patient stones is the possibility of everything you can't see."[5] Appearances melt away and presences emerge.

These prose poems are frequently constructed in dialogic form in order to promote an attitude of respect toward the earth. "Don't bother the earth spirit who lives here. She's working on a story. It's the oldest story in the world and it is delicate, changing" (*Secrets* 54). From the earth there spring forth stories that provide identity for an entire people, from one generation to another. This is the most ancient story, but at the same time it is open to change while displaying the continuity of tradition, in an infinite flux of ceaseless transformations. Physical geology becomes genetic geology, whereby man's relation with the earth becomes spiritual communion. The real landscape and its spiritual essence proceed side by side; reality and myth move toward convergence.

In order to bring to light the secrets the earth holds within, Harjo makes use of a highly evocative tone, one that is far removed from the language of the dominant culture: " . . . something cool as the blues, or close to the sound of a Navajo woman singing early in the morning" (22). The language suggests the musicality of a song free from rigid poetic requirements, since "the most appropriate way to be true to the Native American poetry tradition, when rendered into English, is the flexibility of prose-poetry as opposed, say, to the line break method of European prosody."[6]

A Woman Who Fell from the Sky (1994) and *A Map to the Next World* (2000) constitute a further exploration of Harjo's world as an artist and a woman. What the two collections share is "commentary" by the author following the poetic text. At times this is a means of contextualizing the poem within a specific event; elsewhere it becomes a flow of thoughts that weave a dialogue with the poem itself, broadening its contents or providing a biographical reflection. Some of these prose texts are stories *in nuce*, others short essays. In both cases one notes an attempt at interaction between poetry and prose, between the poet and the storyteller, between the written word and the spoken word of the native tradition.

Even more predominant and explicit in the 1994 collection is the compenetration between mythic space and contemporary reality, strikingly rendered by the poetic re-elaboration of the Iroquois creation myth in the modern world. The woman in "The Woman Who Fell from the Sky" created the world. Her "spirit knew how to climb to the stars." She fell from the sky, yet "she was rather ordinary," an everyday woman who lives in contemporary society but nevertheless finds the fullness of life in contact with the earth, thereby underlining the complex unity of spirit and matter, sky and earth.

In some prose passages (for instance "Northern Lights," "The Flood"), there is a reappearance of themes addressed in earlier collections, and above all there are ancient stories that have a counterpart in the present. One story burgeons into another without explicit delimitations of time or space, a feature that frequently seems to reverberate with the modes of native storytelling. The narrative approach enables Harjo to construct a broader story. Despite the occasional semantic tangle, the language generally maintains an intense evocative power – arising from the process of metaphoric association characteristic of lyrical verse and the use of poetic devices such as synesthesia, alliteration, assonance.

The itinerary the poet charts in *A Map to the Next World* is that of a final reconciliation, revisiting personal or collective happenings: the figure of the father combines tragic personal and tribal stories, highlighted in the long central sequence "Returning from the Enemy." Childhood memories, perceptive analyses of oppressive policies, the insistence on the theme of death infuse a vein of bitter awareness throughout this collection. At times it seems difficult to find that "revolutionary fire" of the earlier compositions which led from fragmentation to completeness, even though "the very act of our beautiful survival" constantly represents the goal that has already been achieved or toward which current efforts are striving.

"Becoming human was the most honorable task of poetry," says Harjo in the preface to *How We Became Human. New and Selected Poems* (2002). This concept runs through all thirteen of the new poems presented in the section that bears the collection's title and tracks the pathway of a life "over the net of eternity" ("Ah, Ah") despite the wounds inflicted by wars and violence. There is also a proud affirmation of her own culture through which a harmonic contact between life and death, seen as natural cycles, can once more be established. The landscape of Hawaii, Harjo's present home, sheds its usual tourist trivialities and is restored to its pristine sacredness becoming a place populated by spirits and native stories. The poetic language appears to be more linear and expansive, the density of the metaphorical fabric is less tight-meshed, as if, in the stylistic rendering, the flow of thoughts were arranged in a more meditative vision.

The medium of expression, English – a language which in Harjo's case does not spring from a shared system of values – cannot always succeed in giving voice to the essence of native culture because "it's very materialistic, and very subject-oriented."[7] Paradoxically, though, "reinventing the enemy's language" bestows on the English linguistic code a new communicative and perceptual channel. This, in fact, is the founding principle underlying the monumental project undertaken by Joy Harjo and Gloria Bird as editors of the anthology *Reinventing the Enemy's Language*, which appeared in 1997. It gathers together prose and poetry contributions by more than eighty Native women writers belonging to almost fifty nations. In the editors' own words, "the language of the colonizers was forced on us ... It was when we began to create with this new language that we named it ours, made it usefully tough and beautiful."[8] Recreating English is thus a veritable process of decolonization. "Something is happening, something is emerging and coming into focus that will politicize as well as transform literary expression" (22).

Such an enterprise truly enshrines the principles that inspire and generate the entire artistic activity of Joy Harjo: a continuous testimony proclaiming, "The poet's road is a journey for truth, for justice."[9]

Notes

1. In a recent interview Harjo provided the following explanation of the horse image: "Maybe the horses picked me. Maybe 'Joy Harjo' is a holographic structure made up of layers of images, streams of languages which don't appear in linear time and space. Horses are one of these images and it grows backwards, forwards, all direction in time and space," Marina Camboni, "Dialogue with Joy Harjo," *RSA Journal* 11 (2001), pp. 92–93.

2. "... the book begins by confessing the poet's fear. It then describes the fate of other 'Survivors' like herself who had to deal with such fear. It introduces intermediary figures ... human and symbolic ... who negotiate between the poet and her fear. It tells a story of the break-up of the poet's relationship with a man and her discovery of the love of a woman. It ends with the freeing of the horses, who are the symbols of her frightened spirit, and the freeing of the poet from old, repressive images to live her own life. The end is a ritual prayer, closing off the matter begun with the first poem," John F. Crawford, "Notes Toward a New Multicultural Criticism," in Marie Harris and Kathleen Aguero, eds., *A Gift of Tongues*, Athens: University of Georgia Press, 1987, p. 166.

3. Joy Harjo, "Weaving Stories for Food," in Laura Coltelli, ed., *The Spiral of Memory. Interviews*, Ann Arbor: University of Michigan Press, 1996, p. 127.

4. See, for instance, "For Anne Mae Pictou Aquash," "We must Call a Meeting," "Resurrection," "Bleed Through," "Mercy," "Summer Night."

5. Joy Harjo, *Secrets from the Center of the World*. Tucson, University of Arizona Press, 1989, p. 18.

6. Bill Aull, et al., "The Spectrum of Other Languages: an Interview with Joy Harjo," *Tamaqua*, 3.1 (1992), p. 19.

7. Joy Harjo, "The Story of All Our Survival," in Coltelli, "*Spiral of Memory*," p. 24.

8. Joy Harjo and Gloria Bird, eds., *Reinventing the Enemy's Language. Contemporary Native Women Writers of North America*. New York, Norton, 1997, pp. 23–24.

9. Joy Harjo, *How We Became Human. New and Selected Poems*. New York, Norton, 2002, p. xxv.

Major secondary sources

Adamson, Joni, "And the Ground Spoke: Joy Harjo and the Struggle for a Land-Based Language," in *American Indian Literature, Environmental Justice, and Ecocriticism*. Tucson: University of Arizona Press, 2001, pp. 116–27.

Allen, Paula Gunn, *The Sacred Hoop. Recovering the Feminine in American Literary Tradition*. Boston: Beacon Press, 1986, pp. 155–64.

Lang, Nancy, "Twin Gods Bending Over: Joy Harjo and Poetic Memory." *Melus* 18 (Fall 1993), pp. 41–49.

Leen, Mary, "Joy Harjo's Poetry and the Survival of Storytelling," *American Indian Quarterly* 19 (Winter 1995), pp. 1–16.

Smith Clark, Patricia and Paula Gunn Allen, "Earthly Relations, Carnal Knowledge: Southwestern American Indian Women Writers and Landscape," in V. Norwood, and J. Monk, eds., *The Desert Is No Lady: Southwestern Landscapes in Women's Writing and Art*. New Haven: Yale University Press, 1987, pp. 174–96.

Wiget, Andrew, "Nightriding with Noni Daylight. The Many Horse Songs of Joy Harjo," In L. Coltelli, ed., *Native American Literatures*. Pisa: Seu, 1989, pp. 185–96.

Wilson, Norma C., "The Ground Speaks: the Poetry of Joy Harjo," in *The Nature of Native American Poetry*. Albuquerque: University of New Mexico Press, 2001, pp. 109–22.

Womack, Craig S., "Joy Harjo: Creek Writer from the End of the Twentieth Century," in *Red On Red*. Minneapolis: University of Minnesota Press, 1999, pp. 223–61.

17

DAVID L. MOORE

Sherman Alexie: irony, intimacy, and agency

Sherman Alexie is the reigning "world heavyweight poetry bout champion" in the second generation of a Native American literary renaissance begun in the 1960s.[1] His popular persona as a comedian, poetry bout heavyweight, experimental writer, filmmaker, and social pundit has itself become a work of art. He shares with many American Indian writers a central motif reaffirming Native lives and Native nationhood, although his direct comedic style and ironic attitude set him apart from the earnest lyricism of the now canonized elder Native writers such as N. Scott Momaday, Leslie Marmon Silko, and Louise Erdrich, and from many of his peers. Unlike many, Alexie rarely points toward the redemptive power of Native community as a direction for his protagonists' struggles. Instead, his bold, sometimes campy, style tends to affirm a more individual agency unique to Native identities, by a distinct artistic pattern of personal affirmation and reconnection. One reviewer marks an ironic balance, writing that Alexie's "dry sincerity leavens the sentiment" of his Indian tales.[2] For all his humor, indeed in the heart of his humor, Alexie invariably circulates the grave themes of ongoing colonial history and its personal effects in Indian country. As 118-year-old Etta explains in his short story "Dear John Wayne," "Having fun is very serious."[3]

Alexie's five genres – poetry, short fiction, novel, non-fiction, and film – weave through such modern and postmodern questions as psychological and social border crossings; internalized oppression; violence; addiction; the absent father; and racial tensions, particularly white guilt. One profile lists Alexie's topics of pain and humor, hunger and survival, love and anger, broken treaties, manifest destiny, basketball, car wrecks, commodity food, US Department of Housing and Urban Development (HUD) houses, small-pox blankets, promises, and dreams.[4] His insider's view of the Indian world, when combined with confessional detail, creates an intimate distance from a non-Indian audience that is one key to the ironic strength of his voice. Although one of his characters in the novel *Reservation Blues* points out that "You ain't really Indian unless there was some point in your life that you didn't want to be,"[5] because of the weariness of difference, Alexie's voice comes from a radical affirmation of diversity. A line in the long poem "The Unauthorized Autobiography of Me" puts that affirmation in lineal terms: "I made a very conscious decision to marry an Indian woman, who made a very conscious decision to marry me / Our hope: to give birth to and raise Indian children who love themselves. That is the most revolutionary act."[6] An America that would erase its first nations would be revolutionized by Indians who assert themselves against vanishing. Alexie's existential expression of indigenous continuance, however conflicted, is at the heart of his art.

Echoing the claims and musings of some of his fictional characters, Alexie affirmed in a conversation with President Clinton during the 1998 "Dialogue on Race," televised on PBS,

> I think the primary thing that people need to know about Indians is that our identity is much less cultural now and much more political. That we really do exist as political entities and sovereign political nations. That's the most important thing for people to understand, that we are separate politically and economically. And should be.[7]

Alexie's emphasis on the political and legal status of tribal sovereignty, rather than the cultural dynamics of tribal life, reflects his own mixed engagement with mainstream and Native cultures. Alexie's is a populist voice, uniquely situated behind enemy lines, of both those tribal changes and that tribal sovereignty. That duality is another source of his irony.

In his first decade of award-winning productions, Alexie has been prolific: eight mixed-genre collections of poems and stories (*The Business of Fancydancing: Stories and Poems*, 1992; *I Would Steal Horses*, 1992; *First Indian On the Moon*, 1993; *Old Shirts & New Skins*, 1993; *One Stick Song*, 2000; *Seven Mourning Songs for the Cedar Flute I Have Yet to Learn to Play*, 1994; *Water Flowing Home*, 1995; *The Summer of Black Widows*, 1996). Three volumes of short fiction (*The Lone Ranger and Tonto Fistfight in Heaven*, 1993; *The Toughest Indian in the World*, 2000; *Ten Little Indians: Stories*, 2003). Two novels (*Reservation Blues*, 1995; *Indian Killer*, 1996). Two films (*Smoke Signals*, 1998; *The Business of Fancydancing*, 2001). This outpouring, plus numerous journalistic essays, and countless interviews in major venues, serves to alert readers to private and public crises in Indian country, and rallies indigenous energies facing those crises. Since it would be impossible to analyze all of these titles in the space available here, I will look at an underlying narrative poetics and ethics that weaves through Alexie's work.

A pattern of intimacy and irony

Throughout Alexie's pained portraits of Indian individuals a recurring pattern links agency or limited power to dramatic intimacy, ever saturated in irony. By imbuing often sexual bodies with a vitalizing sense of humor and the friction of irony, Alexie affirms a sense of subjective will and humanity in his characters that helps set them free in their colonial context.

This dynamic pattern fits one of Alexie's aesthetic proclamations. In *Old Shirts & New Skins* (1993), a peripatetic character, Lester FallsApart, pronounces this crucial equation: "POETRY = ANGER × IMAGINATION" (xi). It is a complex idea woven through Alexie's texts, repeated in other pieces, for instance "The Unauthorized Autobiography of Me" in *One Stick Song* (2000). Each of the factors in the equation affirms an ability to *do something*, a calculus of creative strength suitably blurred and ironized by Lester's last name. Alexie offers here an axiom linking aesthetics to ethics, evidently a dynamic for him on the order of $E = mc^2$ linking energy to matter, connecting art to life.

Storytelling or POETRY for Alexie's characters resonates with creative expression as power, fulfillment of will, proficiency in surviving, an assertion of agency. As one of his most entrapped characters broods in "The Sin Eaters," "With my voice, I suddenly believed, I could explode the walls of that room and escape."[8] ANGER as a positive force for Alexie resonates with passion, authenticity, and the bodily intimacy of sweat and contact. ANGER intimately affirms subjective freedom, though Alexie frequently ironizes ANGER with poignancy by gesturing to oppressive limits: "I pull out my wallet and give them a buck each. I don't feel generous or guilty, just half-empty and all lonely in this city which would kill me as slowly as it is killing these three cousins of mine."[9] "So much has been taken from us that we hold onto the smallest things left with all the strength that we have."[10] Authentic emotions of anger, desire, fear, grief, whether gentle or violent, open an intimate door. IMAGINATION resonates in Alexie with the ability to leap mentally across paradoxes and traps of existence, the pathos of American history. Comedy is an imaginative strategy that both transcends and deconstructs, and thus survives, pain. The liberating value of IMAGINATION is amplified by its absence in a brutal opposite, as a character says of his own warrior nature in the short story, "Saint Junior": "When you resort to violence to prove a point, you've just experienced a profound failure of imagination."[11] If a leap of imagination is the mechanism of comedy, one level of comedy available even to the suffering is irony, as Alexie writes – ironically through the voice of a dogmatic white anthropologist – in the short story "Dear John Wayne," "Irony, a hallmark of the contemporary indigenous American."[12]

This spiraling pattern of intimacy, irony, and agency can be sexual or political, personal or public in Alexie's work. Language plus the body equals purpose, i.e., when the body communicates, when it achieves expression across the intimate borders of bodily difference, then it spirals out of the vortex of alienation. His comedy sparks the surprise of reconnections, and his irony refocuses connections by their lack. The affirmation is tough, facing harsh realities, but it is ultimately enlivening. As he maps the intimate psychological and social violence of Indian–white relations, he not only humanizes that history of grief, but he minimizes it by showing how humor can survive even death. The narration of "Saint Junior" says of six "ghosts" of the Cold Spring Singers drum group, "They understood what it meant to be Indian and dead and alive and still bright with faith and hope."[13] As Alexie explains in an interview, "These aren't happy stories necessarily. But I think they are positive stories."[14]

Poetry of race relations

If POETRY = ANGER × IMAGINATION, we can trace ironic agency through intimate confrontations in a pivotal poem with the dead-pan title "Introduction to Native American Literature." As the first entry in the first section of *Old Shirts & New Skins*, published in 1993 on the momentum of his initial double-barreled success with *The Business of Fancydancing* and *I Would Steal Horses*, it exemplifies three narrative postures in Alexie's comedic aesthetic: assertive attitude, mixed traditions, and historical liability.

The poem proclaims a didactic, revisionary project that Alexie shares with so many American Indian writers who labor to retell history against the triumphalism of manifest destiny. It epitomizes Alexie's early voice, mixing in-your-face polemics with small dreamings of myth. The effect is at once cinematic and sermonic, directly challenging the reader by flashing acute details of poverty and dispossession against fragments of reverie that briefly elevate misery to mythic proportions.

The epigraph, "must I give you / the last words to the story too," quoting a lament by Alex Kuo, Alexie's mentor at Washington State University, slaps the reader with the author's attitude, his mixed literary traditions, and his accusation of the audiences' historical and literary failures. Kuo's public exhaustion with cross-culturally ignorant readers is followed directly by the voice of Alexie's persona echoing the weariness of that task as he addresses his irresponsible audience invested in its own ignorance: "& here you are again (again) / asking me to explain broken glass." That shattered glass follows the drama of the first line: "Somewhere in America a television explodes."[15] Such an opening, asserting its own condescending fatigue, immediately takes on the American audience and its media stereotypes of Indians. An angrily weary Indian is not a vanished Indian, and if not vanished, then he himself, not some manifest destiny, is an agent of change – if not already debilitated.

Alexie's textual persona is explicitly self-conscious of the traditions of Euroamerican literature, the Native American literary renaissance, the painful colonial history and politics that continue to shape such literary outpourings, and of his emerging leadership in that process. An interview asserts that there is "a whole other population out there I want to reach" of "twelve-year-old reservation kids, who ... grew up either with heroes who had been created by the white media or no heroes at all."[16] In his first novel, *Reservation Blues*, Alexie draws on the African American blues tradition, as the musical roots of American culture, to dramatize the failures and survivals of Indian youth in the postmodern world.

That mixed literary consciousness takes many narrative forms, not the least of which is this persona that may be characterized by a tough attitude of confrontation and provocation against a complacent white America and a rallying voice of anger and righteousness for despondent Native youth. This confrontative voice and that attitude is itself his claim to the agency of expression, the power of the word in both oral traditional and biblical senses that N. Scott Momaday and so many other Indian writers invoke.[17]

Relying on both print and film in a visual video age, Alexie's in-your-face approach to the not-so-dear reader reflects his urgent project to reshape Euroamerican audiences' awareness of their liability for history. This enlightened though exhausted voice of an American Indian bard in the poem reads the broken shards of American self-representation like a seer, telling an American readership to clean up after itself, to take responsibility for its brutal inheritance: "Am I the garbageman of your dreams?" That garbage may be the fetishized objects of the voyeuristic colonial gaze: "You scour the reservation landfill / through the debris of so many lives ..." where white readers, like grave robbers, look to Indian stories to fulfill their dreams. For Indians, the effect of white men's curiosity is further erasure and dispossession, as manifest destiny now pursues New Age appropriation of Native cultures. Thus the section finishes in a solitary line: "All you bring me is an empty bottle."

If strong writers create their audiences, Alexie is doing so by educating non-Natives to their own complicity in colonialism, as a sort of indigenous shriver. By affirming his own bardic role to instruct readers through anger and imagination, intimacy, and irony, he reshapes readers' ability to face themselves, America, and American Indians. Further, by enacting that literary battle on the page and on screen, he shows Indian kids how the pen is mightier than the virtual laser.

Yet according to the poem, America, in facing history, cannot recolonize Indians through sympathy. If no definition of another human is adequate, certainly neither the label of victim nor victimizer will suffice. Thus the final stanza accents the ineffable in Native American literature: "Send it a letter: the address will keep changing. / ... Knock on its door: you'll hear voices." Alexie dramatizes an individualistic literary attitude, laying claim to one's own voice and refusing to be defined by others.

That refusal has taken on philosophical dimensions, opening creative agency to randomness. In a preface to *The Business of Fancydancing: the Screenplay*, Alexie explains, "We've all been trained to make movies in three-act structures, as if Aristotle could have somehow predicted how artistically conservative all of these liberal-filmmakers were going to become. 'Resolution! There must be resolution!' Fuck resolutions, fuck closure, fuck the idea of story arc. Embrace the incomplete, embrace ambiguity, and embrace the magical and painful randomness of life."[18] In addition to literary theories of ambiguity, there are other reasons for Alexie's aversion to narrative closure in standard plot patterns. Colonial closure means tragedy for Indians; oral storytelling patterns are often open-ended, even interactive; sit-coms and prequel/sequel movies are open-ended in a more manipulative mode; experience tends to be, for Alexie, random, magical, and painful; so why not art? He says in an interview, "I always want to be a moving target."[19] The extent to which Alexie accomplishes an anti-resolution narrative structure to match his proclaimed anti-Aristotelian poetics is certainly a question. Yet there is no unmediated resolution in his work. Affirmations are invariably tinged or sometimes laden with that characteristic irony of painful incompletion, doubly strengthening the affirmation by making it "a moving target." That humorous effort to elude the effects of colonial mourning is in fact the flip side of what one Spokane critic has called his "exaggeration of despair,"[20] raising complex questions of an author's representation of his own community.

Alexie negotiates political questions of authorship by emphasizing that moving target in the question, *What is an Indian?*, playing with multiplicity, ambiguity, and irony even while asserting tribal sovereignty. "One Good Man," the finale to his collection *The Toughest Indian in the World*, ends, "We laughed. We waited for hours for somebody to help us. *What is an Indian?* I lifted my father and carried him across every border."[21] With no borders, there is no line in the sand. As Spokane elder Etta Joseph in "Dear John Wayne" says to an anthropologist who insists on believing in ethnographies as "the definitive texts on the Interior Salish," "No, there's nothing definitive about them. They're just your oral tradition. And they're filled with the same lies, exaggerations, mistakes, and ignorance as our oral traditions."[22] Purity and authenticity for Alexie do not reside exclusively on either side of cultural or racial divides. "Nothing definitive" *is* the postmodern aesthetic in Alexie, offering nuance and intimation instead of definition. This value in uncertainty is another ironic engine of Alexie's always elusive voice and persona.

Alexie's facility with "both" worlds – the elite literary world and the Indian world of the rez and the cities, that "whole other population out there" – is another key to his literary fascination.[23] As the title of a major interview suggests, "An Indian Without Reservations," that fascination is built on a hint of mutual alienation, yet his work exhibits a singular mastery of double-consciousness.[24] Because of his suspension between those worlds, the locus of his narrative voice drives inward to a singular consciousness. His social agenda, breaking boundaries of class, gender, and race across historically separated populations, is declared in personal terms. For if the "IMAGINATION" factor in his poetry equation is the intimate, internal, imagistic power to break out of one world into another, it accentuates precisely the potency, the AGENCY, of individual consciousness to reach for freedom.

Haunted by salmon

This tendency swings Alexie more toward Louis Owens's critical focus on identity in Native American literature, less toward Jace Weaver's focus on community,[25] and it links Alexie closely to one particular major figure in the first generation of the Native American literary renaissance. The late James Welch, in his prose more than in his poetry, worked through understated language to mark Indian community more as a painful absence than as a promising presence. Welch's novels focus on the identity struggles of individuals sometimes quite apart from community. Owens, in *Other Destinies: Understanding the American Indian Novel*, emphasizes the struggle for individual identity as the key dynamic in Native fiction. In contrast, Weaver, in *That the People Might Live: Native American Literature and Community*, emphasizes the struggle for Indian community survival as the key literary dynamic. Weaver points out that these foci are not mutually exclusive because, "Native peoples find their individual identities in the collectivity of community" (161). However, this contextual difference in emphasis shapes characterizations, narrative perspectives, plot options, streams of consciousness, and other structural prospects of the text, cycling Alexie's personae through that celebration of individual agency.

Alexie is the protégé of Welch in this regard. At readings in Missoula, Montana, where Welch lived, Alexie has said that he feels as though Jim Welch is his literary grandfather – and Welch responded jokingly by saying he wished Alexie had used the term "father" instead.[26] From a later TV generation affirming his own sit-com roots as much as his Spokane reservation roots, Alexie focuses like Welch on Native identities wandering in a sea of loss, "haunted by salmon," looking for islands of human connection. This alienation is balanced in Alexie's work by narratives of often conflicted relations that individuals do indeed have with community, as in *Reservation Blues*, a group weight that is no less communal for being maddening, sometimes mythic and sometimes sinister, always perplexing.

This haunting lack, this loss, is the dark side of Alexie's comedy, reflecting in relief the larger horrors of cultural genocide. As Low Man Smith, the protagonist of the short story "Indian Country," bitterly and ironically contemplates the bigoted, homophobic, self-righteous Indian Christian sneering at him across a dinner table (an absent father alienated from his lesbian daughter), "Low knew for a fact that everything was funny. Homophobia? Funny! Genocide? Hilarious! Political assassination? Side-splitting! Love? Ha, Ha, Ha!"[27] Dark humor hones an ironic edge, like the "funny" title of Alexie's collection, *Ten Little Indians*. The allusion to a children's nursery rhyme not only plays on the infantile projections of mainstream culture that would reduce Native lives to children's ditties, but it also takes seriously the fact that his Indian stories are not heroic, that they reflect lives reduced by history to a scattered and rather arbitrary group of survivors. The seeming arbitrariness and agonized dispensability of Indian lives is reflected further through the book's title because in fact there are only nine stories in the collection, not ten as seemingly announced. Something is missing, the title hints. Completion and resolution are impossible here.

The dark side of comedy leads us to another track in Alexie's *oeuvre*, a bloody trail of gothic horror. Studies of the grotesque in American literature from Poe to Stephen King have pointed to sources of the imagery of horror in the repressed violence of slavery and Indian wars in the nineteenth- and of the uncountable dead in the war-ravaged twentieth-century.[28] Alexie makes that link explicit between repressed history and the repressed psyche of American violence by setting grotesque violence as an outcome of colonial history. His noir mystery *Indian Killer* and his short story "Ghost Dance"[29] are prime examples. By linking murder to imagery of Indian blood rituals, Alexie's second novel plays in nuanced ways against white guilt, trapping the reader into assuming the worst about the Indian protagonist in a mystery murder plot. Alexie keeps the ending ambiguous, reflecting innuendoes in the novel's title (a killer who's Indian? or a killer of Indians?), but by that ambiguity sets up the Anglo reader to scapegoat the Indian and thus experience white guilt yet again. "Ghost Dance" is more direct, locating a *Tales from the Crypt*-like story of cannibalistic ghosts at the Little Bighorn Battlefield Monument on the anniversary of Custer's Last Stand. As ghosts of the 7th Cavalry appear to be avenging past violence in cryptic revenge against racist cops, irresolution again commands the non-finale. Images of blood are enough to carry the "story" where it needs to go: to images of violence, the ultimate critique of the ultimate failure of imagination. Edgar, an FBI agent with painful psychic susceptibility to the violent truth, "felt hunted and haunted, and when he closed his eyes, he smelled blood and he didn't know how much of it would be spilled before all of this was over."[30] Magnifying history's most gruesome details, "two hundred and fifty-six open graves, all of them filled with blood, pieces of skin, and unidentifiable body parts," Alexie again calls his audience to account for the pain of America's racist legacy: " ... Edgar knew he would never truly leave this nightmare."[31]

The short story of gender guilt

If poems like "Introduction to Native American Literature" and Alexie's gothic horrors directly target colonial issues of race, the short story, "Dear John Wayne," published in *The Toughest Indian in the World* (2000), marks his later turn toward unraveling gender in colonial domination. Alexie's comedic approach knocks out America's No. 1 cowboy – another track to literary agency by ironizing intimacy. If John Wayne is the macho monument to everything patriarchal, sexist, homophobic, and delusional about American power and self-proclaimed manifest destiny, Alexie's innovative fantasy shatters his ideological clay feet.

Yet there are other dimensions of his narratives, not defined by that icon, that drive this and many of his stories. A combination of factors behind much of his work moves Alexie to make very personal such an overdetermined political figure. His stories are shaped, for one, by the intimacy of narrative form's requirement of descriptive detail, making the explicit sex in this story not gratuitous. Further, the graphic, straightforward, non-moralistic quality of Native oral traditional storytelling carries Alexie's prose toward the specifics of character past the masks of celebrity. Equally, the graphic, voyeuristic, anti-moralistic quality of pop cultural sexual representations plays out here. In addition, like so many artists, Alexie draws on the primal power of human agency in the body to affirm human connection. Further still, he is dramatizing centuries of de facto miscegenation that constitute Indian–White relations.

Thus Alexie chooses this Hollywood icon on whom to rewrite sexual-colonial relations in a fantasy of reconciliation that sets the real crimes of sexual and colonial domination in sharper relief. In so doing, he echoes Richard C. Trexler's revealing history, *Sex and Conquest: Gendered*

Violence, Political Order, and the European Conquest of the Americas,[32] that brings out of the closet the sexual dimensions of colonial history. Trexler documents the practices of sexual discipline and punishment that permeated sacred and secular colonial institutions of Spain and other nations as they extended their power across the body of the hemisphere and the globe.

Alexie's relentless emphasis on a colonial context renders much of his unflagging irony, by continually playing off the immediate text against a colonial context. In "Dear John Wayne," the elderly, savvy Spokane woman, Etta, says to her interviewer, a cultural anthropologist, "You've colonized Indian land but I am not about to let you colonize my heart and mind."[33] Alexie's poem, "The American Artificial Limb Company," addresses in passing what could be called a colonial poetics of irony: "You have to understand that white people invented / irony," says the first-person narrative voice.[34] He is alluding to treaty-writing and treaty-breaking as ironic by definition, where irony is saying one thing and meaning another. The irony invented by white people erases the very meaning of their own words and their promises tossed across that frontier onto projected stereotypes of Indians. He contrasts irony of political deceit with irony of racial trust.

Pointing to the gender of colonialism, "Dear John Wayne" is a fictional transcript, set in the year 2052, of an anthropologist's interview with 118-year-old but spry Etta Joseph. She reminisces in the St. Tekakwitha Retirement Community about her affair in 1952 with John Wayne on the Arizona movie set of the famous Western, *The Searchers.* After instructing the interviewer in cultural etiquette, "You have a lot to learn. You should listen more and talk less,"[35] Etta goes on to relate the intimate details of her brief and poignant liaison with Marion Morrison (the real name of the actor), with details of his private questions and uncertainties about American history and gender roles.

"I know, I know. I have a public image to maintain," he cries. "But that's not who I really am. I may act like a cowboy, I might pretend to be a cowboy, but I am not a cowboy in real life, do you understand?"[36] The satiric effect is to slay America's icon and all he stands for by imagining his truer, more compassionate heart – and thus to show in stark relief the failure of humanity and imagination that John Wayne's and America's violence perpetuates. It is preposterously refreshing to hear John Wayne say, "I try to embrace the feminine in myself."[37] Alexie imagines an alternative history of human connection rather than domination that redraws the history of oppression. He transforms the imagery of colonial rape, domination, and victimhood into expressions of agency, intimacy, and mutual, loving power. Alexie's imaginative play with this icon matches Gerald Vizenor's revisionary history in the novel *Heirs of Columbus* where The Admiral is a descendant of Mayan voyagers. These writers remaster the arch-colonist and the arch-cowboy.

Parodying a "love in the desert" melodramatic scene, Alexie's story examines some of the sexual dimensions of colonization in a twentieth-century setting. "'Wait, wait, wait,' cried John Wayne as he chased after her. He was not a young man. He wondered if he could possibly catch her." Keeping the character reversal dramatically incomplete, Alexie's third-person narration burlesques nineteenth-century rhetoric of Native romance: "But she was a child of the river and pine tree, of wild grass and mountain." Underlining the alienation of such rhetoric, John Wayne's stream of consciousness then dehumanizes and distances the sexual other to an essential, geologic level – which appropriately turns into farce, then fear: "She understood gravity in a different way and, therefore, tripped in the rough sands of the desert. She fell face first into the red dirt and waited for John Wayne to catch and hurt her." Her colonial history translates into expectations of rape and violence. "Isn't that what he had always done? Wasn't he the man who killed Indians?"[38]

Alexie unmasks the racial cowboy myth as a false cover of sexual domination, while affirming the sexual bond across racial borders. To have John Wayne mouth such expressions of sincere feeling, "Oh, Etta, I'm not going to hurt you," he said. "I couldn't hurt you. I love you,"[39] is to show by absurdity of the mouthpiece the truth of the words, rather like Polonius mouthing wisdom to Hamlet, yet always with a question mark. This ironic technique also reflects back on the bard, establishing his voice yet further as the authority who oversees such distinctions of character.

The fact of intimacy between these two improbable lovers underscores humane interrelationship – and its lack – across race and gender. Human closeness prevails against the strong-man Hollywood stereotype by narration of his and her self-doubts, insecurities, needs, naivetés, contradictions, open hopes – various levels of psychological as well as sexual intimacy. Alexie imagines a way into the ironies of a John Wayne who loves an Indian as much as Alexie would have Indian children love themselves.

This pattern is one trajectory of Alexie's meteoric and prolific writing and filmmaking career, where the text delivers up a sense of humanity by intimately facing poignant loss with ironies of unsentimental imagination. His potion is potent for both his characters and his own public persona as he himself seems to be living ANGER and IMAGINATION consummated in POETRY. He joked in a 1995 interview that he was "the Indian *du jour*,"[40] and he certainly holds that dubious title years later. Alexie's prodigious storytelling talent summons perseverance out of the daily details, the objects and people, the soda cans and sacred songs, the rock-and-roll, country tunes and rez cars, the urban ambitions and warrior hearts, of turn of the twenty-first-century

Indian lives. While his poems and narratives revolve around Indian politics and history, they get to those big themes via the storyteller's gift of imaginative intimacy. He expresses the ways emotions and raw needs play out in American Indian and other lives, the astonishing ways that humans are able to persevere in either wisdom or foolishness, or both. "The following are all good things: the ecstatic and disdainful reviews; the enraptured and bored audiences; the fans and the enemies; the skeptics and the faithful; ... the other filmmakers who think they could have done it better, and the other filmmakers who truly could have done it better ... Trust me. The whole damn universe of response to your art, to your tiny little creation, is a beautiful, amazing thing."[41] Beyond irony, Alexie releases a power of laughter surprised across intimate divides, "a song of mourning that would become a song of celebration."[42]

Notes

1. See Kenneth Lincoln, *Native American Renaissance*, Berkeley: California University Press, 1983.
2. Elvis Mitchell, *The New York Times* (18 October 2002).
3. *The Toughest Indian in the World*, New York: Grove, 2000, p. 193.
4. Susan Berry Brill de Ramirez, "Sherman Alexie," in Kenneth M. Roemer, ed., *Dictionary of Literary Biography*. Vol. *175: Native American Writers of the United States*, Detroit, MI: Gale Group, 1997, pp. 3–10.
5. *Reservation Blues*, New York: Atlantic Monthly Press, 1995, p. 98.
6. *One Stick Song*, Brooklyn: Hanging Loose Press, 2000, p. 17.
7. "A Dialogue on Race with President Clinton," transcript (9 July 1998). Public Broadcasting System. http://www.pbs.org/newshour/bb/race_relations/OneAmerica/transcript.html.
8. *Toughest*, p. 112.
9. "Freaks," *First Indian on the Moon*, Brooklyn: Hanging Loose Press, 1993, p. 49.
10. "Unauthorized ..." p. 13.
11. *Toughest*, p. 175.
12. Ibid., p. 190.
13. Ibid., p. 153.
14. Russ Spencer, "What It Means to Be Sherman Alexie," *Book* (July/August 2000), pp. 32–36.
15. "Introduction to Native American Literature," *Old Shirts and New Skins*. Los Angeles: UCLA, American Indian Studies Center, 1993, pp. 3–5.
16. Spencer, "What it means to be Sherman Alexie," p. 36.
17. See "The Priest of the Sun" section in N. Scott Momaday, *House Made of Dawn*, New York: Harper and Row, 1968; and Momaday's seminal essay, "Man Made of Words," in Rupert Costo, ed., *Indian Voices: the First Convocation of American Indian Scholars*, San Francisco: Indian Historian, 1970, pp. 49–84.
18. "What I've Learned as a Filmmaker," *The Business of Fancydancing: The Screenplay*, Brooklyn, NY: Hanging Loose Press, 2003, pp. 7–8.
19. Spencer, "What it means to be Sherman Alexie," p. 36.

Sherman Alexie

20. Gloria Bird, "The Exaggeration of Despair in Sherman Alexie's *Reservation Blues*," *Wicazo Sa Review* (Fall 1995), pp. 47–52.
21. *Toughest*, p. 238.
22. Ibid., p. 194.
23. Spencer, "What it means to be Sherman Alexie," p. 33.
24. Timothy Egan, "An Indian Without Reservations," *New York Times Magazine* (18 January 1998), pp. 17–19.
25. Louis Owens, *Other Destinies: Understanding the American Indian Novel*, Norman: Oklahoma University Press, 1992; Jace Weaver, *That the People Might Live: Native American Literature and Community*, Oxford University Press, 1997.
26. D. L. Moore notes, Alexie reading at Missoula Children's Theater, Montana Festival of the Book, and personal conversation with James Welch, September 2001.
27. *Toughest*, p. 144.
28. See Geoffrey Harpham, *On the Grotesque: Strategies of Contradiction in Art And Literature*, Princeton, NJ: Princeton University Press, 1982; and Anthony Di Renzo, *American Gargoyles: Flannery O'Connor and the Medieval Grotesque*, Carbondale: Southern Illinois University Press, 1993; and William Van O'Connor, *The Grotesque: an American Genre, and other Essays*, Carbondale, Southern Illinois University Press, 1962; and Kathleen Brogan, *Cultural Haunting: Ghosts and Ethnicity in Recent American Literature*, Charlottesville: Virginia University Press, 1998; Renee L. Berglund, *The National Uncanny: Indian Ghosts and American Subjects*, Hanover, NH: New England University Press, 1999.
29. *McSweeney's Mammoth Treasury of Thrilling Tales*, Michael Chabon, ed., New York: Vintage, 2002, pp. 341–53.
30. Ibid., p. 353.
31. Ibid., p. 348.
32. Richard C. Trexler, *Sex and Conquest: Gendered Violence, Political Order, and the European Conquest of the Americas*, Ithaca, NY: Cornell UP, 1995.
33. *Toughest*, p. 194.
34. *One Stick Song*, p. 33.
35. *Toughest*, p. 193.
36. Ibid., p. 203.
37. Ibid.
38. Ibid., p. 200.
39. Ibid.
40. Kelly Myers, "Reservation Stories with Author Sherman Alexie," *Tonic* 1 (11 May 1995), pp. 8–9.
41. "What I've Learned," p. 7.
42. *Reservation Blues*, p. 306.

Major secondary sources

Bird, Gloria, "The Exaggeration of Despair in Sherman Alexie's *Reservation Blues*," *Wicazo Sa Review* (Fall 1995), pp. 47–52.
Brill de Ramirez, Susan Berry, "Sherman Alexie," in Kenneth M. Roemer, ed., *Dictionary of Literary Biography. Vol. 175: Native American Writers of the United States*. Detroit, MI: Gale Group, 1997, pp. 3–10.

Burkhart, Matthew R., "'Old Maps' and 'New Roads': Confronting Neocolonial Despair in Sherman Alexie's *Reservation Blues*." MA thesis. University of Montana, 2001.

Duran, Bonnie and Eduardo, *Native American Postcolonial Psychology*. Albany: SUNY Press, 1995.

McFarland, Ron, "Sherman Alexie," in Richard H. Cracroft, ed., *Dictionary of Literary Biography. Vol. 206: Twentieth-Century American Western Writers, First Series*. Detroit, MI: Gale Group, 1999, pp. 3–10.

O'Nell, Theresa DeLeane, *Disciplined Hearts: History, Identity, and Depression in an American Indian Community*. Berkeley: California University Press, 1996.

Ruby, Robert H. and John A. Brown, *The Spokane Indians: Children of the Sun*. Norman: Oklahoma University Press, 1970.

"Sherman Alexie," *Studies in American Indian Literature* 9.4 (Winter 1997).

KENNETH M. ROEMER

SELECTED BIO-BIBLIOGRAPHIES

Bio-bibliographies offer beginning places and quick reminders. Hence these entries might best be read before and after reading the rest of the volume. They are highly selective: selective in the choice of authors and in the types of information provided. In keeping with my comments in the Introduction, almost half the entries selected were from the eighteenth, nineteenth, and early twentieth centuries, and I selected titles that reflected the diversity of genres and the mixing of genres. The types of information selected for each entry are rather conventional: name, tribal affiliation, dates, types of writing associated with the author, place of birth (followed by place(s) where the author was raised if it or they differ from the place of birth), education, major awards, brief comments about the authors' contributions, and a short title list of major works. The designation of tribal affiliation follows the guidelines outlined at the beginning of this volume, though I have been selective on this issue also. (For example, Charles Eastman is identified as Santee Sioux; an argument could be made for adding Wahpeton Mdewakanton Dakota.) The awards list and list of titles omit many fellowships and some titles. The selectivity in titles will be most noticeable for prolific authors such as Will Rogers, Gerald Vizenor, and Diane Glancy. My main sources for these bio-bibliographies were autobiographical writing by the authors, the titles listed in "Further readings," and the essays in this volume. To the authors of all these sources I owe a debt of gratitude.

Alexie, Sherman (Spokane / Coeur d'Alene, 1966–)

Poet, fiction writer, essayist, scriptwriter, autobiographer; Spokane, WA; Wellpinit, WA, Spokane Reservation; reservation schools, high school in Reardan, WA, Gonzaga University, Washington State University (BA; mentor, Alex Kuo); PEN / Hemingway Award for Best First Book, Before Columbus Foundation's American Book Award, named as one of Granta's "Best Young American Novelists," Sundance Film Festival awards, Lila

Wallace–*Reader's Digest* Fund Writers Award, a Heavyweight Poetry Championship of the World winner; the celebrity American Indian writer of the 1990s and early 2000s, known for his fast-paced, piercing, and humorous depictions of reservation life in poetry, fiction, and film and on the lecture circuit. Major works: *The Business of Fancydancing*, 1992 (poetry, fiction), *Old Shirts & New Skins*, 1993 (poetry, fiction), *The First Indian on the Moon*, 1993 (poetry, fiction), *The Lone Ranger and Tonto Fistfight in Heaven*, 1993 (fiction), *Reservation Blues*, 1995 (fiction), *Indian Killer*, 1996 (fiction), *Smoke Signals*, 1999 (filmscript for 1998 film), *One Stick Song*, 2000 (poetry), *The Toughest Indian*, 2000 (fiction), *The Business of Fancydancing*, film released in 2001 (filmscript), *Ten Little Indians*, 2003 (fiction).

Allen, Paula Gunn (Laguna / Métis, 1939–)

Poet, editor, essayist, critic, fiction writer, biographer; Albuquerque, NM; Cubero, NM; Cubero mission schools, St. Vincent Academy, Albuquerque, San Fidel Mission School, Colorado Women's College, University of Oregon (BA, MFA), University of New Mexico (PhD); Before Columbus Foundation's American Book Award, Modern Language Association American Literature Section's Lifetime Achievement Award, Native Writers Circle of Americas Lifetime Achievement Award; an important writer, educator, political activist, and critic who pioneered the use of feminist and lesbian approaches to scholarly and creative Native American writing. Major works: *Coyote's Daylight Trip*, 1978 (poetry), *A Cannon between My Knees*, 1981 (poetry), *Shadow Country*, 1982 (poetry), *The Woman Who Owned the Shadows*, 1983 (fiction), *The Sacred Hoop*, 1986 (literary criticism), *Spider Woman's Granddaughters*, 1989 (edited anthology), *Skins and Bones*, 1988 (poetry), *Voice of the Turtle*, 1994 (edited anthology), *Song of the Turtle*, 1994 (edited anthology), *Life Is a Fatal Disease*, 1996 (poetry), *Off the Reservation*, 1998 (cultural criticism), *As Long as the River Flows* (with Patricia Clark Smith), 2001 (biography for children), *Pocahontas*, 2003 (biography).

Apess, William (Pequot, 1798–1839)

Autobiographer, sermon writer, biographer, historian, essayist; in a tent near Colrain, MA; Colrain and Colchester, CT areas; after four, raised by white families, especially the Formans for six years when he received his only formal education; an influential Methodist minister and missionary to and advocate for Northeastern Indians, especially for the Mashpee; *Son of the*

Forest is considered to be the first autobiography written in English by an American Indian. Major works: *A Son of the Forest*, 1829 (autobiography), *The Increase of the Kingdom of Christ*, 1831 (sermon), *The Experiences of Five Christian Indians of the Pequod Tribe*, 1833 (biography), *Indian Nullification of the Unconstitutional Laws of Massachusetts, Relative to the Marshpee Tribe*, 1835 (essays), *Eulogy on King Philip*, 1836 (biography, history).

Callahan, A. Alice (Muskogee, 1868–94)

Fiction writer; Sulphur Springs, TX; Texas and the Creek Nation in Indian Territory (Oklahoma); Wesleyan Female Institute, Staunton, VA; an educator in Indian Territory who wrote what is considered to be the first novel by an American Indian woman; *Wynema* combines romance conventions, assimilation and reverse assimilation plots, and reflections on the effects of recent hostilities (e.g., the Wounded Knee massacre). Major work: *Wynema*, 1891 (fiction).

Cook-Lynn, Elizabeth (Dakota-Crow Creek Sioux, 1930–)

Editor, essayist, critic, fiction writer, historian, poet, autobiographer, journalist; Ft. Thompson, SD; Crow Creek Reservation, SD; South Dakota State College (BA, MA); a leading spokesperson for tribally rooted Native American literature, criticism, and scholarship and the driving force behind the journal *Wicazo Sa Review*. Major works: *Then Badger Said This*, 1977 (multi-genre autobiography), *The Power of Horses*, 1990 (fiction), *From the River's Edge*, 1991 (fiction), *Why I Can't Read Wallace Stegner*, 1996 (essays), *I Remember the Fallen Trees*, 1998 (poetry), *The Politics of Hallowed Ground*, 1999 (revisionist history), *Aurela*, 1999 (fiction), *Anti-Indianism in Modern America*, 2001 (social criticism).

Copway, George [Kah-ge-ga-gah-bowh] (Ojibwe, 1818–69)

Autobiographer, historian, essayist, biographer, speech writer; near the Trent River (now in Ontario); Methodist Mission School, Rice Lake Ontario, Ebenezer Manual Labor School, Jacksonville, IL; a respected Methodist missionary, lecturer, and political activist whose *Life* is considered to be the first autobiographical-tribal history by an American Indian; it initiates a form of Native writing that combines conventions of oral narratives, life stories, and histories. Major works: *The Life, History, and Travels of Kah-ge-ga-gah-bowh* (George Copway), 1847 (multi-genre autobiography-history), *Organization of a New Indian Territory*, 1850 (essays presented to the House and Senate), *The Traditional History and Characteristic Sketches of the Ojibway Nation*, 1850 (history, oral narrative), *Running Sketches of Men and Places*, 1851 (travel literature, biography).

Deloria, Ella C. (Yankton-Nakota, 1889–71)

Linguist, ethnographer, translator, fiction writer; Yankton Reservation, SD; Fort Hayes, Standing Rock Reservation, ND; Episcopalian Saint Elizabeth Mission School and All Saints School, Sioux Falls, SD, Oberlin College, Columbia University (BS; mentor, Franz Boas); Indian Achievement Award; the premier translator and interpreter of Lakota narratives of her day whose novel focuses on detailed accounts of nineteenth-century mostly pre-white contact lives and workings of Lakota women, extended families, and kinship networks. Major works: *Dakota Texts*, 1932 (translations, analysis), *Dakota Grammar*, 1941 (linguistics), *Speaking of Indians*, 1944 (informal ethnography), *Waterlily*, completed in 1944 and published in 1988 (fiction).

Deloria, Vine, Jr. (Yankton-Standing Rock Sioux, 1933–)

Essayist, polemicist, satirist, theologian, legal historian, editor; Martin, South Dakota on the boarder of the Pine Ridge Reservation; Iowa State University (BS), Augustana Lutheran Seminary, Rock Island, IL (BD); University of Colorado, Boulder (JD). Indian Achievement Award, Anisfield-Wolf Award, National Conference of Christians and Jews Special Citation, Wordcraft Circle Writer of the Year Award (personal and critical essays), Native Writers Circle of the Americas Lifetime Achievement Award; influential educator and arguably the best-known spokesperson for Indian rights of his generation whose satiric and piercing critiques of past and present Euro-American worldviews and treatment of Indians in *Custer Died for Your Sins*, *We Talk, You Listen*, and *God Is Red* helped to initiate the Native American Renaissance of the 1970s. Major works: *Custer Died for Your Sins*, 1969 (essays), *We Talk, You Listen*, 1970 (essays), *Of Utmost Good Faith*, 1971 (edited anthology of treaties, court cases, and acts), *God Is Red*, 1973 (essays), *Behind the Trail of Broken Treaties*, 1974 (essays, history), *The Metaphysics of Modern Existence*, 1979 (essays), *The Nations Within*, 1984 (essays, history), *A Sender of Words*, 1984 (edited essays on John G. Neihardt), *American Indian Policy in the Twentieth Century*, 1985 (edited essays), *Indian Education in America*, 1991 (essays),

Red Earth, White Lies, 1995 (essays), *Evolution, Creationism, and Other Modern Myths*, 2002 (essays).

Dorris, Michael (Modoc, 1945–97)

Fiction writer (adult's and children's), scholarly writer (history, anthropology, reference works), autobiographer, scriptwriter, poet; Louisville, KY; Kentucky, Washington, Idaho, Montana; Georgetown University (BA), Yale University (MPhil.); Indian Achievement Award, Guggenheim Fellowship, National Book Critics Circle Award, Writers Guild of America Award; a leading educator, he was best known for his book (adapted for television) describing the experience of raising a child with fetal alcohol syndrome, for his first novel, which introduced a mixed-blood African American-Native American protagonist, and for his writing collaborations with his wife Louise Erdrich. Major Works: *Native Americans*, 1975 (history, anthropology), *A Guide to Research on North American Indians* (co-compiler), 1983 (reference), *A Yellow Raft in Blue Water*, 1987 (fiction), *The Broken Chord*, 1989 (autobiography, essay, 1992, television filmscript), *The Crown of Columbus* (with Louise Erdrich), 1991 (fiction), *Morning Girl*, 1992 (children's fiction), *Working Men*, 1993 (fiction), *Paper Trail*, 1994 (essays), *Guests*, 1994 (children's fiction), *Sees Behind the Trees*, 1996 (children's fiction), *Cloud Chamber*, 1997 (fiction), *The Window* (with Ken Robbins), 1997 (children's fiction).

Eastman, Charles (Santee Sioux, 1858–1939)

Autobiographer, re-creator of oral narratives, historian, biographer, writer of instructional guides; near Redwood Falls, MN; Minnesota, Canada, Dakota Territory; Flandreau Mission School, Dakota Territory, Santee Normal Training School, Beloit College, WI, Knox College, IL, Kimberly Union Academy, Dartmouth (BS), Boston University (MD); Indian Achievement Award; a medical doctor (e.g., on the Pine Ridge and Crow Creek Agencies), educator, and reformer, one of the most popular American Indian autobiographers who raised ethical and cultural questions about assimilation. Major works: *Indian Boyhood*, 1902 (autobiography), *Old Indian Days*, 1907 (recreated narratives), *Wigwam Evenings* (with his wife Elaine Goodale Eastman), 1909 (recreated narratives), *The Soul of the Indian*, 1911 (informal ethnography), *Indian Scout Talks*, 1914 (instructional guide), *The Indian Today*, 1915 (history, essays), *From the Deep Woods to Civilization*, 1916 (autobiography), *Indian Heroes and Great Chieftains*, 1918 (biography).

Erdrich, Louise (Turtle Mountain Ojibwe, 1954–)

Fiction writer (adult's and children's), poet, essayist, newspaper editor, advertising copy writer; Little Falls, ND; Wahpeton, ND; Dartmouth (BA), Johns Hopkins (MA in creative writing); Guggenheim Fellowship, O. Henry Award, Pushcart Prize, National Book Critics Circle Award, Before Columbus Foundation's American Book Award, Publisher's Weekly's Best Books for 1986, Wordcraft Circle Writer of the Year Award (children's literature), Native Writers Circle of Americas Lifetime Achievement Award; one of America's most highly respected novelists known especially for her series, which, like Faulkner's Yoknapatawpha County novels, focuses on a particular region and people – northern and eastern North Dakota, reservation and non-reservation Ojibwe, and non-Indian communities. Major works: *Jacklight*, 1984 (poetry), *Love Medicine*, 1984, 1993 (fiction), *The Beet Queen*, 1986 (fiction), *Tracks*, 1988 (fiction), *Baptism of Desire*, 1989 (poetry), *The Crown of Columbus* (with Michael Dorris), 1991 (fiction), *The Bingo Palace*, 1994 (fiction), *The Blue Jay's Dance*, 1995 (autobiography), *Tales of Burning Love*, 1996 (fiction), *Grandmother's Pigeon*, 1996 (children's fiction), *The Antelope Wife*, 1998 (fiction), *The Last Report on the Miracles at Little No Horse*, 2001 (fiction), *Original Fire*, 2003 (poetry), *The Master Butchers Singing Club*, 2003 (fiction), *Four Souls*, 2004 (fiction).

Geiogamah, Hanay (Kiowa / Delaware, 1945–)

Playwright, scriptwriter, editor, essayist, journalist, autobiographer; Lawton, OK; Anadarko, OK; Fort Sill Indian School near Lawton, Chilocco Indian School near New Kirk, OK, University of Oklahoma, Indiana University (BA); William Randolph Hearst National Writing Award; influential educator and former editor of *American Indian Culture and Research Journal*, recognized as the playwright , director, producer who gained national attention for Native American drama; his own plays range in tone from brutal urban realism (*Indian Body*) to a vaudeville style that undercuts stereotypes (*Foghorn*). Major works: *New Native American Drama*, 1980 (drama), *The American Indian Resources Guide* (co-compiler), 1987 (reference), *Stories of Our Way* (edited with Jaye T. Darby), 1999 (drama anthology), *American Indian Theater in Performance* (edited with Jaye T. Darby), 2000 (essay collection).

Glancy, Diane (Cherokee, 1941–)

Poet, playwright, fiction writer, autobiographer, essayist; Kansas City, MO; Kansas City, St. Louis, Indianapolis; Normandie High School, St. Louis,

University of Missouri at Columbia (BA), University of Iowa (MFA); Native American Prose Award, Wordcraft Circle Writer of the Year (theater play writing), Five Civilized Tribes Play Writing Award, Nilon Excellence in Minority Fiction Award; probably the most prolific Native American writer at the turn of the millennium, respected for her work in several genres, but especially for her poetry and fiction (e.g., *Pushing the Bear*) and for her mixed-genre autobiography *Claiming Breath*, which highlights mixed-blood heritage, feminist, and middle-age issues. Major works: *Traveling On*, 1980 (poetry), *One Age in a Dream*, 1986 (poetry), *Offering*, 1988 (poetry), *Iron Woman*, 1990 (poetry), *Trigger Dance*, 1990 (fiction), *Lone Dog's Winter Count*, 1991 (poetry), *Claiming Breath*, 1992 (mixed-genre autobiography), *Firesticks*, 1993 (fiction), *War Cries*, 1996 (drama), *Pushing the Bear*, 1996 (fiction), *The West Pole*, 1997 (essays, autobiography), *Flutie*, 1998 (fiction), *Fuller Man*, 1999 (fiction), *The Closets of Heaven*, 1999 (poetry), *The Voice that Was in Travel*, 1999 (fiction), *The Relief of America*, 2000 (poetry), *American Gypsy*, 2002 (drama), *Designs in the Night Sky*, 2002 (fiction), *The Mask Maker*, 2002 (fiction), *The Shadow's Horse*, 2003 (poetry), *Stone Heart*, 2003 (fiction).

Harjo, Joy (Muscogee / Cherokee, 1951–)

Poet, essayist, editor, scriptwriter, fiction (children's); Tulsa, OK; Institute of American Indian Arts, Santa Fe, University of New Mexico (BA), University of Iowa (MFA): Pushcart Prize, Poetry Society of America for Best Book of Poetry, William Carlos Williams Award, Before Columbus Foundation's American Book Award, Wordcraft Circle Writer of the Year Awards (recording, poetry, children's literature), Native Writers Circle of the Americas Lifetime Achievement Award, Lila Wallace–*Reader's Digest* Fund Writers Award; educator, performer (saxophone), and narrator of television series (e.g., Turner's *The Native Americans*), one of the most highly respected American Indian poets whose dazzling and piercing imagery and combinations of chant and myth cadences, conversational-personal poetry, and prose poems depict the conflicting forces of everyday life, especially for women. Major works: *The Last Song*, 1975 (poetry), *She Had Some Horses*, 1983, 1997 (poetry), *Maiden of Deception Pass*, 1985 (filmscript), *Secrets from the Center of the World* (with Stephen Strom), 1989 (prose poems and photography), *In Mad Love and War*, 1990 (poetry), *The Woman Who Fell from the Sky*, 1994 (poetry, also a filmscript), *Letters from the End of the Twentieth Century*, 1996 (recording), *Reinventing the Enemy's Language* (edited with Gloria Bird), 1997 (anthology of Native American women's writing), *A Map to the Next World*, 2000 (poetry, prose), *The Good Luck Cat*, 2000 (children's fiction), *How We Became Human*, 2002 (poetry).

Hogan, Linda (Chickasaw, 1947–)

Poet, fiction writer, essayist, autobiographer; Denver, CO; frequent moves but considers Oklahoma her home; University of Colorado, Colorado Springs (BA), University of Colorado, Boulder (MA); Guggenheim Fellowship, Five Civilized Tribes Play Writing Award, Before Columbus Foundation's American Book Award, Wordcraft Circle Writer of the Year Award (fiction, memoir), Native Writers Circle of the Americas Lifetime Achievement Award; in the 1980s, one of the most respected American Indian poets; now she is best known as a novelist of historical fiction that portrays critical turning points in tribal-regional history and concentrates on ecological and women's issues, as does much of her autobiography *The Woman Who Watches Over the World*. Major works: *Calling Myself Home*, 1978 (poetry), *Seeing through the Sun*, 1985 (poetry), *Savings*, 1988 (poetry), *Mean Spirit*, 1990 (fiction), *Red Clay*, 1991 (poetry and fiction), *Book of Medicines*, 1993 (poetry), *Dwellings*, 1995 (essays), *Solar Storms*, 1995 (fiction), *Power*, 1998 (fiction), *Intimate Nature: the Bond between Women and Animals* (coeditor), 1998 (anthology); *The Woman Who Watches Over the World*, 2001, (autobiography).

Johnson, E. Pauline (Mohawk, 1861–1913)

Poet, fiction writer (adult's and children's), essayist; Grand River Reservation of the Six Nations near Brantford, Ontario; Brantford Collegiate Institute; a popular performer, reciting her poetry in Canada, England, and the United States; her stories in the posthumously published *Moccasin Maker* combine romance and protest conventions with a focus on women. Major works: *The White Wampum*, 1995 (poetry), *Canadian Born*, 1903 (poetry), *Legends of Vancouver*, 1911 (recreations of oral narratives), *Flint and Feather*, 1912 (poetry), *The Moccasin Maker*, 1913 (fiction), *The Shagganappi*, 1913 (children's fiction).

King, Thomas (Cherokee, 1943–)

Fiction writer (adult's and children's), editor, scriptwriter; Sacramento, CA; Roseville, CA; Canadian Governor General's Award, PEN / Josephine Award; an educator who works in print, radio, and film media; his engaging satirical fictions undermine Indian stereotypes with trickster wit and humor that often contrast Native and non-Native, reservation (reserve) and returning Indian, and coyote trickster and human worldviews. Major works: *The Native in Literature* (co-editor), 1987 (literary criticism), *An Anthology of Short Fiction by Native Writers in Canada* (editor) 1988 (anthology), *All My Relations* (editor), 1990 (anthology), *Medicine River*, 1990 (fiction), *A Coyote Columbus Story*, 1992 (children's fiction), *Green Grass, Running Water*, 1993 (fiction), *One Good Story, That One*, 1993 (fiction), *Truth and Bright Water*, 1999 (fiction).

La Flesche, Francis (Omaha, 1857–1932)

Ethnographer, translator, autobiographer, essayist, opera librettist; Omaha Reservation, eastern Nebraska; Presbyterian Mission School, Bellevue, NE; National University Law School, Washington, DC (LLB, LLM; mentors, James Owen Dorsey and Alice Fletcher); the first Native American professional ethnologist and the author of an influential mission school autobiography. Major works: *The Middle Five*, 1900 (autobiography), *The Omaha Tribe* (with Alice Fletcher), 1905–06/1911 (ethnography), *Da-o-ma*, 1912 (unpublished opera), *The Osage Tribe: Rite of Chiefs*, 1914–15/1921 (ethnography), *The Osage Tribe: the Rite of Vigil*, 1917–18/1925 (ethnography), *The Osage Tribe: Two Versions of the Child-naming Rite*, 1925–26, 1928 (ethnography), *The Osage Tribe: Rite of the Wa-xo'-be*, 1927–28, 1930, *A Dictionary of the Osage Language*, 1932 (linguistics), *War Ceremony and Peace Ceremony of the Osage Indians*, 1939 (ethnography), *Ke-ma-ha*, (edited by Daniel Littlefield and James Parins), 1995 (fiction fragments, autobiographical accounts), *The Osage and the Invisible World* (edited by Garrich A. Bailey), 1995 (ethnography).

Mathews, John Joseph (Osage, 1894–1979)

Historian, fiction writer, autobiographer, biographer, journalist; Pawhuska, Indian Territory (Oklahoma); Pawhuska High School, University of Oklahoma (BS), Oxford (BA), University of Geneva's School of International Relations; Rhodes Scholarship (declined), Guggenheim Fellowship; one of the first American Indian novelists to focus on the mixed-blood issue, he wrote a complex autobiography, sometimes called the "Osage Walden", was the first Indian to have a book (*Wah'Kon-Tah*) selected by the Book of the Month Club. Major works: *Wah'Kon-Tah*, 1932 (popular Osage history based on diaries by Laban J. Miles), *Sundown*, 1934 (fiction), *Talking to the Moon*, 1945 (autobiography), *Life and Death of an Oilman* (collaborator, Elizabeth Palmour), 1952 (biography), *The Osages* (collaborator, Elizabeth Palmour), 1961 (history).

McNickle, D'Arcy (Métis Cree / Salish, 1904–77)

Historian, fiction writer (adult's and children's), biographer, anthropologist, editor; Saint Ignatius, MT; Saint Ignatius and Chenawa, OR; Indian Boarding School, Chemawa, OR, high schools in Montana and Washington (state), University of Montana, Oxford, University of Grenoble; Guggenheim Fellowship; co-founder of the National Congress of American Indians and Director of the Center for the History of American Indians at the Newberry Library, he was the best-known twentieth-century Native American historian; *The Surrounded* is often considered the most complex treatment of mixed-blood identity before the publication of Momaday's *House Made of Dawn*. Major works: *The Surrounded*, 1936 (fiction), *They Came Here First*, 1949 (history), *Runner in the Sun*, 1954 (children's fiction), *Indian and Other Americans* (with Harold E. Fey), 1959 (history), *The Indian Tribes of the United States*, 1962 (history, ethnography), *Indian Man*, 1971 (biography), *Wind from an Enemy Sky*, 1978 (fiction), *The Hawk is Hungry and Other Stories* (edited by Birgit Hans), 1992 (fiction).

Momaday, N. Scott (Kiowa / Cherokee 1934–)

Poet, fiction writer (adult's and children's), autobiographer, essayist, playwright, scriptwriter, editor; Lawton, OK; Mountain View, OK, Gallup and Shiprock, NM, Tuba City, Chinle, and the San Carlos Apache Reservation, AZ, Hobbs, NM, Jemez, NM; Franciscan Mission School, Jemez, NM, the Indian School, Santa Fe, NM, Bernalillo (NM) high schools, Augustus Military Academy, Ft. Defiance, VA, University of New Mexico (BA), Stanford University (MA, with a poetry thesis, PhD; mentor, Yvor Winters); Returning the Gift Lifetime Achievement Award, Academy of American Poets Prize, Guggenheim Fellowship, Pulitzer Prize for fiction, Premio Letterario Internazionale Mondelo (Italy); respected artist and educator, his Pulitzer Prize for *House Made of Dawn*, the classroom popularity of *The Way to Rainy Mountain*, and his presence as a dramatic speaker have made him the "dean" of contemporary Native American writers and the primary breakthrough writer for the Native American Renaissance. Major works: *The Complete Poems of Frederick Goddard Tuckerman*, 1965 (edited critical collection), *The Journey of Tai-me*, 1967 (recreated Kiowa and family stories), *House Made of Dawn*, 1968 (fiction), *The Way to Rainy Mountain*, 1969 (mixed-genre mythic, tribal, and personal narrative), *Colorado* (with David Muench), 1973 (essays, photography), *Angle of Geese and Other Poems*, 1974 (poetry), *The Colors of Night*, 1976 (poetry), *The Gourd Dancer*, 1976 (poetry), *The Names*, 1976 (autobiography), *The*

Ancient Child, 1989 (fiction), *In the Presence of the Sun*, 1992 (poetry, essays), *The Indolent Boys*, first performed in 1994 (drama), *Circle of Wonder*, 1994 (illustrated children's fiction), *The Man Made of Words*, 1997 (essays), *In the Bear's House*, 1999 (illustrated poetry, dramatic dialogue, fiction, recreated oral narratives).

Mourning Dove (Humishuma, Christine Quintasket) (Okanogan / Colville, between 1882? and 1888?–1936)

Fiction writer, autobiographer, translator-collector of narratives; near Kettle Falls, WA; Goodwin Mission School of the Sacred Heart Convent, Ward, WA, Fort Spokane School for Indians, WA, Fort Shaw Indian School, Great Falls, MT; business school, Calgary, Canada; an important translator of Okanogan oral narratives, she offered an early depiction of mixed-blood identity challenges from a woman's viewpoint in *Cogewea* and of assimilation pressures in her autobiographical writing. Major works: *Cogewea* (edited by Lucullus Virgil McWhorter), 1927 (fiction), *Coyote Stories* (edited by Heister Dean Guie), 1933 (recreated narratives), *Tales of the Okanogans* (edited by Donald M. Hines), 1976 (recreated narratives), *Mourning Dove* (edited by Jay Miller), 1990 (autobiography), *Mourning Dove's Stories* (edited by Clifford E. Trafzer and Richard D. Scheuerman), 1991 (recreated narratives).

Occom, Samson (Mohegan, 1723–92)

Sermon writer, hymnist, collector of hymns, autobiographer, ethnographer; between New London and Norwich, CT; Eleazar Wheelock's home school, Lebanon, CT; New Light Calvinist minister, educator, fund-raiser, whose best-selling execution sermon and his collection of hymns are considered the first books published in English by a Native American; his brief, posthumously published, life narratives may be the first Indian-authored autobiographies in English. Major works: *A Sermon Preached at the Execution of Moses Paul, an Indian*, 1772 (sermon); *A Choice Collection of Hymns and Spiritual Songs*, 1774 (hymns), "An Account of the Montauk Indians, on Long Island" in *Collections of the Massachusetts Historical Society* 9, 1804 (ethnography), "Sam Occom's Diary" (edited by Gaynell Stone) in *The History and the Archeology of the Montauk*, 1993 (autobiography), "A Short Narrative of My Life" (edited by Paul Lauter) in *The Heath Anthology of American Literature*, vol. I, 1990 (autobiography).

Ortiz, Simon (Acoma, 1941–)

Poet, fiction writer (adult's and children's), essayist, editor, scriptwriter, journalist; Albuquerque, NM; McCartys (Acoma Pueblo community), NM; McCartys BIA School, Saint Catherine's Indian School, Santa Fe, Albuquerque Indian School, Ft. Lewis College, Durango, CO, University of New Mexico (BA), University of Iowa (MFA); Pushcart Prize, Wordcraft Circle Writer of the Year Award (anthology / collection), Returning the Gift Lifetime Achievement Award, a Heavyweight Poetry Championship of the World winner; educator and political activist whose early collections, *Going for the Rain* and *A Good Journey*, established the respectability of contemporary Native American poetry; his poetry is known for its conversational style, its deep roots in Acoma landscapes and stories, its experimental blends of prose and poetry, and its indirect and direct attacks on social injustice. Major works: *Going for the Rain*, 1976 (poetry), *A Good Journey*, 1977 (poetry), *Howbah Indians*, 1978 (fiction), *The People Shall Continue*, 1978 (children's poetry, prose), *Song, Poetry, and Language*, 1978 (essays), *Fight Back*, 1980 (poetry, essays), *From Sand Creek*, 1981 (poetry), *A Poem is a Journey*, 1981 (poetry), *Blue and Red*, 1982 (children's fiction), *Fightin'*, 1983 (fiction), *Woven Stone*, 1991 (poetry, autobiography, essays), *Surviving Columbus*, 1992 (television script), *After and Before the Lightning*, 1994 (poetry and narratives in journal form), *Speaking for the Generations*, 1998 (edited collection, essays), *Men on the Moon*, 1999 (fiction), *Out There Somewhere*, 2002 (poetry, autobiography, essays).

Oskison, John Milton (Cherokee, 1874–1947)

Journalist, editor, fiction writer, biographer, autobiographer, collector of oral narratives; Vinita, Indian Territory (Oklahoma); Vinita and Pryor Creek, Indian Territory, and Oregon; Willie Halsell College, Vinita, OK (BA), Stanford (LLB), Harvard; First Prize for Fiction, *Century Magazine*; a prolific writer and editor for the *New York Evening Post* and *Collier's Magazine*, his short stories and autobiographical novel *Brothers Three* were forerunners to the mixed-blood identity novels of the late twentieth century. Major works: *Wild Harvest*, 1925 (fiction), *Black Jack Davy*, 1926 (fiction), *A Texas Titan*, 1929 (biography), *Brothers Three*, 1935 (fiction), *Tecumseh and His Times*, 1938 (biography), *Cherokee Tales* (collected with Rennard Strickland), 1974 (recreated narratives), *American Indian Spirit Tales* (edited by Strickland and Jack Gregory), 1974 (recreated narratives), *Cherokee Spirit Tales and Indian Women Spirit Tales* (edited by Strickland and Gregory), 1974 (recreated narratives).

Owens, Louis (Cherokee / Choctaw, 1948–2003)

Fiction writer, critic, essayist, bibliographer; Lompoc, CA; California, Mississippi, Nevada; University of California, Santa Barbara (BA, MA), University of California, Davis (PhD); Wordcraft Circle Writer of the Year Award (personal and critical essays); wilderness ranger and educator; *Other Destinies* is one of the most important critical studies of the Native American Renaissance; in his fiction, critical works, and autobiographical essays, he addresses complex issues of ecology and mixed-blood identity. Major works: *American Indian Novelists* (compiled with Tom Colonnese), 1985 (annotated bibliography); *John Steinbeck's Re-Vision of America*, 1985 (literary criticism), *The Grapes of Wrath*, 1989 (literary criticism), *Wolfsong*, 1991 (fiction), *Other Destinies*, 1992 (literary criticism), *The Sharpest Sight*, 1992 (fiction), *American Literary Scholarship 1990*, 1992 (general editor, bibliographic essays), *Bone Game*, 1994 (fiction), *Nightland*, 1996 (fiction), *Mixedblood Messages*, 1998 (cultural criticism, autobiography), *Dark River*, 1999 (fiction), *I Hear the Train*, 2001 (cultural criticism, fiction, autobiography).

Posey, Alexander (Muskogee, 1873–1908)

Editor, journalist, poet, essayist, satirist, autobiographer; near Eufaula, Indian Territory (Oklahoma); home tutoring, Creek Eufaula Indian School, Bacone Indian University, Muskogee, OK; an important editor (*Indian Journal* and *Muskogee Times*) educator, lecturer, and poet strongly influenced by the Romantics; he is most often remembered today for his "Fus Fixico Letters," provocative satires often on Indian issues delivered in regionalisms and a Muskogee-English dialect. Major works: *The Poems of Alexander Lawrence Posey* (edited by Minnie H. Posey), 1910 (poetry), "Journal of Alexander Lawrence Posey" in *Chronicles of Oklahoma*, Vol. 45, 1968 (autobiography), *The Fus Fixico Letters* (edited by Daniel Littlefield and Carol Hunter), 1993 (dialect satires).

Ridge, John Rollin (Cherokee, 1827–67)

Editor, journalist, essayist, poet, fiction writer; in the Eastern Cherokee Nation; Cherokee Nation, Fayetteville, AR, Massachusetts; Fayetteville schools, Great Barrington Academy, MA; one of the first American Indians to support himself primarily by writing, began as a journalist and poet, generally accepted as the first Native American novelist; though the novel follows the adventures of a legendary California Mexican bandit, critics have noted parallels between Murieta's life and Ridge's and the unjust treatment of Indians. Major works: *The Life and Adventures of Joaquín Murieta*, 1854 (fiction), *Poems*, 1868 (poetry).

Riggs, Lynn (Cherokee, 1899–1954)

Playwright, scriptwriter, poet, journalist; Claremore, Indian Territory (Oklahoma); Eastern University Preparatory School, Claremore, University of Oklahoma; Guggenheim Fellowship, one of the Ten Best Plays on Broadway for 1931; the best-known American Indian playwright, author of *Green Grow the Lilacs*, which was transformed into the musical *Oklahoma!*; he is also respected for his many other portraits of Oklahoma, including *Cherokee Night*. Major works: *Big Lake*, 1927 (drama), *Roadside*, 1930 (drama), *The Iron Dish*, 1930 (drama), *Green Grow the Lilacs*, 1931 (drama), *Laughing Boy*, 1933 (screenplay), *Stingaree*, 1933 (screenplay), *Andrew's Harvest*, 1934 (screenplay), *Family Man*, 1934 (screenplay), *Wicked Woman*, 1934 (screenplay), *Delay the Sun*, 1935 (screenplay) *Russet Mantle*, and *The Cherokee Night*, 1936 (drama), *The Garden of Allah* (with W. P. Lipscomb) 1936 (screenplay), *The Plainsman* (with Harold Lamb and Waldsmar Young), 1936 (screenplay), *Four Plays*, 1947 (drama), *Hang on to Love*, 1948 (drama), *Toward the Western Sky* (with Nathan Kroll), 1951 (drama), *This Book, This Hill, These People* (edited by Phyllis Cole Braunlich), 1982 (poetry).

Rogers, Will (Cherokee, 1879–1935)

Journalist, humorist, autobiographer; Oologala, Indian Territory (Oklahoma); Indian Territory and Missouri; Drumgoole School, Chelsea, OK, Presbyterian Mission School, Tahlequah, OK, Harrell Institute, Muskogee, OK, Willie Halsell College, Vinita, OK, Scarlett College Institute, Neosho, MO, Kemper Military Institute, Booneville, MO; Spirit of St. Louis Medal; the most widely read American Indian author of the twentieth-century; he developed his grass-roots philosophical and humorous vaudeville monologues on current events into syndicated newspaper columns (e.g., the *New York Times*), and popular books. Major works: *Roger-isms: the Cowboy Philosopher on the Peace Conference*, 1919 (aphorisms), *The Illiterate Digest*, 1924 (sketches), *Letters of a Self-Made Diplomat to His President*, 1926 (fictional letters), *There's Not a Bathing Suit in Russia*, 1927 (travel sketches), *Ether and Me*, 1929 (newspaper columns), *Twelve Radio Talks*, 1930, *The Autobiography of Will Rogers* (edited by Donald Day), 1949 (autobiography, aphorisms), *Sanity Is Where You Find It* (edited by Donald Day), 1955 (newspaper columns), *The Writings of Will Rogers* (edited by Joseph A. Stout and James M. Smallwood), 22 vols., 1973–83.

Rose, Wendy (Hopi / Miwok, 1948–)

Poet, essayist, anthropologist, autobiographer; Oakland, CA; San Francisco area; Cabrillo and Contra Costa Junior Colleges, CA, University of California, Berkeley (BA, MA); an artist and educator; her poetry often addresses social injustices experienced by American Indians and other indigenous people; her mixed-tribal, multicultural background finds voice in defining the frustrations and the flexibility of complex identities. Major works: *Hopi Roadrunner, Dancing*, 1973 (poetry), *Long Division*, 1976 (poetry), *Academic Squaw*, 1977 (poetry), *Aboriginal Tattooing in California*, 1979 (ethnography), *What Happened When the Hopi Hit New York*, 1982 (poetry), *The Halfbreed Chronicles*, 1985 (poetry), *Going to War with All My Relations*, 1993 (poetry), *Now Proof She Is Gone*, 1994 (poetry), *Bone Dance*, 1994 (selected and new poetry), *Itch Like Crazy*, 2002 (poetry).

Sarris, Greg (Miwok-Pomo, 1952–)

Fiction writer, biographer, autobiographer, essayist, scriptwriter; Santa Rosa, CA; Santa Rosa and Stewart's Point, CA; University of California, Los Angeles (BA; mentor, Kenneth Lincoln), Stanford (MA in creative writing, PhD); Sundance Film Festival Award; educator and tribal chair of the Federated Indians of Graton Rancheria, one of the highly regarded new Native voices of the mid- and late-1990s; his fiction and HBO film depict contemporary urban, multicultural, multiracial family life in Northern California with roots going back a century. Major works: *Keeping Slug Woman Alive*, 1993 (literary criticism, ethnography, autobiography), *Mabel McKay*, 1994 (biography, autobiography), *The Sound of Rattles and Clappers*, 1994 (edited anthology), *Grand Avenue*, 1994 (fiction), 1996 (HBO screenplay), *Watermelon Nights* 1998 (fiction).

Schoolcraft, Jane Johnson (Ojibwe, 1800–1841)

Editor, poet; Sault Saint Marie, MI, home schooled; a primary "informant" for her husband, Henry Rowe Schoolcraft, the well-known collector of Native oral narratives; she edited and contributed to the *Literary Voyager* that published articles on Ojibwe history and culture, translations of oral narratives, and her own poetry, which is considered to be the first poetry in English by a Native American woman. Major work: *The Literary Voyager or Muzzeniegun*, 1826–27 (editor and contributor; modern edition edited by Philip P. Mason), 1962 (essays, translations, poetry).

Silko, Leslie Marmon (Laguna, 1948–)

Fiction writer, poet, autobiographer, essayist, scriptwriter; Albuquerque, NM; Laguna Pueblo, NM; BIA schools in Laguna area, Manzano Day School (Catholic), Albuquerque, University of New Mexico (BA and graduate course work in creative writing and the American Indian Law Program); Chicago Review Poetry Award, Pushcart Prize, Lila Wallace–*Reader's Digest* Fund Writers Award, John D. and Catherine T. MacArthur Foundation Grant, Native Writers Circle of Americas Lifetime Achievement Award; an educator and provocative speaker on writing and social issues, the author who established poetry and fiction by Native American women as a significant force in American literature; *Ceremony*'s blend of Native oral and Euro-American literary conventions has helped to make it the prototype of the "Indian" novel. Major works: *Laguna Woman*, 1974 (poetry), *Ceremony*, 1977 (fiction), *Storyteller*, 1981 (poetry, fiction, autobiography, photography), *Arrowboy and the Witches*, 1982 (film workprint script), *Delicacy and Strength of Lace*, 1986 (Silko–James Wright letters, edited by Ann Wright), *Almanac of the Dead*, 1991 (fiction), *Sacred Water*, 1993 (autobiographical vignettes, illustrations), *Yellow Woman and a Beauty of the Spirit*, 1996 (essays), *Gardens in the Dunes*, 1999 (fiction).

Tapahonso, Lucy (Navajo, 1953–)

Poet, autobiographer, essayist, fiction writer (children's); Shiprock, NM; Navajo Methodist School, Farmingham, NM, Shiprock High School, University of New Mexico (BA, MA in creative writing; mentor, Leslie Silko); Wordcraft Circle Storyteller of the Year Award; educator; in contrast to many contemporary Native writers who focus on mixed-blood identity and separation from home, she frequently grounds her poems and prose deep in the clans, families, places, and language of Dinetah (Navajo Country), often from a woman's perspective. Major works: *One More Shiprock Night*, 1981 (poetry), *Seasonal Woman*, 1981 (poetry), *A Breeze Swept Through*, 1987 (poetry), *Sáanii Dahataal: the Women Are Singing*, 1993 (poetry, fiction, autobiography), *Navajo ABC*, 1995 (alphabet book), *Songs of Shiprock Fair* (with Anthony Chee Emerson), 1999 (children's fiction).

Vizenor, Gerald (White Earth Anishinaabeg, 1934–)

Fiction writer, poet, essayist, critic, journalist, scriptwriter; Minneapolis, MN; Minneapolis and White Earth Reservation, MN; New York University, University of Minnesota (BA), Harvard; Before Columbus

Foundation's American Book Award, Fiction Collective Award, PEN Oakland Book Award, Film in the Cities Award, Native Writers Circle of the Americas Lifetime Achievement Award; an educator, postmodern critic, political activist, one of America's premier haiku poets; his screenplay and numerous works of satiric fiction are populated with trickster characters negotiating inventive narrative twists that undermine stereotypes and ossified belief systems, which he labels "terminal creeds." Major works: *Raising the Moon Vines*, 1964 (poetry), *Seventeen Chirps*, 1964 (poetry), *Summer in the Spring*, 1965 (recreated Anishinaabeg songs and narratives), *Thomas James White Hawk*, 1968 (newspaper articles), *Tribal Scenes and Ceremonies*, 1976 (newspaper editorials, articles), *Darkness in Saint Louis Bearheart*, 1978, 1990 (fiction), *Wordarrows*, 1978 (fiction, essays), *Earthdivers*, 1981 (fiction), *Harold of Orange*, 1983 (filmscript), *Matsushima*, 1984 (poetry), *The People Named the Chippewa*, 1984 (revisionist history), *Griever*, 1987 (fiction), *The Trickster of Liberty*, 1988 (fiction), *Narrative Chance*, 1989 (edited critical essays), *Interior Landscapes*, 1990 (autobiography), *The Heirs of Columbus*, 1991 (fiction), *Landfill Meditation*, 1991 (fiction), *Dead Voices*, 1992 (fiction), *Manifest Manners*, 1994 (critical theory), *Shadow Distance*, 1994 (collected fiction and essays), *Native American Literature*, 1995 (edited anthology), *Ishi and the Wood Ducks*, first performed in 1996 (drama), *Hotline Healers*, 1997 (fiction), *Fugitive Poses*, 1998 (critical theory), *Cranes Arise*, 1999 (poetry) *Chancers*, 2000 (fiction), *Hiroshima Bugi*, 2003 (fiction).

Welch, James (Blackfeet / Gros Ventre, 1940–2003)

Poet, fiction writer, historian, essayist, scriptwriter; Browning, MT; Browning, Blackfeet and Ft. Belknap Reservations, Minneapolis, MN; Washburn High School, Minneapolis, University of Minnesota, Northern Montana College, University of Montana (BA, graduate courses in creative writing, mentors, Richard Hugo, Madeline DeFrees, John Herrman); *Los Angeles Times* Award for Best Novel, Pacific Northwest Booksellers Association Book Award, Native Writers Circle of the Americas Lifetime Achievement Award, Knight of the Order of Arts and Letters (French); with Momaday launched the Native American Renaissance; after concentrating on spare, sometimes satiric, typically sharp-imaged reservation portraits in poetry, he turned to fiction; each novel was a new writing experience ranging from taut and realistic representations of contemporary ranch and town settings, to an historical fiction of the late 1860s, to contemporary professional life, to an international tale of Indian displacement and identity recreation in France. Major works: *Riding the Earthboy 40*, 1971 (poetry), *Winter in the Blood*, 1974 (fiction), *The Death of Jim Loney*, 1979 (fiction), *Fools Crow*, 1986 (fiction), *The Indian Lawyer*, 1990 (fiction), *Killing Custer* (with Paul Stekler), 1994 (revisionist history), *The Heartsong of Charging Elk*, 2000 (fiction).

Winnemucca, Sarah (Paiute, 1844–91)

Autobiographer, tribal historian; near the Sink of the Humbolt River, NV; Nevada, California, Oregon; Convent of Notre Dame, San Jose, CA; political activist, popular lecturer; with the support of Boston education reformers, she wrote the first autobiography by an American Indian woman, which combined autobiography, ethnohistory, criticism of government policies, and imagined recreations of historical dialogues. Major work: *Life among the Piutes*, 1883, (mixed-genre autobiography).

Young Bear, Ray A. (Meskwaki, 1950–)

Poet, fiction writer, autobiographer; Marshalltown, IA; Meskwaki Tribal Settlement near Tama, IA; Pomona College, Claremont, CA and in Iowa – Grinnel, University of Iowa, Iowa State, University of Northern Iowa, Cedar Falls; co-founder of the Woodland Song and Dance Group, educator, a boundary crosser whose "novel" blends fiction, autobiography, and poetry and whose poetry is grounded in Meskwaki language and worldviews but also reflects magical realism, surrealism, and existentialism. Major works: *Waiting to be Fed*, 1975 (poetry), *winter of the salamander*, 1980 (poetry), *The Woodland Singers*, 1987 (recording), *The Invisible Musician*, 1990 (poetry), *Black Eagle Child*, 1992 (mixed genre novel), *Remnants of the First Earth*, 1996 (mixed-genre novel), *The Rock Island Hiking Club*, 2001 (poetry).

Zitkala-Ša [Gertrude Simmons Bonnin], (Yankton Dakota, 1876–1938)

Yankton Sioux Agency; the Agency and Wabash, IN; White's Manual Institute (Quaker),Wabash, IN, Earlham College, Richmond, IN, New England Conservatory of Music, Boston; lecturer, educator, political activist, Secretary of the Society of the American Indian, founder of the National Council of American Indians; she is remembered today primarily for her realistic and powerful autobiographical accounts of her experiences as a Yankton child, as a boarding school student, and as a teacher. Major works: *Old Indian Legends*, 1901 (recreated oral narratives), *The Sundance* (with William Hanson), 1913 (opera), *American Indian Stories*, 1921 (autobiography, fiction), *Oklahoma's Poor Rich Indians* (with Charles H. Fabens and Matthew K. Sniffen), 1924 (history, social criticism).

JOY PORTER AND KENNETH M. ROEMER

FURTHER READING

For a comprehensive bibliography consult the forthcoming expanded edition of
A. LaVonne Brown Ruoff's *American Indian Literatures*. This brief bibliography
complements mention of important titles in my Introduction and the Major secondary
sources sections that follow each chapter by listing selected general bibliographies,
encyclopedias, handbooks, dictionaries, histories, and introductions. I have included
recent as well as decades-old reference works. By comparing old and new works,
students can see how the field has developed. Other general works useful to both
beginners and those more knowledgeable about American Indian literature include:
(1) edited collections of essays, such as Laura Coltelli's *Native American Literature*
(1989), Richard F. Fleck's *Critical Perspectives on Native American Fiction* (1993),
Helen Jaskoski's *Early Native American Writing* (1996), Brian Swann and Arnold
Krupat's *Recovering the Word* (1987), Allan R. Velie's *Native American Perspectives
on Literature and History* (1995), Gerald Vizenor's *Narrative Chance* (1989), and
Andrew O. Wiget's *Critical Essays on Native American Literature* (1985); (2) general
collections of essay that are more personal than typical scholarly essays, such as
Roger Dunsmore's *Earth's Mind* (1997) and Greg Sarris's *Keeping Slug Woman Alive*
(1993); (3) broad thematic studies – for example those focusing on sense of place or
region, such as Robert Nelson's *Place and Vision* (1993) and Eric Gary Anderson's
American Indian Literature and the Southwest (1999) – or those focusing on
criticism, such as Elvira Pulitano's *Toward a Native American Critical Theory* (2003).

References

Allen, Paula Gunn, (ed.), *Studies in American Indian Literature: Critical Essays and
Course Designs*. New York: Modern Language Association, 1983.
Brumble, H. David III (comp.), *An Annotated Bibliography of American Indian and
Eskimo Autobiography*. Lincoln: University of Nebraska Press, 1981.
Chapman, Abraham, ed., *Literature of the American Indians: Views and
Interpretations*. New York: New American Library, 1975.
Colonnese, Tom and Louis Owens (comps.), *American Indian Novelists: an
Annotated Critical Bibliography*. New York: Garland, 1985.
Deloria, Philip J. and Neal Salisbury, eds., *A Companion to American Indian History*.
Oxford: Blackwell, 2002.
Hirschfelder, Arlene B. (comp.), *American Indian and Eskimo Authors*. New York:
Association on American Indian Affairs, 1973.

Jacobson, Angeline, *Contemporary Native American Literature: a Selected and Partially Annotated Bibliography*. Metuchen: Scarecrow Press, 1977.

Juricek, Kay and Kelly J. Morgan, eds., *Contemporary Native American Authors: a Biographical Dictionary*. Golden: Fulcrum, 1997.

Littlefield, Daniel F., Jr., and James W. Parins (comps.), *American Indian and Alaskan Native Newspapers and Periodicals, 1826–1924*. Westport: Greenwood, 1984.

    A Biobibliography of Native American Writers, 1772–1924. Metuchen: Scarecrow, 1981.

    A Biobibliography of Native American Writers, 1772–1924: a Supplement. Metuchen: Scarecrow, 1985.

Lundquist, Suzanne Eversten, *Native American Literatures: an Introduction*. New York: Continuum, 2004.

Marken, Jack W. (comp.), *The American Indian: Language and Literature*. Arlington Heights: AHM, 1978.

Roemer, Kenneth M., ed., *Native American Writers of the United States*. Detroit: Gale, 1997.

Ruoff, A. LaVonne Brown, *American Indian Literatures: an Introduction, Bibliographic Review, and Selected Bibliography*. New York: Modern Language Association, 1990.

    Literatures of the American Indian. New York: Chelsea House, 1991.

Stensland, Anna Lee (comp.), *Literature by and about the American Indian: an Annotated Bibliography*, 2nd edn. with Anne M. Fadum. Urbana: NCTE, 1979.

Susag, Dorothea M., *Roots and Branches: a Resource of Native American Literature – Themes, Lessons, and Bibliographies*. Urbana: NCTE, 1998.

Trigger, Bruce G. and Wilcomb E. Washburn, eds., *The Cambridge History of the Native Peoples of the Americas*, vol 1. Cambridge: Cambridge University Press, 1996.

Whitson, Kathy J., *Native American Literatures: an Encyclopedia of Works, Characters, Authors, and Themes*. Santa Barbara: ABC-CLIO, 1999.

Wiget, Andrew, *Native American Literature*. Boston: Twayne, 1985.

    ed., *Handbook of Native American Literature*. New York: Garland, 1996.

Witalec, Janet, ed., *Native North American Literature*. New York: Gale, 1994.

INDEX

Acoma Pueblo, 221–22
  mining at, 226
  Spanish at, 225
activism, 15, 57, 58, 208, 284
adaptation, 15
aesthetics, 71–72
Alaska, 52, 54, 248
  fur trade, 50
Alaska Native Regional Corporations, 66
Alaskan Federation of Natives, 58
Alaskan Native Brotherhood, 55
Alaskan Native Sisterhood, 55
Alcatraz, occupation of, 58, 152–53
alcoholism, 47, 191, 229, 240, 250
Alexie, Sherman, 199, 297–308, 311
  affirmation of diversity, 298
  on anger, 299
  aversion to narrative closure, 302
  confrontation and provocation, 301
  in "Dialogue on Race", 298
  fiction, 184, 186, 298,
  films, 298
  and history, 300–02
  and horror, 304
  and humor, 297, 299, 300, 304
  on imagination, 299, 303
  and irony, 306
  and nationhood, 297
  and oral literature, 305
  poems and stories, 298
  poetry, 157
  on poetry, 299
  publications by, 298
  themes, 297
  titles:
    "The American Artificial Limb
      Company," 306
    The Business of Fancydancing: the
      Screenplay, 302
    "Dear John Wayne," 299, 302,
      305–07
    "Ghost Dance," 304
    "Indian Country", 304
    Indian Killer, 304

"An Indian Without Reservations," 303
"Introduction to Native American
    Literature," 300
Old Shirts and New Skins, 299
"One Good Man," 302
Reservation Blues, 301
"Saint Junior," 299, 300
"Smoke Signals," 184, 199
The Summer of Black Widows, 157
Ten Little Indians, 304
"The Unauthorized Autobiography of
    Me," 298, 299
alienation, 207, 210, 238, 239, 241, 285
Allen, Chadwick
  Blood Narrative, 6, 13
Allen, Lewis Leonidas, 133
Allen, Paula Gunn, 42, 85, 95–96, 122, 312
  collections of Native writing, 96
  *Grandmother of the Light: a Medicine
    Woman's Sourcebook*, 96
  *The Sacred Hoop: Recovering the Feminine
    in American Indian Traditions*, 96
  Song of the Turtle, 186
  *Spider Woman's Granddaughters:
    Traditional Tales and Contemporary
    Writings by Native American Women*, 96
  *Studies in American Indian Literature:
    Critical Essays and Course Designs*, 95
  The Woman Who Owned the Shadows, 95,
    181
Allotment Act
  see General Allotment Act (1887)
American expansionism, 49–54
American Indian
  see Native American
American Indian Development, 169
American Indian Movement (AIM), 57, 261
  "Trail of Broken Treaties," 58, 173
American Indian Self-Determination and
    Educational Assistance Act (1975), 57,
    59
American Revolution, the, 49
Amerindian
  see Native American

CAMBRIDGE COMPANIONS TO LITERATURE

CAMBRIDGE COMPANIONS TO CULTURE